A HISTORY OF THE FRENCH NEW WAVE CINEMA

General Editors
David Bordwell, Vance Kepley, Jr.
Supervising Editor
Kristin Thompson

A HISTORY OF THE FRENCH NEW WAVE CINEMA

Second Edition

Richard Neupert

The University of Wisconsin Press

The University of Wisconsin Press
1930 Monroe Street
Madison, Wisconsin 53711

www.wisc.edu/wisconsinpress/

3 Henrietta Street
London WC2E 8LU, England

1   3   5   4   2

Printed in the United States of America

The Library of Congress has cataloged the first edition as follows:
Neupert, Richard John.
A history of the French new wave cinema / Richard Neupert.
pp. cm. — (Wisconsin studies in film)
Includes bibliographical references and index.
ISBN 0-299-18160-X (cloth : alk. paper)
ISBN 0-299-18164-2 (pbk. : alk. paper)
1. Motion pictures—France—History. 2. New wave films—France—History.
I. Title. II. Series.
PN1993.5.F7 N48   2002
791.43'611—dc21   2002002305

Second edition ISBN: 0-299-21704-3 (pbk. : alk. paper)

Publication of this book has been made possible in part by the generous support of
the Anonymous Fund of the University of Wisconsin–Madison

For Cathy and Sophie

CONTENTS

ILLUSTRATIONS

ACKNOWLEDGMENTS

I have been fortunate to work for two wonderful institutions during the course of this project and owe a great debt to each. At the earliest stages of research, Ken Knoespel and Jay Telotte at Georgia Institute of Technology provided crucial travel funds and access to films. Later, at the University of Georgia, I received valuable support, funding, and advice from Gus Staub and Stanley Longman, with gracious assistance from Yvonne Geisler. It is a bit rare in this state to be able to thank these two rival institutions for help on the same book. At the University of Georgia a number of colleagues have provided information on everything from 1950s automobiles and exchange rates to appropriate translations of particularly thorny French phrases. I thank my French colleagues in the Romance Languages Department including Jean-Pierre Piriou, Doris Kadish, Nina Hellerstein, Francis Assaf, and especially Joel Walz and Jonathan Krell upon whom I have called more than once. Within my own department Antje Ascheid, Mike Hussey, Charles Eidsvik, B. Don Massey, and David Saltz have been very helpful. Deans Wyatt Anderson, Garnett Stokes, and Hugh Ruppersburg of the Franklin College of Arts and Sciences have been instrumental in UGA's commitment to film studies. And, I really appreciate the interest in this project shown by my students in French Film History.

Several archives provided essential assistance and access to rare prints, including Robert Daudelin at the Cinémathèque Montréal, and Gabrielle Claes of the Cinémathèque Royale de Belgique in Brussels. Moreover, the gracious staff at BIFI, the Bibliothèque du film in Paris, offered a welcoming space to work, and Marc Vernet, Director of BIFI, and a true friend, made researching in Paris one of the greatest experiences any scholar could hope for.

I cannot adequately thank Eric Smoodin, Matthew Bernstein, and Kelley Conway for their encouragement and insightful suggestions. Further, there really is no way at all to express the debt and gratitude I owe the series editors, Kristin Thompson, David Bordwell, and Vance Kepley. They have proven to be the most devoted mentors and friends imaginable. At the University of Wisconsin Press, Raphael Kadushin, Sheila Moermond, Adam Mehring, and Terry Emmrich have also been of great assistance. One of the great surprises from this project is my new friendship with Agnès Varda; she has been most gracious and welcoming. Finally, there is my amazing family. I continually marvel at the intelligence and insight offered by my wife, Catherine Jones, whose knowledge of French, history, and narrative criticism make her the perfect reader, while her encouragement, patience, and charm make her the perfect inspiration. Our daughter Sophie's newly discovered love of reading subtitles also helped keep everything in perspective and brought a sense of humor and grace to the entire process of researching and writing this book. I thank you all.

INTRODUCTION

> Despite their differences, these films share connections, a common essence which is nothing less than their notion of mise-en-scène, or a filmic *écriture*, based on shared principles. Just as one recognizes the vintage of a great wine by its body, color, and scent, one recognizes a nouvelle vague film by its style.
>
> —CLAIRE CLOUZOT, *Le cinéma français*

> The New Wave was a freedom of expression, a new fashion of acting, and even a great reform on the level of make-up. I was part of a new generation that refused to wear the two inches of pancake base paint and hair pieces that were still standard equipment for actors. Suddenly, you saw actors who looked natural, like they had just gotten out of bed.
>
> —FRANÇOISE BRION, in *La nouvelle vague*

The French New Wave is one of the most significant film movements in the history of the cinema. During the late 1950s and early 1960s, the New Wave rejuvenated France's already prestigious cinema and energized the international art cinema as well as film criticism and theory, reminding many contemporary observers of Italian neorealism's impact right after World War II. The New Wave dramatically changed filmmaking inside and outside France by encouraging new styles, themes, and modes of production throughout the world. Suddenly, there were scores of new, young twenty- and thirty-something directors, such as Louis Malle, François Truffaut, Jean-Luc Godard, and Claude Chabrol, delivering film after film while launching a new generation of stars, including Jeanne Moreau, Jean-Claude Brialy, and Jean-Paul Belmondo. As a result of new production norms and a cluster of young producers anxious to participate in this burst of filmmaking, roughly 120 first-time French directors were able to shoot feature-length motion pictures between the years 1958 and 1964. Moreover, many of those young directors made several films during those years—Jean-Luc Godard alone released eight features in four years—so the total number of New Wave films is truly staggering. The New Wave taught an entire generation to experiment with the rules of storytelling, but also to rethink conventional film budgets and production norms. A whole new array of options for film aesthetics was born, often combined with tactics from the past that were dusted off and reinvigorated alongside them.

Thanks in part to a renewed interest in the New Wave in France on its fortieth anniversary, increased attention has recently been directed at this movement from a wide range of critics and historians, including prominent figures in French film scholarship like Michel Marie, Jean Douchet, and Antoine de Baecque. The French film journal *Cahiers du cinéma* also organized a special issue devoted to the nouvelle vague.[1]

But given the depth, significance, and variety of the New Wave, much about the movement is still left unexamined. Large survey histories necessarily condense this era and its major figures into simple summaries, while texts devoted to the French cinema or to the New Wave in particular, such as James Monaco's *The New Wave*, Roy Armes's *French Cinema*, and Alan Williams's *Republic of Images*, offer quite different perspectives on the New Wave, though they all end up privileging the directors who had begun as critics for *Cahiers du cinéma* before shooting their first features.[2] For Monaco, the New Wave really amounts to François Truffaut, Jean-Luc Godard, Claude Chabrol, Eric Rohmer, and Jacques Rivette, and he is unconcerned with defining the movement or its dates. Armes divides New Wave–era France into clusters of renewals coming from various new groups of directors. For him, however, New Wave directors have to come directly from criticism; hence he, too, regards the *Cahiers du cinéma* filmmakers as the only pure members. Armes avoids explaining the New Wave as a historical or critical term. Williams does a more complete job, especially for a large survey history, establishing some key influences and classifying the most important directors as the "reformists," including Malle, Chabrol, and Truffaut, in contrast to more marginal directors, like Rohmer, or radical directors, such as Godard.

All these sources help round out a sense of the significance of new directors, themes, and production techniques, but they generally fail to grant adequate space to the cultural context of 1950s France, the history of *Cahiers du cinéma*'s participation, or the resulting films' unusual narrative tactics. Readers are often left without a clear understanding of just what made the New Wave so exciting and challenging to international audiences at the time. The New Wave's "newness" has too often been reduced to a tidy list of representative traits culled from a few canonical films and directors. By contrast, this study lends more depth and breadth to the era while remaining focused on the *Cahiers* directors as exemplary representatives of New Wave filmmaking.

Since every reader will come to this book with overlapping but slightly different perceptions of the New Wave, it is valuable here to lay down a concise working definition of the term, its participants, and its results. While the French film industry had always been much more open to individual producers and writer-directors than were most national cinemas, by the middle 1950s there was a general perception, both in the industry and in the popular press, that French film was losing its direction, bogged down as it was in generic historical reconstructions and uninspired literary adaptations. Individual stylists like Jacques Tati and Robert Bresson were becoming more and more rare. Yet, while the so-called tradition of quality of post–World War II French cinema was earning steady profits with movies like Autant-Lara's *Le rouge et le noir* (*The Red and the Black*, 1954), those traditional films seemed further and further isolated from contemporary life during a time when *ciné-clubs* and new film journals were looking for an exciting modern cinema. Claude Autant-Lara (b. 1901) and his generation of aging leftists became scapegoats of the new young cinephiles and critics like François Truffaut. French cinema was said to be in desperate need of a new direction.

France's cinematic revival came at first from a handful of young directors who found novel ways to fund and shoot their movies, often in direct defiance of commercial and narrative norms. Influenced as much by Jean Renoir of the 1930s, Italian neorealism of the 1940s, and selected Hollywood directors of the 1950s, young directors like Louis Malle, Claude Chabrol, and François Truffaut began to make movies that avoided some of the dominant constraints. They used their own production money or found unconventional producers to make low-budget films set within the milieus they knew best: contemporary France of contemporary middle-class youths. To shoot inexpensively, they followed the lead of the neorealists, shooting primarily on location, using new or lesser-known actors and small production crews. Filming on the streets where they lived or in the apartments where they grew up and without stars or huge professional crews, these directors managed to turn financial shortcomings to their advantage.

Admittedly amateurish on some levels, their tales looked honest and urgent, in contrast to costume dramas set in Stendhal's France. The rule of thumb was to shoot as quickly as possible with portable equipment, sacrificing the control and glamour of mainstream productions for a lively, modern look and sound that owed more to documentary and television shooting methods than to mainstream, commercial cinema. For these filmmakers, glamorous three-point lighting, smooth crane shots, and classically mixed soundtracks were not only out of reach, they were the arsenal of a bloated, doomed cinema. As more producers and writer-directors saw that inexpensive movies not only could be made but also could earn a profit and good critical reviews, the number of first-time feature filmmakers exploded. Suddenly in 1959 and 1960 there were more movies in production by small-time producers and optimistic though untested directors than at any time in the history of the sound cinema. The renewal was now called a wave.

New Wave stories tended to be loosely organized around rather complex, spontaneous young characters. Importantly, unpolished, sometimes disjointed film styles fit these rather chaotic, good-humored tales of youths wandering through contemporary France. Most historians point to 1959 as the first full year of the nouvelle vague—that is the year when the term was first applied to films by Truffaut, Chabrol, and Alain Resnais in particular—and its ending is considered to be anywhere from 1963, the year when the number of new directors declined dramatically, to 1968, the year of the May rebellions. Some critics, however, localize the New Wave so much in specific auteurs that every film ever shot by people like Rohmer, Truffaut, or Godard counts as nouvelle vague: once a "waver" always a "waver," according to some spectators and historians. For reasons that will become clear, this study prefers to summarize the New Wave as a complex network of historical forces, including all films made by young directors exploiting new modes of production as well as unusual story and style options. The New Wave per se lasts from 1958 through 1964. The New Wave era is just that, a time period during which social, technological, economic, and cinematic factors helped generate one of the most intensely creative movements in film history. The New Wave involves more than directors and movie titles; it comprises a whole new interpretation of the cinema and its narrative strategies.

To a certain extent, the unfortunate condensation and canonization of the New Wave into a list of directors began with *Cahiers du cinéma,* itself one of the key historians of the movement, which devoted an entire issue to the nouvelle vague in December 1962. That issue, organized by Jacques Doniol-Valcroze with strong participation from François Truffaut, became a model for how the New Wave has subsequently been described, defined, and summarized. The first sixty pages are devoted to three twenty-page interviews with Claude Chabrol, Jean-Luc Godard, and François Truffaut; the next twenty-five pages are filled with short encyclopedic entries about

"162 New French Filmmakers," typically including a list of their short and long films, one or two paragraphs summing up their contributions, and a snapshot of the director, when available. The final fifteen pages present an interesting roundtable discussion of the industrial climate for French cinema and the hurdles that continued to challenge New Wave production practices and box-office successes.

That *Cahiers du cinéma* should declare that the New Wave involved 162 new filmmakers working in France but devote the bulk of their 1962 special issue to three directors establishes two important trends that will unfortunately persist in most historical summaries of the New Wave. First, while the importance of the Wave lies in its vast size, with scores of first-time directors suddenly getting to make feature films, the most significant participants are really assumed to be the *Cahiers* critics-turned-directors, especially Chabrol, Godard, and Truffaut. Second, the New Wave is presented as a collection of people rather than of films or socioeconomic conditions. The *Cahiers* special issue is arranged, not around a chronology of the *jeune cinéma*, but around the words and faces of young auteurs. The New Wave becomes a list of directors, although even *Cahiers* leaves it unclear whether all of these 162 are nouvelle vague or just new and worth noting.

The *Cahiers* list is particularly weak as a defining tally since some of the 162 directors collected in the *Cahiers* chronicle had begun their careers earlier (Pierre-Domique Gaisseau's first feature was in 1950, Claude Barma's in 1951). Several of the directors, such as Edgar Morin, worked exclusively in documentary, and others on the list, including Michel Fermaud and Henri Torrent, had only so far been codirectors. Noel Burch was included for having written a scenario and serving as assistant on several films; he had not yet directed a feature. And while novelist Jean Giono had just shot his first film, *Crésus*, in 1960, he was hardly young; Giono was born in 1895. *Cahiers* also included the "spiritual fathers" of the New Wave, Roger Leenhardt and Jean-Pierre Melville, who both shot their first features in 1947. Further, the brief summaries for a number of the directors, including Serge Bourguignon (whose *Cybèle ou les dimanches de Ville-d'Avary* [*Sundays and Cybèle,* 1962] went on to win the Academy Award for best foreign film) were quite hostile. Similarly, they dismiss Henri Fabiani's *Le bonheur est pour demain* (*Happiness Comes Tomorrow,* 1960) as an artificial film that looks as if it were made by a sixteen-year old who had misunderstood Soviet montage! Bourguignon and Fabiani are not alone; *Cahiers* dismisses several directors as immature, simplistic, and even embarrassing during this time of aesthetic upheaval and renewal.

Figure 0.1. *Cahiers* nouvelle vague issue

Thus, while on the surface *Cahiers* seems to be championing 162 new directors, its list is hardly an endorsement of all that is youthful in French cinema. For *Cahiers du cinéma*, nouvelle vague possesses connotations of originality and critical value; new directors have the potential to make it into the New Wave camp, but few are actually accorded the label. The *Cahiers* chronicle is very helpful in providing one subjective compilation of people involved in making feature films during this era, but it obviously has shortcomings. Interestingly, this encyclopedic tally includes only three women, Agnès Varda, Paula Delsol (*La dérive* [*The Drift*], 1962), and television writer Francine Premysler, herself a codirector (*La memoire courte* [*Short Memory*], 1962). The *Cahiers* assumption that only directors are worth listing inevitably excludes women by minimizing the effects that the wide range of producers, editors, actors, art directors, writers, cinematographers, and composers had on the amazing look, sound, and feel of these youthful films. Subsequent historians in turn often just fiddle with adapting their own list of most pertinent directors rather than provide a more complex picture of the diverse individuals who helped construct the New Wave cinema.

In contrast, I am particularly interested in a historical poetic approach that reexamines how the New Wave has been variously defined by and for film studies and what nouvelle vague really means today. Hence, I test exactly how the original films were made and received. My initial assumption, however, is that the New Wave is more than a list of people. It is a marketing term, as Chabrol notes, and also an "artistic school," as defined by Michel Marie. But in addition, it comprises changes in economic, social, and technological norms within France in the late 1950s and early 1960s, as well as the narrative contributions from all those new directors making their first feature films in France during these few years, especially 1958–1964. It should also include all the creative personnel who helped make those hundreds of films. Acknowledging the "nouvelle vague spectator" is also a helpful concept since a specific international audience helped ensure that a trickle of new French films led into a mighty wave.

But as I point out in chapter 1, nouvelle vague was initially a blanket term for fundamental social changes that defined an entire post–World War II generation, fifteen to thirty-five years old, who saw themselves as culturally distinct from their parents' generation. By the time of the first New Wave movies, the term "nouvelle vague" was already being applied to everything from juvenile attitudes to a style of living, including wearing black leather jackets and riding noisy motor scooters around Paris. Defining this generation became a national pastime: between 1955 and 1960 at least thirty different national surveys tried to determine "who is French youth today?"[3] Eventually, nouvelle vague was a label that spun out of control in general social use in France; today in film studies it is a fairly coherent term, though various attempts at pinpointing definitive beginning and end dates and comprehensive lists of traits and participants still generate a wide range of competing opinions.

One important, permeating critical opinion that helped motivate the rise of an alternative, New Wave cinema in the 1950s was the broadly accepted notion that post–World War II French cinema was in a stagnant condition and needed a dramatic overhaul. Pierre Billard, head of the French association of ciné-clubs and editor for *Cinéma,* wrote a representative editorial in February 1958, titled "Forty under Forty," which complained about the state of French cinema. He pinned the nation's hopes on forty young directors who were on the rise, including Louis Malle. Billard's editorial lamented that the economic prosperity of top French box-office successes seemed to come at the expense of artistic value: "The depletion of inspiration, sterilization of subject matter, and static aesthetic conditions are hard to deny; the rare exceptions . . . in terms of form and subjects are coming from the periphery of French production. . . . The future of French film progress rests with young directors."[4] Billard's complaints were echoed in many other sources beyond *Cinéma* and *Cahiers du cinéma.* The industry's weaknesses were perceived to be deeply rooted in its structure, not simply in a cautious, aging body of directors.

Even the professional organizations and unions began to draw criticism for being overly protective and hierarchical, posing rigid barriers against easy entry into film production. Popular discourse regularly referred to the film industry as a "fortress," a term that evoked patriotic hopes of storming this contemporary Bastille, overthrowing the current regime, and radically dismantling the unfair conditions for participation. Producers were singled out regularly in the press as lacking taste, vision, and daring. Mainstream producers were condemned for relying upon safe big-budget adaptations of historical novels, in lukewarm compromises between 1940s French style and uninspired, run-of-the-mill Hollywood productions. The label "tradition of quality" had initially been the catch phrase of the Centre national de la cinématographie (CNC) in the days immediately after the war. The CNC and the Minister of Culture were trying to foster a stronger French film industry modeled on British and American classical style, but featuring French themes, historical events, and great

Figure 0.2. Youth stands on old man's beard

literature. But by the middle of the 1950s, angry young critics were using the term "tradition of quality" to deride mainstream output. The phrase now connoted old-fashioned costume epics out of touch with modern life.

Among the few high points in French cinema regularly cited by increasingly impatient critics were individual stylists like Robert Bresson and Jacques Tati, both of whom had trouble finding consistent funding for their films. Another area of hope was the production of daring short films, including documentaries like Alain Resnais's *Nuit et brouillard* (*Night and Fog,* 1955). That the best directors were in financial trouble, while most innovative young directors, experimenting with form and subject matter, were isolated in the marginal field of short films, was often cited as evidence that French cinema was surely headed in the wrong direction. Moreover, French films were winning fewer and fewer international awards, in contrast to the regained prestige among the Italians. The commercial French cinema was regularly condemned in the popular press as teetering, gasping, and even suffering from hardening of the arteries. Throughout the world, cinema was seen as an important cultural barometer, and it was not lost on the French that, while Japan and Italy were earning greater respect each year, France was floundering. As historian Françoise Audé notes of this era, the connections between a rigid cinematic structure and the fixed social structures behind it were becoming obvious to everyone: "Within an apparently frozen society the cinema is inert."[5] Michel Marie sums up the situation most concisely, adopting language right out of the 1950s debates: "Aesthetic sclerosis and a solid economic health—this was the condition of French cinema on the eve of the New Wave's explosion."[6]

Understanding this general sentiment of a French cinema that had lost its cultural significance and artistic edge helps one appreciate that the arrival of what would be announced as a "wave" of new young directors really was an exciting change and even a victory for journalists and film buffs. Already in January 1959, before the label nouvelle vague was even being applied to the cinema, the official publication of the CNC, *Le Film français,* was ecstatic to report that 1958 had seen a sudden spike in the number of features by first-time directors. They cited films just finished or in production by Louis Malle, Michel Deville, Pierre Kast, François Truffaut, Claude Chabrol, and others. More importantly, they foresaw the slate of new features continuing to grow in the new year: "The year 1959 promises the arrival of many new directors. We wish them success and hope they can return the heartfelt youthful vigor our cinema seems to have lately abandoned, but that not long ago permitted our number one ranking in the world. However, it is not by stirring the mud that one makes it go away. Better to ignore it."[7] When *Le Film français,* the voice for the entire French film industry, suggests that current mainstream productions are equivalent to hearts that have stopped beating and mud that is tainting everything it touches, changes in the cinema take on urgent importance. This sort of public scolding of the status quo was highly unusual, and some even considered it unpatriotic. *Le Film français, Cinéma 58,* and *Cahiers du cinéma* were hardly alone in condemning current practice, however, and they, along with daily newspapers and even the Minister of Culture, helped set the stage to welcome newcomers with open arms. The result of all the complaining was to prepare an environment in which change, whether radical or restrained, would be supported and encouraged. New talent came on the scene with a sense of confidence and purpose, trying to deliver the new stories and styles that might save the French cinema from old-fashioned complacency.

But it was more than the critical atmosphere and a shift in taste from carefully crafted historical dramas that helped pave the way for the New Wave. New technological and economic factors as well rewarded fresh ideas and productions. Thus, while this study remains focused on the growth of the New Wave into a strong and varied force, it devotes as much attention to specific generating mechanisms within French culture as to the creative individual auteurs who took advantage of the changing conditions. For instance, while every history of the New Wave, no matter how concise, credits François Truffaut's *Les 400 coups* (*The 400 Blows,* 1959) with helping launch the movement, that film's history should not be limited to Truffaut's personal style, based on his critical past and *cinéphilia.* Although Truffaut's best director award and huge financial success at the Cannes Film Festival in 1959 accelerated the New Wave's growth, the fact that the French franc had lost 20 percent of its value the previous month had an equally important impact. Thus, the international success of French films in 1959 and 1960 was sped along by a better exchange rate for foreign distributors, who could now get an excellent deal on already cheap movies. Small operators like Irvin Shapiro of Films Around the World could subsequently afford the American rights to movies like Godard's *Breathless.*[8] France has always had a strong influx of young individual stylists entering its filmmaking ranks; what makes the New Wave era so special is not so much the rare quality of some of these newcomers but rather the conditions that allowed so many untried people to get a chance at directing feature films within such a short amount of time. The reason that a "wave" rather than simply a new cohort of directors came upon the scene around 1960 is not just a matter of strong personalities. It is the result of an unusual set of circumstances that enabled a dynamic group of young directors to exploit a wide range of conditions that opened up incredible opportunities for inexpensive filmmaking in Paris.

Beyond the historical, social, economic, and technological contexts that affected these marvelous movies, I am ultimately concerned with the resulting narrative innovations. French theater and literature were already changing dramatically during the 1950s, and their shifts away from pre–World War II concerns toward more modern, often theoretically influenced modes of presentation strongly affected the personnel as well as the audiences of nouvelle vague films. Increasingly, narrative experimentation was combined with a renewed interest in telling stories for a younger generation or at least from their perspective. New, sexier themes and actors showed up in important films in the 1950s, such as Roger Vadim's color spectacle, *Et Dieu créa la femme* (*And God Created Woman*, 1956), which featured a daring new representative of amoral female sexuality, Brigitte Bardot. Yet there were also very challenging intellectual movies like Marcel Hanoun's 16 mm *Une histoire simple* (*A Simple Story*, 1958), which concerned a single mother fallen on hard times and was supposedly produced for less than one thousand dollars. The 1950s were rich in storytelling alternatives, some of which were much more influential than others on the core of young directors who would become known as the New Wave filmmakers.

The overall sample of New Wave directors featured in this study is necessarily narrower than the scores of directors who could be said to fit the movement. But I have chosen to concentrate on the rise of the New Wave and examine social forces and influential trends in film criticism as well as the practical influence of exemplary production models provided by Alexandre Astruc, Jean-Pierre Melville, and Agnès Varda. In that way I flesh out rather than remake the canonical list of significant precursors. I then turn to Roger Vadim and Louis Malle, two directors who provide essential narrative and production blueprints for subsequent young directors to copy, revise, or reject. Finally, I take up the core *Cahiers du cinéma* directors, reconsidering their careers and analyzing key films in relation to the many factors that helped shape and determine their movies. Significantly, I also reexamine pertinent financial information on their films, which is occasionally surprising and should raise questions about why some histories have privileged one *Cahiers* critic-turned-director over another. For instance, while Chabrol, Truffaut, and Godard were clearly central to the New Wave as it was understood by 1960, Eric Rohmer and Jacques Rivette were considered marginal. *Cahiers* founder and critic Jacques Doniol-Valcroze and his friend, *Cahiers* critic Pierre Kast, made their first features in the late 1950s as well, and both Doniol-Valcroze's *L'eau à la bouche* (*A Game for Six Lovers*, 1959) and Kast's *Le bel âge* (1958) proved more successful than the first features by Rohmer and Rivette. Thus after detailing the production and narrative strategies that distinguished Rohmer's and Rivette's early careers, I also investigate Doniol-Valcroze and Kast, moving them back into the New Wave subcategory where they belong, as active members of the *Cahiers* critics-turned-directors.

Rather than an encyclopedic account of who is or is not in the nouvelle vague, this history investigates the conditions that gave rise to the phenomenon and the definitions that resulted. I have chosen to discuss films that were integral to the fervor of the New Wave, especially those that shared a role in revitalizing film language as well as motivating further experiments in film. The bulk of the book remains organized around directors, since this was an auteur-centered era, with individual directors struggling hard to devise their own personal styles while fighting for the economic means to remain as independent as possible. Nonetheless, whenever possible this study reminds the reader that these movies are not one-person shows, for all directors depended upon friends, producers, actors, editors, cinematographers, and composers, among others, to get their films made; the characteristic nouvelle vague look was produced by groups of people working within specific small, minimally industrial teams. Limiting the scope of this book allows for a valuable depth of historical and narrative analysis that will, I hope, inspire others to reinvestigate some of the hundreds of worthy New Wave films not touched on here. The so-called Left Bank Group warrants its own book-length study to reinvestigate the production, reception, and narrative strategies of Resnais, Varda, Alain Robbe-Grillet, Chris Marker, and Jacques Demy in particular.

For the purposes of this history, the New Wave should be seen as a large cinematic phenomenon that includes the earliest signs of changes in the industry (such as Vadim and Malle's films and the new Film Aid rules); the first successful new, younger directors and their films (Chabrol, Truffaut, and Godard, among others); the talented pool of bold producers, ac-

tors, editors, and cinematographers; but also the "wave" of first-time directors, working hard to get their films finished and into domestic and international distribution. The New Wave is precisely a wave of productions,
some very successful, some now forgotten, and some demonstrating the
risk of failure that always faces new, youthful experiments in narrative
film. But what finally makes the New Wave's significance so enduring is
that it has marked all French film production ever since. No one looks to
Germany for a revival of expressionism. No one would expect Italy this
year to explode with a new era of pure neorealism, but every French film
is to a certain degree measured against the New Wave, and not a year goes
by without some critic somewhere asking whether two particularly interesting young French directors might not be the harbingers of another nouvelle vague. Would that they were.

A few explanations concerning the book's overall format might prove
helpful. I have tried to reduce the number of French phrases whenever
possible in the interest of clarity and readability, though certain terms that
have become part of the standard vocabulary of film studies, such as auteur, mise-en-scène, and cinephile, are used frequently. Film titles are
given in original French on initial citations and their American, and occasionally British, release titles are also included. Subsequent references
are typically made with the English-language title, especially if that name
is very commonly used already in survey histories of French cinema. For
instance, *The 400 Blows* has been more widely used than *Les 400 coups*
(and it is much easier for non-French speakers to pronounce), so I employ
the translated title most of the time. Films released abroad with their
French title, such as *Hiroshima, mon amour,* are rare. Unless otherwise
noted, all translations from French sources are mine.

The illustrations from the movies are all frame enlargements shot directly off the films, not inaccurate publicity stills. Those images that may
appear a bit compressed, such as frames from *The 400 Blows* and Malle's
Les amants (The Lovers, 1958), are from anamorphic wide-screen prints.
Since the book is aimed at intermediate-level film students who have already been exposed to introductory film analysis and perhaps the basics of
film history but not necessarily the concepts and vocabulary of the most
daunting of film theory, I have endeavored to minimize unnecessary jargon; I hope the resulting format proves clear and convincing. The ultimate
hope for this overview, of course, is to generate renewed interest among
French film fans, motivating the reader to go back to lesser-known films by
favorite directors or, better yet, to retest assumptions about films that may

have disappointed in the past. The New Wave may have officially ended in 1964, but while many observers continue to search for other New Waves on the horizon, it proves just as fruitful to return attention to the scores of films that created all the furor in the first place. There is nothing like rediscovering a nouvelle vague masterpiece and remembering why it is one does film history in the first place.

A HISTORY OF THE FRENCH
NEW WAVE CINEMA

1

Cultural Contexts:
Where Did the Wave Begin?

In 1958 and 1959, my buddies at *Cahiers* and I, having moved into
directing, were promoted like a new brand of soap. We were "the nouvelle
vague." . . . But if the popular press spoke so much of us it was because
they wanted to impose a formula: De Gaulle equals renewal, in the cinema
like everywhere else. The general arrives, the Republic changes, France is
reborn!

—CLAUDE CHABROL, *Et pourtant je tourne*

A number of guys arriving from very different places ended up finding one
another at *Cahiers du Cinéma*, like metal shavings attracted to and then
organized around a magnet.

—PIERRE KAST, in *La nouvelle vague 25 ans après*

THE FRENCH New Wave was much more than a tally of titles or an
encyclopedic list of directors. The New Wave was first and foremost a cultural phenomenon, resulting from economic, political, aesthetic, and social trends that developed in the 1950s. Changes in the other arts, including literature and theater, anticipated some of the shifts in cinema, and
the role and even domain of art criticism shifted during this time as well.
The New Wave cinema was shaped by forces as abstract as the growth
of film criticism that stressed mise-en-scène over thematics and as concrete as technological innovations in motion-picture cameras and sound
recorders. This chapter investigates some of the most profound mechanisms that influenced the rise of the New Wave. For instance, the excited
reception of movies like Louis Malle's *Les amants* (*The Lovers*, 1958)
or Claude Chabrol's *Le beau Serge* (*Handsome Serge*, 1958) can only be
fully understood in relation to the conditions that fostered and rewarded
these unusual productions. France was undergoing unprecedented industrial growth and self-evaluation, both of which put new pressures on the
cinema and its place in the larger national sphere. Moreover, the average

3

moviegoers of 1960 were already quite different from those of 1950. Political conservatism, consumerism, television, *ciné-clubs*, popular film journals, and a new generation of movie producers all affected the stories and styles that would mark this daring movement. To understand what it meant to "be" nouvelle vague, it is essential to consider the social, critical, economic, and technological backgrounds that helped determine the films and their significance. Thus, rather than starting with the cinema, one must begin with the social realm; by getting a clear sense of what French life and culture were like in the 1950s, one can comprehend better why this unique event in world cinema took place when and where it did, while the rest of international cinema could only look on in curious awe at the revival of French cinema.

A New Society, a New Audience

France had changed dramatically in the late 1940s, and these far-reaching transformations continued into the 1960s. Obviously, every nation involved in World War II was deeply affected by it for some time afterward, and France, in particular, came out of the war afflicted with widespread war damage and debt. But the French also shared a strange mixture of national shame for France's military loss and Vichy collaboration and an exaggerated national pride in their country's role in the resistance and ultimate victory over Germany. Further, all the conflicting views of France held by the international community at the war's end—France as a helpless victim, a lazy and ineffective military force, a valued ally, a crippled industrial power—were also felt within its own borders. For historians of this era, it is often tempting to fall into simple personifications of France as a unified, biological entity; it is easy to find articles and books devoted to postwar reconstruction that refer to France "standing up," "awaking from its slumber," or "shaking off its recent past." These sorts of metaphors were common in popular history texts, but they also came directly from the political and cultural discourse of the days. Most political parties struggled quickly after the war to prove that they, more than all the other competitors for power and national respect, had fought for and helped regain France's liberty. The political discourse of the day was built on themes of reviving past glories and moving France triumphantly forward with purpose, unity, and pride. Every politician and newspaper seemed to want to speak to and for a unified France, and the French people were often addressed as a single team that now had to get back to basics in order to simultaneously make up for lost time and join the modernizing world.

Thus, the years after World War II saw a France desperately trying to assert, or reassert in the eyes of many French citizens, its cultural, political, and even economic clout in Europe and beyond. From the day the Germans were pushed out of Paris, on August 19, 1944, the French film industry literally rushed to reclaim its domain from the collaborators and to foster a newly reborn cinema that would regain the glory of the 1930s, the golden years of Jean Renoir, René Clair, and Marcel Carné. With the liberation, the famed offices of the Vichy government's Comité d'organisation de l'industrie cinématographique (COIC) were ransacked and claimed by the cinematic arm of the resistance as the last Nazis were being chased from the Paris streets. Legend has it that the omnipresent Henri Langlois, cofounder of the Cinémathèque française, even took over the desk of the former COIC director and pounded his boot on the desktop, calling for executions in the name of French cinema.[1] The era of purification and revitalization of the film industry had begun in earnest.[2]

The tale of the dynamic changes in French cinema, however, cannot begin without first taking time to understand how the demographics, economics, and general cultural climate of France developed during this era. The prospects for the film industry as a whole, as well as for individual filmmakers, writers, and producers, were motivated and also constrained by the larger generating mechanisms of the society at large. France was undergoing a tense era of change with its left-center coalition Fourth Republic, which gradually took shape from 1944 to 1946. And while political infighting forced the nation's overall political trajectory to move in often contradictory fits and starts until Charles De Gaulle's Fifth Republic came to power in 1958, there was nonetheless a real sense of urgency to rebuild every facet of French life, from constructing more electric power plants to exporting more perfume. As Jill Forbes writes, "After the war, Paris was determined to regain its position as the leading center of fashion worldwide, and to counter the growing competition from Britain and the U.S."[3] The various interest groups that desired a stronger cinema fit squarely within this national sense of destiny. As the 1950s progressed, France underwent fundamental, far-reaching changes that would eventually help establish a "New Look" in fashion and, by 1958, favorable conditions for the rise of new faces and production practices in the French film industry; these changes occurred at roughly the same time that the nation was getting its new Fifth Republic—a "coincidence" that was lost on almost no one.

At the close of World War II, France's population was just 39 million people, or nearly the same as it had been in 1900. The two world wars had killed and displaced vast numbers of young men and disrupted innumerable families; the relative drop in the number of children born in France during the 1930s also decreased the number of potential filmgoers during the war years and just after.[4] Between 1945 and 1960, however, the population increased more than it had in France's previous one hundred years. Thus, while the United States, a nation built on immigration and rapid population growth, could lay claim to having undergone a post-World War II baby boom, "le boom" in France was indeed unprecedented. According to Maurice Larkin, the dramatic population increase was not simply a result of a predictable, immediate rise in births among traditional young French families, from new marriages, or from the reunion of young couples separated by the war. Rather, sample maternity hospital surveys in the 1950s "revealed that a third of pregnancies were unwanted, and that without them there would have been no population increase at all."[5] Larkin argues that throughout the 1950s, birth control in France was minimal (paralleling shortcomings in many technical, health, and household commodities), and thus the lack of widely available contraceptives serves to highlight very real tensions between contemporary women's lives and the social norms of traditional France. But a much more telling statistic is that another one-third of the population increase resulted from France's growing immigrant population. The large numbers of Italians, Portuguese, and North Africans living and working in France to help fuel its economic revival accounted for ever higher percentages of the French population. By 1960 an estimated 10 percent of Portugal's entire population was working in France on a seasonal or full-time basis.

Nonetheless, the political discourse of a France getting back to work and moving forward was not entirely hollow campaign rhetoric, for a steady economic boom accompanied "le baby boom." By 1950, France was operating with a perfectly balanced budget (thanks in large part to a devalued franc and war debt that was excused by the United States). In 1951, France's gross national product was only two-thirds that of Great Britain, and its exports only one-half of Britain's. By 1965 (the end of the New Wave period), France had surpassed Britain in every category, including average wages paid. But as Larkin explains, "Contrary to the hopes of many contemporaries, the economic changes of the postwar decades saw no particular upswing in social mobility."[6] The foreign labor force remained at the low end of the pay scale, and France became increasingly stratified into several distinct social ranks. Even the public education system continued to enforce two very divergent tracks from the earliest grades on: some students were channeled toward professional and intellectual fields, while most were directed toward practical jobs without hope of pursuing education in specialized lycées, much less universities.

Nonetheless, as many institutions within France struggled to modernize and rebuild, the standard of living of all classes improved steadily, thanks in part to strong labor unions and the active roles played by the Socialist and Communist Parties, even though the gap between upper middle class and lower middle class widened. As Forbes and Kelly observe, economic progress brought a new era to France, one borrowed mostly from American and British business models: "The economic boom of the 1950s was a remarkable achievement. . . . Production grew by 41 percent between 1950 and 1958, fulfilling the targets of the [Fourth Republic's] Second Plan a year ahead of schedule. France entered the consumer age of detergents, plastics, private cars, washing machines. . . . The 'jeune cadre dynamique,' or thrusting young executive, was becoming a familiar figure, with a commitment to business success, modern (American) managerial attitudes, and a life-style of personal development and conspicuous consumption."[7] Not only was this new copycat spirit lampooned by Jacques Tati in *Jour de féte* (1949) and *Mon oncle* (1958), but American and British cultural influences provided unsettling backdrops for many of the subsequent New Wave films as France entered into a long era of love-hate obsessions with American and British culture and lifestyles.

If the dramatic changes resulting from this rapidly growing economy produced a general trend for 1950s cinema spectatorship in France, it was, ironically, to create a gradually smaller, more elite audience. This study will investigate the specific economic and industrial changes in the cinema itself later in this chapter, but it must confront here the connections between large changes in French society and the resulting shifts in the audience. While overall economic conditions were improving throughout Europe, there was nonetheless a shared crisis in motion-picture attendance during the 1950s. Immediately after World War II, a boom in exhibition had occurred when American films and other domestic and international motion pictures, long banned from French, German, and Italian screens, came back with a vengeance, allowing Europeans finally to witness such already famous movies as *Gone with the Wind* (1939), *The Wizard of Oz* (1940), and *Casablanca* (1943), as well as the recent films noirs and others. But by the 1950s, as Europe's national industries were cranking out increasing numbers of high-quality films to compete with American imports, cinema-going ran head-on into other competitors for leisure time. With the expanding economies of the mid-1950s, European film attendance peaked in 1956, a full decade after it did in the United States. France reached its highest box-office numbers in 1957. From 1956 to 1961 Western Europe's film audience declined by 473 million spectators. France alone saw a drop from 412 million tickets sold in 1957 to 328 million by 1961, and this during the largest increase in French population in a century.[8]

Movies were losing nearly one-third of their audience for a variety of reasons, but the most important competitors were two consumer products: the automobile and the television. The number of people buying automobiles in particular was a "marker of changes in lifestyles and spending habits," according to Jean-Claude Batz.[9] He does not propose that people who bought a car were simply too busy driving around to stop for a movie, nor that they were necessarily so broke from buying a Citroën that they could not afford to see *M. Hulot's Holiday*. Rather these new purchases indicated an upwardly mobile family with many more options for leisure time, beyond watching TV or driving. The potential film audience was able to go on more frequent and longer vacations, attend more sports events, or spend more evenings in restaurants and nightclubs. Increased disposable income and the parallel increase in manufacturing and imports also led to people spending additional money on new appliances, ranging from radios for every family member to washers and dryers, or even on a second home in the country. As Colin Crisp argues, "The period of the fifties saw a dramatic increase in all forms of consumer spending related to the individual and to the home and it was those forms of spending related to public or community activities which showed decreases. This move away from a population which expects to go out for its services and entertainment, and toward a population which expects services and entertainment to be delivered to the home . . . was one of the essential factors in the steadily growing pressure on cinema throughout this period to transform itself."[10] The trade paper *Variety* concisely summed up the problems confronting Europe's film industry in the title of a 1963 article: "Box Office Foes: Cars, TV, Prosperity."[11]

Studies in both England and the United States in the late 1940s, when film attendance in these countries began to drop rapidly, showed a perfect symmetry between the increase in automobile ownership and the decline in film attendance. American studies suggested that 42 percent of the decline in attendance was attributable to car purchases, which was almost as much as for television. Accordingly, Italy, with the smallest percentage of cars per citizen in Western Europe, saw the smallest decline in film attendance during the 1950s. France, by contrast, which saw the number of automobiles and drive-in campgrounds double between 1955 and 1960 (reaching nine people per car in 1961 versus twenty-four in Italy, but only three in the United States), followed the American example by losing movie attendance swiftly after 1957. In fact, France's concerned film industry spent a great deal of time looking over the border at Germany, whose fascination with the automobile was quickly becoming a national craze. Germany provided an example of what France was trying to avoid: over two hundred German theaters closed in 1960, another three hundred in 1961, and twenty-five hundred more were considered near bankruptcy.[12] A 1960 front-page editorial in *Le Film français* titled "Autos et 'deux roues' concurrent no 1 de cinéma" ("Autos and Mopeds Are Cinema's Number 1 Competitor") argued that the French film industry needed new initiatives to ensure that this newly "motorized public" would remain faithful to the cinema in winter and summer alike.[13] The authors realized that new affluence, unfortunately, did not necessarily translate into more money for the cinema's coffers. The automobile had a dramatic impact on France; in 1963, Roland Barthes wrote that the French were so obsessed with the automobile that within popular discourse and family relations in France, it ranked as the second most common topic, trailing only the more traditional debates concerning food. Barthes even suggested that Oedipal struggles between father and son were now being played out over selection and control of the family's automobile purchase![14]

Television, however, became an even more direct competitor for the cinema's audience and the family's attention. American box-office receipts dropped 23 percent between the peak years of 1946 and 1956, even though ticket prices increased 40 percent over those same ten years. According to Tino Balio, the profits for Hollywood's ten leading movie studios dropped 76 percent while over four thousand theaters closed their doors.[15] Already in 1953, André Bazin warned in *Esprit* about the dire economic circumstances in Hollywood and how newly unemployed actors and technicians, laid off by the major studios, were struggling to retool and find work in the new television boom.[16] Thus, it should come as no surprise that French film professionals and critics alike were worried about how post–World War II changes that had an economic powerhouse like Hollywood on the ropes would affect their own, weaker national cinema.

Television did not burst into French homes as rapidly as it had in the United States and England, but it did make steady inroads, especially during the late 1950s and early 1960s, as movie attendance dropped accordingly and also began its biggest shift in demographics. Television's gradual pace was attributable in part to the slower economic expansion in the late forties and early fifties in France but also to the government's heavy user tax on sales of television sets and the relatively slim offerings of broadcast shows. In 1950, for instance, France had just one state-run television channel, and it broadcast a mere twenty hours per week. Only in 1964 did the second channel appear; not until 1967 was color available in France. According to Jill Forbes, "The survival of the French film industry benefited enormously from the slow spread of television."[17] For instance, in 1949 the United States already had 1 million television sets while France had only several thousand. In 1958 that number had increased to 683,000 sets; by 1959 it had climbed to just under 1 million (versus 55 million for the United States), and by 1962 there were 2.5 million sets in France. Nonetheless, one of the more pathetic signifiers of the new crisis for French film was cited in a front-page editorial by *Le Film français* titled "La recherche d'un public" ("In Search of a Public"), which mentioned that only one in thirty people in France went to a movie theater in 1959, the same ratio as people owning a television.[18] By the end of 1960, the balance between going to the movies and owning a television shifted permanently in television's favor.

While French television offered much less made-for-television entertainment than did American commercial networks, the French did augment their news, documentaries, and variety shows by airing motion pictures on television almost from the start. Television thereby directly cut into the perceived need or desire to go out to movie theaters in a way that other consumer distractions did not. Moreover, as television became more widespread among the lower middle class and middle class, it affected family disposable income for leisure activities more dramatically than did automobiles, which tended to be owned by upper middle class, urban families. As Batz explained, "TV is not only a huge family expense, cutting into other entertainment purchases; it tends to keep the head of the household home, so families no longer go to the movies together as often. It therefore changes audience behavior patterns permanently."[19] France would have to learn, as American motion picture and even radio producers had, that the days of a mass, generalized family audience were ending, and their products would have to be pitched more keenly at increasingly fragmented segments of the population (children, teenagers, college students, and women). The New Wave could obviously appeal to a specific niche audience in a way that many of the earlier "tradition of quality" historical epics or literary adaptations would not. The cinema's entire function within a new society was changing, and the rise of affluence, education, television, and other consumer products provided tough new challenges to an industry that had always remained rather decentralized, undercapitalized, and artisanal. One unpleasant but necessary option for the French, as will be examined in detail later, was to enter into more international coproductions with American producers. But to many this alternative seemed like a fast track to oblivion, leading toward the demise of the spirit and independence of France's national cinema. As Batz lamented in 1963, "If tomorrow our European film market finds itself submerged by the flood of televisions, as most of the current warning signs suggest, the companies already allied with Hollywood will become, for better or worse, islands where everyone will try to find refuge."[20]

In his influential book, *Le cinéma exploité*, René Bonnell examines the industry's cynicism and frustration. Bonnell argues that French cinema had faced nearly endless crises since the 1930s, but the decline of audiences by 1960 deepened the problem: "Film has gradually changed from the dominant popular form of entertainment to its current status as another form of artistic and cultural activity. The decline in attendance has not been universal, but rather has affected most the lower end of the scale, as the audience becomes more elite."[21] He also cites the sobering conclusion of a study of the French cinema's relative health by the Société d'études et de mathémathiques (SEMA) covering the years of 1957 to 1964: "'Cinema is no longer the art of the masses or the popular entertainment it was. The social profile of the film audience is nearing that of live theater. The young, well-educated 'enlightened fanatic' is replacing the average spectator.'"[22] This new dependence on a concentrated core of young, urban moviegoers made the industry as a whole especially vulnerable, because by the early 1960s, roughly 20 percent of the audience provided 80 percent of the annual box-office revenue, while the working class's attendance dropped over 60 percent during that decade. And although the largest portion of the audience remained fifteen to twenty-four year olds, Bonnell points out that even that previously reliable group's attendance depended largely on socioeconomic status: "Overall demand for movies shifts toward an increasingly selective audience. Higher than average income, a privileged professional background, and solid education increase one's attendance. . . . Even the attendance of young people fits these traits."[23]

By the early 1960s, study after study was confirming the French industry's worst fears: like England, the United States, and most of Western Europe, France's motion-picture industry, which had long been a source of national pride and export income (like fashion, wine, and perfume), no longer served the average citizen. By 1961, the commercial French cinema was clearly feeling the financial pinch from these changes in demographics. Two of every three film technicians were unemployed for some or all of 1961; this fact also explains why the unions were so quick to condemn New Wave location shooting practices, which further channeled the decreasing production money away from underutilized studio space. Batz explains that national Film Aid, which accounted for roughly 20 percent of French production budgets, kept France in the international production business: "French . . . productions would be condemned to failure if their subventions, which assure the economic feasibility of the majority of their films, were removed without some other form of compensation."[24]

Consequently, the late 1950s and early 1960s must be seen as a complex and contradictory time for the French film industry and its spectators: On the one hand, the New Wave was bringing renewed attention and respect to the French industry as perhaps the most exciting place on the earth for making movies. On the other hand, the traditional bases for the French and European cinemas were nonetheless crumbling, and as this study will demonstrate, the notion of a truly national cinema was being weakened even as the power of the individual auteur seemed to be on the rise.

The Cultural and Aesthetic Setting

Transformations in demand deeply affected the nature of the cinema's clientele, as an ever more elite audience comprised the most active moviegoers, but these changes also were part of shifts in the larger cultural sphere of 1950s France. The lively and occasionally vicious aesthetic debates in film circles were part of a general rethinking of the connections between various arts, critical models, and political commitments. World War II had demonstrated on many levels that aesthetics, education, sociology, economics, and politics played parallel and competing roles in modern society; the war had reminded everyone of the high stakes involved in ideology, cultural theory, and media practice. The rise of a wide array of popular media after World War II contributed to a monumental reshaping of the cultural realm; this phenomenon, plus the expansion of France's universities, motivated traditionally isolated "high culture" critics to rethink their place in the modern world. Many contemporary sociologists, art critics, and philosophers began to write more consistently of "changing intellectual landscapes" and "broken academic barriers" as they tried to map out this new cultural terrain. From the halls of the Sorbonne to the pages of weekly news magazines, recurring motifs of a rapidly changing face of France gradually developed, and the popular media were always cited as catalysts of these changes. The rising status of aesthetic and cultural criticism as a significant factor in French intellectual and political life helped in turn fuel "French Theory" as an up-and-coming international export.

In the media, the 1950s saw a definitive breakdown of conventional divisions between high and low cultural products and the ways they were interpreted. One striking development was the emergence of mass circulation weekly magazines, such as *Elle* (1945), *Paris-Match* (1949), and *L'Express* (1953), that replaced smaller, more specialized reviews and journals as barometers of social and intellectual change. *L'Express*, in particular, strove to represent this new, transitional France by combining coverage of contemporary lifestyle issues with an academic, or cultural studies, stance. Cover stories often focused on "high art" figures such as Samuel Beckett and the twenty-eight-year-old "painting sensation" Bernard Buffet, but one also featured thirteen-year-old Jean-Pierre Léaud, star of *The 400 Blows*, just before the film's premiere at the 1959 Cannes Film Festival. Meanwhile, these magazines' articles covered topics ranging from the war in Algeria to Camus's novels to the latest women's fashions.

A telling example of this fascinating mixture of consumerism and culture can be seen in the March 1, 1957, issue of *L'Express*, which featured an article titled "La Machine à laver tourne-t-elle dans le sens de l'histoire?" ("Is the Washing Machine Spinning in History's Direction?"). This article highlighted France's rush for more household appliances (vacuums, washing machines, refrigerators) and noted with concern that consumer spending on them had doubled from 68 million francs in 1954 to 121 million in 1956. "This rise in comfort has interesting industrial and economic implications. But is it sane for our nation? It also touches on serious sociological and psychological issues. How does increased comfort affect a person's mindset? How does it modify our social behavior?"[25] The magazine then enriched the discussion by featuring an interview with a number of sociologists and cultural experts, including Edgar Morin, of the Centre national de la recherche scientifique, author of sociological anthropology books such as *Stars* and *Le cinéma ou l'homme imaginaire*.[26] Another contributor to this discussion, Colette Audry, a home economist, pointed out that washing laundry by hand had the advantage of creating a shared bond between French women and hardworking women in Africa and the rest of the world: "Once this continuity is removed, we lose a feminine connection. . . . That is a significant issue."[27] It is hard to imagine *Time* magazine, on which *L'Express* was modeled, inviting social scientists from Harvard to debate the national and international cultural consequences of buying vacuums and washing machines during the 1950s.

It was, of course, *L'Express* that launched the term "nouvelle vague" and used it almost relentlessly during the late 1950s as its own battle cry. In the fall of 1957, *L'Express*'s Françoise Giroud initiated a national survey of "the generation who will create France's future": "We have prepared a vast questionnaire for young people from all locales, all social classes, designed to reveal for the first time, in depth, just what our new French generation—*la nouvelle vague*—is like. Their ideals, their beliefs, their education, their desires . . . what are they? *L'Express*, which has a large audience among those who make up this 'nouvelle vague' is well positioned to distribute and evaluate this survey."[28] *L'Express* asked young people between the ages of eighteen and thirty to respond to twenty-four questions ranging from "What is France's number one problem?" to "Are you happy?" and "Do you think people like you will have any real influence over France's fate?" The responses, published on December 5 and 12, 1957, included both the raw data (25 percent wished France had a socialist society, 69 percent thought women should concentrate on home and family) and selected comments from the surveys ("In modern life today, we have no god. . . . We are isolated and independent.")

Professional social scientists evaluating the data offered cautionary conclusions. They pointed out, for instance, that the majority of young people felt unable to influence current events and that only a few people in their twenties were interested in the top literary figures of the era. Rather, contemporary youth were preoccupied with more accessible sources like detective novels and the sports page, and their immediate goals were to establish their own families and careers. Such a survey is important today not because it gives any clear sense of a unified generation but because it reveals how deeply France's popular press believed that younger people lived and thought differently than previous generations. These observations paralleled the research and theories of American sociologists, who were also busy studying and documenting "youth culture" after World War II. It is startling to recall that the term "teenager" first entered everyday language in 1945, and it was really the 1950s that saw young people identified as a separate, definable age group falling between childhood and adulthood. According to *A History of Young People in the West*, "The fifties saw the appearance of 'teenagers,' who were different from their predecessors due to their numbers, their high level of resources, and their group consciousness."[29] Young people constituted a distinct community, and as American sociologist James Coleman wrote in 1955, "a youth subculture in industrial society" had emerged: "These young people speak a different language . . . and the language they speak is becoming more and more different."[30] While sociologists, psychologists, and community leaders debated the potential social dangers of this new lifestyle, its perceived existence and differences helped fuel a widespread fascination with all things young and new. In addition, older people suddenly tried to learn about this generation to appear "hip" themselves; marketing powers shifted into high gear, trying to gauge and exploit the newfound subculture. The topic was so lively in France that Giroud published an expanded version of the *Express* articles in book form, titled, *La nouvelle vague: Portraits de la jeunesse.*[31]

L'Express's initial response to its groundbreaking survey was an opportunistic attempt to summarize and speak to this new market audience— "the eight million French people between the ages of eighteen and thirty-five who make up the *nouvelle vague*"[32]—but it also offered a cautionary warning that France's future lay with a generation that might not respect or follow the established rules and rituals of France's past. In the process, a new generation, whether it really was all that different or not, was being defined and represented. Now the emphasis in advertising, fashion, literature, and cinema would be on novelty, change, and breaks from the past, while the cultural observers would create a new business of combing the horizon for concrete signs of any major upheavals. As French historian Jacques Siclier wrote in 1961, "For a press that has to uncover striking new trends, all that was young and animated by a new spirit became part of *la nouvelle vague*."[33] But everyone seemed to agree that the mid-1950s was indeed a challenging new era where new detergents were needed for new washing machines, new shopping routines were determined by new cars and new refrigerators, and a new generation was reading new novels and watching new, sexier films like *And God Created Woman* (Vadim, 1956). Even older, long established directors like Marcel

Carné offered their own cautionary tales on this new youthful, sexually active milieu with films such as *Les tricheurs* (*The Cheats*, 1958). It is also a sign of the times and a warning that the students in *Les tricheurs* spend a great deal of time drinking scotch, driving around, and listening to American records, but almost no time going to the movies. Already in 1959, *Le Film français* ran an article by Maurice Bessy arguing that there was a "*nouvelle vague de spectateurs*" that French filmmakers had to comprehend and address immediately: "Understanding their general thoughts, preoccupations, hopes, and fears, upon which the health of the cinema depends, seems essential and URGENT."[34] Young people were thus granted a cultural importance and power never before seen in French society.

The marketing of culture and blurring of the lines between high and low culture were also reinforced during this decade with the 1953 launching of the *livre de poche*, paperback versions of French classics, which made the great works of literature cheaper and more accessible. But while these inexpensive classic novels may have helped students, they were far from the essence of literature for this generation: "The 1950s were not only 'modern,' they were assertively 'new,'" write Forbes and Kelly. "Modernity was characterized by the constant search for novelty, as the consumer-driven boom imposed the values of change and innovation . . . increasingly in daily life."[35] Thus, effects of consumerism pushed even the academic presses to pursue new forms, new talents, and new modes of public relations. The most radical of modern novelists distanced themselves from the classics by aiming for a young, impatient audience, incorporating contemporary events and realism into their fiction while avoiding stylized, academic narration. As historian Georges Duby writes, "The 1950 novel was marked by a transformation of both style and technique. This revolution was inaugurated, as all must be, with a radical attack on traditional structures. It threw into question the concepts of plot, character, and psychological analysis: hence the label 'antinovel' proposed by Sartre."[36]

The *nouveau roman*, or New Novel, as one literary subgenre became known, was a novel "under construction," balancing itself between telling a story and destroying the possibility of fiction at the same time. But one should not fall into the trap of assuming a simple, unified youth movement served by a single narrative wave. The 1950s saw at least two contradictory trends in modern literature. On one side were the so-called New Novelists, Alain Robbe-Grillet, Natalie Sarraute, Claude Simon, and Michel Butor in particular, who threw novelistic conventions like characterization and cause-effect out the window, substituting subjective personal styles or even cold lists for psychological realism or motivated description. On the other side were the new realists, who often exploited popular fiction norms. These new popular novelists were typified in the meteoric success of Françoise Sagan's novel *Bonjour tristesse* (published in 1954, when Sagan was nineteen years old) and Christiane Rochefort's *Les petits enfants du siècle* (*The Century's Children*, 1954), both aimed at youthful and, especially, female readers.

The rise of the New Novel fit comfortably within larger intellectual debates over the search for new modes of representation for a new generation, and thus it too should be understood in relation to pertinent national and international generating mechanisms. Germaine Brée and Eric Schoenfeld define the New Novelists as writers who struggled to renovate 1950s French literature by moving away from the commercialization but also away from the tragic themes of wartime existentialism: "In a world transformed by the rapid advances of physics, biology, biochemistry—to say nothing of technology—the novel, they claimed, was lagging far behind, content to repeat ad nauseum what the nineteenth-century novelists had said. The new novelists wished to experiment with narrative techniques that would correspond with the new conceptions we had of ourselves and our world."[37] The New Novel had only arrived on the international scene in 1955, but by the early 1960s many of its titles were already considered part of the canon for twentieth-century French literature courses throughout the world. According to Jill Forbes, two social institutions helped fuel this rapid insurgence of the *nouveau roman*. First was the publishing industry, which, hoping to discover and market youthful writers, aggressively pursued novelty. Editions de Minuit's new director, Jerome Lindon, sought a niche market and hired young Alain Robbe-Grillet as his literary advisor. Born in 1922, Robbe-Grillet was nearly twenty years younger than Jean-Paul Sartre and the same age as filmmaker Alain Resnais. Robbe-Grillet became a perfect choice for Lindon, since he brought fame and profit to Editions de Minuit, gradually becoming the most prominent of Lindon's writers, publishing *Les gommes* (*The Erasers*), *Le voyeur*, and *La jalousie*, before following Marguerite Duras's example from *Hiroshima, mon amour* and writing a script for Resnais, titled *L'Année dernière à Marienbad* (*Last Year at Marienbad*, 1961). Robbe-Grillet helped turn a tiny publishing house (he explained that as few as eight people generally worked at Edition de Minuit) into a major international cultural force and further broke the barriers between high art, literary theory, and New Wave cinema.[38]

A second determining factor in the rise of the New Novel was the accelerated growth of colleges and universities in the 1950s, not only in France but also in England and in the United States. Comparative literature and French language departments taught more contemporary literature, and the *nouveau roman* provided a daring, coherent literary movement that new faculty and graduate students could easily build into the expanding twentieth-century literature canon. Thus, the New Novel gained from the considerable cultural attention on all things "youthful." Publishing houses picked up on this sudden interest quickly; they were helped along by the rapid expansion of academia, where more courses meant more book sales, and more book sales in turn meant more public attention and validation of a youthful export from France, as Robbe-Grillet became a new, highly exportable, cultural icon.[39]

Robbe-Grillet became particularly significant as a representative of the New Novel because, in addition to his personal flair for public relations, including interviews, lecture tours, and visiting professorships, he was both a novelist and a narrative theorist. He wrote a number of essays, beginning in 1955, which were collected in his *Pour un nouveau roman* (published in English in 1965 under the title *For a New Novel*), providing critics with a sort of manifesto outlining the spirit of change in literature. For instance, at the very beginning of *For a New Novel* Robbe-Grillet writes that one thing that surprised him in the many reviews of his novels, whether the reviewer was praising or attacking books such as *Les gommes* or *Le voyeur*, "was to encounter in almost every case an implicit—or even explicit—reference to the great novels of the past, which were always held up as the model on which the young writer should keep his eyes fixed."[40] The influence of Robbe-Grillet was felt beyond French language classes or specialized literary reviews such as *La Nouvelle revue française*, however, as he was interviewed and even wrote a series of essays for *L'Express* in the mid-1950s. In fact, *L'Express*'s desire to be equated with "newness" is clear in its interview with him in October 1959: "Two thousand copies of your most recent book, *In the Labyrinth*, were sold in its first two days alone. We are happy for you since we had recommended it to our readers interested in 'pure literature.'"[41] The popularity of *In the Labyrinth* thus validated the cultural power of both the New Novel and *L'Express* as voices of the New Wave generation.

Interestingly for this study, Robbe-Grillet complained that his theoretical arguments caused many popular and serious critics alike to crown him king of a new literary youth movement that they variously labeled the New Novel, the Objective Novel, the School of Minuit, and *ecole du regard* (school of the glance). Robbe-Grillet, however, wrote that he did not believe any unified school or movement existed. He was troubled when critics began to lump him together with any young writer whose work did not seem traditional, discussing Robbe-Grillet's novels alongside others that shared nothing except their unconventionality. Similarly, some *Cahiers du cinéma* filmmakers would later complain about the tendency to group together Vadim, Truffaut, and Resnais under the same New Wave heading. The unsatisfactory and uneven reception of Robbe-Grillet's novels and essays motivated him to rework some of his essays in an attempt to clarify his own positions on contemporary literature and the *nouveaux romans de Robbe-Grillet*: "These reflections in no way constitute a theory of the novel; they merely attempt to clarify several key lines of development which seem to me crucial in contemporary literature. If in many of the pages that follow, I readily employ the term New Novel, it is not to designate a school, nor even a specific and constituted group of writers working in the same direction; the expression is merely a convenient label, applicable to all those seeking new forms for the novel, forms capable of expressing (or of creating) new relations between man and the world."[42]

Here one finds additional justifications for discussing the New Novel in a book on the New Wave: both movements are loosely organized around youthful searches for new ways to tell new stories that engage the modern world. As Robbe-Grillet argues, New Novelists "know that the systematic repetition of the forms of the past is not only absurd and futile, but it can even become harmful: by blinding us to our real situation in the world today, it keeps us, ultimately, from constructing the world and man of tomorrow."[43] Those critics championing the New Novel argued convincingly that Balzac's era involved traits such as faith in cause-effect and individuality that were missing in the modern world. Just as modern notions of space, time, and the human condition had changed by the mid-twentieth century, humanity's modes of representation and inquiry should change as well. Modern man and modern fictions no longer belonged to the world of Balzac and Dickens, so there was no point in retelling the tales that Balzac and Dickens had told. Many of these arguments resurface in debates over the French New Wave as well, since, in large part, these films are about renovating cinematic *écriture* or the very process and difficulty of narrating something unexpected. Modern novelists wanted to break free of the links to nineteenth-century literature just as the New Wave filmmakers needed to isolate themselves from literary adaptations and the traditional conventions of classical cinema.

Further, both New Novel and New Wave are handy historical terms that conjure up immediate, if exaggerated, images of unified movements creating groundbreaking books and movies that were changing French culture daily. Unlike earlier modernist movements, such as Symbol*ism*, Impression*ism*, or Surreal*ism*, which each suggested itself as a sort of variation or fine tuning of modern art, "New" movements suggested vast ramifications for the future, producing connotations of irreversible, revolutionary change. Even the occasional designations of "young novel" or "young French cinema" suggested a passing moment that would soon mature like all others. But to be "New" gave novels and films a very real degree of cultural power, especially in an age transformed by marketing and a distrust of or even disgust with some of humanity's past. Rather than offering a range of optional artistic camps (for example, Existentialism, Expressionism, Minimalism) France now had only two options: there was the "New," and there was everyone else. For instance, in response to novelist Henri Clouard's complaint that New Novelists "want to saw off the branch we are sitting on," Robbe-Grillet replied, "The branch in question is already dead of natural causes (and the passing of time); it is not our fault if it is now rotting."[44] The battle cry of innovation and youth became so dominant that eventually cigarette maker Peter Stuyvesant adopted the slogan "*Jeune, dynamique, et international!*" which grew out of this frenzy for novelty that not only helped sell cigarettes but also helped launch both the New Novelists and the New Wave.

Because of the boom in popular and specialized magazines, radio, and eventually television, artists and writers saw their visibility and social role change in the 1950s. Moreover, the New Novel was closely connected with other new trends in literary and cultural criticism, partly because writers such as Robbe-Grillet were rapidly becoming public figures. Culture was being revived as a French national treasure and an important intellectual export. Cultural figures, from Sartre and Picasso to Sagan and anthropologist Claude Lévi-Strauss, saw unprecedented wealth and celebrity heaped upon them as they became part of the new "culture industry," which carried them far beyond the traditional intellectual circles more common to 1930s and 1940s artists and academics.[45] The ideological ramifications of such large-scale gaps between lived experience and representation, in rhetoric, novels, cinema, and even advertisements, came to the center of intellectual activity in the decade after World War II. Lévi-Strauss in par-

(Dessin de Tim)

Figure 1.1. Cartoon from *L'Express,* April 30, 1959, 29; unborn child kicking elderly gentleman

ticular helped bring together the study of literature and social science by combining his study of myths with an enlivened brand of anthropology.

Lévi-Strauss argued that language lays the foundations for culture since both are made of the same material: structural relations, systems of difference, signs, and relations of exchange. Lévi-Strauss played a crucial role in the 1950s for igniting a new era of structural and semiotic analysis that sought to understand how language determined the human mind, which in turn determined culture and history. His inspiration came from Ferdinand de Saussure's *Course in General Linguistics*. Saussure argued that linguistic structures, including the sign, made of a signifier and its signifieds and combined in codes, were the bases of all human activity. The belief that linguistics was essential in studying other cultural phenomena was rooted in two fundamental insights: first, society is not simply a collection of material events, but consists of events with meaning or signs; and second, that lived events do not have essences, but are defined by systematic internal and external networks of relations, or signifying code systems, that the analyst must work to uncover and understand.[46] As Rosalind Coward and John Ellis explain, "Structuralist thought bases its analysis of the social process upon this analogy between society and language. . . . For Lévi-Strauss, linguistics presents itself as a systematic science, whose methods are exemplary for the human sciences."[47]

The significance of Lévi-Strauss and of the rise of structuralist and semiotic analysis, both of which were fueled by the impact of his 1958 book, *Structural Anthropology*, was far reaching. Suddenly, the novel's social function went beyond Sartre's engaged literature to become part of the fabric of social formation. If language provided the rules and production of meaning and was made concrete in social structures, then all language was worthy of careful study and all modes of communication could be analyzed in linguistic terms. The world was a rich network of sign systems, and social scientists, art historians, film critics, and literature professors could all share common vocabulary, methodology, and goals. Everyone's task was to evaluate signification in all its forms; as Roland Barthes, the most influential cultural critic of them all, would prove, "reading" a spaghetti advertisement or a wrestling match was as valid for professors at the Sorbonne as analyzing the novels of Flaubert or even Robbe-Grillet.

Barthes argued that all literary and cultural history was really a history of signs. Beginning in 1947 until his death in 1980, his criticism moved gracefully from discussing Flaubert's *écriture*, to the New Novel, to images from Sergei Eisenstein's *Ivan the Terrible*, to the excessive qualities of the 1950s Citroën automobile, and back to the codes at work in Balzac. His object of study was the entire cultural world that literary theory opened up for structural, semiotic, and eventually poststructural analysis (as seen in his *The Pleasure of the Text*). One of his most amazing collections was *Mythologies*, published in 1957 from articles written over the preceding several years. As he explained, *Mythologies* was "an ideological critique bearing on the language of so-called mass-culture" that unmasked the very real, mystifying signs that work to naturalize bourgeois culture via mass culture *myths,* which people accept as universal.[48] Lévi-Strauss had burst on the scenes writing about distant cultures and their myths; Barthes brought myth and its functions full circle, turning them back upon French culture and discourse. By the early 1960s, Barthes was an international sensation, leading a new generation of theorists to prominence. As Forbes and Kelly write, "Critics such as Roland Barthes, Jean Starobinski, Jean-Pierre Richard, Jean Ricardou, Serge Dubrovski, and Gerard Genette sought to replace the traditional humanist approaches to literature with new ones drawing on the theoretical resources of the human and social sciences. . . . The role of the critic is therefore not to narrow down the possible meanings, but rather to multiply them . . . and to analyze the textual structures which make meaning possible."[49] A new sense of significance, as well as of poetics, inspired novelists and filmmakers to think in terms of the history, connotations, and multiple functions of the signifiers they used. Not surprisingly, the French New Wave regularly referred to past film practice (via irises, direct camera address, pantomime, and so on), allusions inspired in part by a renewed desire to reassess current and past arsenals of "cinematic signs."

Barthes wrote for many specialized journals, such as *Communications,* where his influential "Elements of Semiology" and "Rhetoric of the Image" first appeared in 1964, in the same issue in which film theorist Christian Metz launched his study of the semiotics of cinema with "The Cinema: Language or Language System?" Thus, literary and cultural criticism expanded during the late 1950s and early 1960s, not just because of lively new novels and growing universities, but because a whole new generation of scholars was bringing "high" art criticism to bear on every aspect of daily life, including the cinema. As French departments in the American and British universities had seized on the New Novel, their English departments now followed suit, studying French literary theory, if not literature. Everyone's life was suddenly part of innumerable cultural codes, and every "text," whether a Native American folk tale, a 1930s Pagnol film, or a striptease act at a local club, was seemingly worth analyzing for what it could reveal about the societies human beings built around themselves. Readers, too, were now walking sign systems, living according to codes they did not always perceive or acknowledge. Artists, as the creators of representations, became newly aware of their cultural power and the constant danger of being coopted by unseen "bourgeois conventions." Thus, it became more imperative for artists to work critically to anticipate and

shape the many potential significations their work could evoke. The job of
the critic was to decode modern culture in all its forms. George Duby acknowledged this revolutionary scholarly attention to culture in the final
volume of his *Histoire de la France*. Duby explained that the mere presence of his chapter on culture in a survey history of France marks a shift
in the significance of culture in contemporary life and a redefinition of history itself: "Here substituted for [revolutions, wars, and social crises] in
this history text is the vast and vague term *culture*."[50]

Nor surprisingly, literature and cinema were not the only arts undergoing rapid and radical changes in the 1950s. All the critical, cultural, and
economic factors that affected these art forms held true for live theater in
France as well. French theater of the 1940s was very popular, but right after the war few top dramatists seemed to break any new cultural or representational ground. Gradually, however, new playwrights and the so-called
Theater of the Absurd began to fill in the intellectual gap. Sartre and Camus had written plays to point out social crises, but they also had illus-
trated the correct direction for positive action. In contrast, the Absurd
dramas held out no such hope for action, positive or negative. New theater
was more engaged in the formal investigation of the medium than in the
conventions of an engaged or epic theater of the earlier twentieth century.

Writing in 1960, Wallace Fowlie called attention to this dramatic revival of French theater after World War II and especially during the 1950s:
"During the past ten or fifteen years, the number of successes, both literary and commercial, almost warrants the use of the new term *Ecole de
Paris*. Pichette, Beckett, Ionesco, Adamov, Schehadé, and Ghelderode are
writing new types of plays, so opposed to the successes of the first part of
the century that it is possible to see in their work a renaissance of the theater. . . . Already during the 1940s the very marked commercial successes
of Sartre and Anouilh and Montherlant threw into disrepute the older fixed
formulas of the thesis play and the adultery play of Henry Bernstein and
Henri Becque. But in the 1950s, the successes of Ghelderode, Beckett,
and Ionesco made the Bernstein play the product of an era that is over."[51]
Other drama historians, including Jacques Guicharnaud, would go on to
label these 1950s experiments "new theater."

With plays like *The Bald Soprano*, *The Chairs*, and *Rhinoceros*, Eu-
gene Ionesco broke away from the conventionalized "committed" drama of
Brecht and Sartre. His plays helped Martin Esslin define the essence of
Theater of the Absurd. Others labeled them "antitheater," to parallel the
"antinovels" of Robbe-Grillet. By the early 1960s, Ionesco's avant-garde

works of the 1950s were already part of a new canon. As Guicharnaud writes: "'Anti-theater of the 1950s has quite simply become the theater of our times. Sketchy characters being carried away by words, changing identities, having three noses, laying eggs, talking without communicating, become preys to organized disorder . . . being brainwashed by monks who are not really monks—none of that seems baffling any longer."[52] Theater of the Absurd, defined as tragicomic, joyously pessimistic plays evoking godless worlds with no pertinent answers or guidelines to help the surreally lost characters, is most closely identified with Samuel Beckett's 1953 premiere of *Waiting for Godot*, considered by many historians the most important play of the twentieth century.

Theater of the Absurd became the immediate catchphrase for many of these plays, but subsequent historians have tended to retain the label New Theater. Forbes and Kelly define this era concisely: "'*Le nouveau théâtre* serves both to recall the pervasive concern with the new, and to indicate a parallelism with the contemporaneous emergence of the *nouveau roman*. The radical developments in both genres were animated by common concerns, in particular to challenge the concept of unitary meaning."[53] Thus, these new plays not only fit the New Novel's notion of radical youthful forms pushing aside respected traditions (here Sartre and Brecht were being surpassed instead of Balzac and Proust), but they also proved that experimentation could make money. Just as specialized presses such as Editions de Minuit or Editions du Seuil were successfully marketing new novels and critics, the New Theater began in tiny Latin Quarter theaters in Paris, where low overhead decreased initial financial risks. Moreover, these small theaters, located near the Paris universities La Sorbonne, Jussieu, and Censier as well as tourist sites, proved there was a strong new audience made up of urban, educated young people—the same sort of audience that bought Robbe-Grillet novels and would frequent new films by young New Wave directors. By 1960, *Waiting for Godot*, which initially premiered at the Théâtre de Babylone, had moved to the large state-run Odéon Theater, and, as Forbes and Kelly point out, "The success of the new theater in displacing a dominant cultural form heralded a new wave of experimentation in dramatic styles and practices which was to gather momentum throughout the 1960s."[54] New forms, new modes of production, and new audiences proved that French culture was indeed undergoing what *L'Express* called a nouvelle vague, and that Wave was now proving significant to every aspect of Parisian life. No medium of this new activity would prove more exciting or marketable than the French New Wave cinema.

From *Ciné-Clubs* to Film Journals

The film culture of the late 1940s helped jump-start the nearly fanatical *cinéphilia* that came to characterize 1950s Paris. After the war, previously banned or heavily edited films played prominently in French theaters and *ciné-clubs*, including *L'Atalante* (Vigo, 1933) and *La règle du jeu* (*Rules of the Game*, Renoir, 1939) as well as many revivals of American and other international motion pictures from the past. Between 1946 and 1955, young cinephiles such as Eric Rohmer, François Truffaut, and Jean-Luc Godard, among scores of others, immersed themselves in moviegoing but also in the parallel activities that made *"cinéphilia"* so rich in France. *Ciné-clubs* and journals were popping up all over Paris and even sprouting up in many provincial towns. One of the most famous *ciné-clubs* was Objectif 49, which was organized by André Bazin, Jacques Doniol-Valcroze, and Alexandre Astruc, along with Jean Cocteau, Robert Bresson, and Roger Leenhardt. At another, Studio Parnasse, young cinephiles met regularly on Tuesday nights and debated the films after the screenings. Rohmer's own Ciné-Club du Quartier Latin met on Thursdays and attracted many of the same participants.

Rohmer also went on to publish his *Gazette du cinéma* in 1950 as a sort of outgrowth of his *ciné-club*. While his journal lasted only one year, it marked an important transition in French film criticism by combining an older generation of critics from *Revue du cinéma* (including Astruc) with new writers, such as Godard, Truffaut, and Rivette.[55] When Bazin, Doniol-Valcroze, and Joseph-Marie Lo Duca created their first issue of *Cahiers du cinéma* in 1951, it was merely one of many French voices on world cinema, but it, like Rohmer's *Gazette*, helped bridge a gap between the past (they dedicated their first issue to *Revue du cinéma*'s Jean George Auriol, who had vanished one year earlier) and the future of film studies. Interestingly, Bazin and Doniol-Valcroze learned too late that in Rouen there was already a small publication titled *Cahiers du cinéma*. It is important to note that much of the New Wave's eventual audience sat right alongside the young critics and future filmmakers in the *ciné-clubs* and the Cinémathèque française, or read about the debates over film history and film style in the many new film magazines. The New Wave would not fall from the sky in the late 1950s, nor would its audience appear magically out of thin air. Serious film buffs were carefully nursed along and encouraged by the conditions of postwar film culture.

France has a long history of critical and historical writing about the cinema, dating from the 1910s. By the end of World War II, however, the number and quality of French film journals were at an all-time high, picking up where many 1920s journals and publications had left off. Post-World War II magazines and journals devoted exclusively to cinema included titles such as *Cinévie, Cinévogue, Cinémonde, Ciné-Miroir, Paris-Cinéma, Raccords, L'Age du cinéma*, and even *Saint Cinéma de près*. Cinema was seen as the most modern of all art forms, and its recent pivotal role in both propaganda and resistance had clearly proven to everyone the cinema's dynamic cultural power, which was occasionally exaggerated into mythic importance. During the war, the cinematic wing of the French Resistance, Comité de libération du cinéma français (CLCF), had even published its own underground film journal, *L'Ecran français* (The French Screen). Begun as a newsletter in 1943, *L'Ecran* continued as an important cultural force after the war, publishing until 1953. During the war, *L'Ecran* was used to inform cinema personnel about practical issues, review films, and remind everyone that some day a purification of collaborators in the industry would seek revenge. It was in *L'Ecran* that Georges Sadoul wrote many of his famous reviews and that Alexandre Astruc wrote about the *"caméra-stylo."* Even Jean-Paul Sartre, writing in *L'Ecran*, entered into debates with film critic André Bazin over films such as *Citizen Kane* (Welles, 1941). Writing in 1945, just before *Citizen Kane*'s premiere in Paris, Sartre criticized Welles's movie as overly fatalistic and a pure example of bankrupt bourgeois American filmmaking, while Georges Sadoul dismissed it as excessively expressionistic and a mere *"exercice du style."* Later, in *Temps modernes*, Bazin disagreed with Sartre and Sadoul, championing *Citizen Kane*'s modernity and democratic traits.[56]

Battle lines were thus defined by political as well as aesthetic alliances, and the pages of French film journals, like the question-and-answer sessions at local *ciné-clubs*, featured impassioned and often eloquent praise and criticism. One of the dividing lines was whether American films should receive the same critical attention as French or other national cinemas. The Blum-Byrnes agreement of 1946 had further fueled the issue by increasing the number of non-French films that could be shown on French screens to 70 percent. There was a resulting leap: during the first half of 1946, only 38 American films were shown in France; during the first half of 1947, the number jumped to 338. French intellectuals, interested in the artistry and power of the cinema, had to take a stand as open to or opposed to American cinema. The two leading camps were defined by *L'Ecran* (whose editorial board included Jean-Paul Sartre and

Georges Sadoul, as well as André Malraux, Marcel Carné, and Henri Langlois) versus Bazin, Doniol-Valcroze, and Roger Leenhardt, among others, who wrote in a number of journals, including *Revue du cinéma* and eventually *Cahiers du cinéma*. The Communist *L'Ecran*, which had long editorialized against Hollywood films, charged after the war that Hollywood was seducing away French audiences with big budgets and Technicolor the way American soldiers had seduced French women with chocolates and nylons. Then in 1949 they viciously attacked Hitchcock, whose *Rope* (1948) had just been praised by Jacques Doniol-Valcroze in *Revue du cinéma*.

L'Ecran considered Hitchcock a talented craftsperson churning out overly polished Hollywood products, and, like William Wyler and other supposed Hollywood auteurs, he was contrasted to the real artistry of modern European auteurs. In one of many counterattacks, Jacques Rivette eventually wrote in Rohmer's *Gazette du cinéma* that "Hitchcock is the only director to have understood that the cinema can evoke a Dostoevski-like world, which is a purely moral world."[57] When *Cahiers du cinéma* was begun in 1951, it was precisely to champion a wider brand of film criticism that allowed serious critical attention to Hollywood as well as to all other vibrant modes of film production. André Bazin and Jacques Doniol-Valcroze, with significant aid from Léonide Keigel and Joseph-Marie Lo Duca, launched *Cahiers du cinéma*. But while *Cahiers* would become the most internationally famous of all these journals, it should not be considered as an isolated source of film criticism. Rather, one of the best ways to understand the role of *Cahiers* in relation to film culture and the New Wave is to see it as one voice among many that were reshaping the discourse around film criticism.

While *Cahiers du cinéma* is typically identified as Bazin's venture, and he certainly did dominate its aesthetic range in the 1950s and help determine the apprenticeship and directions for many of its young critics, the journal owed its initial success and even its existence most heavily to Jacques Doniol-Valcroze's efforts. Bazin, already ill with tuberculosis in 1950, relied on Doniol-Valcroze to put together the initial financing and the original team of critics. Doniol-Valcroze wanted to continue the work begun by Jean George Auriol at *Revue du cinéma*. With his postwar experience as a journalist and critic for *Cinémonde* and *Revue du cinéma* and simultaneously as editor-in-chief for the fashion magazine *Messieurs*, Doniol-Valcroze had learned well the tasks of organizing a journal, locating sponsors, and preserving harmony among the contributors.[58] He was also actively involved with Jean Cocteau in organizing Objectif 49, where he met Léonide Keigel, then an exhibitor, who would provide the initial financing for a small publishing company, Editions de l'Etoile, to prepare the new cinema review. Bazin was resting in a sanitarium and Doniol-Valcroze retained his principal job at *Messieurs*, so they hired Joseph-Marie Lo Duca, also a "new critic" from *Revue du cinéma*, to organize the first issues. Not only did Lo Duca prove an excellent writer, with access to the latest American films guaranteed by Keigel, but he also designed the format and "look" for the first yellow *Cahiers du cinéma*, though Doniol-Valcroze chose the name (over Bazin's suggested *Cinématographe*).

From the first issue, *Cahiers* established its tone with a brief dedication to the memory of *Revue du cinéma* and its editor, Auriol. The editorial promised that *Cahiers* would provide faithful and rigorous attention to all of world cinema, a cinema, they noted, that had just provided such amazing titles as *Journal d'un curé de campagne* (*Diary of a Country Priest*, Bresson, 1950), *Miracle in Milan* (De Sica, 1951), and *Sunset Boulevard* (Wilder, 1950), among others, in only the preceding few weeks. The first issue included André Bazin on depth, Doniol-Valcroze on Edward Dmytryk, an article on cinema versus television, and a letter discussing cinema from Uruguay. Further, while histories often reduce the contributions of *Cahiers du cinéma* to its unified call for auteurism and a new cinema, throughout the 1950s it printed a surprisingly rich variety of articles and perspectives. Doniol-Valcroze and others strove to maintain the notion of a true "*cahiers*," or notebook, in which many different documents could coexist. Antoine de Baecque's mammoth history of the journal, *Les cahiers du cinéma*, helps clarify the policies at *Cahiers*, revealing that opposing perspectives were allowed since the editorial board considered each article for its own coherence rather than for whether it fit some narrow polemic or aesthetic agenda. Obviously, however, simply offering so much attention to American films was in itself a sort of aesthetic manifesto, and *Cahiers* never shrank from openly explaining and defending some of its editors' controversial positions.

Regardless of the practiced diversity, *Cahiers* established a set of favorite auteurs early on, including Charlie Chaplin, Jean Renoir, F. W. Murnau, and Edward Dmytryk. Yet the new young critics who joined the roster from the earliest days of the journal—Maurice Schérer (a.k.a. Eric Rohmer, who began writing for *Cahiers* at age thirty-one), Jacques Rivette (twenty-four years old), Jean-Luc Godard (twenty-two years old), Claude Chabrol (twenty-two years old), and François Truffaut (twenty years old)—

began, controversially, to shift increased attention to directors such as Alfred Hitchcock and Howard Hawks, who were not as popular with some of the editors. These critics quickly earned the label "young Turks" for their fiery, often ruthless brand of criticism. Jean Douchet argues it was precisely because of these young critics, beginning in earnest in 1954, that the auteur concept became firmly entrenched at *Cahiers*. Rohmer and his friends began with short reviews but then quickly moved on to presenting lively interviews with directors, proving their passion for cinema and detailed knowledge of film history. "The directors (especially the Americans who were little accustomed to people discussing their work with such accuracy and depth) were dumbfounded and deeply impressed by these young writers' ideas. . . . The reputation of *Cahiers du Cinéma* began to grow. In Hollywood the review became essential reading and Fritz Lang, Joseph Mankiewicz, Samuel Fuller, and Nicholas Ray often posed for photographs with a copy of the magazine in their hand."[59] Their gift of auteur status to Hitchcock and Hawks as equivalents of Renoir and Bresson amounted to incendiary criticism during this era, but it also proved how quickly these young men had made their mark, building on Bazin's brilliant groundwork to move *Cahiers du cinéma* criticism firmly into the analysis of mise-en-scène.

Internal debates among critics were commonplace at *Cahiers du cinéma*, though the editors preferred to feature positive reviews and articles over negative ones, believing that only good cinema should receive attention. Before *Cahiers* critics could get reviews and articles published, they first had to convince their own colleagues that their arguments were valuable, while the editorial board regularly asked for revisions, if they did not reject the piece altogether. To a certain extent, the real labor of reshaping film criticism took place within the offices of *Cahiers du cinéma*, where some of the more impassioned and reckless articles were discussed, argued out, and finally revised before being printed. Belonging to the *Cahiers du cinéma* team in the 1950s brought with it a great deal of notoriety, but it also demanded a clear aesthetic perspective, long hours of highly focused dedication, and a strong enough personality to fight for one's ideas to be understood and finally printed. Truffaut's controversial "A Certain Tendency of the French Cinema" proved an excellent test case for the processes, critical challenges, and discursive power of *Cahiers* in the 1950s. But it should be noted that this sort of blunt attack on long lists of films and filmmakers was quite rare at *Cahiers*.

Truffaut's article, published in 1954, provided a scathing denunciation of some of the most respected films, writers, and directors of postwar France; his criticisms were generally leveled at titles such as *Les jeux interdits* (*Forbidden Games*, Clément, 1952) for moral as well as stylistic reasons. Unusual as "A Certain Tendency" was, its attack on the French "tradition of quality" was actually anticipated by Michel Dorsday's review of Christian-Jaque's *Adorables créatures*, in *Cahiers* number 16, in October 1952. Dorsday's review was titled "Le cinéma est mort" ("French Cinema Is Dead") and included the line, "Dead under the weight of its impeccable, perfect quality." Moreover, Dorsday listed other guilty parties in the overly polished recent French cinema, singling out directors Julien Duvivier and Jacques Becker, among others.[60] When Truffaut began writing for *Cahiers* in March 1953's issue 21, he defended several of Dorsday's targets, especially Becker, but he had already been at work on his most famous article, which would prove to be his own manifesto against dominant French cinema and would further establish the phrase "tradition of quality" as a derogatory label.

In December 1952, Truffaut, recently dishonorably dismissed from military service, gave his editors an initial version of his tirade against mainstream French cinema, with which Bazin "was not unsympathetic." Yet, Bazin suggested drastic reworking of Truffaut's proposed article and allowed Truffaut instead to write brief reviews to begin learning the trade of criticism.[61] It was not until January 1954, after more than one year of revisions and deliberations, that Doniol-Valcroze and Bazin agreed to publish "A Certain Tendency of the French Cinema"; even then, Doniol-Valcroze published a careful editorial preparing the readers for Truffaut's "massacre," as de Baecque terms it. In his essay, Truffaut complained primarily that "tradition of quality" cinema depends too heavily on scriptwriters, especially Jean Aurenche and Pierre Bost, rather than on directors. He singled out these writers for their practice of seeking "cinematic equivalents" to "unfilmable scenes" from the novels they adapt. Truffaut, by contrast, argued they are betraying the spirit of their sources and adding their own "profanity and blasphemy" whenever possible. In marked contrast to these betrayals of both literature and cinema stand Truffaut's great auteurs, including Jean Renoir, Jean Cocteau, Abel Gance, and Jacques Tati, who all write their own dialogue and most of their stories.

Articles like Truffaut's bold "A Certain Tendency" should be seen as part of a very diverse and rich outpouring of reflections on the cinema, and not as the norm or the only perspective to come from *Cahiers du cinéma* in the 1950s. Nonetheless, the "Hitchcocko-Hawksians" gradually gained power and attention, and Eric Rohmer even became coeditor alongside Doniol-Valcroze by the time of Bazin's death in November 1958. By then, *Cahiers* had earned a reputation as the single most influential magazine on world cinema. Jim Hillier asserts that one reason *Cahiers* was so important was that it remained relatively apolitical, a stance that fit the prevailing trends in Western culture by the late 1950s.[62] Regardless, one should heed historian Pierre Billard's warning not to accept the clever but subjective conclusions forged by *Cahiers*'s young Turks as historical fact: "What we should object to is the untested reprise of their dated and polemical arguments thirty and forty years later, as if they represented valuable historical facts."[63] Their often subjective perspective should never be accepted on face value, and many of the movies condemned rather shamelessly by Truffaut are among the most interesting titles of the late 1940s and early 1950s. Yet the journal that began in order to fill the gap left by *Revue du cinéma* not only thrived, and far outlived *L'Ecran français*, but it continued to expand its influence when the young "Rohmer team" of Truffaut, Godard, Chabrol, Rivette, and Rohmer moved from being critics to filmmakers. By 1959 images from *their* films began to adorn the journal's covers, and the popularity and critical success of many of those motion pictures fueled the perception that *Cahiers* not only provided an accurate perspective on past and present auteurs but demonstrated a firm grasp of the future as well.

Nonetheless, *Cahiers* was hardly the only journal calling passionately for a revitalization of French cinema. *Positif*, which began during 1952 in Lyons, went on to become *Cahiers du cinéma*'s most successful rival for the hearts and minds of French cinephiles. In the opening statement of its first issue, "*Pourquoi nous combattons*" ("Why We Fight"), *Positif*'s editors, proud to write from the critical distance of Lyons, acknowledged that launching a new journal might seem foolhardy: "Another film journal (and another preface!) when so many have come and gone?"[64] To justify *Positif*'s existence, they explained that, in contrast to *Cahiers du cinéma*, they did not want to define their journal as a review for youth only, though their writers were mostly young. Rather, *Positif* would look back to *Rules of the Game* and other classics, saluting their elders. The editors pointed out that rather than revel in audacity, they would write about films only after many viewings, so as to prove the unknown auteurist qualities of directors such as John Huston. Throughout their opening issue, *Positif*'s editors seemed bent on following *Cahiers*'s lead, while distancing themselves from some of

Cahiers's key arguments. They reviewed Claude Autant-Lara's *L'auberge rouge* (*The Red Inn*, 1951) and were obviously referring to Truffaut's "A Certain Tendency of the French Cinema" when they wrote that they would "avoid rash judgments and public executions."[65] *Positif* also promised to celebrate French cinema for the most part, and into the 1960s they continually sparred with *Cahiers du cinéma*, criticizing their competitor's choices of auteurs, the value of the New Wave, and eventually their political conservatism. Years later, former *Cahiers* critic André S. Labarthe would claim that there were two sorts of *cinéphilia* in the 1950s: "At *Positif* they liked films without taking sides, or for fetishistic reasons or political views; *Cahiers* came up with the notion of applying a moral perspective onto films."[66]

But *Positif*, which boasted successful future directors such as Lyons-born Bertrand Tavernier among its writers, had a tough time economically compared to *Cahiers du cinéma* in the late 1950s. During the pivotal years of 1958 and 1959, its output nearly ground to a halt (much like *Cahiers* fifteen years later in the early 1970s). Supposedly a monthly journal, *Positif* published issue number 28 in April 1958, but only one more issue appeared that year, labeled "rentrée 1958." Issue number 30 finally arrived in July 1959, while number 31 came out in November. Thus, at the very moment when François Truffaut and Claude Chabrol were getting attention for jump-starting the young French cinema, *Positif* was almost invisible, though always present in its absence, just off screen, to *Cahiers* critics. This difference in the fates of the two journals may be what motivated *Positif*'s blistering attacks on the New Wave figures and some of *Cahiers*' favorite directors, such as Alfred Hitchcock and his latest film, *Vertigo*. In particular, *Positif* struck out against Claude Chabrol, whose *Le beau Serge* and *Les cousins* were reviewed in the long overdue July 1959 issue. *Positif*'s Michèle Firk attacked Chabrol's low-budget filmmaking as insincere (what little money Chabrol did spend came from an inheritance) and his style as "nonexistent" and full of mismatches and incorrect syntax. But Firk especially criticized his themes, which she condemned as tender tributes to "Goebbels, the Gestapo, racism, and anti-Semitism." The review article closes with "Young nation, Nazism, doesn't that tell you something?"[67]

In their November editorial, *"Quoi de neuf?"* ("What's New?"), *Positif*'s editors complained that "[t]he young cinema is certainly the chief topic of conversation these days. The young people who are suddenly deciding that technique means nothing are happily taking the place at *Arts* of

people who formerly thought style was everything."[68] In June 1962, when
Positif was on much firmer economic ground and building a strong following, they issued their own assessment of the young French cinema with
what they labeled a "*partiel et partial*" (incomplete and biased) dictionary
of new filmmakers, which anticipated *Cahiers*'s own much more complete
tally of new directors in December. *Positif*'s Raymond Borde summarized
Godard as "a disgusting misogynist" who had salvaged the unwatchable
Breathless by convincing the public that badly made movies were now in
style: "Godard represents the most painful regression of French cinema."
Chabrol was dismissed as "a *petit-bourgeois* director for a snobbish audience looking for exoticism," and he, like Godard, was attacked as "mili-
tantly misogynist."[69] *Positif*'s favorite New Wave directors were Philippe
de Broca and Jacques Rozier, both of whom were unconnected with
Cahiers. While much of *Positif*'s New Wave-era criticism was obviously
overly determined by its reactions against whatever *Cahiers* was arguing,
they did nonetheless build their own aesthetic tastes, championing surreal
and Marxist tendencies in French cinema and defining their own list of important auteurs (they preferred Orson Welles to Hitchcock, but also Jean
Rouch to Godard). Even today one can see the vibrant antagonism live on;
during 1998, for instance, *Cahiers du cinéma* put out special issues dedicated to *la nouvelle vague* and also Claude Chabrol, while *Positif* devoted
an issue to Orson Welles.

Perhaps the new journal most connected with contemporary issues in
French film, however, was *Cinéma 55* (whose title changed with each new
year, a tactic that cleverly identified it as the most up-to-date chronicle of
current trends). *Cinéma 55* was the house organ for the Fédération françáis
des ciné-clubs and, as such, concerned itself with speaking to and for the
sixty thousand audience members who regularly attended one or more of
France's 180 clubs. The opening editorial proclaimed that the continual
growth of *ciné-clubs* since the liberation was one of the most important
events in French film history: "Up until now, this movement has lacked an
outlet to help enrich, enhance, and bring to light even further its actions.
That is the goal of *Cinéma 55*." The editorial also promised to serve the
vast collective interests of this avid cinephile audience: "*Cinéma 55* will
inform our readers of all the people, films, and events that make up the cinema of our times."[70] This journal also went to great pains to include all
film industry talents, providing interviews with technicians as well as producers and distributors, and not just favorite auteur directors. It reported
industry information, such as average production costs, problems with

box-office attendance or returns, and international competition. When it expressed concerns that production costs were climbing too high and shutting out average producers in the late 1950s, it was not afraid to print the photos of "overpaid" talent such as Fernandel and Marcel Carné, branding them "the ones responsible!"[71]

Beginning with its first issue, in fall of 1954, *Cinéma 55* asserted its broad-based appeal immediately: the first issue featured Lotte Eisner writing on German cinema, an excerpt from the late Jean Epstein's final book, *Esprit du cinéma*, but also reviews of films ranging from Chaplin's *Modern Times* (1936) to Otto Preminger's *River of No Return* (1954). The second issue included a tribute to Jean Renoir, but also praise for one of Truffaut's favorite targets, the scriptwriter Pierre Bost. Bost, who had just been savagely attacked in January in Truffaut's "A Certain Tendency of the French Cinema," used *Cinéma 55* as a forum to defend his adaptation tactics; he protested that, although some people believed it wrong for the cinema to retell stories from novels, good writers adopt and then adapt the literary material: "'When you adopt a child you make it yours. But no one expects adopted children to resemble their adoptive parents.'"[72] Yet while *Cinéma 55* worked conscientiously to deepen the historical understanding of films, filmmakers, and critics of the past who were pertinent to the revivals featured in so many *ciné-clubs*, they also struggled to keep abreast of new trends enlivening French screens.

Throughout the New Wave era, this journal championed new talent. When *Cinéma 58* listed "forty under forty" directors, editor Pierre Billard explained the serious need for new faces and tactics in French film: "It seems our cinema's current economic prosperity has been accompanied with a deep artistic crisis. It is hard to disagree that inspirations have run dry, subject matters are sterile, and film aesthetics ever more static. . . . It is thus with great interest that we look to young French directors of today for the chance that tomorrow's cinema will evolve and progress."[73] Billard and his journal would give due attention to films by the *Cahiers* directors while also complaining that the equally fascinating films by other young directors, such as Pierre Kast's *Le bel âge* (1958) or Michel Drach's *On n'enterre pas le dimanche* (*They Don't Bury on Sunday*, 1959), were receiving too little attention. The articles in *Cinéma*, whether appeals to protest the censorship of Godard's *Le petit soldat* (*The Little Soldier*, 1961), reviews by the busy and passionate Bertrand Tavernier, or industry summaries by Billard, offered the New Wave era a consistently rich source of information. All four of these important voices—*L'Ecran, Cahiers, Positif,* and *Cinéma 55*—were part of a burgeoning critical excitement that helped catapult film studies forward in France and internationally during the 1950s, simultaneously raising the level and rigor of discourse for serious film lovers.

New Modes of Film Production

If more established disciplines such as literature, theater, social science, and even film criticism were seen as undergoing revolutionary changes, with a revitalized culture overturning so many conventions, then it seemed plausible that film production, the newest art form, should be experiencing transformations as well. Many observers were actively scanning French film for signs of its own new wave, even before one had taken on coherent shape. Initially, signs of rebirth were noticed in the irreverent themes of young directors Roger Vadim and Louis Malle, while the truly radical contributions by Agnès Varda, Jean-Pierre Melville, and the 16 mm shorts and documentaries of Alain Resnais, Jean Rouch, Chris Marker, Jean-Luc Godard, and François Truffaut were less visible to the critics of mass culture. But if the aesthetic and social conditions helped set the stage for a New Wave in cinema, France's economic context provided equally significant generating mechanisms. While it certainly was anticipated, the French New Wave hardly burst onto the scene fully grown.

Colin Crisp argues for a comprehensive view of the New Wave as rising rather logically from the long-standing diversity of French productions: "What is not adequately emphasized in most accounts of the origins of the New Wave is the debt owed by [these new, young] directors to the industrial and financial mechanisms put in place during the classic period to foster just such filmmaking practices. This process had been complemented by the commercialization of wartime technological breakthroughs which transformed work practices in the cinema during the period 1945-1960."[74] Crisp fears that most contemporary histories overemphasize the New Wave's "break from the past," when in fact French cinema had always retained a sizeable portion of nongenre, "personal" films from directors as diverse as Jean Vigo, Jean Renoir, Marcel Pagnol, and Jacques Tati.

How then should one summarize the New Wave's effects on the modes of production in French cinema? Is there a decisive break, or is this simply another stage in an ongoing series of variations in film production? The question has been variously answered. Some historians argue that the New Wave liberated the cinema from the weight of the established rules of studio production; others claim that the New Wave unfairly criticized and then crushed the standards and economic stability of the industry. Without a doubt, the actual production mode employed by most New Wave films was directly opposed to most industrial norms. While the New Wave certainly did not obliterate the commercial French cinema, its new production methods did create much more lasting effects on the rest of the industry than the individual innovations of directors such as Vigo or even Tati ever mustered. The New Wave did motivate decisive changes in film production, and, importantly, it came along at a decisive moment for the CNC, which needed a shot in the arm to prove that its economic and administrative policies were helping improve the quality and quantity of French movies.

There were certainly many warning signs throughout the 1950s that France's film industry needed to become more dynamic, both economically and aesthetically. *Cinéma 55* complained that the number of French films had dropped 45 percent in only three years, from 1952 to 1955, while the increase in international coproductions was not picking up the slack for French technicians, actors, or directors. When French studios were rented, it was often by American or other foreign television or film companies. During 1955, for instance, at Billancourt Studios, two soundstages were rented to American television, while two more were simultaneously rented for *Gentlemen Marry Brunettes*; Joinville rented three stages to an American movie company, while Epinay rented three stages to American television, and all of Neuilly's soundstages were being rented to American television studios.[75] The same *Cinéma 55* editorial went on to argue that France's problems were complex and included the need to find new administrative ideas, better import and export conditions, and revolutionary rethinking of storytelling and directing ideas. Coproductions were also prompting some people in the industry to warn that soon no true national cinema might be left to save. "We need to *counter* this denationalization by producing more ambitious films . . . projecting the real face of France to the world and reviving the prestige of our cinema."[76]

One of the more famous strategies of this era was precisely the revamping of the CNC's Film Aid program. During the mid-1950s, CNC Aid accounted for roughly 40 percent of a film's budget. Producers could receive subsidies, the money coming from taxes on movie tickets. Filmmakers would be paid a percentage based on their profits, but the money then had to be invested in a new film project, which in turn could apply for Film Aid. The plan was to provide incentive for producers to become stable enough to continue making films, and to help guarantee profitability, which is not easy in a small national market. But about one-half of all Film Aid money also went to help remodel theaters, with some funds designated to upgrade studio space. By 1959, André Malraux, minister of culture, helped Antoine Pinay, minister of finance, revamp the Film Aid rules to bring cinema in line with government policies in other industries. But in the process, Malraux, who was calling openly for a "rejuvenation" of French cinema, wrestled more control for financing and administration of the cinema away from Pinay, thereby strengthening the CNC and eventually helping the New Wave.

Under the new plan, Film Aid money to exhibitors was to be reduced over the next two years, with special loans and subsidies still available to small exhibitors of *art et essai* films or in tiny rural markets. The biggest change was to drop the notion of guaranteed subsidies based on box-office returns of completed films in favor of low-interest loans, or "advances on receipts," to producers, which had to be paid back before the producers could earn profits. But the CNC also retained and strengthened Film Aid for riskier, low-budget films: there was a juried quality subsidy, based on a script or *découpage* of the proposed film. The jury for 1959 was composed of roughly thirty members, including older directors such as Abel Gance, Marcel Pagnol, and Marcel L'Herbier, the veteran actress Françoise Rosay, but also modern novelist Raymond Queneau and established critics Georges Sadoul and Henri Agel. Their quality prize was to encourage more productions "that enhance French film prestige both at home and in the foreign market."[77] These changes in the Film Aid rules, however, brought many complaints. Producer Robert Dorfmann, who made profitable films such as *Forbidden Games* (Clément, 1952) and *Les tricheurs* (Carné, 1958), feared a loss of subsidies for commercial cinema, arguing ironically that Malraux's encouragement of "quality" was bad for business and would hurt exports.[78] Louis Malle, however, was typical of directors wary of losing creativity: "It is going to make French film very conventional. Nobody can tell on the strength of a script what kind of a picture is going to emerge; it implies script control."[79] The new Film Aid law did produce many positive effects, however, encouraging a whole new breed of producers to become involved in French film production, in part because of these shifting rules for government funding. Moreover, in early 1960, Finance Minister Pinay, who often disagreed with Malraux about Film Aid, was replaced by De Gaulle, partly because of Pinay's objection to subsidies for quality films: "I do not subsidize groceries so why should I subsidize films?"[80] His removal safeguarded the Film Aid program into the middle 1960s and was a victory for Malraux and, some argued, for "Culture" over "Finance."

The increased access to funds motivated increased optimism and experimentation, often bringing producers and directors active in producing short films over into feature production, but the amounts of Film Aid were insufficient to cover more than a fraction of the cost of an average motion picture. Thus, it was the combination of new, less expensive filming techniques, stories set in the streets that could appeal to young audiences, and new portable production equipment that allowed the New Wave to take off. As Francis Courtade notes, "The first contribution of the nouvelle vague was to create a new financial atmosphere and exceptional conditions of production."[81] He cites the use of small production budgets, location shooting, and short shooting schedules as the initial keys to New Wave production norms; add to these factors the lack of expensive stars, and one has the recipe for quick, cheap, youthful films. As François Truffaut explained to *Variety*, the New Wave was not necessarily against using stars, but big names made movies too expensive and many of the offbeat scripts that New Wave filmmakers favored did not need stars.[82] Typically, the budget of New Wave films ranged from fifty thousand to one hundred thousand dollars, while average French films cost two hundred thousand dollars and prestige productions were over a million dollars. The effect of forty thousand or seventy thousand dollars in Film Aid money on smaller productions was thus immense. By 1960, the heart of the New Wave era, one in three French productions was filmed entirely on location, and the number of productions costing less than two hundred thousand dollars increased dramatically. Films such as *Breathless*, shot in just four weeks, provided the new blueprints for quick, cheap, exciting modes of production. As René Prédal points out, "Before the New Wave directors could modify the profound *nature* of the cinema, they had to attack its *structures* so as to shake up the system."[83]

New Wave filming techniques depended on more than shooting quickly on location, however. They altered the conventions of their shoots, looking back to neorealist techniques, but combining what they learned from Rossellini with what they could learn from new documentary filmmakers such as Jean Rouch. Jean-Pierre Mocky, whose first feature, *Les dragueurs* (*The Chasers* in the United States, *The Young Have No Morals* in the United Kingdom, 1959), was one young director who urged everyone to "eliminate all the dead weight the cinema drags behind it," which meant not just heavy, overly clichéd stories, but also "tradition of quality" production norms. Mocky urged new directors to follow his model and shoot silent, like the neorealists, and put the sound together later in the sound studio to save time and money.[84] New Wave directors did shoot silent when appropriate, but some also followed documentary practice, using new lightweight portable magnetic-tape recorders for sync-sound on location. In 1959, the Swiss Nagra III, a new fourteen-pound version of earlier models, became available; it caused an immediate sensation within the cinéma vérité community and was adapted right away by some New Wave directors. Recorders such as the Nagra simply used standard quarter-inch magnetic tape, unlike studio machines, which used 16 mm- or 35 mm-wide tapes. Ironically, it was the rise of 16 mm production for the huge new markets of television news and location work that helped fuel the increased invention and diffusion of lightweight equipment for film-making, providing new options just when the New Wave filmmakers were looking for cheaper techniques.

These young French directors also used newer, more portable 35 mm and 16 mm cameras, such as the Auricon, and Eclair's Cameflex and NPR, which allowed them more hand-held options and the freedom of avoiding standard, heavy camera mounts such as dollies and tracks. Truffaut regularly perched his camera on a light tripod on balconies or rooftops, while Chabrol set the camera and operator in the trunk of his car or on motorcycles for traveling shots. Shooting a movie was suddenly casual and fun, resembling the mobile news crews covering the Tour de France bike race. Moreover, the escape from heavy cameras mounted on heavy tracks or tripods liberated production crews from depending on established camera operators and their crews. Instead, a new cadre of operators appeared on the scenes, and New Wave productions returned to the early cinema norm of a two-person crew of cinematographer and camera operator. The hand-held camera became a distinctive marker of New Wave images, adding a casual, contemporary look that found a bit of shake and jitter in the image not just acceptable, but lively and desirable. As Jean Douchet writes, "Aesthetically, a new and unexpected style exploded across the screen and added a sense of buoyancy to otherwise serious issues. It was as if the law of gravity had been temporarily suspended. . . . An intentional technique of making the camera shake to convey veracity was introduced."[85] It is difficult to imagine today, in the age of the Steadicam, how amazed critics were that Godard and cinematographer Raoul Coutard used a mail cart and a wheelchair for dollies in *Breathless*; review after review marveled at such revolutionary simplicity. Of course, by the mid-1960s almost every film school in the world adopted the practice.

New, faster film stocks, including Kodak's 250 ASA black-and-white Tri-X, allowed different lighting requirements as well. Since most of the young directors were reacting against the status quo, they also did not worry about having to use the commercial norm of quality images created with multiple lighting units that required time, labor, and studio facilities. Films that were about modern youth, set in modern Paris, did not want to look like Balzac adaptations or Hollywood melodramas, and this disdain helped them further cut corners. Chabrol's *Le beau Serge* has an exterior night scene lit exclusively by a lamp in actor Jean-Claude Brialy's hand. And Louis Malle's *L'ascenseur pour l'échafaud* (*Elevator to the Gallows,* 1958), like Truffaut's *Tirez sur le pianiste* (*Shoot the Piano Player,* 1960), lights whole night scenes with the available light from streetlights and store windows. Suddenly, the very definition of a film crew was challenged, which, of course, angered and threatened the technician unions in France. More importantly, however, the new smaller production crews and simpler equipment broke down many barriers determining when and where one could make movies. Once some of the financial and technical hurdles had been knocked lower, there was an influx of eager new talent that could re-think just what sort of subject matter would be most appropriate for this new mode of production. As Claude Bernard-Aubert, director of *Shock Patrol* (1957), explained, "We were all forced to begin with tiny budgets because most of us had no money. So we filmed subjects we were interested in and that fit with our budgets."[86] The generating mechanisms of finances and technology dramatically affected the stories and styles of this new generation.

One aspect of French exhibition that also helped provide a welcoming marketplace for offbeat new movies was the circuit of designated *art et essai* theaters, which showed both avant-garde films and documentaries. In the 1950s, several critics, including Joseph-Marie Lo Duca, convinced the owners of one Paris cinema chain to turn their Les Reflets theater into a specialized house modeled on dramatist Jean Tardieu's Théâtre d'essai. Gradually a number of other theaters followed suit and a small circuit, including famous movie houses such as Studio des Ursulines, Studio Parnasse, and Studio 28, formed the Association française des cinémas d'art et d'essai in 1955, with the goal of expanding the diffusion of both old and new films. By 1961, the CNC regulated the Art et essai theaters by giving them special Film Aid for renovations and tax breaks since they served the "national interest" by projecting quality prints of shorts and features that might otherwise receive no commercial distribution. CNC and the association drew up specific rules for member theaters, including the prohibition against showing more than 50 percent classics and more than 10 percent "amateur," or nonunion, films. Eventually, there were thirty-seven Art et essai houses in Paris and forty in the rest of the country, which helped many first time directors find early audiences. But these houses, like the earlier ciné-clubs, also relied heavily on established auteurs; of the twenty most frequently screened directors in 1963, Resnais, Truffaut, and Godard were the only French directors on the list, with Ingmar Bergman, Alfred Hitchcock, and Luis Buñuel dominating the Art et Essai circuit.[87]

All these new cultural, economic, and technological changes underway in France motivated a new generation not only of writers, actors, and directors but of producers as well. As this study will demonstrate later, the autoproductions of Jean-Pierre Melville, Louis Malle, Claude Chabrol, and François Truffaut would prove incredibly important, but for a real "wave" of productions to appear, more outside financing had to be found.

Three bold entrepreneurs in particular helped launch many of the New Wave features with their clever strategies developed specifically for the new cinema culture of 1960. Pierre Braunberger (b. 1905), Anatole Dauman (b. 1925), and especially Georges de Beauregard (b. 1920) helped remake the face of French cinema. "These producers did their job brilliantly, investing part of their own money, negotiating for advances from distributors, playing their credit to the maximum with labs and banks, and betting on a CNC *prime à la qualité*."[88] Braunberger, fittingly, began his career producing early Jean Renoir films, including *Charleston* (1927) and *Une partie de campagne* (*A Day in the Country,* 1936), but he made his reputation as a patron of young directors in the late 1940s and early 1950s when he produced short films by Alain Resnais, Agnès Varda, Jacques Rivette, and Jean-Luc Godard. He helped Jean Rouch with *Moi, un noir* (1958), among others, before producing Truffaut's *Shoot the Piano Player*, Jacques Doniol-Valcroze's *L'eau à la bouche* (*A Game for Six Lovers,* 1959), and Godard's *Vivre sa vie* (*My Life to Live,* 1962).

Anatole Dauman founded Argos Films in 1951 to specialize in art films and documentaries, and he, too, helped produce short films by Resnais (*Nuit et brouillard* [*Night and Fog,* 1955]) as well as by Chris Marker (*Letter from Siberia*, 1957, and *La jetée*, 1962) and the big Resnais features of *Hiroshima, mon amour* (1959), *L'année dernière à Marienbad* (1961), and *Muriel* (1963), in addition to the exemplary *vérité* documentary *Chronicle of a Summer* (Morin and Rouch, 1961). Dauman, who also produced several films by Godard as well as by Robert Bresson in the late 1960s, "made some of the major films of the modern cinema," providing funding and marketing for some of the greatest talents in France, who would otherwise have had great difficulty making the films they wanted to make.[89] But it was Georges de Beauregard who caught the attention of young directors and the popular press alike, thus becoming a nearly mythical figure as the stereotypical New Wave producer.

Georges de Beauregard had been trying to establish himself as a commercial director during the 1950s when Jean-Luc Godard convinced him to abandon risky, expensive, and adventurous big productions and to produce instead *Breathless*. Beauregard and his new partner, Carlo Ponti, formed Rome-Paris-Films and produced not only Godard's first feature but also Jacques Demy's *Lola* (1961) and Jacques Rozier's *Adieu Philippine* (1962). According to Agnès Varda, Beauregard earned so much from *Breathless* that he asked Godard if he had any friends interested in making movies, so Godard sent him to Demy.[90] But the courageous Beauregard lost money as well: Rozier went way over budget and *Adieu Philippine* was delayed several years, Godard's *Le petit soldat* (1960) was banned completely for three years because of its reference to the Algerian War, and Chabrol's *L'oeil du malin* (*The Third Lover,* 1962) sold only eight thousand tickets in Paris. Nonetheless, Beauregard's contribution was so vast—he produced Agnès Varda's *Cléo de 5 à 7* (1961) and a total of seven films by Godard and several post-New Wave Rohmer and Rivette films—it makes him the exemplary New Wave producer. Godard agreed; when Beauregard died in 1984 he wrote, "For a producer, he was a real worker . . . he fought against the ogres at the bank and the dragons of the CNC. . . . He also produced Belmondo's first smile and Bardot's last."[91] All of which reiterates that the New Wave included, in addition to a new journalistic catchphrase, a group of new filmmakers, a cohort of new actors, a set of new narrative and cinematic techniques, also a new way of producing and marketing motion pictures in France.

The term "New Wave" thus incorporates many dimensions and meanings involving generational, cultural, economic, and technological components and mechanisms. That French film, of all the other national cinemas, saw the most dramatic revitalization during the late 1950s is an amazing phenomenon. There was just the right combination of critical, industrial, artistic, and political forces at work to make France the most fertile battleground of film aesthetics. A complex convergence of factors helped ensure those skirmishes would spill over into the larger production realm. Not least among these generating mechanisms was the young cadre of individual agents who, shaped by their milieu, knew how to exploit the many changes in demographics, finances, and attitudes. This was an era of daring auteurs and new government policies, and the results were stunning, if confusing, to many observers at the time.

Variety, the most internationally read trade paper of the post-World War II period, proved representative in the way it struggled to chronicle and comprehend the rapid changes underway in French filmmaking in the late 1950s. One of its recurring motifs during the New Wave years is that, at least from the perspective of its American correspondents in Paris, France's industry upheaval was just plain puzzling. *Variety* argued in 1959, for instance, that for all the talk of a New Wave, the box-office take in France that year was down 5 percent from the previous year and off 17 percent from 1957. How could there be anything to celebrate, it pondered. Yet, it also reported that French films were suddenly earning more of those decreasing ticket sales, with eight of the top ten box-office hits that year coming from French productions: "So as usual, French film biz shows its paradoxical nature with a crisis being opposed by the renaissance, and optimism mixing with pessimism."[92] It is precisely the paradoxical and surprising sides of the French film industry and its New Wave in particular that make this era in French filmmaking so exciting and worthy of historical and aesthetic investigation.

2

Testing the Water:
Alexandre Astruc, Agnès Varda,
and Jean-Pierre Melville

In the work of Astruc and Varda we find the first stirrings of the New Wave.
—KRISTIN THOMPSON AND DAVID BORDWELL, *Film History*

Melville's characters are always caught between good and evil and even the
most negative have some good in them. Melville is a God to me. His manner
of telling a story is always "cool," calm, and touched by philosophy.
—JOHN WOO, "Le Style Melville"

AMONG THE most important generating mechanisms behind what
was to be called the New Wave were three precursors: Alexandre Astruc,
Agnès Varda, and Jean-Pierre Melville. Each of these directors contributed in unique ways to the context of experimentation in modes of
production and storytelling that helped create the New Wave's initial
successes. They provided various blueprints for subsequent directors,
even though all three produced films that were fundamentally different
from one another. Astruc has certainly gained the most attention historically for his revolutionary article, "Naissance d'une nouvelle avant-
garde: La caméra-stylo," ("The Birth of a New Avant-Garde: *La
Caméra-Stylo*"), published in *L'Ecran* in 1948.[1] Yet he also shot short
and feature films, including *Une vie* (*One Life*, 1958), based on a story by
Guy de Maupassant. Agnès Varda, who was a trained photographer but
knew little of the cinema, shot her first feature film, *La Pointe Courte*, in
1954 at age twenty-seven, and though this feature was never commercially distributed in France, it proved a minor sensation among the rabid
cinéphilia of 1950s Paris. But it was Jean-Pierre Melville who provided
the initial model for post–World War II directors, proving, first, that
Astruc's complaints about the excessive barriers to entry into the
French film industry were all too true, and second, that individuals

could nonetheless manage to serve as their own producer and director and succeed despite those industrial constraints.

Astruc and the *Caméra-stylo*

Alexandre Astruc (b. 1923) is one of those mythical figures of the New Wave era who is mentioned in every history as a key inspiration but then is generally too quickly passed over. Jean-Luc Godard points out in several interviews that Astruc was an influence on the New Wave, not simply for his critical articles calling for a more personal cinema and a new film language, but also because he was the first critic Godard knew who moved from film criticism to film directing. Thus, Astruc's critical perspective not only helped set the stage for many of the key concepts championed by André Bazin and *Cahiers*, but he helped revive the viability of critic-filmmakers. Combining written criticism with film production had been a relatively common practice in the 1920s among people such as Louis Delluc, Germaine Dulac, and Jean Epstein, but such creative overlap had gone out of fashion with the coming of sound cinema. Alexandre Astruc's significance for young cinephiles in the 1950s was indeed vital.

The twenty-two-year old Astruc published his first novel, *Les vacances* (*The Vacation*) in 1945 at the same time that his career as a film critic took off. He, like André Bazin, became a central figure in post–World War II Parisian film culture; he regularly wrote articles and reviews for journals such as *Combat, L'Ecran français,* and *Les temps modernes.* As early as 1945, Astruc praised American auteurs such as Preston Sturges and Orson Welles alongside Jean Renoir, and he was a founding member of the Objectif 49 *ciné-club,* along with Bazin and Jacques Doniol-Valcroze. Moreover, in 1952 Astruc directed a forty-five-minute film, *Le rideau cramoisi (The Crimson Curtain),* then two more features that decade, *Les mauvaises rencontres (Bad Encounters,* 1955), and *Une vie,* all of which motivated French film historians to call him the "Louis Delluc of the sound cinema." But for film students today it is primarily Astruc's most famous article, "The Birth of a New Avant-garde," that stands as evidence of his significance.

Astruc wrote regularly for *L'Ecran* and, along with André Bazin in particular, occupied one of the two poles of that journal's critical slant. After the liberation, as *L'Ecran français* shifted to serving a wider readership than its initial audience of leftist members of the resistance, it split into two opposing camps: "One, fundamentally political, promoted the idea of film's commitment in the ideological struggle between East and West. The other, basically aesthetic, led by Alexandre Astruc and André Bazin, continued the work of artistic criticism."[2] By the early 1950s, Astruc and Bazin's critical views, on preferred directors and American cinema in particular, were no longer welcome at *L'Ecran,* and both critics moved to other journals. Astruc went on to write for Eric Rohmer's *Gazette du cinéma* in 1950 and helped with the very first issue of *Cahiers du cinéma,* while Bazin was recuperating from tuberculosis in the mountains. Astruc was therefore a highly active member of pre–New Wave film culture. Further, as Alan Williams argues, his writing helped shape French cinema: after the war a small group of individualistic directors, including René Clément and André Malraux, was on the rise, and they needed a new sort of critic to weld them together, calling attention to their alternative film practice. Astruc helped form this "new variety of film criticism—an activist, often theoretical discourse aimed at a new kind of cinema as yet rarely realized in images and sounds. Its critical ideal was not a cinema of reality, but a cinema of *authors,* of creators who 'wrote' in images."[3] Certainly, the most famous articulation of this new brand of criticism is Astruc's article on the "*caméra-stylo,*" or camera-pen.

Along with Bazin's "Evolution of Film Language" and François Truffaut's "A Certain Tendency of the French Cinema," Astruc's *caméra-stylo* piece is among the most cited articles in French film history. While it only occupied one large, three-columned page in *L'Ecran*'s issue number 144 (March 30, 1948), the article's twelve paragraphs provide a virtual manifesto for the New Wave. Moreover, many of Astruc's ideas were later repeated in various forms by subsequent critics and filmmakers alike. Jean Douchet sums up the article's significance succinctly: "Astruc, whose elaborate and flamboyant style marked the article as his own, dared to claim that like literature and philosophy, film could tackle any subject, that the subject was part of the writing, and the camera the pen of modern times."[4] Astruc begins the article by claiming a revitalization of the cinema is underway, but most critics are blind to it. He points out that *Rules of the Game* (Renoir, 1939), *Citizen Kane* (Welles, 1941), and Bresson's *Les dames du bois de Boulogne* (*Ladies of the Bois de Boulogne,* 1945) had recently established the foundations for a new future for the cinema. These films are "prophetic" of future film practice and thus worthy of the label "avant-garde" in its most literal sense. He adds, "To come to the point: the cinema is quite simply becoming a means of expression."[5] Students of Bazin will recognize the parallels between Astruc's list of exemplary films and those celebrated by Bazin during the same era. Further, Astruc shares with Bazin a faith in and an excitement about these films that point a way out of what Bazin called "the equilibrium profile" of 1930s and 1940s classical cinema.

Astruc writes that cinema was in the process of breaking free of its limiting role as visual anecdote or mere spectacle: "The cinema is gradually becoming a language. By language, I mean a form in which and by which an artist can express his thoughts, however abstract they may be or translate his obsessions exactly as he does in the contemporary essay or novel. That is why I would like to call this new age of cinema the age of *camérastylo*."[6] Astruc even suggests that his vision of future cinema is more complex than Sergei Eisenstein's belief that he could illustrate Marx's *Das Capital* in silent images, since the *caméra-stylo* would "write ideas directly on the film stock" without recourse to montages of falling leaves and then trees in blossom to indicate the passage of time. He also finds a perfect example of this new cinematic language in André Malraux's *L'espoir* (*Days of Hope*, 1945), "in which, perhaps for the first time ever, film language is the exact equivalent of literary language."[7] Here again are reverberations with Bazin's later article on the evolution of film language, which closes with the phrase, "The filmmaker is no longer the competitor of the painter and the playwright, he is, at last, the equal of the novelist." In 1951, Bazin would also compare *L'espoir* favorably with *Citizen Kane*.[8]

Astruc not only points to and calls for radical new aesthetic trends in cinema, he also anticipates Truffaut's famous attack on conventional literary adaptations, "A Certain Tendency of the French Cinema," published in 1954 in *Cahiers du cinéma*. Truffaut, like Astruc, prefers auteurs who do not simply look for cinematic equivalents of literary devices but who rework the very language of narrative with cinematic techniques. It may surprise contemporary students that Astruc's brief attack is much more convincing than that by Truffaut, partly because Astruc does not attack specific films on the narrow moral grounds that Truffaut employed.

> Scriptwriters who adapt Balzac or Dostoevski excuse the idiotic transformations they impose on the works from which they construct their scenarios by pleading that the cinema is incapable of rendering every psychological or metaphysical overtone. In their hands, Balzac becomes a collection of engravings in which fashion has the most important role, and Dostoevski suddenly begins to resemble the novels of Joseph Kessel [who wrote *Belle du jour*, among others] with Russian-style drinking-bouts in night-

clubs and troika races in the snow. Well, the only cause of these compromises is laziness and lack of imagination.[9]

Astruc continues by arguing that directing should no longer be considered simply a means of presenting a scene but rather become "a true act of writing." He also cautions that in a world of talented auteurs, the cinema no longer has to "rehash" the poetic documentaries or surreal films of the 1920s just to escape the constraints of commercial filmmaking. Rather, Astruc points toward a new cinema with lively, experimental new techniques, for a broader, clearer new cinematic language. His words have the fire and vitality of many New Wave critics five and ten years after him, who would also call for turning a back on "daddy's cinema" in order to create a vibrant new film language. As proof of the prophetic quality of Astruc's article in anticipating new productions, René Prédal cites Jean-Pierre Melville's *Le silence de la mer* (*Silence of the Sea*, 1949), while Kristin Thompson and David Bordwell point out that Robert Bresson serves as a good example of Astruc's aesthetic: he uses written documents as sources for his films, but composes the narratives in very cinematic ways.[10]

Astruc's writing provided a critical foundation for his own film directing. As Williams explains, "Astruc composed his famous essay 'The Birth of the New Avant-garde' in frustrated reaction to many of the obstacles to entry into the industry. 'One had to have one's card—like prostitutes do,' he later recalled."[11] But eventually, after making two 16 mm shorts, Astruc managed to secure financing through Argos Films to shoot the medium-length *Le rideau cramoisi* and put his theories into practice. The twenty-eight-year-old Astruc worked with the famous cinematographer and lens maker Eugène Schuftan to adapt a short novel set in the nineteenth century. He also chose a friend, Jean Mitry, to edit the film with him and cast twenty-year-old Anouk Aimée as the bourgeois daughter who falls in love with a soldier billeted in her family's home. The resulting film is a unique production, with one foot in classical literature and the other in a modern, almost pretentious mise-en-scène that tries to evoke emotion in instances when the characters are not allowed, for personal or narrative reasons, to explain themselves. The novelette by Barbey d'Aurevilly recounts the action through a conversation between two soldiers years later, as an old man explains this startling tale from his youth. While he was staying with a family, the young daughter at first flirted with him, then seemed to rebuff him, but finally slipped into his bed, where she eventually died later that night.

This strange Gothic romance tale is adapted by Astruc, who tried to preserve the atmosphere dominated by impending death but also to maintain the original internal narrator's sense of distant memory. Its neoromanticism and first-person voice-off narration impressed later New Wave directors.[12] Long takes and significant props, camera movements, and intricate sound effects attempt to replace unspoken dialogue, and denote the obscure emotions, guarded so carefully by these characters. As Georges Sadoul observes, "*Le Rideau cramoisi* is striking and stylish; in it Astruc makes more use of the dramatic setting of the interior of the house (the ornate dining room, the complex iron stairways, the mirrors) than of the actors. . . . It enjoyed considerable success, won several prizes and helped pave the way for the future *nouvelle vague.*"[13] *Le rideau cramoisi* even earned Astruc the prestigious Louis Delluc Prize in 1952. This triumph for Astruc helped bolster the value of his criticism and launch his name as a new critic-filmmaker in an era when such a combination was almost unheard of.

Astruc's first feature, *Les mauvaises rencontres,* came out three years later and continued his penchant for excessively stylized and moody tales. Based on another novel, *Une sacrée salade,* by Cécil Saint-Laurent, and adapted by Astruc and friend Roland Laudenbach, this film again starred Anouk Aimée, this time as a young woman accused of procuring an abortion who then recalls all the unfortunate relations with men she has had. Claire Clouzot cites this film as a strong precursor to the spirit and themes of the New Wave, especially with its contemporary account of relations between young men and women that combine the sexual, the psychological, and the intellectual. Further, Astruc centers his tale in the neighborhood of Saint-Germain-des-Prés, which will figure in so many subsequent New Wave films.[14] Astruc tries to map a heavily novelistic atmosphere onto this melodramatic world, but the highly charged mise-en-scène and expressive camerawork make the narration look like an uncomfortable mix of old and new styles or occasionally a French version of *Brief Encounter* (Lean, 1945) rather than *Rules of the Game.*

Nonetheless, *Les mauvaises rencontres,* with its mobile camera and depth of story information, won Astruc the best director award at the Venice Film Festival in 1955. Jacques Rivette, in his review in *Cahiers du cinéma,* justifies the film as "a young film, by a young director, for the young," and he defends the formalism of Astruc's camera movement, charging "every movement of the camera is subject to the movement of the soul."[15] But while many of Astruc's contemporaries would benefit from young, talented cinematographers, such as Henri Decae, who were happy to experiment with new film stocks and lightweight cameras, Astruc here worked with Robert Lefebvre (b. 1907), whose first production was in 1926. If Astruc wanted his films to look like contemporary versions of Balzac or Flaubert's themes, they too often ended up resembling updated German Expressionism. Yet, both black-and-white films, *Le rideau cramoisi* and *Les mauvaises rencontres,* fit comfortably within art cinema norms and encouraged a new generation to debate stories and styles, while proving that the leap from criticism into production was possible. Importantly, like the later *Cahiers* critic-directors, Astruc also maintained a strong critical presence, writing about films in between making them.

Astruc's biggest achievement was certainly *Une vie,* shot in Eastman color with a major international star, Maria Schell, paired with Christian Marquand in the starring roles. Astruc recalls, "I didn't choose the subject. The film was offered to me on the condition that Maria Schell was the lead. I re-read the novel and felt I could do it. For Maupassant, *Une vie* was the story of an unhappily married woman who couldn't obtain a divorce because divorce then was impossible. I insisted on what was still relevant in it: the difficulty of two people living together."[16] *Une vie* is a beautifully sentimental film. But it was another literary adaptation, again written with Laudenbach's help, initiated by an external production company, and starring Schell and Marquand, all of which distanced it from other youthful, or *"jeune,"* films of 1958. Schell was a firmly established star of commercial cinema, having just made *Gervaise* (Clément, 1956) and *White Nights* (Visconti, 1957). Marquand was more easily identified with the youth market, but his recent role as the insensitive lover in Vadim's *And God Created Woman* seemed worlds away from the pompous and unfaithful Julien, dressed in frilly period-piece costumes. Nonetheless, *Une vie* was championed by *Cahiers du cinéma,* though even Godard had to begin his review by admitting there were problems: "I don't give a damn about the merry-go-round decorated by Walt Disney, the lunch on the grass with imitation plastic cloths, the chewing-gum green of a ball of wool. I don't give a damn about any of the lapses in taste piled up by Astruc. . . . *Une vie* is a superbly constructed film."[17]

Une vie is indeed a rather odd, if carefully constructed, production, with a strange charm and beauty that seem simultaneously to attract and to offend. The bold color scheme, filmed by Claude Renoir, lends the story an additional thematic strategy, but it also works too hard to appear more than natural. Astruc did not want this big budget costume drama to be taken as "realistic." Thus its detractors might complain that *Une vie*'s visual look hovers somewhere between Douglas Sirk's melodramas and a perfume commercial, though Godard prefers to see it combining the decadence of Baudelaire with the daring color schemes of Manet: "People talked of painting without realizing that *Une vie* was a novelist's film; and of taste without noticing that it is a barbarian's film."[18] Not everyone, however, recognized Astruc's adaptation of the elegant Maupassant novel as a modernist "barbarian" work, and for many its lush Normandy locations and stylized acting recalled romantic pulp fiction more than ironic transformation.

Une vie is the tale of an overly protected wealthy young woman, Jeanne (Schell), who marries the brooding, handsome Julien (Marquand). But while the naive Jeanne is overwhelmingly happy on her wedding day, Julien admits to others that he had to marry her to help pay off his heavy debts. Things decline relentlessly between them from that point on.

Increasingly, Julien feels trapped with his loving wife in her beautiful château, while Jeanne feels it must be her fault that Julien spends less and less time at home. Eventually, Julien's brazen affair with Jeanne's maid, Rosalie (Pascale Petit), results in a child. Julien demands that Jeanne send the maid and the "bastard" away, and the crushed Jeanne eventually tries to protect the mother and child by sending them to another of her sev-

Figure 2.1. Julien is glum at his wedding (*Une vie*)

eral farms. Jeanne's sense of betrayal is doubled by the fact that Rosalie is virtually her only friend, having lived with her for thirteen years. In one of her multiple voice-over commentaries on the action, Jeanne regrets that Julien will not even apologize or admit his mistake. She also acknowledges that the unfaithful Rosalie is lucky; at least she gets to live with Julien's child, while Jeanne is left in the huge château alone with a husband who despises her.

As the years pass, Julien and Jeanne continue their stormy marriage, and in one rare moment of mutual disgust and passion, they make love, producing a son, Paul. But Julien meets and falls for another married woman, Gilberte de Fourchville (Antonella Lualdi), who tells him, "We have a thousand days ahead of us and nothing to do but lie, deceive, and hide. You are playing with fire, and I only love such fire!" Eventually, Gilberte's husband, who is a sensitive, long-suffering spouse like Jeanne, discovers that Julien and Gilberte have slipped off during a picnic to make love in an abandoned wagon. He pushes the wagon over a cliff, and the two lovers are crushed to death in each other's arms. Jeanne, alone with Paul, brings the maid, Rosalie, and her daughter back, and the four continue to live together in the château. Jeanne ends the film with another voice-over observation: "Time polishes memories. . . . Life is never as good or as bad as we imagine it."

The story line, which is much more judgmental and sarcastic in Maupassants' tale than in Astruc and Laudenbach's version, is here offered as a stylish telling of a period-piece melodrama. Astruc shifted the story away from what he called "the sad, gray, realistic tale of a woman becoming troubled," toward a more lyrical tone and replaced the small, shifty Julien of Maupassant to a tall, handsome, and violent Julien, who towers over everyone and seduces them naturally with his good looks and silence. Such transformations led to complaints that the film slipped away from Maupassant's comic world-view and closer to popular romance. Godard, interviewing Astruc for *Arts* in 1958, asked the obvious, nagging question: "You preach modernism, and yet you make a costume film?" Astruc replied, "Costume or not is irrelevant. . . . We tried to convey the fantastic atmosphere of the book rather than its bourgeois drama."[19] But however Astruc tried to gloss over the subject matter, *Une vie* remained a strange film that fell somewhere between the so-called tradition of quality and Elia Kazan, whom Astruc praised highly in the 1950s. As a critic, Astruc wrote much of modern cinema and its future direction, but his *Une vie* became a disappointing tribute to the past.

Figure 2.2. Jeanne is proud of Paul, while Julien ignores them (*Une vie*)

Stylistically, *Une vie* depends heavily on Jeanne's internal subjective monologues to lend characterization, fill in plot points, and summarize huge leaps in time: "Six years passed—father died; mother returned." But Astruc's visual style, while striking, was not exactly what critics looking for a vital alternative cinema expected of the man who had written about the *caméra-stylo*. "*Une vie* displays a nostalgia for classicism, balanced on his explicit admiration of Orson Welles and intense faith in the shot sequence," according to Jean-Michel Frodon.[20] Astruc's fascination with elaborate long takes becomes most successful in the painful scene where Rosalie goes into labor. The shot sequence begins with an establishing shot of the ice on the trees and Jeanne exiting the château. Her voice-over begins, "The days were peaceful and long, but I never forgot Julien's words [that I had ruined his life]." But then Rosalie's screams interrupt her reflections. Jeanne, stunned that Rosalie is in labor, is confronted by Julien, who tries to drag her away from Rosalie in the barn and sends Jeanne instead for the midwife. Julien then tells Rosalie she cannot keep her bastard here. The midwife arrives, and Jeanne cries over the entire situation. Such long shots (though the film overall has an unremarkable average shot length of fourteen seconds) prove Astruc's technical virtuosity. But because the subject matter derives more from mainstream melodrama than from the modern novel, and the melodrama is set in the nineteenth century with suffering wives, pregnant maids, and dastardly, handsome husbands, any real sense of a potentially radical style is doomed.

Figure 2.3. Julien looks out over the bay (*Une vie*)

Astruc's career did not end with *Une vie*, but his prestige and significance among many of his contemporaries decreased with its release in 1958, despite Godard's efforts to celebrate his auteur traits. The context of volatile new changes within French film culture made *Une vie* seem less than exemplary. As Alan Williams points out, unfortunately for Astruc, *Une vie*'s release "coincided with the first, striking impact of a new generation on the film community. *Une vie* failed commercially and even today is seldom screened despite its remarkable qualities. Its potential impact was eclipsed, even for those in search of alternatives to mainstream filmmaking, by Louis Malle's *Les Amants,* Claude Chabrol's *Les Cousins,* and praise of a new wave that would quickly pass Astruc by."[21] Historians typically, and with good reason, refer to Astruc in the 1950s as someone who begins moving toward the future of French film but then has to "get out of the way" as others charge ahead. Frodon echoes that Astruc is "a precursor who is quickly overtaken by the very events that he, more by his lively and clairvoyant writings than by his filmmaking, helped to launch."[22] Prédal also describes Astruc as having "broken a chink in the wall of French cinema" only to be pushed aside by the rush of New Wave filmmakers charging through and leaving Astruc on the outside.[23] *Une vie* looked stagy and relatively old fashioned—after all it looked back to Welles at a time when post–World War II filmmakers were finding newer influences or forging new syntheses. The fact that his Eastman color spectacle lost money while low-budget black-and-white films by Malle and Chabrol earned prizes and strong box-office success further isolated Astruc, reducing his pertinence for his colleagues in the young French cinema. Frodon summarizes Astruc's predicament by arguing that he was too "literary" at a time when being highly "cinematic" was in vogue.[24] The irony is more biting since Astruc had been one of the loudest critics calling for a new cinematic language to arrive.

Agnès Varda's Elegant Realism

While Astruc was a highly visible player in shaping the debates within the French film community by the early 1950s, Agnès Varda (b. 1928) proved a more subtle but equally inspiring role model for the New Wave that would arrive a few years later. If Astruc provided an example of a critic-turned-director for the New Wave, Varda proved important for two reasons: First, she showed how an "outsider" could make a movie despite the industrial barriers, bypassing the normal production or distribution routes. Second, her first feature became an exemplary demonstration of Astruc's concept of the *caméra-stylo* in practice. Agnès Varda thus became a highly significant precursor to New Wave film practices, but she was also a new auteur who saw filmmaking as a specialized *écriture* process, synthesizing literary and cinematic codes and strategies. Varda even coined the term *cinécriture* for her brand of filmmaking, which features carefully constructed image-to-sound textual relations. Moreover, Varda's importance was eventually felt beyond France's borders, encouraging other young women to pick up the camera and begin making personal films.

Agnès Varda, born and raised in Belgium, came to Paris to study art history but shifted over to photography, attending classes at the influential Ecole de Vaugirard. Once finished with her studies, she was fortunate enough to land a job as official photographer for the Théâtre national populaire (TNP) in the beautiful Palais de Chaillot in the heart of Paris. Earlier, during the war, Varda's family had fled to the southern French town of La Pointe Courte, near Sète on the Mediterranean Sea. One of her close friends from that experience later married Jean Vilar, who became a vibrant young force in French theater after World War II, helping establish the Avignon Theater Festival's reputation for youthful experimentation. Vilar became director of the TNP in Paris and hired Varda to work with him.[25] This is also where she met the talented young actors she would use in her first feature, *La Pointe Courte* (1954), Philippe Noiret and Silvia Monfort. Varda worked for the TNP for ten years, from 1951 to 1961. Her background in art, literature, and theater was much stronger than her knowledge of film history or techniques, so it has always struck historians as somewhat bizarre that, in contrast to the wild *cinéphilia* of people such as Astruc, Melville, or the *Cahiers* critics, Varda initially began filmmaking from a rather naive perspective.

Varda is a rare director in many ways: She entered the cinema via still photography, and was one of only a few women to direct French films in the 1950s, but she also followed an unusual trajectory in the sort of film projects she pursued. Unlike Alexandre Astruc, Jean-Pierre Melville, or most of the New Wave filmmakers, she made a feature film, *La Pointe Courte*, *before* she made short films. Initially, according to Varda, she visited her old haunt, La Pointe Courte, to record images and sounds of it as a favor for a terminally ill friend who could no longer visit his home. If this was indeed the case, then her later project, *Jacquot de Nantes* (1990), a tribute to her dying husband, Jacques Demy, would mirror the event that initially motivated her to move from a still camera to a motion-picture camera. In any case, nostalgia, memory, and reflection figure in all her work.

Soon after seeing the footage she had shot with a borrowed 35 mm camera, Varda inherited enough money to allow her to consider shooting a very inexpensive feature film about a young couple, set in La Pointe Courte. She established her own tiny production company, Ciné-Tamaris, forming a cooperative with the principal actors and crew members. Roughly 35 percent of the budget came from the cooperative. No one was paid during the production, and Varda has always said that the film was accomplished only because of the generosity and enthusiasm of everyone involved in the project, including the principal actors, Noiret and Monfort, the young technicians, and the local inhabitants of the fishing village. They eventually completed the production with the extremely low production cost of fourteen thousand dollars (seven million old francs), or roughly one-quarter of the budget of later New Wave films such as *The 400 Blows* or *Breathless*. Several years later, Claude Chabrol followed in Varda's footsteps: he received an inheritance and shot his first feature, *Le beau Serge*, in a small town where he had spent time during World War II, and he also used local residents to act in the project, most of them for no payment.

La Pointe Courte is a highly unusual and personal project that firmly established Varda's reputation as a transitional figure in French cinema.

Alison Smith notes that since Varda's first feature was shot on location, with local, nonprofessional people playing all but two roles, Varda carries on the spirit of the Italian neorealists and anticipates the New Wave.[26] She also strongly parallels the neorealists in that her film, like Visconti's *La terra trema* (*The Earth Trembles*, 1948), was shot in a tiny fishing village. But Varda is also a transitional figure in bridging the gap between documentary and fiction film practice, creating a highly distinctive text. As Pierre Billard explains, "Her first film had all the markings of the avant-garde, but she was the only person who did not recognize them. She thought that was how one made movies."[27] Billard, like many historians, overly romanticizes Varda's innocence in the ways of the cinema, but he is accurate in claiming that her film was closer to experimental cinema than to conventional narratives, and next to *La Pointe Courte*, Astruc's *Une vie* now looks incredibly commercial and dated.

La Pointe Courte begins with the arrival of a mysterious government official who is watching to see whether the local fishermen in this tiny seaside village are fishing without having purchased the proper permits and are also illegally harvesting shellfish from the bay, which is apparently infested with disease. But this narrative thread involving the menace of the public health officials, which recurs occasionally throughout the film, is downplayed as the camera wanders through the streets and alleys, recording the mundane details of laundry flapping in the breeze, cats meandering in and out of doorways, and children playing. After ten minutes, the young man played by Philippe Noiret is introduced; he is walking to the train station to check whether his Parisian wife has taken the train to see him. She has. From this point on, Varda alternates between slice-of-life filming of the slow-paced, daily life of the village, and the poetic and obscure discussions by this young couple, whose marriage is in a crisis.

There is no real exposition of story information, but bits of their conversations gradually reveal enough information for the viewer to begin piecing together story events and character traits: After four years of marriage, the unnamed couple (Monfort and Noiret) has been having some unexplained difficulties, and the wife could not decide whether to leave on a vacation with her husband. The man has returned to the fishing village where he was born; he had left the village twelve years earlier and apparently has no family left there. He has been going to meet the train every day hoping she would join him, and on the fifth day, the day the plot time begins, she arrives. During the bulk of the film, the couple speaks in brief, calm passages, trying to understand each other's feelings and determine just what is wrong with their relationship and what will happen next. While he leads her on walks, pointing to people and places he knows ("What I find here is mine alone"), she regularly derails his discourse ("But you always told me there is nothing to see here"). They thus broach difficult issues tangentially. All the while, the villagers' working-class lives go on around this attractive, isolated couple. She is obviously undergoing a nervous strain, and seems disappointed that he always remains so calm. She may also be dealing with the guilt of having been unfaithful to him ("Do you recognize me? Hasn't my face changed?"), and it remains unclear just what he does or does not know. For all their talking, solid details and accusations are never raised.

Intermittently, the husband and wife drift through the striking, gritty landscape of fishing nets, piers, and boats as they discuss their lives without ever really settling anything. Early on, for instance, she states that she will live apart, but they end up sharing the bed in the room he has secured for them. Later, at the Sunday water festival where gondola-like boats compete in bizarre jousting matches, the husband suddenly finds the chair next to him empty. He appears sad and dejected, but his wife soon returns with ice cream cones for each of them. He looks relieved but then gives the cone away to someone else. Only later that evening will he tell his wife he thought she had left him as she warned she would, and she laughs indulgently at him as if he were a silly little boy. Eventually, he does take her back toward the train, but it is unclear whether they will continue to try to work out their problems in the future, or whether the audience has just witnessed their final days together. In the meantime, in alternation with the couple's vague story, one local child has died, a young man has been ordered to jail for five days for having fished without a license (which is, of course, the same amount of time the husband had waited for his wife), and the parents of the young man have arranged his future marriage to his sixteen-year-old girlfriend. The villagers' lives go on, untouched by the problems of the couple from Paris.

Like many young French directors during this era of authorship and personal expression, Agnès Varda contributes valuable critical insights into her own films. One interview in *Positif,* upon the 1962 release of her *Cléo de 5 à 7,* condenses many of her earlier statements about her first feature's story strategies:

> I had a very clear plan for La Pointe Courte: it was to present two themes, that, while not really contradictory, were problems that canceled one an-

other out when set side by side. They were, first, a couple reconsidering their relationship, and second, a village that is trying to resolve several collective problems of survival. The film was made up of chapters, so while the two themes were never mixed together there was the possibility for the spectator to oppose or superimpose them. I have always thought it very difficult to integrate private matters with more general social problems. . . . I was inspired by William Faulkner's Wild Palms. If you remember the novel, there is no connection between the couple, Charlotte and Harry, and the former slave from Mississippi. It was neither allegorical nor symbolic, but there is a sensation produced by the alternating reading of these two histories. . . . In La Pointe Courte, I presented a couple in crisis; they are not only in the process of breaking up but also of splitting off from society.[28]

What makes this a stunning movie, beyond its loose, alternating narration, is its visual style, most particularly the camerawork, framing, and staging of actors. There is a strange and haunting visual quality to *La Pointe Courte* that uses the local light, setting, and inhabitants as if they were simultaneously carefully crafted elements of mise-en-scène and chance, found objects. André Bazin was a big fan of Varda's first feature, in part because of its unlikely mode of production. He wrote that the first miracle of *La Pointe Courte* was that it was actually completed; the second miracle was the resulting style: "There is a total freedom to the style, which produces the impression, so rare in the cinema, that we are in the presence of a work that obeys only the dreams and desires of its auteur with no other external obligations."[29] And while many critics have complained about what Billard labels "the embarrassing stasis of the actors," Bazin finds their meanderings through the environment to be as beautiful as those in a Rossellini movie, and their dialogue admirable: "These protagonists only say things that are both useless and essential, like the words that escape us in our dreams."[30] Bazin also seemed to find it appropriate that the 1956 Paris premiere of *La Pointe Courte* was at the Studio Parnasse, which played it along with Jean Vigo's experimental documentary, *A propos de Nice* (1930).

The parallels between neorealist film and portions of *La Pointe Courte* are quite clear: Varda's film has an open story structure; location shooting; nonprofessional actors; anecdotal, slice of life scenes; and a sensitive portrayal of the poor fishing village's existence. These aspects of the film certainly resemble Luchino Visconti's *La terra trema*, though Varda and her historians have always claimed she was ignorant of neorealism when she made this movie, and she insists she had only seen a few movies in her life. Yet *La Pointe Courte* is such a group project, like many of the neorealist films, that Varda even lists the scenario and direction credits as herself "and the inhabitants of La Pointe Courte." The mise-en-scène and camerawork also make it a modern, transitional film, since her visual style recalls Visconti and Rossellini in many places but also anticipate the intellectual, formal narrative strategies of Alain Resnais's *Hiroshima, mon amour* (1959). The opening shot, which has a duration of one hundred seconds, provides a perfect example of this distinct, modern, and transitional style. Most of the titles are superimposed over a close-up of a slab of roughly grained wood, which turns out to be the back of a chair sitting in the sun. The wood grain initially resembles a long shot of a desert landscape as well, but then the camera pans across the wood chair back to reveal an adjacent narrow street of doorways, windows, drying laundry, and sharp shadows. The camera travels slowly down the empty street; the opening clarinet music ends, and the viewer studies the street as if it were a starkly beautiful photograph, as deserted as an Atget photograph, come to life. The port—its cats, boats, inhabitants, fluttering laundry, labyrinths of drying fishing nets, and all—will be the subject and setting for the film. Many shots of the small boats going out to fish or of men wandering amid the rubbish recall Lumière as well as the Rossellini of the Po River episode in *Paisan* (1946). Thus, the film as a whole looks, feels, and sounds like a New Wave collection of pastiches, homages, and tributes to earlier film practice, integrated with the highly modern narrative structure.

La Pointe Courte also looks very modern because of the way it composes in depth. Even though Varda alternates the couple's scenes with those involving the villagers, the village and its environs are ever present during the couple's conversations, adding aesthetic unity to the narrative space. At one point, when the husband is trying to explain to the wife that he wants a pleasurable life with her, there is a cut to what appears to be an old, abandoned, and worn-out train car, sitting on overgrown tracks. But the train is actually moving slowly toward the camera. The grinding sound of its wheels becomes incredibly loud as the couple walks into the shot and must wait for the train to pass before resuming their halting conversation about her fears and doubts. Not only is the depth of field typically evocative here, but it anticipates, strangely enough, Marguerite Duras's use of large trucks in *Le camion* (*The Truck,* 1977) to stand in for the words of women during difficult discourses with men. Several critics have commented on the way that shots in *La Pointe Courte* begin and end in carefully composed static images, as if Varda thought of the scenes as a collection of photographs that awake briefly before closing off the action once again. This strategy lends an unusual halting rhythm to the narrative. And every image seems potentially metaphorical, yet naturalistic. Over and over in *La Pointe Courte,* the seeming debris of the man's childhood village—barrels of stagnant water, broken pitchforks, even a dead cat washing up on the rocks—stand as enigmatic, often ambivalent backgrounds to the couple's discussions. Moreover, the husband is constantly associated with wooden objects and fishing nets, while the wife is connected to sharp steel objects, such as the pitchfork, train tracks, and fishhooks.[31] It is never possible to see the pair as separate from their setting, which often divides the characters within the frame, blocks their path, or even makes them stumble.

An elegantly restless camera, deliberate character gesture and motion, crisp use of shadow, long shot durations (the average shot length is sixteen seconds), and evocative depth of field make Varda's film one of the most unusual and beautiful motion pictures of 1950s France and a wonderful example of what could be produced by this new era's calls for personal cinema. It was, like Resnais's later *Hiroshima, mon amour* and *Last Year at Marienbad,* a great blending of a New Novel–style narrative with the *"jeune cinema."* Unfortunately, for all its potential significance, *La Pointe Courte* also proved that the industrial hurdles to new filmmakers and unconventional projects, lamented by Astruc and so many others, were indeed restraining French film practice. Because the film was shot without authorization from the CNC, it was designated "amateur" and could not be exhibited in a commercial cinema. Hence its brief premiere at Cannes, and then the Art et essai Studio Parnasse. No distributor was interested in picking up a film that could not be shown nationally, and according to Michel Marie, "Varda's is certainly not the only movie in this situation: several dozen features produced within or outside the industrial circuit remained in their cans during the 1950s." But Marie adds, "This experience proved valuable in teaching future directors the central importance of the distributor."[32]

The Paris premiere for *La Pointe Courte,* combined with the praise it earned from André Bazin and her new friendship with Alain Resnais, opened new doors for Varda, as she moved from photography and theater into the French film scene. She now came into regular contact with the "young turks" at *Cahiers du cinéma.* Varda recalls her first encounter with these young fanatical critics: "Chabrol, Truffaut, Rohmer (who had a different name then), Brialy, Doniol-Valcroze, and Godard were there that evening. They quoted thousands of films and suggested all sorts of things to Resnais, they all talked fast, chatted brightly, and sat everywhere including on the bed. I seemed to be there by mistake, feeling small, ignorant and the only woman among the guys from *Cahiers*."[33] Varda would always have a tangential relation to the *Cahiers* critics; her more literary and modernist film practice and her shift into documentary shorts for the next eight years placed her more in the camp known as the "Left Bank Group," along with Resnais, Demy, and Chris Marker, among others. Nonetheless, historians rightly label her a key precursor or even retroactive first true member of the French New Wave. Perhaps the best summary of *La Pointe Courte*'s place in history is offered by Gerald Mast and Bruce Kawin, who argue that Varda's film is to the New Wave what *Ossessione* (Visconti, 1942) was to neorealism.[34] It had all the traits that would be recognized several years later as New Wave, so pointed their way, but one isolated film is not yet part of a movement or school.

Jean-Pierre Melville, the Renegade Role Model

Jean-Pierre Melville's post–World War II filmmaking career provided yet another path for later New Wave directors to follow, but while he served as a model and inspiration, he, like Astruc, would seem tangential to that movement by 1960. Melville, born Jean-Pierre Grumbach in 1917, was ten to twenty years older than most of the New Wave directors, and thus World War II had a more direct effect on his life and films. At the age of six, he was given a Pathé-Baby camera. Later, he regularly skipped school to see the latest movies, and he proved to be a fanatical filmgoer all his life. But from the time he was drafted in 1937 until the end of the war in 1945, Grumbach, who was Jewish, put his plans to make movies on hold and took an active role in the regular and, later, the Free French armies, eventually traveling to London and joining the Allied invasion of Italy before returning home in Paris. As soon as the war ended, Grumbach changed his name to Melville as a sign of his respect for the storytelling of Herman Melville, whose works he had read during the war. Like René Clair after World War I, Melville made a break with his own past, in part motivated by the psychological trauma of the war years, as he adopted a new name and followed his passion, trying to make his postwar life worth living. Melville was fond of Hollywood cinema as well as of many of the contemporary French

auteurs, such as Jean Renoir, Jean Cocteau, and Robert Bresson. His synthesis of these impulses would affect his whole career.

Even though Melville had no experience in filmmaking and had never
taken courses or assisted anyone in production, his first act after the war
was to establish his own production company, Melville Productions, re-
taining the English label to suggest it was an international enterprise.
Colin Crisp cites Melville as the most dramatic example of a director striv-
ing for economic autonomy: "Unable to enter the industry on demobili-
zation because he was refused an industry work card, Melville decided
to reject entirely the established procedures, with their built in constraints."[35] In 1946 he shot a short film, *24 Hours in the Life of a Clown,*
which was shown successfully at some *ciné-clubs.* Next he adapted a famous novel of the French resistance, *Le silence de la mer,* and found some
financial assistance from Pierre Braunberger, who eventually helped distribute the finished film. During its production, Melville further developed
his own distinct persona, donning a Stetson hat that he always kept on in
public, forging a recognizable figure for the press. Like Hollywood's Samuel Fuller, he came off as a tough veteran, and interviews typically touched
on his violent war background. It is no surprise that his first feature was
about World War II.

The novel, *Le silence de la mer,* was written secretly by Jean Bruller under the pseudonym Vercors during the Nazi occupation and printed illegally by his clandestine publishing house, Editions de Minuit, in 1943.
Melville's adaptation was shot in 1947, premiered privately in 1948, and
commercially shown in the spring of 1949. The film's final version was slow
to be shown for many reasons, not least of which were that he had adapted
the novel without the author's permission, and he had shot the film with no
authorization from the newly organized CNC. As Susan Hayward points
out, the clandestine book became a clandestine film, made under a
truly resistant mode of production.[36] The movie even begins with a little
documentary-like scene in which one man, walking along an obscure
bridge, sets down a briefcase, which another man then picks up. He opens
the case, and hidden under the shirt is a pile of resistance newspapers and
also a copy of the book, *Le silence de la mer.* As he opens the book, there is
a perceptual point of view shot of the title page and the dedication to the
memory of Saint-Pol-Roux, "an assassinated poet." Next, the movie titles
are inscribed on pages of a book. Eventually Melville had to pay a fine before this illegal movie could be shown, and even then the labor unions
fought its premiere. Thus, *Le silence de la mer* would prove to be an un-

usual project, produced completely outside the conventional constraints of the French industry, and this radical practice impressed the rebellious, independent impulses of French cinephiles and future filmmakers alike.

Le silence de la mer was completed with a low budget of only nine million old francs, or roughly eighteen thousand dollars, which was 10 percent of an average French feature budget for that era. He shot the entire movie in twenty-seven days, but the shooting dates were drawn out across several months, from August to December 1947 since, like Roberto Rossellini with *Rome Open City* (1945), he could only shoot when he had gathered enough money and film stock. Moreover, since Melville did not have authorization to shoot from the CNC, he was forced to purchase his 35 mm film stock on the black market, and reportedly used nineteen different varieties of film![37] Young cinematographer Henri Decae, shooting his first feature as well, borrowed old equipment to edit the developed footage. In this way, *Le silence de la mer* was a truly "amateur" production, as the CNC branded it. But Melville did not object to being labeled an amateur since he was proud to be working outside the system he found so closed and artificial. His attitude anticipates that of Jean-Luc Godard, who would later brag that the best thing that ever happened to him was being turned down by the French film school, Institute des Hautes Etudes Cinématographiques (IDHEC). Other strategies Melville used for saving money (and cutting crew positions) included shooting on location in an unglamorous fashion with available light or very spare lighting set-ups, and without any make-up on the principal actors. Much of *Le silence de la mer* is also shot silent, with the narration, sound effects, and music added later. Melville's film, on every level, was an indictment of contemporary mainstream French cinema.

Melville was able to complete this film partly because of the simplicity of the story, which includes only three major characters, while the bulk of the action is set in one room of an average provincial house. The story concerns the billeting of a Nazi officer, Werner von Ebrennac (Howard Vernon), in the home of an elderly man (Jean-Marie Robain) and his niece (Nicole Stéphane). The "silence" of the title comes from the fact that the old man and his niece refuse to acknowledge the soldier's presence the entire six months that he lives in their home. During the course of those months, the German tries to explain himself to the pair, and each evening, he enters into long monologues in the main living room of the provincial house. He is incredibly polite and well read; he even tells them that he is sorry to disrupt their lives, but he tries to convince them that Germany is correct in launching this war. Gradually, however, the woman, who knits most evenings by her uncle's side and in front of the fireplace, struggles to avoid looking at the German, who is apparently beginning to fascinate her. Near the end, the German receives permission to take a short leave to see Paris, where he discovers just how ruthless the Nazi machine really is. He returns briefly to announce that he has learned that the German army is like the devil and is about to put the flame of French culture out forever. Devastated by the truth of this now unjust war, Werner announces that he has volunteered for duty at the hell of the front lines and wishes them farewell. The uncle's only real communication with Werner takes place when he leaves open an Anatole France book to the passage, "It is good for a soldier to disobey criminal orders." The final scene reveals the elderly man and his niece eating alone, in silence as usual, but the uncle's voice-over states that outside it seemed awfully cold that day.

Melville's style is strikingly spare, and the novelist Vercors liked the ascetic look of the film, partly because it avoided the artifice and spectacle of the usual war films, so he granted Melville permission to show the film and asked a relatively small fee for the rights. Once the CNC allowed Melville to screen the film (which involved petitions from famous members of the resistance, pleading Melville's and Vercors's case), it received very favorable reviews.

Melville's bare-bones crew included several young talents: in addition to Decae, his second assistant director was future filmmaker Michel Drach. The film maintains a slow, thoughtful, almost grim pace, reminiscent of Robert Bresson's work. Moreover, Melville asserts that he in turn influenced Bresson: "I once had this conversation with André Bazin. Bazin had noticed some shots in *Diary of a Country Priest* (1950) were from *Le silence*, there were things right out of my movie, like Laydu's voice commenting on the images."[38] Melville lives up to Astruc's call for a *caméra-stylo* since his film uses cinematic strategies to communicate both subtle and overt aspects of the novel. For instance, the night Werner arrives, he is shot from low, close camera positions, since he is a menacing Nazi, "occupying" their home; by the end of the film he is shown much more sympathetically with longer takes and softer lighting.

The voice-over mentioned by Melville is the dominant narrative tactic. The uncle begins the film in a voice-over just after the story's end, as Werner leaves. He is trying to understand what has happened during these last six months; thus the overall style is inscribed as subjective memory, and the film moves at the slowly meandering pace of the old man's recollections. Yet the visual style contributes heavily to the mood, with many long takes capturing the contradictions between Werner's long monologues on music, literature, and his life, and the old man and his niece sitting passively, pretending not to listen or care. The camera often pans or tracks from Werner across the room to the family members, or stages them in a triangular composition with lateral space and planes of action in depth separating them out while a ticking clock reinforces the silence and subtle tension between them. The spare, naturalistic mise-en-scène of objects, snow-covered roads, and books on the shelf is infused throughout with an elegantly simple camera and a richly significant soundtrack.

Typical of Melville's "ascetic style" is the first morning of Werner's visit; this eighty-second scene, filmed in two shots, has Werner entering the kitchen, where the woman and her uncle eat in silence. Werner explains that he slept well and hopes they did as well. Meeting no response, nor offers of food or coffee, he politely heads to the door. The second shot has great depth, à la *Citizen Kane,* with the stove's steaming pots and pans looming huge in the foreground, the silent family eating slowly in the middle ground, and Werner exiting behind them through the outside door left, then pausing in front of the window, screen right, to salute them before disappearing from the background altogether. David Bordwell argues this shot was a direct homage to Welles.[39] *Le silence de la mer* was hailed by many as the greatest film about the German occupation of France. Melville, veteran of the resistance, sporting a Stetson hat, and with no cinema training other than having watched thousands of movies, demonstrated that a low-budget, highly independent production made outside the norms could prove a real critical and financial success. Moreover, Melville's success in adapting Vercors's novel won Cocteau's permission to allow Melville to adapt *Les enfants terribles (The Strange Ones,* 1950). It was actually the raw, low-budget feel of *Le silence de la mer* that encouraged Cocteau to accept Melville's offer: "Cocteau believed the low budget, free style, and use of natural settings would allow this project to escape the usual heavy look of literary adaptations."[40]

Melville's adaptation of Cocteau's novel was excessively faithful to the book and even included Cocteau himself reading long passages in voice-over. Melville retained more than *Le silence de la mer*'s voice-over technique for this adaptation; he also kept the actress Nicole Stéphane (born de Rothschild) to play the eccentric sister Elisabeth, alongside Cocteau's selection of Edouard Dermithe (from *Orphée,* 1949) as Paul. But while *Le silence de la mer* was heralded as a great adaptation and true film of the resistance, *Les enfants terribles* was neither a critical nor a commercial success. Though some scenes and actions have a bizarre, irreverent charm and an occasional burst of humor, the bulk of the film tends toward a tedium that the more static *Le silence de la mer* somehow avoided.

Next, Melville accepted a commercial assignment, *Quand tu liras cette lettre* (*When You Read This Letter*, 1953), for which he had very little input in the story. In taking on this project, Melville inadvertently pointed to one of the other problems many New Wave filmmakers would also face: the fact that a small producer constantly risked all his or her resources on each individual production. One weak movie, or one that was not immediately successful, could derail the ability to create another "personal" work. Nonetheless, the moderate financial success of this commercial movie allowed Melville to purchase a new apartment as his home and studio space on rue Jenner in Paris and also provided a chance for him to swing back to auto-production and direct his own script of a gangster tale, called *Bob le flambeur* (*Bob the Gambler*, 1955).

The fascination with *Bob le flambeur* shown by John Woo and Quentin Tarantino during the 1990s helped revive interest in this "pre–New Wave" film. In interviews, Tarantino encouraged a new generation of international film buffs to investigate Melville's caper movie, which he acknowledged as a key influence on his *Reservoir Dogs* (1992). Similarly, Woo regularly referred to Melville as one of his great inspirations for movies such as *The Killer* (1989), *Hard Boiled* (1992), and *Face/Off* (1997). But for New Wave directors such as Godard, Pierre Kast, and Jacques Demy, Melville had already become a cult icon by 1960, as they adopted his mixture of the French *policier* with Hollywood-style noir influence and even parody. Melville appears in person in *Breathless* (1960), portraying a famous novelist, and in Demy's *Lola* (1961), the returning lover Michel drives a white Cadillac and wears a Stetson cowboy hat, a clear reference to Melville as a cultural hybrid. While Melville went on to make many more excellent "hard-boiled" detective tales, none has the influential edge, restrained sense of self-awareness, or cult value of *Bob le flambeur*.

Melville's intricate gangster movie was shot for only about thirty-six thousand dollars (eighteen million old francs), which was double the budget for *Le silence de la mer*, but again roughly 10 percent of the average feature cost for that year. This time he was shooting his own script, so he had to pay no royalties. For his lead actor Melville employed Roger Duchesne, a supporting actor type who had averaged five pictures a year in the late 1930s and early 1940s. Duchesne, now forty-nine years old, had never played a leading man, nor had he acted in a major film for thirteen years. He worked for a low pay scale, but also gave Bob a fascinating impression of someone past his prime who nonetheless is desperately confident that good times are just around the corner or on the next spin of the roulette wheel. Melville continued to shoot on locations, in local bars and night-clubs, and most "studio" set-ups, like Bob's apartment, complete with the slot machine in the closet, were filmed in his own space on rue Jenner. The locations, often shot at dawn when the streets were deserted, reminded audiences of the beautiful use of Paris settings in Poetic Realism of the 1930s, but the action owed more to Melville's love of American movies such as *Dead End* (Wyler, 1937) and *The Asphalt Jungle* (Huston, 1950).[41] He cut costs everywhere he could, even reading the voice-over narration himself. He again employed the brilliant Henri Decae to capture the documentary style images of Paris and Deauville, this time with a new film stock, Gravaert 36, which other cinematographers feared, but Decae used to great advantage.[42]

Melville opens "the very strange story" of *Bob le flambeur* with a tongue-in-cheek monologue about the Montmartre neighborhood, which is Bob's world. Melville's mock poetic voice-over claims this setting offers both heaven and hell . . . "but let's get to Bob." Bob is introduced gambling at the crap tables in a small back room, and he moves from one game and gambling joint to another, even after telling his friends he was finished and is going home. When he returns to the first place, admitting to losing two hundred thousand dollars, he turns down a drink, but orders one moments later. Bob is established as a cool, obsessed gambler, moving through the dark predawn underworld of Paris, but he is also torn between wanting to "do good" and not really wanting to carry through on his promises to himself. He is also respected by the police inspector (Guy Decomble), because Bob protected him in a shoot-out years earlier, and the inspector feels a debt of honor and friendship toward him.

During the course of the movie, Bob befriends a beautiful young streetwalker, Anne (Isabelle Corey), who is rapidly moving from amateur status to becoming a real professional. Bob is attracted to her, but she ends up sleeping with his young protégé, Paolo (Daniel Cauchy), who accidentally spills the news to her that Bob has organized a "last job" of robbing the casino at Deauville. Bob assembles a gang, but Anne and others betray enough information for an informant to tell the inspector about the scheme. Unable to warn Bob in time, the inspector races off to Deauville, arriving just in time to stop the robbery before it begins. But Bob is the inside man, gambling the night away in the casino while the gang prepares and waits for their early morning attack. He forgets the time as he continues to win ever higher amounts at roulette and blackjack. Bob rushes outside as the police and gang exchange gunfire, only to see young Paolo shot dead in the street. Bob and his buddy Roger are arrested by the inspector as the casino staff loads Bob's millions of francs of winnings into the police car's trunk. The inspector tries to reassure his old friend Bob: "Criminal intent will get you five years; with a good lawyer, three." Roger responds, "And with a very good lawyer: No criminal intent, acquitted!" To which Bob adds, "With a really top lawyer, I could sue you!" The inspector smiles wryly as the jazz music swells, and a relaxed Bob is driven off.

Thus, *Bob le flambeur* proves a terrific precursor to many of the later New Wave films: It synthesizes images and characters from Poetic Realism and American films noir, with a raw, low-budget style that mixes documentary style with almost parodic artifice, all set to a jazzy, contemporary score. Alan Williams enumerates the story's surface-level debt to Hollywood detective B-movies: It is populated with "tired professional criminals and callow young ones, and the policemen who know them all too well; young amoral women out for thrills who betray the men without thinking, and older, jaded ones who can predict the deceptions to come; a perfect crime that will go wrong."[43] It is precisely this fascination with the shift in generations—from the older bar owner, Yvonne, who warns Bob against any last jobs and offers to take care of him, to the wild and careless young Anne, whom Bob wants to protect but cannot—that would make this a popular hit during the decade of France's fascination with youth. Anne in particular anticipates the free sexuality of Bardot's Juliet in Roger Vadim's upcoming *And God Created Woman* (1956); Anne and Juliet share a penchant for sexual independence, but both also identify with modern jazz music and perform startlingly exhibitionistic dances. Historians such as Peter Hogue have pointed out that, while Melville's world here is resolutely male, one of its best characters is nonetheless Anne: "Isabelle Corey's uninhibited gall as the teenaged streetwalker in *Bob le Flambeur* is somnambulist movie acting of an extraordinarily high order."[44] She typified a young generation that was becoming lost in its excessive freedom but has no intention of being "saved" by its elders. More so than Varda's Sylvia Monfort or any of Astruc's women, Melville's Anne provided a blueprint for the defiantly sexy new young women who would fascinate so many young New Wave directors and their audiences into the 1960s.

Beyond the character archetypes and iconic underworld images of

Paris, *Bob le flambeur* offers the New Wave a virtual menu of stylish low-budget devices to adopt. In addition to the claustrophobic sets and locations with low ceilings, low-key lighting, and heavily patterned shadows borrowed from film noir, Melville's visual style depends on a modern, playful mix of transitions, montages, and shot sequences. Decae's famous intimate style provides a wide array of angles, pans, reframing, and starkly lit contrasts, and it all comes at a rather rapid pace, with an average shot length of nine seconds. Since Melville films typically feature only occasional brief scenes of violence, the style becomes more about gradually building character relations and a fatalistic tension. Mere conversations between friends, as in the scene where Bob tells his friend Roger that they will rob the casino at Deauville, is filmed as if it were a duel. The room has large black-and-white checkerboard walls to remind the viewer that Bob, with his flowing white hair, sees the world as one big board game. But even casual conversations or the mere act of Bob returning home to put a coin in the slot machine and pour himself a glass of wine are choreographed as if a crime has just been committed or is pending. Thus the lighting, descriptive passages of the neighborhood, nostalgic use of wipes, personal voice-overs, and bursts of jazz help establish the tired world of Bob, a fellow who can look in the mirror and say, "That's a good face for a thug." These devices will inspire Godard, Truffaut, and Demy, among others.

Melville became a highly publicized mentor for the New Wave, but he also headed in a different direction from them in the early 1960s, swinging more toward the conventions of the popular detective film and further from his stylish personal dramas of the 1940s and 1950s. Pierre Billard compares Melville to the swallow who announces spring; Melville anticipated the New Wave, "not just in his relentless pursuit of new economics, but also by his taste for technical experimentation and the frantic energy he displayed in conducting his projects."[45] Yet it is his economic model that Melville emphasized as his biggest influence on the new young filmmakers: "Since these [young directors] did not have much money, they decided they could do it 'like Melville.' They were inspired by our 'economy' in production but that's the only point we have in common. Moreover, once the New Wave directors got their second or third film, these films became tainted with intellectualism, something I distrust greatly."[46] Yet, in a *Cinéma 60* interview, Melville defined the New Wave as "an artisanal system, shot on location, without stars, without a standard crew, with a very fast film stock and with no distributor, without authorization or servitude to anyone."[47] This definition easily summarizes his own *Le silence de la mer*

and the spirit of *Bob le flambeur;* even though Melville preplanned carefully and ruled out spontaneity on the set, he was his own boss for his best
movies. With *Le doulos* (*The Finger Man,* 1961) and later *Le samourai*
(1967), among others, Melville aimed at a larger public and distanced
himself more and more from his followers. But he had shown young directors that a personal director-package system not only worked but should
be the norm for low-budget art films.[48]

It should be clear that Astruc, Varda, and Melville each offered distinct
cues for other young, unconventional directors to follow. They, as much as
the atmosphere of *cinéphilia,* the influence of *Cahiers du cinéma,* and the
rise of a national fascination with all things youthful, shaped the cultural
environment from which more and more young directors would arise. Yet,
the lessons provided by these directors were valuable but also cautionary,
teaching those who followed in their paths to pay attention to their failures
as well as to their successes: Astruc's personal brand of romanticism was
quickly seen as out of date, and he lost most of his personal freedom;
Agnès Varda could never apply for Film Aid for *La Pointe Courte,* since it
was produced in violation of CNC rules, and she had to wait eight years to
find money to shoot her next feature; Melville pulled away from New Wave
aesthetics at the very moment that others were proclaiming them the only
way to make important movies. The idea that low-budget films could be
highly marketable did not become a reality until transitional figures, especially Roger Vadim and Louis Malle, added examples and helped encourage even more directors to come forward and launch a "wave" of such
productions.

3

New Stories, New Sex:
Roger Vadim and Louis Malle

And Vadim Created Woman

An impeccable craftsman and elegant stylist of the widescreen color film
. . . Vadim, more than any other single figure in the French cinema, opened
the doors of the industry to his generation and provided the economic
justification for the New Wave.
> —DAVID A. COOK, *A History of Narrative Film*

Roger Vadim owed his reputation as a modern director to Bardot's breasts.
> —PIERRE BILLARD, *L'age classique du cinéma français*

R O G E R V A D I M was celebrated by the popular French press as yet another harbinger of the growing youth movement and the rejuvenation of the
French cinema. His debut film, *Et Dieu créa la femme* (*And God Created
Woman*, 1956) fed right into the sort of nouvelle vague being discussed
by *L'Express* magazine and other cultural barometers in France. Vadim
(b. 1928) lived a colorful life, some of which he embellishes in his chatty
autobiography, *Memoirs of the Devil*. Vadim built his life story around tales
of the women in his life and worked to market his relationships with his famous partners, who were often his leading actresses as well. Moreover, like
Roman Polanski, Vadim exploits the close ties between his personal and
professional lives, creating a fascinating and mythical self-image, though
Polanski's talent and real suffering surely surpass those of Vadim. Many
French historians consider Vadim, along with Malle, Alexandre Astruc,
and Pierre Kast, as a "fifth cohort" of directors, who brought a new relevance to the cinema and eased the industry into the New Wave aesthetic.
Unlike these and other important young French directors considered precursors to the New Wave, however, Vadim generally comes up short in
many historians' evaluations and receives the harshest criticism. While
directors such as Jean-Pierre Melville and Agnès Varda are celebrated for

their intellect, novel creativity, and love of the cinema, Vadim is often dismissed as a poser with great potential who only disappoints. But his first feature film proves he deserves more attention than routine French histories generally grant him.

In his teens, Vadim enrolled in Charles Dullin's drama school, which had earlier trained Jean Marais, and Vadim studied alongside Marcel Marceau. He frequented the legendary Saint-Germain-des-Près neighborhood of Paris, where he mingled with the famous, from Colette, Ernest Hemingway, and André Gide to a young Marlon Brando. "I doubt whether a boy of less than twenty arriving in Paris today without any connections . . . would have any chance of living the kind of adventurous existence that I enjoyed after the Occupation."[1] But his most significant early encounter was with director Marc Allégret (b. 1900), when Vadim was working as an extra. As early as 1948, when Vadim was just twenty years old, he sold a script idea to Allégret. In preparation for the initial screen tests, Allégret asked Vadim to locate a young woman whom he had seen featured as the "ideal young French girl" on the cover of *Elle;* her name was Brigitte Bardot. Bardot, as well as newcomer Leslie Caron, tried out for the movie. The film was ultimately never made, but Vadim began to pursue the fifteen-year old Bardot, who came from a very bourgeois family in Paris's fashionable sixteenth arrondissement. Meanwhile, Vadim found steady work as a reporter for *Paris-Match,* the French equivalent to *Life* magazine, where his charm and confidence allowed him to make more contacts throughout France. But he took time off from *Paris-Match* when Allégret hired him to help write *Maria Chapdelaine* and then *Blackmailed* (both released in 1950). During this same period, Bardot became an actress, and Vadim, who became her husband in 1952, when she turned eighteen, was often hired to write dialogue for her films.

With his first screen credit coming at age twenty-two, Roger Vadim became something of a poster boy for the post–World War II generation, for whom anything seemed possible. In contrast to the popular image presented in the later 1950s, that French cinema was a completely closed shop, Vadim proved that young talent was indeed welcome. But his background also differs strongly from that of many of the eventual New Wave directors. Rather than working as a film critic for *Arts* or *Cahiers du cinéma,* Vadim wrote for the glossy, popular *Paris-Match.* Moreover, he had studied at a traditional drama school and spent eight years as a scriptwriter and then assistant director for the very conventional Marc Allégret. Allégret, famous for helping launch the careers of many suc-

cessful actors, served as a close model and mentor for Vadim, even standing up as best man for the Vadim-Bardot marriage. Thus, Vadim was a re-
sourceful fellow who followed fairly established patterns of making good
connections in order to work his way into the French film industry.
Through Allégret he managed to meet Pierre Braunberger; Allégret and
Braunberger dined together every Sunday for forty years. Vadim had written several of the movies Braunberger produced, but even that daring producer refused to finance Vadim's pet project of directing his own script.
Vadim recalls, "I was twenty-six years old and, at the time, youth was not
a marketable commodity."[2] But he did meet up with a small-time producer,
Raoul Lévy, who took a chance on his idea for a melodramatic story about
love, marriage, and betrayal set in Saint-Tropez.

Lévy had produced only one film, four years before *And God Created
Woman*. When he and Vadim met, Vadim proposed a love story starring
Brigitte Bardot, in color and wide-screen. Once won over, Lévy set to work
to locate additional partners and sign an advance distribution contract. As
Vadim recalls, "In 1955 Raoul was a hard-up young producer and I was a
novice writer. Our first project brought shrugs of disbelief from film people,
who advised us to buy a lottery ticket instead."[3] But Vadim, who was a big
fan of *East of Eden* (Kazan, 1955), wanted the French industry to recognize the value of color, wide-screen, and young Method actors, arguing that
their films would sell at home and abroad. Eventually, a former band-
leader, Ray Ventura, agreed to coproduce the film; once they signed up veteran actor Curt Jurgens (b. 1915), and Columbia agreed to distribute the
final film, they had enough capital to begin shooting. To counter Vadim's in-
experience, Lévy hired Armand Thirard (b. 1899), who had been cinematographer on such French classics as *Hotel du nord* (Carné, 1938), *Wages
of Fear* (Clouzot, 1952), and *Diabolique* (Clouzot, 1955). Thirard, cinematographer of over fifty films before *And God Created Woman*, had worked
with many of France's most celebrated directors and had shot several of
Bardot's early films. The music was composed by Paul Misraki (b. 1908),
who had also worked on roughly fifty films at this point in his career, beginning with Jean Renoir's *On purge bébé* (1931); more recently he had composed the score for *Mr. Arkadin* (Welles, 1955). In his long career, Misraki
went on to write the music for many early Chabrol films, including *Le
beau Serge* (1958) and *The Cousins* (1959), as well as Godard's *Alphaville* (1965).

Vadim's project can be summarized as a fairly typical, moderately
priced production for a first-time director: the project mixes established,

classically trained personnel with young talent, while aiming to exploit the new technologies of color and wide-screen as well as the fame and beauty of Brigitte Bardot. Bardot had already appeared in fourteen feature films, working with directors such as Allégret, Sacha Guitry, and René Clair as well as appearing in international coproductions in England and Italy. Moreover, even before the Paris premiere of *And God Created Woman*, Bardot had been featured on the cover of *Elle* twelve times. She was already enough of a sensation that, by 1955, Vadim was often referred to as Monsieur Bardot, a label he resented.

Lévy built a budget of two hundred thousand dollars for their project, which, while a moderate cost for France in this period, amounted to only one-third the budget of comparable European color films. Where later New Wave filmmakers often argued for auteur films with few compromises, Vadim was eager to please anyone who could help him get his directing debut. For instance, Lévy needed to get an international star in the package before Columbia would enter the deal, so he and Vadim took a train to Munich to meet with the forty-year-old Jurgens. But there was no part in the script for a middle-aged German at Saint-Tropez, so Vadim adapted the story on short notice, creating a small but important part for Jurgens. In the end, Vadim revised his story in such a way as to market the beauty, sexuality, but also amoral independence of Juliette, whose passionate world stood in sharp contrast to the stiff, mature elegance of Jurgens's character.

And God Created Woman is built around the effect Juliette (Bardot) has on the small, sunny fishing town of Saint-Tropez. Juliette was adopted from an orphanage by an older couple who own a bookshop, where Juliette works, barefoot in her loose dress. The adoptive mother threatens to send her back to the orphanage until Juliette is twenty-one years old because the whole town is gossiping about her sexual escapades. The wealthy, middle-aged Eric Carradine (Jurgens) owns a nightclub in Saint-Tropez and flirts with Juliette, but his central concern is secretly to buy up land and build a large casino.

The only obstacle to Carradine's plan is the Tardieu family's dock, where they build and repair fishing boats. The oldest son, Antoine (played by Vadim's former roommate, Christian Marquand), has a full-time job in a different city but does not want to sell the unprofitable family business to Carradine. Michel (Jean-Louis Trintignant), the middle of the three Tardieu brothers, is timid and hardworking and the only one to understand that there is no future for their small boatyard. But their mother, who prefers Antoine over Michel, refuses to move.

Figure 3.1. Carradine and Juliette hover over a jukebox (*And God Created Woman*)

Meek Michel secretly loves the flirtatious Juliette and even compares himself to the earthworm who fell in love with the moon. But Juliette, who likes the tall, handsome Antoine, overhears Antoine telling his buddies that Juliette will be an easy conquest that night, and then he will just leave town again tomorrow and forget her. Angry, she flirts with Carradine, who decides to keep Juliette from leaving for the orphanage by trying to find someone to marry her, but timid Michel is the only one interested in doing so. When Michel takes her home to tell his mother, Juliette stands provocatively eating carrots while the mother curses her. Antoine laughs at Michel, and even the priest tells Michel he is not the man to break in a wild horse like Juliette. Michel nonetheless marries Juliette. He has to defend Juliette's honor on the walk home from the wedding ceremony but gets beaten up by one of the men from Juliette's previous affairs.

Carradine, getting impatient to consolidate his business deal, decides to offer the Tardieu family a part of the new business, so Antoine agrees to return to town to help manage the new dockyard portion of the business. But once he moves back home, Antoine's jealousy and Juliette's longing create tense and embarrassing scenes in the Tardieu home. One day, when Michel is in Marseille on business, Juliette who was too lazy to get up and go with him as she had promised, instead eventually takes out a boat that is not safe. Antoine chases after her in his jeep along the beach and sees her struggling with a fire onboard. After swimming out to rescue her, Antoine makes love to Juliette on the deserted beach. At home that night,

Figure 3.2. Michel and Juliette are married (*And God Created Woman*)

Juliette tells the youngest brother, Christian, about her mistake with Antoine, but a jealous Antoine comes in on them and tells Juliette "Not both of us in one day!" He warns Christian to stay away from the tramp Juliette. On his return, Michel's mother recounts the incident to him; the naive Michel asks "What am I to do?" His mother tells him he must make Juliette leave their house right away.

But Juliette has already left to wander the town. As if in a daze, she goes to a bar to look up her old friends, as Michel chases after her. Drunk and wondering aloud whether the barman would put poison in her cognac for her, Juliette goes downstairs to hear a salsa band practicing and performs an exhibitionistic and finally hysterical dance to their music. Looking for her, Michel fights with Antoine at their office. He takes his brother's gun, comes to the bar, and finds Carradine trying to lead Juliette away. Even as Carradine tells Michel that Juliette really loves him, Michel fires a shot. Carradine intervenes to make sure Juliette does not get hit, but he is wounded in the process.

Though he says, "Lucky for you it only made a hole in my jacket," the bleeding Carradine gets Antoine to drive him to another town for treatment, to avoid scandal in Saint-Tropez. As he remarks, "The police don't understand about love affairs." Still angry and thwarted by Carradine in his revenge, Michel slaps Juliette, and she seems calmed. On the road, Carradine admits to Antoine that he let Juliette go because he was afraid

Figure 3.3. Michel fires (*And God Created Woman*)

that *she* would tame *him*. He then tells Antoine not to return to Saint-Tropez, so that perhaps Michel will be able to hold the marriage together. The final shots, accompanied by melodramatic music, reveal Michel leading Juliette back into the Tardieu family home.

This melodrama is fairly conventional in some of its plot points, but it was the audacity of Bardot's performance and the bits of frank conversation and nudity that made contemporary reviewers react strongly. For most 1950s audiences, this was a bold new vision of French youth and sexuality. Bardot's Juliette was not just another beautiful baby doll; rather, she shattered past norms while establishing new conventions for female sexuality. For viewers today, however, Bardot's Juliette provides a puzzling, even contradictory performance. Yet, Simone de Beauvoir, author of *The Second Sex* and an international voice for women's liberation in the 1950s, praised Bardot and her Juliette: "Her eroticism is not magical, but aggressive. In the game of love, she is as much the hunter as the prey."[4] Bardot was as important a role model for teenage girls in the 1950s as Madonna would become in the 1980s. Her unabashedly sensual poses became iconic. And even though her personal style of dress, featuring loose, revealing clothes and sandals with no stockings, flew in the face of more conservative female dress codes of the Paris fashion industry, they were quickly adopted by thousands of young women. "B. B." had arrived.

Cahiers du cinéma critics, among many others, were ecstatic over

Bardot's natural acting style, which was far removed from the theatricality of her contemporaries: her spontaneous manner of walking, speaking, smiling, and kissing, as well as the way she could caress the soil with her bare feet, fascinated young audiences.[5] As feminist critic Françoise Audé explains, Bardot spearheaded a sort of global revolt against moral hypocrisy among a large segment of young women: "Brigitte Bardot was disrespect itself." Audé even suggests that while the New Wave proper may have begun in 1959, for women it began in 1956 with *And God Created Woman*, "creating an immediate impact on the cinema as well as on real life." Juliette's amorality somehow seemed honest and independent and provided liberating effects that were discussed in many popular magazines for young women. Yet, as Audé adds, though Bardot at the time seemed an ideal model for independent-thinking women, no contemporary feminist can identify with her image today.[6]

That much of the so-called honesty of Juliette's character is hard for today's viewers to perceive, much less celebrate, should be motivation to determine how contemporary reactions to Vadim's story can be so different from those of his 1950s audiences. Antoine de Baecque points out that Juliette did not fit any of the existing categories for women of the period: "She created her type: she is neither venal nor fatal, instead she is a 'pure sinner' who can be brutally frank."[7] For de Baecque, the real novelty of *And God Created Woman* lay in the relation between Bardot and Vadim's mise-en-scène: "Vadim conceived of Juliette as an incarnation of a lively, desirable youth, carefree and comfortable in her body, which is endowed with radical new liberty and expressions."[8] Vadim worked closely with Bardot to create his script around many of her real life traits, but he also allowed her a great degree of flexibility in dialogue, so that many of Juliette's quirky expressions and physical poses are Bardot's personal additions. One should keep in mind, however, that Vadim also tried to direct some of the film's critical response by stating in interviews that he was a sort of ethnographer, documenting a new sort of woman with her own desires, gestures, and beauty. It is safe to say that Juliette is a sort of synthesis of Vadim's and Bardot's visions, which were often competing. In fact, during the filming, Bardot began to drift away from Vadim and began a physical relationship with her costar Trintignant. Many of the scenes where Juliette exhibits independent desire were being matched by her sexual independence off the screen as well, and some of Trintignant's pouting performance can be tied to his discomfort being directed by the husband of his new girlfriend and costar. The Vadim-Bardot marriage ended with *And God Created Woman,* while, ironically, the careers of all three principals took off simultaneously.

For the year 1957, when *And God Created Woman* first became a sensation in France and then abroad, Juliette's character was more ambiguous than any other female characters in competing films. Her role was contrasted favorably with Carroll Baker's thumb-sucking lead character in Elia Kazan's *Baby Doll* (1956), since Juliette remains beyond family control for most of the film. Juliette expresses her desire fairly clearly, and her presence reveals the hypocrisy around her. For instance, her adoptive father strains from his wheelchair to peek at her sunbathing in the nude outside his window, but later sits quietly as his wife calls Juliette a tramp and vows to see her punished. One scene that seemed particularly radical to contemporary audiences was the wedding breakfast. Just after Michel has returned bruised and bloody in his wedding suit, Juliette takes him upstairs, makes love to him, and then comes back down to gather food from the table to take back to the bedroom, in front of Michel's mother and the other snubbed wedding guests. She treats her elders with scorn, revealing a previously unknown disdain for basic social codes of conduct.

Beyond dismissing social norms, Juliette, of course, is most famous for violating sexual taboos. She is consistently unconventional; as Françoise Audé writes, "In 1957, Juliette-Brigitte Bardot forced a revision of the fixed old languages of the love story and film criticism."[9] Audé points out that 1957 was the year of the first Planned Parenthood office in France, and for many young women in the audience, Juliette's daring role, displaying no concern with pregnancy or motherhood, combined with Bardot's real-life sexual adventures, including her affair with Trintignant, provided a stunning new perspective on modern sexual autonomy. As Carradine explains in the movie, "She has the courage to do what she wants, when she wants." For many parents in the audience, however, Bardot became a dangerous role model. In particular, showing Juliette openly seduce Antoine on the beach, with no sign of concern for the future or what this might mean for her marriage, provided a radical break from the moralizing indiscretions of more conventional French dramas. Beyond the idea of Juliette openly having sex in broad daylight with her husband's handsome brother, there was Vadim's staging, which in the original version revealed Bardot's bare breasts as she lay under Antoine. This scene was edited for a censored version in markets such as the United States. In many scenes, from the opening, where Bardot stands behind a sheet on a clothesline, to scenes in her bedroom with Michel, Vadim proves to the viewer that the actress is really naked on the set, exceeding many conventions for representing nudity on screen. Thus, when Juliette combined her physical freedom with lines such as "Oh, the future, they just invented that to keep us from having fun now," she was offering movie-goers a new character type that would be explored further and reworked by subsequent young actresses as well as their young male directors over the course of the New Wave.

Yet, while Juliette does choose the men in her life, she also submits to Michel's slap at the end of the film, just before he leads her back to his mother's house, towing her along like a disobedient child. *And God Created Woman* is troubling in that it finally reinforces the cautioning comments of the older generation, as Juliette ultimately does cause too many problems and needs to be "tamed" by Michel; his shooting of Carradine and slapping of Juliette reveal both his frustration and his maturing. Earlier in the film Carradine told Juliette, "What you need is a beating," to which she giggled, "I'd like that." When Michel does strike her, there is even a long take of her rubbing her hair, looking longingly at Michel, and sighing, as if his violence were merely foreplay. Hence, there is a consistent "taming" motif that undercuts the frank sexual freedom enjoyed by Juliette. For the resolution, Carradine suddenly changes from a predator

Figure 3.4. Juliette sunbathes (*And God Created Woman*)

to a benevolent uncle, whisking Antoine off with him so as to remove any temptations, leaving Michel to try to make the marriage work. The narrator seems finally to believe in the value and benefit of Michel's patriarchal rights and control of Juliette. For instance, in the next-to-last scene, as Juliette dances frantically and Michel pulls a gun, Carradine tries to comfort him: "You imbecile, don't you see she loves you?" He suggests Juliette is now a "one-man woman." With Antoine, Carradine explains he gave up pursuing Juliette out of fear she would make a puppet out of him, and then he tells Antoine that Michel is young and might still be able to "win." This conversation is followed by the final images of *And God Created Woman* as Michel leads Juliette into the family house. Further sexual freedom for Juliette seems unlikely, and Michel's victory is dependent upon her changing her ways.

Susan Hayward reduces this tale to a lesson that women who try to follow their sexual desire will be punished, since Juliette is first "locked up" in her adoptive father's gaze and then nearly killed by her husband.[10] As this discussion has made clear, however, Juliette's behavior for the bulk of the film establishes contradictory and ambiguous interpretations and visions. For young women in the 1950s, who were busy adopting Bardot's hair and clothing styles, Juliette's behavior seems to have rung truer than the ending that forces Juliette into submission. That she did not seem to mind being struck by Michel adds an unsettling perversity to her character that seems alternately to satisfy and to defy bourgeois norms. As Audé suggests, even to the end, Juliette is making most of the choices. Juliette realizes that she is really dancing for her husband, his arrival gives her pleasure, and her exhibitionism is finally aimed at his gaze. Juliette, it could be argued, is once again making her own path, forcing the men in her life to react in response to her lead.[11]

The visual style in *And God Created Woman* provides another valuable glimpse into mid-1950s notions of modernity. Rather than looking to the gritty naturalism of Italian neorealism or to more formal art cinema experimentation, Vadim is inspired by both the polish of classical Hollywood spectacle and a highly stylized but authentic use of locations. As he explained in a 1959 interview, "Our generation does not want to retell stories with the same vocabulary that has been used for so long and that not even the neorealists could escape: long shot, medium shot, close-up, shot/reverse shot. It has become a nightmare. All films look the same. I feel that Malle, Astruc, Chabrol, and Truffaut share this same new desire with me."[12] Vadim's mise-en-scène inserts his melodramatic characters into a

very contemporary version of small-town France on the verge of modernization and late capitalism. On the side of the past, there is the family
home, which looks as if it came right out of a 1930s Marcel Pagnol film,
with its cracked exterior walls and its minimal, rough-hewn furnishings.
The Tardieu family dock, the narrow, old city streets, and the city's sea-
shore cemetery are all used as highly significant yet traditionally realistic backdrops. But just down the street is the bar where Juliette's aimless
young friends hang out, drinking excessively and listening to jazz on the
jukebox, a Caribbean salsa band plays downstairs, and the German Carradine's yacht parks just beyond the old fishing boats that Michel Tardieu
scrapes and repairs. It is an elegant synthesis of old, picture-postcard
France and the new, colorful life opening up to youth at a transitional moment of history. Similarly, Vadim's use of lush color, wide-screen composition exploiting lateral staging, smooth and functional camera movements, and reliance on long takes (there are 325 shots for an average shot
length [ASL] of sixteen seconds) add up to a transitional film as well. He
has learned from Allégret and Pagnol as well as Elia Kazan. Subsequent
New Wave filmmakers, especially those from the *Cahiers* auteurists, will
simply shift their allegiances to a different collection of French and American influences.

   And God Created Woman was startling on an economic level as well,
reportedly earning four million dollars in its United States release alone,
which was more than Renault's automobile exports that year.[13] This precedent shook up the French industry, accomplishing something few would
have believed possible for a young, first-time director and his marginal
producer. Thus, Vadim offered a transitional cue for French cinema with
And God Created Woman that the rest of his career never quite matched in
importance. But the fact that his subsequent oeuvre was so uneven does
not mean that one should follow strict auteurists' leads and, with hindsight,
minimize the historical significance of this first feature. When the journal
Cinéma 58 published its list of forty "*nouveau*" directors, it argued that
they "generated new ways of talking and thinking, new ways of representing and categorizing people" and that Vadim, like Varda, Kast, and Astruc,
presented some of the most sincere and modern studies of male-female relations.[14] Similarly, Jean-Luc Godard, then a critic for *Cahiers,* wrote that
Vadim's great gift was to "breathe the air of today" with *And God Created
Woman.*[15] And Bardot was launched not simply as yet another bombshell
actress but rather became the representation, for better or for worse, of a
new woman and "the symbol of a new freedom recognized by a young au-

dience that had grown up during these first years of a new consumer society."[16]

Truffaut also saw Vadim's film as a good omen: "In *Arts,* I wrote during a festival and without quite having recovered from the euphoria of *And God Created Woman* . . . 'From now on, films no longer need to tell stories, it is enough to describe one's first love-affair, to take one's camera to the beach.'"[17] And of course, Truffaut would take his camera onto a beach for the final scene of his own first feature, *The 400 Blows.* The twenty-eight-year-old Vadim's combination (and commodification) of Bardot, location shooting, glossy production values, and a tale about amorality or at least new perspectives on morality fit everything *L'Express* had labeled as nouvelle vague. The critical success and enormous financial profits of *And God Created Woman* pointed the way for other young actors, directors, and also unconventional producers to capitalize on youth, sexuality, and the mythical French sophistication, in marketing a new trend to a world hungry for alternative product in their booming art houses. As Jean-Pierre Jeancolas concludes, "*And God Created Woman* is probably not a great film, but it was a sign. It announced the imminent mutation of French cinema."[18]

Louis Malle and the Nouvelles Editions de Films

In 1957 . . . Louis Malle had already moved into the house that would be
the nouvelle vague and opened the doors wide for the newcomers.
                                    —JACQUES SICLIER, *Nouvelle vague?*

Louis Malle, who is completely outside the nouvelle vague, may be counted
among those film artists—from von Sternberg to Minnelli—who make
cinema come alive thanks to their incessant formal quests.
                                    —*Positif*

Louis Malle is an even better test case than Roger Vadim for examining the historical challenges involved in defining the shift from a *nouveau* young French cinema to the New Wave proper. As the epigraphs to this section indicate, Malle was a pivotal player in late 1950s France, but discussions of his significance and whether he actually counted as a member of the New Wave reveal a wide range of opinions and reactions. Moreover, since the writers at *Positif* were openly suspicious of and hostile to the New Wave, their praise for a young French director would logically have to distance him from that group. Yet, even though François Truffaut praised Malle's early films, the famous 1962 *Cahiers* summary of New Wave directors remains cautious: "He speaks intelligently about the cinema and his intentions; if his films resembled his claims he would be the nouvelle vague's phoenix."[19] Therefore, it should come as no surprise that contemporary historians are still divided about just how to contextualize Louis Malle. Survey histories tend to minimize Malle's significance, set him on its fringes, or place him at its heart: Kristin Thompson and David Bordwell's *Film History: An Introduction* follows many others by labeling Malle a "mainstream" director who borrows New Wave style when he needs to; David A. Cook's *A History of Narrative Film* places Malle firmly in the New Wave and discusses him between Chabrol and Rohmer; Alan Williams considers Malle "the very heart of the nouvelle vague."[20]

Most historical accounts acknowledge his role as a precursor and even a model for young directors who followed his example in the late 1950s and early 1960s. As Ginette Vincendeau summarizes, "Malle's early features place him in an odd position vis-à-vis the New Wave; he is a precursor to it with *Ascenseur pour l'échafaud / Lift to the Scaffold* (1957), with his use of locations, Jeanne Moreau and a Miles Davis score, and *Les Amants* (1958), and already marginal to it with the zany comedy *Zazie dans le métro* (1960)."[21] In an effort to clarify Malle's status in the 1950s, this section lends context to his early career, explaining the sources of uncertainty over his ultimate effect on new French cinema and detailing important and distinctive narrative strategies in his first two features, *Elevator to the Gallows* and *The Lovers*.

Part of the problem in summarizing Malle's place as a charter member of the New Wave is that his personal background differs from that of the *Cahiers* group in many ways. While Malle was the right age—he was born in the northern town of Thumières in 1932, which made him the same age as Truffaut, but younger than Vadim, Chabrol, Rohmer, and Godard—he came from a much higher social class than any of his peers. Mademoiselle Malle's maiden name was Beghin, of the famous sugar processing company. The Beghin-Say Company, whose name can still be found on sugar-cube wrappers in many French cafés, also supplied raw sugar to large beer producers in Belgium, France, and other countries. Louis's father was a manager at the Beghin plant, and the Malle children, much like those in the families in *Le souffle au coeur* (*Murmur of the Heart,* 1971) and *Au revoir les enfants* (1987), were raised in very luxurious fashion, attending some of the best schools in France. The immense wealth and stature of Malle's family certainly marked his career just as strongly as poverty and a dysfunctional childhood affected Truffaut's. But while Truffaut would become a sort of mythical Cinderella of the New Wave, Malle's wealth affected negatively many critics' initial responses to his work. Some saw him as just a rich kid whose personal fortune and connections allowed him to buy his way into the film industry. Yet Malle was much more progressive politically than most of the *Cahiers du cinéma* critics and directors, a factor that helped generate some strong initial support from leftist journals.

Unlike the more famous *Cahiers* directors, Malle never wrote film criticism. Furthermore, he *did* attend the much-maligned IDHEC's film production program (like Alain Resnais), he did work very briefly as an assistant director (one month with Robert Bresson on *A Man Escaped,* 1956), and he did work in documentary before making his first feature film. If one overestimated these steps in his career, it would be easy to dismiss Malle as much more conventional in his preparation than the *Cahiers* directors. Malle never completed the program at IDHEC, however, and his work in documentary and then with Bresson reveals a deep love of all kinds of cinema—the sort of love that historians generally ascribe to the *Cahiers* critic-directors more than to other filmmakers. That Malle never wrote for *Arts* or *Cahiers du cinéma* does not mean that he spent any less time watching movies at the Cinémathèque or elsewhere, than did Truffaut, Rohmer, or Godard. Moreover, the fact that Malle managed to have such a full career by the time he was twenty-five years old attests to his youthful passion and a very real talent in the cinema.

During the summer of 1953, the twenty-year old Malle was hired by Jacques Cousteau as a technical assistant for a documentary on his revolutionary oceanic studies. By the fall, Cousteau and Malle embarked on a two-year voyage aboard the *Calypso* filming what would become the award-winning documentary *Le monde du silence* (*The Silent World,* 1955). As Malle recalls, "We had to invent the rules—there were no references; it was too new. The camera by definition—because we were underwater—had a mobility and fluidity; we could do incredibly complicated equivalents of what, on land, would be a combination of crane movements plus enormous tracking shots."[22] Malle wanted to maintain very austere Bressonian touches, with long takes that require the spectator to reflect on the details before the camera, while Cousteau leaned toward more manipulation, melodramatic themes, and even lighthearted touches. The synthesis of their temperaments resulted in a stylish and often moving film, and *The Silent World* won codirectors Cousteau and Malle the Palme d'or prize for best film at Cannes in 1956, when Malle was still just twenty-three years old.

After spending several weeks as an assistant director to Robert Bresson on *A Man Escaped,* Malle decided that his idol Bresson remained too
independent and aloof to teach him much about fiction filmmaking, and
that Malle's background from *The Silent World* had taught him enough
about cinematic technique to enable him to direct a feature. The impatient
Malle therefore decided to strike out on his own: "That autumn and winter
of 1956 I wrote one of those autobiographical screenplays—a love story
set in the Sorbonne. I did a treatment, took it around to producers and was
turned down everywhere—this was before the New Wave. Two years later
they would have taken it immediately . . . but in those years somebody
who had never directed fiction and wanted to do a personal film had
no chance."[23] Just why Malle never subsequently produced this script is
unclear, but he apparently decided to compromise slightly by selecting a
preexisting novel to adapt, while adding as many personal touches in
the adaptation as he could. Malle selected a crime novel, *Ascenseur pour
l'échafaud* by Noel Calef, and hired his friend, writer Roger Nimier, to help
revise it into a shooting script.

At this stage Malle provided the strongest blueprint for later New Wave
directors. Rather than continue as a first assistant director, he followed
Melville's model and became his own coproducer along with Jean Thullier,
who also produced *A Man Escaped.* After *Elevator to the Gallows,* Malle
bought Thullier's company, Les Nouvelles Editions, and produced *The
Lovers* by himself. His family fortune allowed him a great deal of independence, yet Malle decided to begin with a low-budget film. An average
French production in the 1950s could anticipate a return of eighty thousand to one hundred thousand dollars, so Malle, like Chabrol, Truffaut,
and others after him, decided to keep the budget limited to that range.
Moreover, *Elevator to the Gallows* was one of five French films in 1957 to
be awarded one of the new *primes à la qualité,* thus Thullier, who had also
received CNC aid for *A Man Escaped* a year earlier, helped show Malle how
to exploit the new economic possibilities of French film production even
before Chabrol or Truffaut. Malle realized that even a moderate box-office
return on a small budget, combined with the Film Aid, guaranteed he
could break even and then quickly begin making another inexpensive film
right away. Waiting for box-office returns to trickle in to cover a more expensive film was much riskier and demanded more patience than young
men like Malle could muster.

While Malle's selection of a pulp-fiction crime novel as source
material seems to anticipate so many other New Wave projects, such as

Truffaut's *Shoot the Piano Player* or Godard's *Breathless*, it was actually another rather cautious move. It was fairly standard for first-time directors in France in the late 1940s and early 1950s to shoot a B-grade detective story, or *polar*, loosely following American noir patterns. But Malle's adaptation varies from the model in his reworking of the crime drama, his addition of personal and art cinema traits to what would otherwise be a conventional genre film. Even Louis Malle liked to quip that for this first film he was split between being influenced by Bresson and by Hitchcock. Malle's project thus has many New Wave characteristics from the beginning: it is a low-budget film; it refers to Hollywood as well as to European art film traditions; it reworks an established genre with personal touches that will eventually be defined as auteur traits; it uses Melville's cinematographer, Henri Decae; it involved extensive location shooting; it has a soundtrack featuring improvised jazz music by Miles Davis; and it simultaneously launched the careers of several talented, young, up-and-coming actors. As Alan Williams writes, "Jeanne Moreau and Maurice Ronet, playing the film's doomed lovers, became the New Wave's first ideal couple, and two of its most striking and charismatic stars."[24] Moreover, *Elevator to the Gallows* was highly influential and successful, winning the prestigious Prix Louis Delluc in 1957, when Malle was only twenty-five years old. This sort of success, of course, turned the relatively small financial risk, thanks to Film Aid support and the frugal low-budget, into a highly profitable venture that ensured Malle even more flexibility on his next production.

The adapted story of *Elevator to the Gallows* involves a former French Army intelligence officer, Julien Tavernier (Maurice Ronet), who has served in the Vietnam and Algerian conflicts (presumably, to shore up France's slipping colonial power) and now hires out to perform "delicate" jobs for major corporations. But Julien is in love with Mme. Florence Carala (Jeanne Moreau), the wife of his current boss, M. Carala (Jean Wall).

Julien and Florence hatch a plan in which Julien kills Carala in his office at the end of the business day, making it look like a suicide. In the process, however, Julien gets stuck in the company elevator, where he spends the night trying to escape (with reference here to Bresson's *A Man Escaped*), while Florence roams Paris in search of him. Intercut with their story is the tale of a young florist, Véronique (Yori Bertin), whose young-tough boyfriend Louis (Georges Poujoly) steals Julien's flashy Chevrolet convertible and takes her for a ride around the outskirts of Paris.

Figure 3.5. Julien (*Elevator to the Gallows*)

Figure 3.6. Florence (*Elevator to the Gallows*)

Figure 3.7. Julien trapped (*Elevator to the Gallows*)

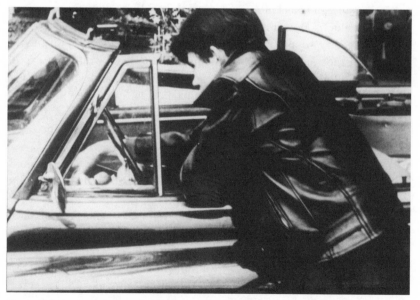

Figure 3.8. Louis steals the car (*Elevator to the Gallows*)

Complicating things further is the fact that Florence glimpses Véronique riding in Julien's car and assumes Julien has run off with the cute florist and chickened out on killing her husband. The stunned Florence decides to look for Julien in the usual clubs for an explanation. Later that night, while Julien struggles to free himself from the stalled elevator and Florence searches from café to café, Louis and Véronique stop at a motel, meet a couple of German tourists, get drunk, and take some photographs with Julien's spy camera. But later, as Louis steals the Germans' Mercedes, he kills them both with Julien's gun and then flees back to Paris, leaving Julien's gun, coat, and car at the scene of the crime. Louis and Véronique then unsuccessfully attempt to commit suicide to escape justice and separation. Finally, after pursuing several wrong paths, the police tie Julien and Florence to Carala's "suicide" and Louis and Véronique to the murder. Florence and Julien never actually get to meet during the plot time, but are only seen together in the last shots as an incriminating photograph of the two of them develops in a photographer's lab with Florence and the police inspector (Lino Ventura) looking on.

So much of what one expects to find in a New Wave film is present in both the story and the narrative style of *Elevator to the Gallows* that it deserves careful study as both a prototypical New Wave text and a personal "auteur product." Many reviews at the time referred to the film's mix of realism and poetry, set in a strange, new, and modern France and displaying formal elegance and complexity. Jacques Siclier even wrote that *Elevator to the Gallows,* with its brilliant exercise in style molded onto a basic detective-story structure, provided a model that "every new filmmaker used as his touchstone."[25] For historians such as Siclier, Malle, in his first several films, proved a concrete example of what André Bazin, Alexandre Astruc, and *Cahiers* in general had been preparing on paper: *Elevator to the Gallows,* and later *The Lovers,* showed the viability of a personal, independent cinema, which in turn encouraged others; only then did the New Wave "revolution" begin in earnest.

Many story elements in *Elevator to the Gallows* became central Malle auteur traits, resurfacing repeatedly throughout his career. Philip French, in *Malle on Malle,* argues that *Elevator to the Gallows* is typical of Malle's oeuvre because it interweaves conventions from documentary and fiction filmmaking alike into a rare synthesis. French also provides what is surely the most exhaustive list of Malle's auteurist "themes, tropes, and preoccupations." These narrative traits all first appear in *Elevator to the Gallows:* "a fascinated contempt for the hypocrisies of the middle class; jazz music;

Figure 3.9. Julien is grilled for the wrong murder (*Elevator to the Gallows*)

Figure 3.10. Julien and Florence in the photograph (*Elevator to the Gallows*)

suicide; the adult world observed by the dangerously innocent young; a political background that frames and is reflected in the protagonist's conduct;
characters trapped in some web of fate; the destructive power of sexual
passion; a gift for seizing a society at a precise moment of social change;
the urge to disrupt and disconcert; a refusal to make direct moral judge-
ments."[26] Thus, *Elevator to the Gallows* holds historical interest as representative of the beginning of both the New Wave aesthetic and Louis
Malle's auteurist style, which even the ailing André Bazin recognized and
praised.[27]

The story structure for *Elevator to the Gallows* weaves together the
three narrative trajectories: First, there is Julien, who kills Carala, gets
stuck in the elevator, and eventually flees, only to be wrongly arrested initially for the murder of the Germans, which he did not commit. Second,
Florence, who is waiting for Julien, wanders the city, eventually hunting
down the florist Véronique to learn what really happened that night. Third,
there is Véronique's bizarre parallel, and equally doomed, love story as
she accompanies the impatient Louis, a sort of French rebel without a
cause, who is always in trouble and has now graduated from pinching
scooters to stealing luxury cars and committing murder. This intricate alternating narrative retains many traits from the crime melodrama genre,
typical of film noir, but it also pushes character complexity and ambiguity
closer to European art cinema traditions, abandoning classical unity and
psychological realism.

The opening shots of Malle's thriller exploit a primacy effect, establishing Florence and Julien as passionate and frustrated lovers, even before the audience knows anything else about them. The opening shot, a
tight close-up of Florence's face, features her, in a very breathy delivery of
her dialogue, explaining to what the viewer assumes is a man just offscreen, "It's I who cannot wait any longer. . . . I love you." Slowly the camera pulls back to reveal that she is in a phone booth rather than a bedroom,
as she says, "You know I'll be there with you." Then Malle cuts to a close-
up of Julien repeating and continuing the conversation, "I love you. If I
didn't hear your voice, I'd be lost in a world of silence [*pays de silence*]."
This opening exchange establishes a sort of Romeo and Juliet devotion,
with two dedicated and desperate lovers who cannot tolerate whatever barriers separate them at the moment. Interestingly, the scene also includes a
referential in-joke since Julien does not want to be plunged into a silent
world, which corresponds precisely to Malle's previous film, *The Silent
World*. Florence's response, in the film's third shot, which also includes the

title "Jeanne Moreau," is that being lost is not very courageous. The fourth shot shows Julien (with a rapid title for "Maurice Ronet") replying that love is rarely courageous and then Malle cuts back to Florence saying, "Be quiet." But while she appears to continue speaking, the diegetic soundtrack stops abruptly and Miles Davis's trumpet begins its mournful "Night on the Champs Élysées," undercutting their shared passion with a tone of desperate isolation. This disorienting opening, beginning as it does in midconversation and tagging the actors with their names even before any other opening credits, functions to exploit a narrative code for frustrated lovers before the audience learns that Julien is upset not simply because they are physically separated, but because he is about to kill her husband. So the claim that Florence "will be there" has a double implication that is only clear retroactively: she will be "with him in spirit" to lend courage during the murder, and she plans to be waiting for him at their usual café when he is through. Malle thus manipulates the audience from the beginning by withholding information and creating connotations that help blur characterization throughout the film, all the while foregrounding his heavy-handed use of titles, editing, framing, and the soundtrack. *Elevator to the Gallows,* much more than Vadim's *And God Created Woman,* announces from the start that it is as much about how to tell a story as it is about the story itself.

The Miles Davis soundtrack is a highly distinctive feature of this Malle film, and every reviewer of *Elevator to the Gallows* mentions the music's radical nature, while Davis's biographers call it a pivotal moment in his jazz career as well. There are several stories about how Malle and Davis ended up working together on this project, with many people subsequently claiming credit for arranging the collaboration. Malle explains that he met Davis, who was in Paris on a limited engagement, through his friend Boris Vian. Vian, in addition to being an important wild, young literary figure, was the jazz editor for Philips Records. On Miles Davis's one night off, he and his band recorded all the music used in the film: "We worked from something like ten or eleven that night until five in the morning. . . . It's one of the very few film scores which are completely improvised. . . . We would run those segments that we had chosen for music, and he would start rehearsing with his musicians."[28] Jeanne Moreau was also in attendance, discussing the film with the musicians and staffing an improvised bar in the recording studio. Boris Vian, also present, claims that the entire evening was a very relaxed session with Malle encouraging the musicians simply to be themselves and see where his images took their music.

During this one-night improvisation, December 4, 1957, Malle projected a loop of each of the ten sequences to be scored, and Davis gave the musicians a couple of chords and a tempo to follow.[29] Richard Williams, a Miles Davis biographer, writes, "Of the ten separate tracks that were eventually used, nine are based on the same two chords, D minor and C7; the tenth is a variation on the harmonic sequence of 'Sweet Georgia Brown.' But the nine provided evidence of perhaps the most profound and remarkable of the changes that Miles Davis would impose on his music: the paring down of harmonic material practically to nothing. . . . As a result, the soundtrack of *Ascenseur pour l'échafaud* took on a completely novel flavor, one that Davis would spend some years exploring."[30]

Williams argues that the somber images on the screen affected Davis deeply as he improvised with his eyes glued to the screen: "Davis created an unusually graphic mood; listening to the soundtrack . . . the listener has little difficulty summoning fugitive images of rain-washed Paris streets at dawn, of empty nightclubs, of lonely figures prowling the shadows. . . . Never had Davis's music been so poised and assured, so stark and so spare; and the starker and sparer it became, the more power it exerted. . . . Miles Davis had discovered his true characteristics—tragic, solitary, impenitent."[31] Thus, images of Julien, stuck in an elevator, Florence wandering empty streets, and a lone car driving on the Parisian perimeter all seem to have helped Davis explore and expand central traits of his own music.

Even though only about eighteen minutes of the eighty-six-minute feature have musical accompaniment, most critics agreed that the music transformed the film aesthetically. It also provided Malle with another marketing angle for young audiences. With *Elevator to the Gallows* coming on the heels of *And God Created Woman,* in which Bardot danced to the jazzy salsa band, it became almost a convention to include lively, often discordant jazz scores in youth-oriented French films of the late 1950s and early 1960s. The loose jazz music fit the structure of these loose narratives, and subsequent directors as diverse as Godard, Jacques Rozier, and Jean-Pierre Mocky would often move beyond contemporary popular music to jazz, which lent dangerous and hip connotations to images of Paris rather than allow it to remain majestic and traditional. The music showed that something new was afoot. The new music fit the new generation, and it was an appropriate accompaniment for *Elevator to the Gallows* with its young, streetwise punk Louis, who seems as chaotic and jarring as the Miles Davis soundtrack.

As the opening blast of music dies down, it turns out the lovers have continued their conversation during the credit sequence. The camera dollies back to reveal Florence isolated in a phone booth and then Julien in a generic, modern glass-and-metal office building, looking out the window as he speaks. The diegetic environment of a cold and modernizing Paris is quickly established, and this element too was noted by many contemporary reviewers. For instance, Georges Sadoul wrote that Malle was "the first to bring a new perspective onto certain corners of Paris and onto modern life."[32] Then, as Florence asks Julien what time it is, he picks up a strange sort of predigital clock with a seven and a four on it. After he hangs up, he goes out into the large secretarial office space and asks the remaining secretary to stay a few more minutes on this Saturday evening while he finishes up one final project. Since the film does not offer access to Julien's thoughts, the audience must assume he wants a witness as an alibi to prove he was in his own office. The secretary, who works over a modern telephone exchange and intercom system to receive calls and check on M. Carala, agrees and spends the next few minutes sharpening pencils in an electric pencil sharpener. In fact, it is this grating sound that helps cover the noise of Julien's escape through his office window onto the ledge and his tossing of a grappling hook and rope to get up to his boss's office one floor above. France at the time was rapidly modernizing, and the Paris in *Elevator to the Gallows* becomes a place of new buildings, appliances, and cars, mirroring the new wave of French consumerism.

Malle went to great pains to deromanticize the City of Light: "I was trying to portray a new generation through . . . a description of the new Paris. Traditionally, it was always the René Clair Paris that French films presented, and I took care to show one of the first modern buildings in Paris. I invented a motel—there was only one motel in France. . . . I showed a Paris not of the future, but at least a modern city, a world already somewhat dehumanized."[33] Even the cafés Florence will pass through reveal a bored and drunken populace; no one is heading to the theater or cinema or discussing art, philosophy, or love. They merely drink, play pinball, and wander. Julien, Florence, Véronique, and Louis are all out of control and thinking of nothing beyond the moment, and Malle's Paris becomes the perfect place for such disconnected people. Just before Florence hangs up the phone in the opening scene, she proves that these characters are simply acting without thinking, for she says she will wait in their usual café for him to drive up in his big car in thirty minutes and drive them away to freedom. Once the audience realizes Julien is about to kill her husband, the notion of their meeting at their usual place and simply riding off

Figure 3.11. The modern secretary (*Elevator to the Gallows*)

Figure 3.12. Julien scales the office building (*Elevator to the Gallows*)

happily together seems more insane than naive. Unlike the carefully plotting murderers in *Double Indemnity* (Wilder, 1944), Julien and Florence have no intention of "lying low" to dispel suspicion. Moreover, Malle never presents any classical character motivation. These characters speak, but they never really explain, and this chronological, interwoven narrative does not show any events from the past that might justify the central story events. Unlike so many films noir, *Elevator to the Gallows* does not use subjective voice-overs or flashbacks to reveal how these characters got to this doomed point in their lives.

The only care Julien takes in committing the murder is to wear gloves, and once he has killed his boss, he locks all the doors from the inside to help support the assumption that it was a suicide. The ten shots of Julien moving from his office to Carala's increase the editing tempo, with an average shot length of six seconds, compared to the pace of the rest of the film, which has 313 shots for an ASL of nearly seventeen seconds. Thus this crime-preparation sequence seems like a pastiche of a Hitchcock crime scene, complete with Julien's perceptual point of view down onto the street to see whether any of the scores of possible witnesses are paying attention. The confrontation between Carala and Julien is brief, but it does establish some characterization: Julien is a former paratrooper whom Carala calls his "angel" for helping obtain secret business information, but once Carala recognizes his own revolver, Malle cuts away to the secretary sharpening yet another pencil in close-up, followed by a graphic match to a close shot of Julien placing the pistol into the dead Carala's hand. Malle often inserts such flashy editing strategies in *Elevator to the Gallows,* and this match allows the viewer to compare the "tools of their trade," equating the cutthroat world of big business with the gun of a mercenary, while also allowing the noise from the sharpener to cover the pistol shot. Then Julien quickly slides back to his office and exits the building with the secretary and Marcel, the security guard, having forgotten in his haste to remove the rope and grappling hook from the balcony.

The story structure is complicated once Julien leaves his modern office. As he walks to his Chevrolet, which has been parked in a crosswalk all day, the camera stops on Véronique and Louis as she prattles on like an eccentric about all the fantastic thoughts she has and points out how bold Julien Tavernier is: He scoffs at rules and police tickets. In a deep space shot with Véronique and Louis in the foreground and the Chevrolet in the background, she also points out the fancy convertible top that Julien retracts with the touch of a button.

Figure 3.13. Carala is killed with his own pistol (*Elevator to the Gallows*)

Figure 3.14. Julien in deep space (*Elevator to the Gallows*)

Véronique apparently has quite a crush on Julien and tells Louis that Julien has "English chic" and was in Vietnam and now is in business: "That's the life I dream of." But Julien looks up to see that he absent-mindedly left the rope dangling on his balcony, so he jumps out of the car, and hurries back to his office. As he ascends in the elevator, however, Marcel, the guard, cuts the building's current and locks the front door. Julien is plunged into darkness and has to use his cigarette lighter to look for ways to escape. Adding to the viewer's feeling of his isolation and frustration is the nearly silent soundtrack here. There has been no music since the title sequence; Malle uses it sparingly rather than follow classical conventions to use pervasive nondiegetic music to heighten tension or direct the audience's emotions.

The interconnection of all three lines of action now has Julien exclaim to himself: "Florence is waiting for me, and I left my motor running!" Next, the jealous Louis hops into Julien's car and drives off with Véronique, and as it begins to rain he puts up the top just as Florence, waiting at their café, sees the passenger side of the car and recognizes Véronique. As the stunned Florence sits back down at the café, her disorientation is reflected in a discontinuous pair of shots that cross the axis of action, and a car salesman recognizes her and asks how her new luxury French car is doing. But she turns away, the man's continuing conversation decreases to a low level, and the audience hears Florence's internal voice-over exclaim, "I recognize that little florist. . . . Julien's a coward." Gradually all diegetic sound disappears as the sound around her begins to reflect her psychological isolation. For much of the rest of the film Florence will speak in internal dialogue as she wanders Paris, confused and disappointed but still proclaiming her love for Julien and trying to find him.

Now, however, the plot returns to Véronique and Louis; as they drive they rummage through Julien's coat pockets and glove compartment where they find his gun and spy camera. Rapid Miles Davis music returns softly for their wild ride, but stops abruptly with a cut back to Julien struggling to unscrew portions of the elevator. Next, Florence leaves the café amid a thunderstorm to begin her night-long meanderings. She shows up at the office building, oblivious to the fact that he is stuck inside, and rattles the locked gate; Julien hears the sound but stays quiet, fearing it may be the guard. But as Florence turns away, a little girl finds the rope and grappling hook on the ground, apparently disconnected by the storm, and runs off with them, so the entire reason for Julien's return to the building is eliminated, making his entrapment all the more frustrating and absurd.

As Florence searches Paris, Henri Decae's trademark cinematography becomes more evident. Decae, who made his reputation earlier by shooting Jean-Pierre Melville's films, became, along with Raoul Coutard, central to the look and production style of the New Wave. Decae was hired by Malle and then employed by Chabrol and Truffaut for their first features as well. He excelled at shooting on location, with new lightweight equipment, and using available light. Malle explains: "The first scenes we did with Jeanne Moreau were in the streets, on the Champs Élysées. We had the camera in a pram, and she had no light—it was black and white of course; we were using this new fast film, the Tri-X, which serious filmmakers thought too grainy. We did several long tracking shots. . . . She was lit only by the windows. That had never been done."[34] Moreover, some reactions to *Elevator to the Gallows* anticipated reactions to Godard and Coutard's *Breathless,* with critics complaining that the night shots looked amateurish and ugly. But the grainy documentary style, with the camera almost randomly positioned—sometimes it observes Florence as she walks from across a street, other times it was right under her chin in a low angle shot from a tracking wheelchair—created a strange effect when combined with her subjective, dreamy voice-over and determined gestures. Many of these same types of shots recur in Chabrol's *Le beau Serge* and *The Cousins* and especially in Truffaut's *The 400 Blows,* as Antoine Doinel wanders through Paris at night. Decae had a way of turning Paris into a modern maze of reflecting surfaces, electric signs, and moody puddles that made it an oneiric place caught in black-and-white images just as modernization took away some of its famed picture-postcard charm.

Thanks to the combination of Decae's images, Moreau's acting, and Malle's editing, Florence's simple act of walking around nighttime Paris became mythical and disorienting. For instance, in one shot she looks offscreen left; next is a cut to what one assumes is her perceptual point of view of some young men playing pinball, but then Florence walks into that very shot.

Furthermore, whether there is only diegetic sound or Miles Davis's music in the background, the film has many shots of Florence in which her lips are moving but the audience hears no words, suggesting that perhaps some of her voice-over may have been spoken aloud at a slightly different time in the evening than it is heard on the soundtrack. In one shot Florence looks into a mirror in a crowded café, and the audience hears her voice say, "I've lost you this night, Julien," but her lips do not move here, while other times, when the audience does not hear her voice, her lips seem to be speaking.

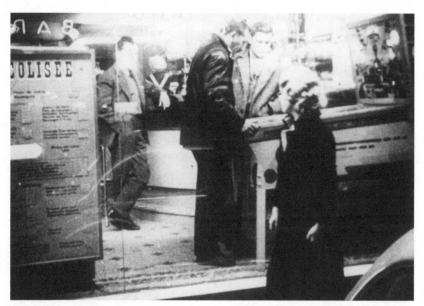

Figure 3.15. Florence walks past the café window (*Elevator to the Gallows*)

Figure 3.16. Florence speaks into the mirror (*Elevator to the Gallows*)

This slippage between diegetic sound (sometimes she speaks in sync with appropriate wild, diegetic sounds; at other times there is no diegetic sound or all the sounds seem postsynchronized) and the occasional voice-over and Miles Davis score further challenge norms of image-to-sound relations that will later typify many of Malle's films and much of the French New Wave. If this were a Godard film, critics would argue he is fore-grounding the materiality of the recording process, moving sound from one scene to another; Malle seems to be carrying out the same sort of experimentation here, though historians have been much less inclined to search for such strategies in his oeuvre. In the years just before *Hiroshima, mon amour, The 400 Blows,* and *Breathless, Elevator to the Gallows* broke new ground and appeared disconcerting and quite modern in its story and style.

The next section of this film that deserves special attention is the meeting of Louis and Véronique with the Germans, Horst Bencker and his wife. Bencker, who races Louis in a new gull-wing Mercedes sports car, pulls into a strange, hybrid motel, which has attached cottages with their own garages. Malle's bizarre motel even has room service driving around with a little three-wheel scooter to deliver champagne and dinner and a next-day photomat on the premises. Looking on, and serving later as a witness for the police, is another young tough in a black leather jacket played by future star Jean-Claude Brialy. Louis and Véronique check in next door to the welcoming Germans, and the older German with his beautiful younger wife entertain the young couple, who pretend to be M. and Mme. Julien Tavernier. During the evening, as Horst offers vintage champagne, he remarks, "We didn't see the likes of this during the occupation," to which the sulking Louis replies, "Our generation has other things than champagne to think about—the occupation, Indochina, Algeria." In Calef's novel, adapted by Malle, the model for Louis, named Fred, is more obnoxious and violent, complaining that the older generation put work before pleasure, but today's new young generation is in a hurry with no time to lose as they "destroy and reconstruct" the world around them.[35] Malle has made Louis a bit more sympathetic than Calef's Fred, but he still creates an ambiguous character, and Malle withholds motivation or judgement from the audience. It is unclear whether Louis is just an antisocial punk or a representative of a lost generation made confused and bitter by France's political blunders. Malle, who was actively involved in social issues such as stopping the war in Algeria, confuses the film's cultural politics with Louis and Horst Bencker's meeting. While Véronique and Mme. Bencker giggle, get drunk, and take pictures with Julien's camera, Horst has figured out that this rude young man is a fake, but he seems amused anyway. It is unclear why he spoils them and unclear just what Louis wants from Horst or even from Véronique, for that matter. Only later, after they have all gone to bed, does Louis hatch the plot to steal the Mercedes and drive Véronique back to Paris. Horst arrives in the garage laughing because he has a special gearbox that is tough for Louis to figure out, but he and his wife are gunned down by Louis.

Once again, there is ambivalence: Horst is simultaneously a comically drunken German industrialist, a nice guy, and a former Nazi who occupied France. His murder is more an inconvenient twist of fate that will doom Julien than an immoral crime, especially since part of the thematic structure of *Elevator to the Gallows* allows the audience to sympathize with the plight of careless lovers who may be repugnant in many ways but still remain faithful and tragically romantic. Malle's plot aligns the audience in a basic way with all four central characters; thus the viewer may not feel allegiance to any of them since the film grants limited access to their lives and feelings, but one can readily identify with their clumsy devotion.

In a panic, Louis and Véronique drive back to Paris, abandon the Mercedes and Julien's coat on the Bir Hakeim bridge, the dividing line

Figure 3.17. Horst and wife are shot (*Elevator to the Gallows*)

between the fashionable sixteenth and less trendy fifteenth arrondisse-
ments (this bridge becomes another icon of New Wave filmmaking). Back
in her *chambre de bonne,* Véronique returns to the somewhat loony romanticist she was at the beginning, complaining that if they go to prison
they will be separated, which she could not stand, just as she could never
allow Louis to be guillotined. Thus they must commit suicide: "We'll never
part. . . . Our photo will be on the front page of the paper. . . . Tragic lovers
die together. . . . We'll be an example." She hands out sleeping pills and
puts on a Brahms record, excitedly stating: "The music will continue and
we'll be dead." In the meantime Florence has been arrested in a sweep of
prostitutes; when she explains who she is, Inspector Cherrier (Lino Ventura) tells her that her husband's employee Julien Tavernier just killed two
tourists at a motel. Julien's photograph appears on the front page of the papers, and the police search both the motel and his office. But since they
must get the guard, Marcel, to turn on the electricity, Julien's elevator
moves and he escapes while the police head up to his office. Once upstairs,
Marcel and the police discover Carala's "suicide."

The final scenes of the film pull together both story and narration
strategies as Julien, acting cool if rumpled, shows up at his usual café and
orders breakfast, oblivious to the fact that (like Godard's Michel Poiccard
in *Breathless* a few years later) his photo is on the front page of the newspaper and everyone has seen it. Moreover, in a shot with great depth of
field, the woman behind the counter calls the police in the extreme background, while in the middle ground a little girl looks at Julien in the right
corner of the frame and announces to her father that Julien is the same
man. This "betrayal" combines a fatalistic shot, reminiscent of Bresson,
with a comic Hitchcockian child.

As the father rushes off with his child and Julien sees the newspaper,
the sirens announce the police's arrival. There is a fade to a film noir-like
scene where Julien is grilled about where he spent the night. Malle accel-
erates the "rescue" now. A cut to Florence shows her reading the paper as
well and then locating Véronique and Louis in Véronique's apartment.
Florence mocks the sickly couple for not knowing how to kill themselves.
After calling the police from a phone booth outside the apartment (in a shot
that recalls her first loving conversation of the title sequence and mirrors
the woman calling the police at the café), she follows Louis and his stolen
scooter back to the motel. There she meets the inspector, and the crimes
are resolved, in Julien's absence. When the inspector tells her she will get
ten to twenty years in prison, Florence ends the film with a voice-over that

It's the same man, Dad!

Figure 3.18. A girl recognizes Julien (*Elevator to the Gallows*)

shares some of the same words and concerns Véronique had spoken to Louis earlier that morning: "Twenty years . . . twenty days. . . . What will they mean? I'll wake up alone." As she looks at a developing photo of Julien and herself she continues, "I'll be aging in prison, but we'll always be together somewhere. Nothing can separate us." Miles Davis punctuates these final shots with a rapid, bitter horn blast as the photos come into focus in the developing bath. The final image is the photograph of Julien hugging Florence, just coming into view in the photomat's bath while Florence's tears drop onto the surface of the solution. As this image fades to the end title, the trumpet fades out just as rapidly.

Rather than bracketing his film at the end with solid closure devices and story termination points, Malle continues the 1950s art cinema trend toward ambiguity and ambivalence. The narrator in *Elevator to the Gallows* refuses to return to Julien, last seen being grilled by the police, or to Véronique, last seen in her room, depressed and groggy after her unsuccessful suicide attempt. The narrative, which has been alternating in unrestricted fashion from character to character across eighteen hours or so of plot time, simply stops once it is clear that both couples are doomed. Yet there has been no substantive delivery of psychological background to support any motivations other than the blind love that guides these characters. Neither Julien nor Florence speak of wanting Carala's money, only of the desire to be rid of him and "free." Beyond Véronique's expressed desire for excitement and escape, the film offers no suggestion of why she hangs around with Louis, who is the opposite of her idol, Julien, in every way, treats her poorly, and has no goals at all. Finally, the story is also typical of a 1950s French (and indeed international) fascination with the asocial, aimless youth sporting black leather jackets, who seem spoiled and moody in the aftermath of their parents' Depression and World War II experiences. The irony of this new "lost" generation, of course, is that they seem to feel doomed amid the prosperity of the highly capitalized, postwar economy. Malle's ambivalence runs counter to some of the more leftist French films and novels that try to blame a greedy society for the ills of such young characters. Rather, for the four principals in *Elevator to the Gallows*, love seems to guide and doom everyone in a world where old-world romanticism and new-world pessimism do not allow any happy synthesis. The older, richer generation, represented here by the arms dealer Carala and the former Nazi Bencker, are killed off, but there is no clear gain or purpose other than selfish or even senseless motives. Julien may want to run off with Florence and Louis wants to steal the Mercedes, but neither of these acts justifies the violence or presents any coherent stance for the audience. Thus viewers can revel in the telling of the story without ever forging any strong allegiances to the characters since the narration withholds so much information. *Elevator to the Gallows* provides a rather unresolved story, while establishing key production and narrative trends that will be pursued further by Malle in subsequent films, but also by many later filmmakers of the New Wave.

Malle's next project, *The Lovers*, proved even more successful financially than *Elevator to the Gallows*. *The Lovers*, with 451,000 entries, was France's fourth biggest hit that year, while *Elevator to the Gallows* had been thirty-eighth at the box office. In New York City, *The Lovers* earned $195,000 during its first run, compared to $52,000 for *Elevator to the Gallows*. According to Malle, "*Ascenseur* was very well received, but *Les Amants* was a phenomenon. All over the world the film was shown and thought scandalous. . . . So, at the age of just twenty-six I was an international director, suddenly appearing on the scene."[36] But *The Lovers* also provided auteurist critics with consistent markers of story and style, proving that Malle could display a mature virtuosity for so young a director. Pierre Billard's mammoth history of French cinema calls *The Lovers* "the crown jewel" of the new French cinema.[37] Jacques Doniol-Valcroze wrote the *Cahiers du cinéma* review, proclaiming *The Lovers* even closer to the spirit of the Louis Delluc award than was *Elevators to the Gallows* and celebrating its social criticism, perfect mise-en-scène, and stunning acting: "This very rare and personal work shared the Silver Lion Award at the Venice Film Festival, but merits the whole animal, covered with the heaviest gold."[38] Bazin added that Malle's moral intentions and audacity were "irreproachable."[39] And it was precisely the seeming amorality of *The Lovers* that helped catapult this film into something of a scandal, getting a "no one under sixteen admitted" status in France and landing one theater manager in Dayton, Ohio, in court with obscenity charges and a sentence of six weeks on a prison farm.[40]

If *Elevator to the Gallows* owed equally to Bresson and Hitchcock, *The Lovers* resembles more a mix of the work of Jean Renoir and Jean Cocteau. Initially based on a loose updating of Vivant Denon's 1777 *conte libertin*, or libertine tale, *Point de lendemain* (*No Tomorrow*), the story barely retains any story material from that source text, which documented the abduction of a young man by an older woman who then whisks him off to her remote château for a dreamlike encounter. Rather, novelist Louise de Vilmorin, whose popular novel *Madame de* had recently been filmed by Max Ophuls, joined Malle in reworking Denon's novella and updating it into a combination of a modern comedy of manners and a daring, even oneiric love story that played with and defied many conventions of the romance genre. In their story, Jeanne Tournier (Jeanne Moreau), the pampered wife of a newspaper editor in Dijon, drives herself regularly to Paris to stay with her childhood friend Maggy (Judith Magre), who married well and now leads a "brilliant life" in Paris (though the audience never sees any evidence of her husband).

Maggy and Jeanne attend polo matches and fancy dinner parties, accompanied by one of the smartest men in this set, polo player Raoul Florres (José-Louis Villalonga). On Jeanne's return home, it becomes clear that her husband of eight years, Henri (Alain Cuny), finds her absences annoying and her Parisian friends ridiculous. Even the maid seems disappointed in Jeanne's frequent trips, since she fears Henri spoils their young daughter, Catherine, too much while his wife is away. But Jeanne decides that Henri is no longer pertinent to her life and decides to travel to Paris even more often.

Back in Paris, Jeanne begins an affair with Raoul, until Henri, angry by her increasingly frequent trips, forces her to invite Maggy and Raoul for a weekend in Dijon so he can get a good look at them. On her return drive

Figure 3.19. Maggy and Jeanne (*The Lovers*)

from Paris, Jeanne's elegant Peugeot convertible breaks down; she is helped by a young archeologist, Bernard (Jean-Marc Bory), in his cheap and tinny two-cylinder Citroën (popularly called a "*deux chevaux*" or "two-horse" car).

Bernard agrees to drive her home, but warns her that he drives slowly and has to stop by a former professor's home with some books on the way. When they finally arrive shortly after eight o'clock, Raoul and Maggy, who raced down in Raoul's flashy sports car, are already waiting with Henri. Bernard is asked to spend the night; a rather uncomfortable dinner follows, in which Henri pretends great affection for Jeanne, so as to embarrass her suave lover, Raoul. There are many intertextual parallels with Renoir's *Rules of the Game* here: the Tourniers live in a remote château; the wife's lover is invited for a visit; and Gaston Modot, who played the groundskeeper, Schumacher, in Renoir's film, is their butler, Coudray. Moreover, Henri, Maggy, Raoul, and Jeanne all decide to go to bed early so they can wake up at four o'clock for an early fishing trip, which recalls Renoir's famous rabbit hunt. As T. Jefferson Kline points out, "Malle leaves little doubt that *Les Amants* is to be read through the 'grid' of Renoir."[41]

After dinner, Jeanne goes to her own room, even though both Henri and Raoul have tried to entice her to stay with them. Restless and disgusted by the behavior of both her husband and her lover, Jeanne descends to the library where Bernard has left a record playing. Outside in the moonlight, she encounters Bernard. The final third of the film turns to a dreamlike night of erotic attraction and nearly constant sexual activity between Jeanne and Bernard as they wander about the lovely park, liberate some trout captured by Henri's traps, make love in a boat in the pond, and finally

Figure 3.20. Bernard helps Jeanne (*The Lovers*)

return to the château. In the house, Jeanne checks on her daughter. Then in the next room, Jeanne and Bernard resume their physical encounter, and Jeanne makes it clear that she has never felt so satisfied. Moral outrage from many critics centered on the shameless joy found by these lovers, who only met that afternoon and now make love next door to Jeanne's daughter while her husband and "official" lover are just down the hall. But the most controversial element is one long take in which Jeanne is alone in the frame while Bernard remains just off screen. As the reviewer for *Films in Review* writes, "The camera records at length the facial reactions of a woman during cunnilingus. . . . They should be ashamed."[42]

At four in the morning, when the others are rising to go on a fishing trip, Jeanne and Bernard walk right past them and drive off together in his 2CV. They stop for breakfast; then as the sun rises, they drive off on their "uncertain journey," proclaiming their love for each other, with no regrets.

The Lovers continues many of Malle's personal story and style traits, while it also creates more options for future New Wave filmmakers to follow. This story chooses a very restricted range of story information, rather than juggling three separate actions like *Elevator to the Gallows,* but it does contain many similar thematic traits: The upper-class wife takes a lover and discards her husband, Moreau's character wanders around trying to recover a sense of purpose, a young rebel does not respect social constraints, the morally bankrupt world is filled with fancy cars, and so on. Most important for the overall feel of these two stories, however, is the continued refusal to make specific moral judgments. In this way, Malle's films share narrative traits with later Chabrol films in that they observe society with disdain but have ambiguous endings that offer neither judgment of the characters nor better models of behavior.

Figure 3.21. From bed (*The Lovers*)

The ambivalence and ambiguity result from the complex representation of Jeanne; as will be demonstrated throughout this study, even though nearly all New Wave directors are men, and partly *because* they are men, their films are fascinated with women characters. The restricted story structure follows Jeanne, and every scene involves her. Jeanne drives all the action, and she motivates all the men's activities, almost as a prototype of Jeanne Moreau's later, more famous role, as Catherine in *Jules and Jim* (Truffaut, 1962). Here, rather than being part of a love triangle as in *Elevator to the Gallows*, Moreau's character is at the center of a sexual quadrangle that resembles a La Fontaine fable without a moral lesson attached. For the first two-thirds of *The Lovers*, Jeanne moves between the realms of Henri (a sort of country rat) and of Raoul (the city rat), and it is only after the disastrous dinner party that she comes to realize they are both disappointing. In her room alone, sitting in front of her vanity mirror, where she spends much of her screen time, Jeanne Moreau, in voice-over, says: "Her world crumbled; her husband was odious, her lover had become ridiculous. Jeanne, who had thought herself in a melodrama, realized it was just silly vaudeville. She suddenly wanted to be someone else." This self-realization motivates her to leave her room, perhaps in search of Bernard. That night she begins to remake herself as she discards all her past, including her husband, her lover, her best friend, Maggy, her daughter, and all the trappings of her elegant life, including her clothes, home, and car.

The voice-over narration functions to help the viewer fully understand the centrality of Jeanne and the complexity of *The Lovers*. Unlike Florence's internal dialogues presented via voice-over in *Elevator to the Gallows*, here Jeanne's words defy simple codification. For one thing, the words are spoken by Jeanne Moreau and hence should conventionally

Figure 3.22. To bath (*The Lovers*)

reflect the simultaneous thoughts of Jeanne the character, but they are also presented in third-person, and their temporal links to the action vary dramatically. The most conventional use of voice-over in the film includes the two times when the audience hears Jeanne remembering Maggy's comment that love has made Jeanne unrecognizable. These words obviously affect Jeanne strongly so she recalls them twice. But in ten instances when the audience hears Jeanne Moreau's voice-over, the relation between Jeanne the character and Moreau the actress/narrator becomes problematic. In the script, the voice-over narration is simply marked "voice"; it does not specify "Jeanne's voice" or anyone else's. If *The Lovers* had used a different actor's voice, or Louis Malle's, or that of the scriptwriter Louise de Vilmorin, the voice-over would have a more conventional, distant narrative authority. Instead, it is Jeanne Moreau's own voice referring externally to Jeanne Tournier, a situation that allows the narration to teeter between diegetic internal and nondiegetic external information. While the distinction may seem academic, analyzing the functions of this voice helps understand Jeanne's possible psychological dysfunction (is one to interpret her as seeing herself as an object, from the outside?), but also her centrality to this narrative world and the ultimate modernity of Malle's storytelling.

The first instance of Moreau's narration comes in the opening scene just after Jeanne has told Maggy she understands nothing of polo, and Maggy tells her she should at least pretend she understands. This bit of conversation actually has deep reverberations in the story, since Jeanne often seems confused about her life and will spend great amounts of screen time gazing into mirrors, either out of pure, shallow vanity or as if trying to fathom who she is. Jeanne's opening narration begins with her responding

Figure 3.23. Jeanne narrates her own story (*The Lovers*)

in internal dialogue to Maggy; in a conventional cue for a voice-over, the wide-screen camera reframes and dollies in to isolate Jeanne in close-up as she lights a cigarette and looks distracted: "No. Jeanne knew nothing about polo; she sometimes accompanied her friend Maggy." But then the voice-over shifts to take on the function accorded normally to a narrator as it introduces the two women, mentions Henri, who "loves his wife but is devoted to his newspaper," and explains that recently Jeanne has begun coming to Paris. The narration then concludes by looping back to the present polo context and mentioning that Jeanne met Raoul at Maggy's home. The narration becomes a novelistic third-person summary of Jeanne's thoughts while it also privileges Jeanne as both character and her own narrator and provides the audience with story information from the past. Malle often admitted being influenced by both Flaubert and Stendhal, and Jeanne's characterization seems to owe a bit to their nineteenth-century narrative strategies.

The ten instances of Moreau's narration alternate between these poles of a rather formal internal dialogue in the third-person that seems simultaneous, and a nonsimultaneous voice-over from a more distant narrator's perspective yet with Moreau's voice. Often, as in this first example, there is a blurring of character and narrator functions, as Malle lives up to Astruc's challenge to tell a story in a truly personal way. He has forged a new cinematic form of narration, collapsing the lines between diegesis and nondiegesis, character and narrator, via this sound strategy that decenters the soundtrack from the image, adding a novel polyphony.[43] Sometimes the voice-over does function as an approximation of internal dialogue, such as on the night when Jeanne returns home from Paris after Maggy told her that

Strangely enough, Jeanne suddenly felt a deep jealousy rising in her...

Figure 3.24. Jeanne the narrator explains Jeanne the character (*The Lovers*)

love has made her unrecognizable: The maid and daughter both comment upon Jeanne's different appearance, but Henri mentions nothing. As Jeanne walks slowly up the staircase, looking reflective, the audience hears "Henri hadn't noticed anything." And several moments later, with Jeanne looking into her vanity mirror, the audience hears "Jeanne suddenly felt a deep jealousy."

These bits of voice-over dialogue seem to fit perfectly with Jeanne's current mood, and act as mental monologues to explain her vulnerability and her subsequent actions, though, of course, they remain in third-person. Yet later, in Paris, when Jeanne returns to Maggy's apartment after spending the night with Raoul, the voice-over is more like a narrator opening a new chapter of a book: "The uneasy double life of Jeanne Tournier did not last long. One evening before leaving for Paris . . . " During the voice-over, the camera fades out on Paris and then fades up on Jeanne, now back home in her bed in Dijon, as the drunk and angry Henri enters and demands that her friends come to their home for a change. Most of the voice-over interventions fit this model of reflecting Jeanne's frame of mind, while also commenting on the action from a narrative level that seems superior to the diegetic knowledge or immediacy of Jeanne. That Moreau's voice will also refer to the character she interprets as "Jeanne Tournier" further establishes a strange dividing line between Jeanne/Moreau.

The final voice-over commentary, "They left on an uncertain journey. . . . Jeanne already doubted her decision. She was afraid but regretted nothing," functions as a closure device—conclusive words are followed by a quick fade to black and the end title—but resolves little. All the viewer knows is that Bernard and Jeanne are driving off together, but there is no narrative certainty about whether this is a good or bad thing and no suggestion of what might happen down the road. The voice seems to be relatively simultaneous with Jeanne looking thoughtful as she rides off with Bernard during part of the narration. By the time Moreau says, "She was afraid," however, Jeanne can be seen laughing comfortably with Bernard in the car. As a further counterpoint, the somber Brahms music swells ominously just as the couple seems happiest. Malle thus leaves the authority and functions of this concluding voice-over ambiguous. He undercuts the conventional uses for a voice-over and forges a new synthetic narrative option for the soundtrack, mixing diegetic and nondiegetic elements that build the visual and sound space around the character of Jeanne Tournier and the face and voice of Jeanne Moreau.

To a certain extent, *The Lovers* is as much a tribute to Malle's relationship to Jeanne Moreau as it is to Jean Renoir. The review in *Cinéma 58* even calls this "a beautiful poem offered up to Jeanne Moreau."[44] Not only does the character, whose first name matches that of the actress, inspire love in every man she meets, but Malle and Moreau had been lovers since *Elevator to the Gallows* and then split up near the completion of *The Lovers*. Moreau explains one of the text's more interesting touches—the white horse that stands alone beside the road as Bernard and Jeanne drive away in the final shot sequence—as a result of their affair. According to Moreau, her mother had taught her a song with the refrain "White horse, white horse bring me some luck," and it was used as a farewell song. She claims she told Malle to show her a white horse when their relationship was ending, so he inserted that horse in the last shot to signal that "it was over."[45] However romantic this tale might sound, it seems fairly implausible. A much more likely motivation is that the lone horse reverses the opening shots where Raoul is playing polo, riding hard across the playing fields. At the end, the audience sees the church and the horse left behind, signifiers of her provincial married life and lover, both now abandoned, much like her car left at the side of the road where Bernard picked her up the day before. As the couple drives down an empty country road, the camera tracks backward so that the viewer can see their faces as they drive but also to observe what they have left behind without glimpsing where they may be headed.

Beyond its use of frank sexuality and sound, *The Lovers* is also significant for its unusual visual concept, which splits the film into two distinct styles. Many critics praised or attacked the film for its establishment of a scathing, realistic portrayal of upper-class excess, followed by a more poetic treatment of physical love between Jeanne and Bernard. According to Malle, "the first half is a comedy of manners, a satire on the mores of the upper class in France in the late 1950s; the second part is almost an homage to the German romantic painter Caspar David Friedrich."[46] The first two-thirds of the film, however, owe the greatest debt to Renoir, while the Friedrich-inspired night of love also seems to lean on Jean Cocteau's surreal environments with characters who almost float through the gardens. It is important to note that the latter section of the film was treated differently by the script as well as the camera and the soundtrack, and some reviewers criticized the sudden shift in sensibility. Yet, as Eugen Weber wrote, during that night of lovemaking in Malle's film, "Dialogue is almost nonexistent: it is replaced by the very haunting music of Brahms and by the touch of the camera which fulfills the ideal Astruc once expressed of using the camera as one uses a pen."[47] *The Lovers* found a way to parallel the observational qualities of the new novel, exploiting very cinematic language. Louise de Vilmorin disliked the concept of this erotic night, so little of it was written in the script; much of that segment was improvised during production and postsynchronized when the characters did speak. The rare frankness of Jeanne's sexual liberty is matched, therefore, in a strange lyricism as romanticism replaces realism in her life, and in the mode of production, a detailed script gave way to a series of nearly anecdotal events.

Throughout *The Lovers*, Malle's use of camera movement, wide-screen framing, and mise-en-scène create a particularly stunning and significant visual world built around Jeanne. With an average shot length of nearly twenty-eight seconds, Malle relied on very long takes, deep-focus staging, and dynamic, lateral wide-screen shot composition, all combined with a very mobile camera. Malle claimed he used little editing because in part, for new critics and filmmakers, long takes were "very fashionable at the time." Responding to Astruc's and Bazin's writings, Renoir's cinema, and even Hitchcock's recently released *Rope,* Malle felt that avoiding classical continuity editing was essential. His debt to Renoir is clear in most of the scenes filmed in the château: "For all of us, my generation of French filmmakers, *Rules of the Game* was the absolute masterpiece."[48] These long takes helped present a realistic narrative space that built on Malle's documentary experience while confronting contemporary trends in art cinema composition. Much more than for *Elevator to the Gallows,* the mise-en-scène and camera work in Malle's second feature force the audience actively to interpret the image, in keeping with the *Cahiers du cinéma* agenda. As David Bordwell writes, the revolution in film language after World War II changed staging options: "The viewer will have to scan the image, seek out salient points of interest, and integrate information into an overall judgment about the scene."[49] Malle's use of these techniques reinforces the thematic ambiguity with an attention to open, cinematic space that is a very successful synthesis of homages to past practice and contemporary film criticism.

A number of flashy camera movements and long shot sequences establish the rhythm of the film and demand that the audience search for spatial orientation and even comic effects. Malle's camera movement of choice is an arcing camera that not only reduces the need for eyeline matches and shot/reverse shots but keeps the wide-screen image from becoming too flat or theatrical. Within the Tourniers' château, Malle often mimics *Rules of the Game* by allowing characters and the camera to peer down long halls while panning, tracking, and/or dollying. For instance, when the dinner is served, the camera waits in the empty dining room with the butler, Coudray, as Henri, Raoul, Maggy, and Jeanne walk down a hall, all dressed elegantly in black. But Bernard simultaneously becomes visible down a different hall and enters from a separate door at the right, wearing a contrasting light gray jacket. He does not fit into their world, so the framing and costuming signal his uniqueness. Furthermore, the camera also arcs around the dinner table in this sixty-eight-second shot as the guests take their places and begin conversation.

Even in exterior shots in Paris, Malle's camera rarely stays still. After one dinner party, when Raoul convinces Jeanne to ride with him to the carnival at Invalides, the forty-three-second shot sequence begins with an establishing shot of two cars, then dollies toward the six dinner guests as they approach the cars. Next, the camera stops temporarily in front of Raoul's car, framing Raoul, Jeanne, and Maggy in a medium shot. Then, the camera dollies and pans, arcing around as it follows Raoul and Jeanne to the passenger side of his car where he opens her door, then jogs around the front to his door as the other car, now in depth, starts up and pulls away. The shot began showing the front door at the left of the courtyard but ends revealing the gate entrance at the opposite side of the courtyard, in a carefully choreographed sequence. Moreover, in the next scene at the Invalides carnival, Decae even sits with the camera in the seat on one ride; thus, the audience watches Raoul and Jeanne travel high above the ground in the "Hurricane" ride, as if they were simply turning their heads to see the happy couple laughing behind them. The intricate camerawork becomes playful as well as functional and begins a long run of Decae films that include flashy camerawork in rotor rides or bumper cars at carnivals.

Figure 3.25. Jeanne and Raoul (*The Lovers*)

Malle's most comical framing occurs when Jeanne, driven by Bernard, stops at a small village garage to seek help in recovering her stalled Peugeot. In the first shot, fifty-seven seconds in duration, Malle sets up a gag worthy of Jacques Tati. The camera is placed in the shop, with a man crouched at the left edge fixing a bicycle wheel, while Bernard's 2CV pulls up in the background, and Jeanne descends and walks toward the camera and into the garage. Jeanne calls out, asking if anyone is there, and a man shouts, "Present!" She walks into the dark shop and up to the man on the left, facing the camera, as she explains several times, louder each time, that she needs help with her car. Finally, frame right, a man, standing in the shadows responds, "Don't bother, he's deaf." The man on the right had been visible all along but with his back to the audience and his head under the tow-truck hood; yet it is easy to follow Jeanne's line of sight and miss altogether the fellow on the right, not noticing that the other man's mouth never moved when he replied, "Present!" The topper comes, however, when she asks the man on the right if he has a phone, and the supposedly deaf man on the left replies, "Right over there." Jeanne looks confused, the man looks embarrassed, and Bertrand in the deep background looks on, amused. But no one ever explains what sort of game the two men are up to, and nothing really comes of this scene, except to make Jeanne the brunt of a practical joke that amuses Bernard. Further, the garage owner is repairing his tow truck, so he cannot help her, and Jeanne decides against making a phone call. Narrative space is truly a playground, as Malle exploits Jeanne's central status, depth, and wide-screen width to mislead and entertain the viewer, in a playful tribute to Tati that is quite in keeping with the New Wave's famous good-natured sense of humor.

The mise-en-scène is also highly significant in developing and commenting on Jeanne. While *The Lovers* can hardly be labeled a feminist text since Jeanne simply replaces two men with another, it does contain some traits typically assigned to liberal feminism. Jeanne is not only the central character, motivating all scenes, but she is shown as unsatisfied with the few paths society has carved out for her: mother, wife, and/or mistress. Malle's mise-en-scène reinforces systematically Jeanne's objectified status, not simply by dressing her in elegant gowns, but also by surrounding her with door frames and especially picture frames all around her château. Repeatedly, Jeanne stands in front of portraits hanging in the château, presumably of the majestic, noble women of Henri's family. These are the upper-class, female role models that Jeanne does not or cannot follow. Moreover, while Florence, in *Elevator to the Gallows*, looked self-consciously at her reflection on occasion, for the uncertain Jeanne, mirrors become something of an obsession. Throughout *The Lovers*, Malle stages Moreau in front of mirrors, especially at her vanity table but also throughout her home. She searches for answers but in a futile, vain way, staring at herself. Once she falls for Bernard, however, the mirrors in her bedroom are more likely to reflect him, so his image replaces hers in the wide-screen compositions. During one exchange of dialogue in her room, Jeanne can be seen in a mirror behind Bernard, and then he is reflected in her mirror, in a sort of parody of a shot/reverse shot. Yet if Malle's use of mirrors can be said to connote Jeanne's discovery of happiness (Bernard will fill the void in her life and become the object she sought), then the final mirror shot, of the fleeing Jeanne looking at herself in the café, returns the ambiguity, since she turns away from Bernard temporarily before getting back in the car with him as the sun rises and they drive off. By reverting to the earlier pattern of Jeanne feeling alone with her image, the mise-en-scène and the framing here lend a subtle uncertainty to her final frame of mind.

In addition to proving that a young director could produce and direct successful feature films and tell novel stories in lively, modern ways, Malle's greatest legacy for the New Wave might well be Jeanne Moreau's two performances, as Florence and then as Jeanne, which combine to present a prototype for New Wave female characters beyond the shallow, pouting little sex kitten offered by Bardot's Juliette. Rather, Moreau's characters struggle against patriarchal constraints; in *The Lovers*, Jeanne fights against objectification and decides to give her own pleasure priority, even if that means abandoning her young daughter. But the sexual independence of Jeanne, coupled with Malle's frank exploration of its effects on her person rather than upon the young man, Bernard, added a new option to the cinematic canon. Unlike Juliette's exhibitionistic dance in *And God*

Figure 3.26. Jeanne literally reflects upon her decision (*The Lovers*)

Created Woman, Jeanne's pleasure is personal. Furthermore, review after review, whether horrified or pleased, remarks upon the revolutionary nature of Jeanne's erotic behavior. *Le Film français,* for instance, warns, "This passionate adventure has an audacity and realism almost unknown to the screen."[50] It is also important to note that if the final image, of an unsure Jeanne leaving her family with a man she met the day before shocked many, that ending should be interpreted in relation to the opening title sequence, which was shot over a *carte de tendre,* a seventeenth-century text by Madeleine de Scudéry.

The *carte de tendre,* or map of tenderness, is an allegory that represents spatially the desire by women to chart out and in some ways control their own lives, especially in romantic relations. The geography consists of bodies of water such as the Lake of Indifference (where Jeanne's marriage to Henri perhaps flounders), the Dangerous Sea, or towns such as New Friends. In her own way, Jeanne is trying to navigate the space of bourgeois France in the 1950s and break away from traditions that have endured for hundreds of years. When her husband disappoints her, she can drive herself to Paris for a romp with her dashing lover. But in the end she decides to leave "her country" for a new place, in an uncertain crossing with Bernard, perhaps to the Unknown Land, or *Terres inconnues,* drawn at the top of the map.

Thus, while the New Wave would, for all intents and purposes, be a "boys' club," there was a very real tendency to feature tales about young women as much as young men and to concentrate on just what it meant to be nouvelle vague women in nouvelle vague France. While *Rules of the Game* forced Christine (Nora Gregor) back into her rule-bound role

Figure 3.27. The *carte de tendre* (*The Lovers*)

supporting her husband at the end, by the time Malle arrived, women were
given more complex character traits and could test more options than wife,
mother, or mistress. And one of the fascinating themes of the New Wave
that develops across the length of this history is the excitement, irony, and
ambiguity with which these young male directors construct their fictional
young women.

For historians of Malle's career, Malle's third fiction film, *Zazie in the
Metro,* is either a puzzlement, a disappointment, or proof of his uneven and
unusual career. This film, which was an adaptation of the popular Raymond Queneau novel, was brightly colored, silly, with some scenes shot in
fast motion, and did not seem to fit what one expected of Malle, much less
the New Wave. By contrast, his fifth feature, *Le feu follet* (1963), is often
cited as a perfect example of his new maturity and a welcome return to the
successful combination of his most personal themes and previously established stylistic markers. Certainly, both these films deserve much more
careful attention than they have received from film history. Yet for this
study of the development and narrative strategies associated with the New
Wave, Malle's first two features prove more about the conditions surrounding the birth of the New Wave. By the time of *Zazie,* many critics were already narrowing their lists of who or what was New Wave, and Malle was

being purged from most of these lists for a number of reasons. But the real break in the critical reception of his career does seem to owe much to this popular, gaudy, colorful *Zazie,* a film that did not fit the strict demands of auteur criticism, and Malle is one of the first casualties of the rigid auteurism of *Cahiers du cinéma,* among others, that was quick to condemn a film because it did not fit what was expected of its director. Nonetheless, Malle's contributions to French cinema in the mid-1950s clearly earn him a key spot in the transition from a *nouveau cinéma* to a nouvelle vague, and *Elevator to the Gallows* and *The Lovers* figure prominently as examples of rich and successful storytelling by an auteur still in his twenties. From a historical perspective, it would seem ridiculous now to argue that Malle would be a bit "more New Wave" if he had only written an article or two for *Cahiers du cinéma* instead of spending a few months studying filmmaking at IDHEC or earning the Palme d'or at Cannes for *The Silent World.*

Both Roger Vadim and Louis Malle can be justly credited with proving the enormous critical and financial potential of new stories, new styles, and even new modes of production in the 1950s transition to the French New Wave. Vadim and Malle are both significant for making their discordant voices heard even within the remnants of France's classical system of production.[51] According to Peter Graham, "Like *And God Created Woman, Les Amants* helped to pave the way for the New Wave films, proving that controversial and innovative low-budget films made by a young director could be successful at the box-office."[52] And it is precisely this emphasis on economic success that helped catapult subsequent young French directors onto the international marketplace. Critical success was one thing, but unlike the 1950s films of Robert Bresson or Jean Renoir, which were, indeed, important to contemporary critics, Vadim's and Malle's films tapped into the popular media's interest in youth and French cultural renewal. As Malle argued, "The one thing people always forget to mention about the New Wave—the reason that the New Wave was taken so seriously— is that our first films (or even first two films) were very successful commercially."[53]

Beyond the box office strength, both Vadim and Malle were initially celebrated for providing concrete examples of the personal cinemas prescribed by Alexandre Astruc, *Cinéma,* and *Cahiers du cinéma,* among others. *And God Created Woman, Elevator to the Gallows,* and *The Lovers* were all praised by serious critics for their mise-en-scène, and Malle's films in particular were recognized for their highly novel *écriture.* The combination of their audacity, thematic ambiguity, youthful passion, and elegant cinematic techniques, all on a low budget and aimed at a new international audience of educated young people, provided the French cinema as well as film buffs throughout the world with hopes for more groundbreaking films to come from more young men and women in Paris. They would not have to wait long for the revolutionary excitement that would be called the French New Wave.

4

Claude Chabrol:
Launching a Wave

For me, Mozart has always been a composer engaged in a search for
minuscule, scarcely palpable beauty. He is also a composer who sensed
putrefaction and decadence in the simplest things.

    —CLAUDE CHABROL, in "Chabrol's Game of Mirrors"

WITHIN A fifteen-month period, from January 1959 to March 1960,
Claude Chabrol premiered four feature films in Paris: *Le beau Serge, Les
cousins* (*The Cousins*), *A double tour,* and *Les bonnes femmes* (*The Good
Girls*). At a time when the French press was full of accounts of a New Wave
in the cinema, Chabrol was promoted as the central agent of change.
Chabrol was leading the way for his *Cahiers du cinéma* cohorts François
Truffaut and Jean-Luc Godard and trying to get others such as Eric
Rohmer, Jacques Rivette, and even Philippe de Broca on track by producing their first features. In fact, in Paris theaters, the New Wave's real
testing ground, *The Cousins* proved to be the second most successful film
by a *Cahiers du cinéma* filmmaker during these years, with 416,000 entries. Only Truffaut's *The 400 Blows* later surpassed it, with 450,000 tickets sold, while Godard's *Breathless* came in third with 380,000.

As historian Claire Clouzot points out, Chabrol represented the novelty, success, and euphoria of the New Wave for that era: "Chabrol was living the unbelievable adventure of a director who knows nothing of filming
and then overnight becomes the rave of Paris, the darling of all critics."[1]
Consequently, Chabrol is often acknowledged as the "first" New Wave director by most historians today, with *Le beau Serge* and *The Cousins* recognized as "the breakthrough films of a new generation" or "the lightning
bolts" announcing the New Wave.[2] Yet after such a promising beginning
Chabrol directed a string of poorly received films, lost his independent
production company, and by 1964 had to look hard to find commercial
projects such as *Le tigre aime la chair fraiche* (*Tiger Likes Fresh Meat*).

The uneven commercial value, inconsistent aesthetic success, and vague ideological slant of Chabrol's oeuvre have left many historians confused about how to summarize the contributions of this prolific charter member of the New Wave. Chabrol's sudden fall from grace with many critics and the resulting confusion over his long-term significance are part of the reason his career is so fascinating. One can approach Chabrol's early career from three directions: his production practices, his narrative strategies, and his troubling thematics, all of which shed light on what makes Chabrol so puzzling yet essential for any history of the New Wave.

First, Chabrol's groundbreaking economic practices helped provide a new blueprint for filmmakers who wanted to make commercially viable feature films yet lacked patrons, massive private fortunes, or a traditional preparation for filmmaking. It is important to point out that Chabrol was not interested in forging a purely alternative personal cinema along the lines of an Agnès Varda or even an Alain Resnais. Chabrol, like Louis Malle, wanted to be a major new player in the French cinema, and his financial good fortune and marketing savvy allowed him not only to enter into the world of inexpensive production but also to point the way for others to play the production game as well.

The initial funding in 1958 for Chabrol's film career came in the form of an inheritance from his wife's grandmother. With the bulk of the inheritance (thirty-two million old francs, or roughly sixty-four thousand dollars) he staked his own company, AJYM (named after his family), thereby modestly following Louis Malle's model of establishing his own production house.[3] He surpassed Malle's autoproduction, however, by helping produce films by other directors as well. Moreover, Chabrol, like a good tax lawyer, knew how to work the new French *prime de qualité* rules to his advantage, and he argued for and won major concessions from the Centre national de la cinématographie, all in the name of encouraging young outsiders to revitalize the cinema. For instance, Chabrol appealed to the CNC and won an exemption during production of *Le beau Serge:* Chabrol could eliminate three union positions from the crew in order to keep his costs low.[4] The jobs cut from the downsized production included set designer, sound engineer, and make-up person. These exemptions not only helped keep costs lower for *Le beau Serge*, but once the CNC approved them for Chabrol's first film, a new precedent was set to which others could, and would, appeal. As a result, Truffaut and Godard were also allowed to drop the same three positions from *their* first features.

In addition to the anger such cuts caused within some professional guilds, the actors' union was not happy with Chabrol's cost-cutting trends either; it complained that he was exploiting too many nonprofessionals for *Le beau Serge* (such as hiring the local baker Michel Creuse to play the main character's old friend and the fictional town's baker, Michel). Other rather unusual touches to Chabrol's crew included using friends for walk-on roles or as assistants, to learn the trade. For instance, Chabrol himself plays one of the central character's old friends, recently come into an inheritance, and Philippe de Broca (the assistant director) plays his buddy, named Jacques Rivette, a soldier home on leave.[5] In reality Rivette was off shooting his own film with funding from Chabrol's AJYM. Such good-natured clowning and the Hitchcock-style appearance of the director in his own film created a casual, familial, and joking tone in *Le beau Serge*, but these practices also violated contemporary industry standards.

Once *Le beau Serge* was finished, at a cost of seventy-six thousand dollars, Chabrol submitted it to the Film Aid board (administrated as well by the CNC) and was granted a *prime de qualité* of seventy thousand dollars.[6] As René Prédal points out, earning such a sum on a more expensive film, such as an average French feature, which in 1959 cost $240,000, would have produced nowhere near the same effect.[7] Chabrol's inexpensive mode of production, as well as many of his aesthetic choices, therefore, were intertwined with his novel financial strategies. *Le beau Serge* was initially chosen to represent France at the 1958 Cannes Festival, but then another film replaced it. Nonetheless, that publicity, plus the very favorable audience it received at its Cannes premiere (out of competition), helped Chabrol find a domestic commercial distributor *and* foreign distribution contracts with advances totaling $50,000. Thus, before *Le beau Serge* was ever shown on a commercial film screen, it had earned Chabrol $120,000 and rave critical attention, including the Jean Vigo Award and best director award at Locarno. Chabrol used that money to begin shooting *The Cousins* immediately. This second feature cost about $115,000 to produce and won a *prime de qualité* of roughly $90,000. The real payoff for his financial wheeling and dealing, however, arrived as the box-office receipts for *The Cousins* rolled in—it became France's fifth largest success of 1959, earning $180,000 in its first run.[8]

Chabrol's filmmaking style satisfied the government's institutional demands for artistic quality, thereby ensuring financial security independent of the box office. The critical excitement over Chabrol's triumphs (fueled by the popular press, *Cahiers du cinéma*, and festival awards) ensured high profits in turn. Moreover, once his first two films played well commercially and critically, both Chabrol and the CNC were vindicated (despite complaints from more progressive voices such as *Positif* that the CNC was unfairly rewarding a small group of directors at the expense of true cinematic experimentation, industry tax revenues, and union jobs). Chabrol had proved to be an exemplary producer of the era by following the self-production strategies of Jean-Pierre Melville and Louis Malle, yet he improved upon their example, backing up his own money by finding diverse funding sources inside and outside the film institution as well. Chabrol even sought funding for *Le beau Serge* from national campaigns against alcoholism.[9] Such "financial gymnastics," as Prédal calls them, plus Chabrol's basic mode of production featuring friends and family (he even promised to make his friend Jean-Claude Brialy a "star" if he worked cheap), provided a daring alternative to norms of commercial French production. As Charles Ford writes, Chabrol's methods were quickly adopted by other newcomers as well as some frustrated veterans wanting to begin directing their own productions.[10]

By using AJYM to help friends such as Rohmer, de Broca, and Rivette, Chabrol gained a reputation as a minipatron of the art cinema and provided the press with another striking, nearly mythical New Wave trait to celebrate: unselfish interdependence and camaraderie. The notion of new production practices coupled with tightly intertwined crews and finances among the *Cahiers* critics-turning-filmmakers (for example, Rivette shooting *Le coup du berger* with AJYM money and in Chabrol's apartment, or Chabrol serving as technical advisor for Godard as he shot *Breathless,* based on a story by Truffaut) fueled this image of pure art and generosity in a field associated more typically with barriers to entry, cutthroat competition, and greedy producers. Thus, as a risky but generous producer, Chabrol functioned as one "carrier wave" that propelled the New Wave forward. He had turned his sixty-four-thousand-dollar inheritance into a small production company, generated several hundred thousand additional dollars, shot four features himself, and helped get the *Cahiers* band of the New Wave on track and running—and all within two short years.

If Chabrol had remained one of the more critically and commercially successful of the *Cahiers* filmmakers over the next several years, his position in French film history would be much easier to summarize. Instead, Chabrol lost his power to produce despite his recent successes and had to turn to outside producers. This shift in practice resulted in part from his gradual loss of AJYM because of the divorce from his first wife, Agnès—

a divorce initiated by his relationship with actress Stéphane Audran. Chabrol, who had risen quickly in the press's eyes as the model New Wave producer-director, shot eight features between 1958 and 1962, but the last six films were commercial and critical failures, especially compared to *The Cousins*. None of these—*A double tour* (1959), *Les bonnes femmes* (1960), *Les godelureaux* (*Wise Guys,* 1960), *L'oeil du malin* (*The Third Lover,* 1961), *Ophélia* (1962), and *Landru* (*Bluebeard,* 1962)—earned any major film-festival award. Such a rapid shift in his fortunes led many to dismiss Chabrol and center on Truffaut and Godard by 1960. Jacques Siclier, writing in 1961, is representative of critics suspicious of Chabrol's future: "This director seems to have exhausted with his first two films everything personal he had to say."[11]

This dramatic change proved to Chabrol's harshest critics that the New Wave was over, and it certainly provides one motivation to date the movement's close as 1964, the year Chabrol needed a commercial producer. But several of these recent "troubling" films, especially *Les bonnes femmes* and *L'oeil du malin,* are certainly among his more interesting works. Nonetheless, for historians who reduce Chabrol's contributions to his having proved how to escape the established production and distribution norms of France's old "studio" system, the loss of money on such films signals the end of his usefulness. By contrast, it is interesting to note how little criticism is ever aimed at Godard for failing to make money during this same period. In fact, Godard's failure to attract huge crowds with films such as *A Woman Is a Woman* (1961) or *Les carabiniers* (1963) was used more typically as proof of his radical aesthetic vitality; when Chabrol lost money, he was seen as betraying the spirit of the New Wave. Similarly, when Godard took money from Carlo Ponti to make *Une femme mariée* (*A Married Woman,* 1963) or *Le mépris* (*Contempt,* 1963), he was said to parody the studio system, but when Chabrol shot *A double tour,* a color, international coproduction, his importance for the New Wave was over for historians such as Charles Ford and Roy Armes.[12]

From an economic standpoint, Chabrol does cause problems for historians of the New Wave, and viewed aesthetically, too, he is among the more difficult figures to synthesize or summarize. From one corner come the antagonistic voices of political critics, such as the writers at *Positif,* charging that *Le beau Serge* and *The Cousins* were dragging the cinema back to the suspect bourgeois narratives of Balzac and Julien Duvivier. From other directions detractors such as Francis Coutarde complain that Chabrol's films were coldly formal, artificial, sexist, and cruel. Yet for many, he is a great and ironic storyteller. Historians and critics as varied as Georges Sadoul, Robin Wood, and Luc Moullet sing Chabrol's praises. Sadoul, for instance, wrote that *The Cousins* was not only the event of the 1958 film season but of the decade.[13] Robin Wood argues that Chabrol studies many of the same themes as Hitchcock but more naturally and rigorously.[14] Moreover, *Cahiers* critic Luc Moullet wrote that Chabrol belongs alongside Griffith, Ford, Pagnol, and Fassbinder, as one of the few great narrators of the cinema.[15]

Because of Chabrol's prolific and uneven output (and even Chabrol likes to quip that he made some of the worst movies in cinematic history), critics, whether favorable or antagonistic, often simplify Chabrol's themes and style around one or two central issues. But it is precisely the tension between the auteurist consistencies and his challenging diversity that makes Chabrol such an interesting test case. One of the least-studied dimensions of Chabrol's cinema is his use of excessive narrative strategies. While Godard's cinema is more typically analyzed for its formal play, intertextual layering, and parodic overcoding of visual and audio representation, Chabrol's films, too, offer many examples of self-conscious filmmaking. The resulting contradiction between Chabrol's "realist tendencies" and his artificial stylization provides a satirical and often ambiguous perspective on a concrete, diegetic world, and the spectator is caught between identifying with the characters and being distracted from them by an obvious narrative presence. Joel Magny identifies one result of such tension when he writes that Chabrol parallels Hitchcock in his ability to lead the audience through a series of increasingly outrageous shocks until in the end the audience is left only with the "real" situation of sitting in a theater, watching a film.[16] The diegesis is always undercut while the narration is always foregrounded.

One way to get a handle on Chabrol's distinct and troubling style is to reveal how he interrupts "realistic" action with sudden subjective, often parodic, interjections of exaggerated sound, editing, camera work, or mise-en-scène elements. Chabrol constructs a complex and individualized narrative space that shifts between a functional, realistic use of location, and a metaphorical or even comically parodic sense of place. The resulting contradictions and confusion are reflected in critical reactions to Chabrol's early films; for example, Don Allen writes that *Le beau Serge* and *The Cousins* "were so difficult to classify and therefore extremely disturbing."[17] Similarly, for some critics these opening films were "too personal" and for others "too cold."

Even critics writing fondly of early Chabrol have often been at odds about what the essence of his stories and style involves. Some, such as Joel Magny, have maintained that these films stylistically are direct descendants of neorealist traditions. For example, *Le beau Serge* features "purely descriptive scenes" of the town and the empty church, populated at least partially with "such emblematic neorealist characters" as the baker, the curate, and even random, wandering dogs.[18] Such a view of Chabrol as objective observer resurfaces throughout his career, fueled partly by his references to Rossellini in his own critical articles and interviews. Moreover, because *Le beau Serge*'s Marie (Bernadette Lafont) accuses François (Jean-Claude Brialy) of looking down on everyone in the provincial town "like they were bugs," the quasi-scientific metaphor of Chabrol as cultural entomologist has informed critical perspectives and led to conclusions such as André S. Labarthe's that Chabrol's fiction honestly "observes and describes" characters from outside "without extracting them from their own environment."[19] Jacques Siclier, as early as 1961, summed up Chabrol's most important trait as "a unique entomologist's style, observing contemporary reality from a new angle of vision never before seen in classical French cinema."[20]

Yet while reference to this metaphor and touches of neorealism are often useful in analyzing Chabrol's particular vision, they are not easily paired with his narrator's perspective, which is often mocking and excessive, rather than coolly detached and scientific. When New German director Rainer Werner Fassbinder discussed Chabrol's cinema, therefore, he overturned the entomology analogy. Fassbinder saw Chabrol rather as "a child who keeps a collection of insects in a glass case and observes with alternating amazement, fear and delight the marvelous behavior patterns of his tiny creatures."[21] This image of a *méchant* Chabrol, cruelly fascinated with his strange character/specimens, is clearly a productive analogy to be added to his loftier portrait as scientist-observer. The scientist versus child analogy is complicated again by Charles Derry, who makes Chabrol much more than an entomologist; for Derry, Chabrol's viewpoint is that "of a god who, with compassion but without sentiment, observes the follies of his creations."[22] The best way to summarize Chabrol and his unusual films is as contradictory combinations of traditions and strategies rather than unified works that can be easily interpreted, and therein lies part of the pleasure that is Chabrol: He may be a neorealist scientist crossed with a cruel child, who in reality delights in a godlike control, but he has no clearly defined divine plan to back it all up.

The complex thematics of Chabrol's films further challenge critics and spectators alike who attempt to isolate the ideological stance of this "first New Waver." In fact, one of the more fascinating and troubling aspects of Chabrol's cinema is that his films do not always fit what critics *want* to see from the New Wave filmmakers. On the one hand, he is not as humanistic and sentimental as Truffaut or Rohmer; on the other, he is not as modernist and political as Godard. Too often his stories seem misogynist, cruel, and even silly, and no one is sure where to place him on the political spectrum. For critics celebrating the *Cahiers* critics as young revolutionaries pushing aside the tired stories, styles, and production policies of an older French cinema, these filmmakers are too often assumed to be progressive on every level. But more radical (and often more perceptive) critics antagonistic to the New Wave, such as Raymonde Borde and Jacques Siclier, charge that Chabrol returns French cinema to conservative nineteenth-century narrative traditions, masking reactionary themes under cynical contemporary melodramas.

The critical problem involves sorting out whether Chabrol has a unified political agenda, or whether he is permanently ambiguous, which in turn, of course, is a very different ideological tactic. For instance, with *The Cousins* it is difficult to tell whether Chabrol offers the tale of country cousin Charles (Gérard Blain) and city cousin Paul (Jean-Claude Brialy) as a sort of pathetic, cautionary parable of modern France, or as a vicious critique of Paul's inherent fascism, or to ridicule Charles's outdated, romantic naiveté, or to mock and shame the insincere, immoral behavior of modern young women like Florence. Finally, any pertinent discussion must involve deciding whether Chabrol is laughing *at* or *with* his characters.

Moreover, the quest to isolate Chabrol's perspective and politics is not merely a game inspired only by the reviewers' need to summarize. It is also inscribed within the texts' stories and styles as well as in Chabrol's often farcical extratextual comments.[23] For instance, many of Chabrol's films *look* as if they are meant to serve some message or purpose, especially since *Le beau Serge*, *The Cousins*, *A double tour*, *L'oeil du malin*, and even *Landru* appear deliberately to resemble La Fontaine fables. Guy Braucourt's monograph even organizes itself around painting Chabrol as a sort of La Fontaine character himself, calling him a "provincial Parisian."[24] Thus, fairytale structures often hide just beneath the surface, and the films seem to cry out to be unraveled by the spectators as object lessons, but of what exactly?

Some who think they have figured out Chabrol, such as Borde, Marcel

Martin, James Monaco, René Prédal, or even Fassbinder, attack him as just another pessimistic, bourgeois imposter, with, as Monaco puts it, "insipid politics."[25] Prédal writes that Chabrol's politics follow an "amoral cynicism": "His films are even more pernicious than they seem: Chabrol, like his characters, merely secretes his venom behind the reassuring screen of a refined [bourgeois] aesthetic."[26] Similarly, Borde charges that "Chabrol wanted to be the French Fellini, but instead he is a *petit-bourgeois* of 1930."[27] Fassbinder goes further, charging "complete fascism": "The question is: is he knocking [bourgeois values] in order to overcome them or to maintain them? I think the latter is more likely."[28] For critics such as these, Chabrol's ideological concerns not only belong to "old wave" politics, they also become particularly dangerous when passed off as "new wave" ideals.

The engaging aspect of Chabrol's ideological implications, however, is that others disagree strongly with such blanket condemnations. Some critics praise Chabrol for what they see as his "no holds barred" attacks on the bourgeoisie. Braucourt, for instance, warns against confusing a cinema *about* the bourgeoisie with a bourgeois cinema: "With Chabrol . . . the glance is always critical of the object. . . . He is the only one [of the New Wave] to represent the bourgeois class with sufficient detachment . . . not to fall into either an ineffectual Punch and Judy show or into the complacency of offering an attractive spectacle."[29] While Braucourt here appears to be contrasting Chabrol with Godard and Truffaut, respectively, he finds Chabrol's perspective that of a politically engaged social critic. Don Allen seems to agree: "How else should he condemn wealth and the idle middle classes, other than by 'giving the audience a good look at them first.'"[30] Chabrol, in an interview with *Sight and Sound,* seems to echo their concerns when he asks, "Does making a film about fascism make one a fascist?"[31]

There are, therefore, two firmly divided camps and perspectives on Chabrol's ideological implications, and like the debates over whether to consider him a realist or a romanticist, a detached entomologist or a fascinated child, neither viewpoint seems adequate, nor particularly fruitful, for analyzing his ambiguous and troubling oeuvre. It is this very tension between Chabrol's reveling in and attacking social norms that delights Robin Wood. He finds Chabrol unwilling to affirm a belief in anything: Chabrol rejects the bourgeois world yet finds all alternatives empty and ridiculous. It must be noted that the perceptiveness of Wood's comments, written in 1970, will be supported over and over throughout Chabrol's career by films as diverse as *Nada* (1973), *Story of Women* (1990), and *La cérémonie* (1995).

The purpose of this discussion is not to end all debate on how to interpret Chabrol's cynical, satirical, exaggerated characters and the foolish worlds they inhabit but rather to examine how these films could possibly create and even encourage such conflicting interpretations. Two of Chabrol's strategies actually work hand in hand to reinforce confusion over what the audience is supposed to think about characters and their actions: he limits the depth in his characterization while further distancing the audience via his artificial, often boldly formal, manipulation of narrative devices and point of view. Together, these tactics shift attention from one character to another and finally to the narrator, while they distance the audience from identifying easily with any individual perspective throughout a film. As Robert Kolker points out, "We are permitted to view the conflict, not partake in it or resolve it."[32]

Le beau Serge: Chabrol's Return to the Country

Chabrol's first feature, *Le beau Serge* is the tale of a Parisian, François (Brialy), who returns to a village where he spent time as a youth (perhaps during the occupation, as Chabrol did). François is recuperating from a disease, but he finds that his best friend, Serge (Gerard Blain), is now an embarrassment, drunk and mistreating his wife, Yvonne (Michèle Méritz), who recently gave birth to a dead child. Yvonne's kid sister, Marie (Lafont), still lives with their disgusting father, Glomaud (Edmond Beauchamp), who turns out not to be the biological father of Marie. Serge has been unfaithful with Marie, and François will be drawn to her as well. During his extended stay, François takes an active interest in the family, though his efforts to help often backfire. Eventually, Yvonne gives birth to a new son, and Serge is brought to see the mother and child, though, as will be demonstrated, exactly what effect this might have on everyone remains unclear.

Chabrol's particular brand of New Wave filmmaking involves a constant reworking of story and style, with a variety of end results. Analyzing this deliberate effort to distance, satirize, and parody requires looking at the use of one formal parameter not often studied in Chabrol's films, the soundtrack, to see how even the audio functions to create yet undercut these unusual diegetic worlds. In *Le beau Serge*'s opening scene, Chabrol uses and defies realistic parameters while he also signals the spectator to join the narrator's complex game of leaping from one narrative tradition to another, overturning the neorealist conventions it echoes, while parodying the classical cinema's functionally coded sound aesthetics.

Le beau Serge opens with a "direct" soundtrack of the natural countryside sounds interrupted by a bus honking in the distance. Once the camera moves inside the bus to reveal François, nondiegetic sound presents one thread of theme music, whose melody and timbre are so serious as to become ominous. When the bus stops and François is met by his old friend Michel and landlady Mme. Chaulnier, the music halts, too, and "natural" noises return as the only sounds. But the camera, now stationed on the bus roof to record the driver retrieving François's luggage, suddenly reveals Serge standing below on the other side of the bus, and the music booms out a very brief, heavily staccato theme that will become the most overcoded motif of the film. Thus, as the driver moves out of his medium shot and Serge is revealed in long shot, the soundtrack not only blasts out a warning, it also connects the audience's attention and this highly parodic, evocative strain of music to Serge before François has even seen him.

This use of music typifies Chabrol's heavy-handed style, which simultaneously undercuts moments of neorealist direct recording while it exaggerates the music to the point of parodying melodramatic sound practice. The sudden and brief booming sound here is even more outrageously excessive than many of Douglas Sirk's blaring staccato accents since it is abrupt and unmotivated. Most significantly, however, the soundtrack also foregrounds Chabrol's playful presence and marks the alternation of diegetic versus nondiegetic and realistic versus artificial stylistic techniques that will continue to structure the narrative itself, as well as other stylistic parameters ranging from camera to editing. The narrator is preparing the viewer for a mixture of genres, techniques, and traditions that will alternately reinforce and undercut the narrative.

Throughout *Le beau Serge* the music serves this narrative mélange and continues the sense of parody and intertextuality. For instance, often the music signals story events too abruptly: it becomes wildly excessive when Serge races his truck to menace François and Marie or drinks wine excessively for breakfast. But the soundtrack also becomes tritely romantic when François and Marie walk hand-in-hand to music that could be from a Hollywood romance. Moreover, the sound is often overcoded as *obviously* expressive, as when François sees Glomaud leaving his house after raping Marie, and only one loud, jolting note booms on the soundtrack.

Within *Le beau Serge,* Chabrol also manipulates film style and theme to forge diegetic conflicts whose end results remain vague. While the constantly shifting perspective and formal play are not always immediately obvious, they are partly responsible for the shallow, often contradictory characterizations. Just before *Le beau Serge* was released Chabrol wrote in *Cahiers du cinéma* that he had eliminated most shot/reverse shots in favor of long takes, pans, and tracking shots so that "subjective takes suddenly become objectified."[33] He seems here to refer to the unexpected stylistic flourishes wherein what begins as one character's view of an object—a perceptual point of view shot—is suddenly revealed as "objective" when the character somehow appears in what began as his or her own field of vision. Such play with perception will, as will be demonstrated, occasionally operate on the level of the shot as well as in larger narrative structures.

Joel Magny argues that such shifts and the resulting "objectified subjectivity" disrupt the diegetic world and distance the audience from the characters by undercutting its ability even to share their view. But they also serve to complicate the story's contradictory themes. Magny cites a number of instances in which Chabrol's camera begins a shot focused straight on a character's face, then pans or tracks in a half-circle until the viewer sees what the character sees: "The one looking becomes the one looked at, and vice versa."[34] In fact, *A double tour*, with its systems of subjective flashbacks, employs many such variations on seeing and being seen that are not simply empty formal play but integral techniques intertwined with characterization and the complication of story events.

Despite the clunky sound of the term for Chabrol's technique to manipulate and shift point of view in midshot or midscene, "objectified subjectivity" is a central device in all his early films. In *Le beau Serge*, a story built around François's often skewed perception of his old village and the villagers' perception of him, the central tension becomes not simply this exchange of glances but also how they affect the *audience's* vision of François and others. The camera work signals the importance of following and interpreting vision in this film as it privileges key plot points with fancy movements that shift one's point of view and develop the film's motifs of circularity and repetition or the "exchange of redemption" theme.[35]

For example, the moment François notices Serge, Serge looks back accusingly from his drunken stupor, though there is no sign Serge recognizes François. As François and his old buddy Michel head toward the hotel and François asks what has happened to Serge, the audience sees them both stopped in a medium long shot, looking just off right. The film then cuts to Serge in a long shot looking back at them as he stumbles into the doorway of a café, then cuts back to François and Michel in a nearly identical medium long shot framing that graphically matches their earlier point/glance as they now turn to walk up the street. But now the camera is *behind* them, and they walk toward, instead of away from, the viewer. The editing and camera position have shifted so that François and Michel's vantage point in space, the point/glance, as they looked "down" on Serge, the object/point, has become another point/object as the audience now looks down on them looking.[36]

This subtle complication of the narrative space signals not only the centrality of perceptual points of view but also that in the end the narrator's vantage point will turn everyone into an object of a textually inscribed glance. Much like Hitchcock's narrative space, Chabrol's space is built around camera positions anticipating, rather than following, the action. Another example occurs early in *Le beau Serge* as the camera tracks backward while the men follow it to the hotel. What has been signaled is not only François's overly charged vision of Serge, but also that the camera is looking at the concerned "tourist" François just as he looks at everyone else. Thus, while François and Michel discuss who lives where and look off screen right and left on their stroll, the camera does not cut to more point of view shots; Serge and François are the only real objects of study for this narrative, while the town remains a mere backdrop, never fully clarified in terms of spatial continuity.

The entire narrative structure echoes and reinforces this circularity and exchange of views at key plot points. Circular pans, in fact, not only signal significant moments in the story, they also communicate characters' mental states. For instance, the first sexual encounter between François and Marie provides a central example of how the circularity of story and style are intertwined. François has followed Marie home in midday, but just outside the door of her house, he asks Marie again whether her father, Glomaud, might not be home. She smiles and begins opening the door. The next shot is a pan of the ground-floor interior of Marie's house. It could be assumed that this pan, scanning the interior, represents the perceptual point of view of the worried François or the confident Marie, especially since it is accompanied by her voice-off proclaiming, "No, he is not there." But by the end of the scene one sees clearly that it is *not* a subjective point of view shot since the couple walks into the shot and the camera stops panning as they embrace in a medium close-up at the foot of the stairway. Somewhere in the middle of the scene, the actors left the point/glance position in the doorway to enter as point/object of their own gaze.

   The confusion and circularity continue: as François and Marie climb
the stairs, the church bell begins to toll, and there is a three-second dissolve into another circular pan of a room, which begins by revealing only
clothes tossed on the floor but slowly tilts and pans to show the two lovers
on Marie's bed. Not only have the rather disorienting pans enhanced the
notion of François being "swept away" by Marie's passion, but during this
second pan the church bell continues for a total of ten chimes. The time of
the dissolve and pan, ten seconds, is contradicted by the tolling bell. Has
the bell simply begun to ring again one hour later or has it continued?
Either way, the bells complicate rather than clarify the diegetic time, and
one cannot be sure whether one hour or only a few seconds passed during
that dissolve. In the end, perhaps it is also a narrator's joke that for these
two, making love really does make bells ring.
   Later at the church the curate asks François why he did not come to
mass when he heard the bells earlier, and François answers that he never
noticed them. Thus, the bells take on additional implications: one option
is that François is lying to the priest (after all the *audience* heard bells); another is that the bells were a nondiegetic warning to the audience, signal-
ing the severity of François' actions; a third option is a further gag in that
rather than "hearing bells" when he met with Marie, he was so overwhelmed by her sexuality that he did *not* hear bells or anything else. In the
latter case, his sexual escapade would have made him forget his moral
obligations. The camera work and soundtrack combine here to blur dis-
tinctions between objective and subjective time and space in this scene.
Dialogue, too, never clarifies the action since François is never in a position to explain whether he felt guilty about being seduced by Marie, or
missing mass, or lying to the priest.
   In another scene that day, just after François has been with Marie and
while he is on his way to the church, the narration provides one of only two
scenes in which the audience follows Serge, instead of François. The range of
story information is exchanged for a short time. The drunken Serge hollers at
Yvonne that François has returned to find them living a stupid life, like
vermin. He runs from the house, kicks the chickens, but then sees François
in the distance. Serge watches from behind a tree, in a conventional
point/glance, point/object exchange, but Serge's point of view and range of information both abruptly end as François enters the church. There is a cut on
the dark door closing (accompanied by an exaggerated bang on the soundtrack), and the camera is now placed inside the cathedral, with François established at the point/glance as he scans the nearly empty interior.

This brief shift to seeing Serge when François, for once, does not, helps verify François's suspicions that Serge and Yvonne lead a miserable life, but it also signals that François's arrival is significant for Serge and motivates him to reflect on his current state and even spy back at François. Nonetheless, the motive for his excessive drinking is now unclear; later, in fact, Yvonne will explain to François that it has become worse since François returned. Is his drinking prompted by embarrassment? Is it some sort of revenge? Or is it related more to his fear of another potentially disastrous childbirth? Serge's tendency to speak in incomplete phrases that burst out during drunken fits further disrupts the viewer's ability to define his character and specify what he thinks about himself or anyone else. As the film continues and scenes again limit themselves to François's depth of story information, any positive effects of François's intrusions into Serge's life become more and more doubtful.

What makes the characters so difficult to summarize, therefore, is a combination of inner circles of characters' lives that are never fully revealed. Unlike flat but motivated classical, melodramatic characters, Chabrol's characters do not suddenly explain their deepest fears. If the audience never fully comprehends their maladies it is difficult to envision any resolving cure that might happily conclude the story. Serge behaves monstrously toward Yvonne: he mocks her appearance; makes a distorted face to mimic their dead first child, who was affected with Down's syndrome; damns her new pregnancy and her family; openly dances with and runs off with her little sister, Marie; and finally abandons the frail, pregnant Yvonne to scrounge for firewood alone in the cold woods.

Yet Serge seems often on the verge of explaining his actions to François: As François leaves the church, Serge is lying outside the door and screams that when Serge needed help, the priest only gave him an empty sermon. It is unclear whether the curate helped create Serge's current problem or to which occasion Serge is alluding (did the priest convince Serge to marry the pregnant Yvonne, console him after the child's death, or scold him after a confession). Later, the drunken Serge seeks out François, talking to himself as he searches: "The kid did it all—lousy kid Glomaud's daughter had. . . . Help me François." Thus, the film suggests that something in the story of this first child ties in the priest and Glomaud. Whether it is all a narrative ploy or a carefully constructed story point that must remain open and unsaid is unclear, but one detects another suggestion of incest: the first child is referred to more frequently as Glomaud's and Yvonne's than as Serge's. This possibility may also explain Serge's wild fears about the second birth (will it be his or Glomaud's?) and his own seduction of Marie (as retaliation and/or in-law incest). But the audience cannot discover any more about Serge's mental state here since François is off romping in the fields with Marie rather than hearing Serge's story at the one point Serge wants to tell it. Therefore, when François finally has opportunity to get an explanation from Serge, he is busy enjoying Marie's company instead of helping Serge. Not only does this scene show François, the self-proclaimed Christ-figure, as a disappointment, it also mirrors the fact that the priest, too, could not help Serge when he needed it.

While such play with point of view and narrative information functions to obscure characterization and identification, one can see the ultimate results of Chabrol's ambiguities by analyzing how different critics have interpreted *Le beau Serge*'s ending. Throughout the film, François's role shifts slightly, leading up to his final, obsessive behavior. Chabrol claims that he bathed François in light and even dressed him in light colors to privilege him over the darker Serge from the start, allowing the film to *pretend* that François has the moral right and obligation to interfere in Serge's life and world.[37] Yet as the story unfolds, François's actions begin to affect everyone negatively: Serge's behavior gets more vicious, Glomaud rapes Marie because François tells him he is not her real father, François offends the curate, and finally, having angered Serge to the point of violence at the dance, François isolates himself in his room, awaiting a chance to vindicate himself.

During the final scene, featuring what Chabrol proudly asserts is a paradoxical mixture of light and dark, the snow and night combine with character gesture and music to leave final interpretations incomplete. François does get to play saint and run out for the doctor to aid Yvonne as she goes into labor. But the doctor is visiting Glomaud, who may have been sick ever since the angry François chased him into the cemetery. The doctor sees no point in going all the way to Yvonne's home just to deliver what will undoubtedly turn out to be another dead child. But Glomaud magnanimously sends the doctor to his daughter while the scowling Marie stays by his bed to comfort Glomaud. Earlier, Serge had told François that Glomaud's rape of Marie was almost natural and that Marie had probably secretly wanted to have sex with her old "papa" too. At the time that line had stunned François, but the image of Marie staying behind with the bedridden Glomaud, rather than running to help her sister, seems to confirm that Serge knew more all along about these people than did François. Moreover, if one further tests the double incest hypothesis—that Glomaud may have had an incestuous relationship with Yvonne that was responsible for the first child's condition—perhaps Glomaud sends the doctor away because he knows the second child is *not* his and has a better chance of survival.

François, having secured the doctor's reluctant aid, has to search out Serge and drag him home in what becomes a reversal of their earlier fight scene: previously Serge dragged and kicked the immobile François around town in front of Marie and the revelers at the dance; now it is François's turn to drag Serge through the streets. The end is complicated, however, by the final series of shots of Serge and François as Yvonne gives birth to the live, healthy though small child ("Well," the doctor admits, "it's no giant"). To the accompaniment of heavy nondiegetic music, François appears to feel vindicated as he sinks down saying, "J'ai cru [I believed]." Serge laughs loudly in an extreme grimace, and the final shot goes out of focus.

The central questions surrounding this ending concern interpreting Serge's expression (is it a cruel laugh, or ecstasy, shock, drunkenness, mockery, disbelief?) but also François's final words. For Alan Williams, the ending is simple: *Le beau Serge* concludes with "an uplifting affirmation" of life and the justice of François's mission.[38] Paul Monaco tends to agree: "Suddenly recognizing his healthy son, Serge screams in agitated delight, as if this awareness has suddenly purged the effects of the alcohol from him. . . . Serge triumphs in the last scene in an elemental and life-giving manner."[39] But Monaco does note that the loss of focus on Serge leaves any final interpretation open. Robin Wood's version of the ending retains more ambiguity; François has helped reunite Serge's family via "a gesture of grandeur and perversity." Nonetheless, the end has something of the effect of "a divine miracle" for Wood.[40]

But given Chabrol's thematic complexity, it is hardly surprising to find strongly divergent interpretations of the end of *Le beau Serge*. T. Jefferson Kline's interpretation is the polar opposite of those offered by the above-mentioned critics, since for him both Serge and François unquestionably die at the end. Kline's interpretation of the entire film is that it closely and even faithfully retells the Icarus myth; thus, the prideful François, who has flown too high, sinks down to his death while Serge's face is distorted into a skull as the image loses focus. For Kline, both friends must die to prove his claim that the myth of Icarus structures *Le beau Serge* intertextually. Thus, while Williams finds the end uplifting, Kline sees the same sequence as a dance to the death for Serge and François.

Chabrol deliberately overturns the classical happy ending here with

Serge's exaggerated face and laugh, the loss of focus, and the collapse of
François. The only solid information delivered is that the child is alive and
normal. The viewer *is* distanced from the closing actions as the fiction signals itself as excessive, and the only reality remaining is that the audience
is left sitting in a theater, watching a fictional construct. Chabrol claimed
that the ending was indeed double, with François saving Serge and Serge
saving François by teaching him "to dig into the truth of things."[41] Gradually, according to Chabrol, a truth emerges that François is less stable
and more mixed up than Serge, who at least understands why he acts as
he does. Yet as this study has demonstrated, there is hardly *a* single truth
here, and the ending remains puzzling, thanks in part to the oneiric narration of this end sequence, which differs so strikingly from the rest of *Le
beau Serge* and its neorealist style. In the end, Chabrol personally may be
laughing at François, but the text seems to laugh at and with everyone, including the spectator.

What this discussion of the vagaries of Chabrol's themes demonstrates
is not simply that reviewers can easily disagree over his films, but that in
order to make decisions about the film, one must weigh ambivalent gestures
and actions constantly against stylistic interventions. If the music at the
close of *Le beau Serge* were not so heavy-handed, if Serge's grimace and
laugh were not so grotesque, if the shot did not lose focus before fading out,
it would be much easier to adopt Williams's interpretation that all is well by
the end. It should be clear from such widely disparate aesthetic readings of
Chabrol, however, that it is rarely easy to categorize his cinematic traits. His
style and characters undercut the neorealist world as readily as they evoke
it, and they refer to Balzac, Hitchcock, and Lang as regularly as they defy
them as models; *Le beau Serge*, like other Chabrol films, is more complex
and ambiguous than many historians admit. Marc Ruscart agrees, warning
that too many critics underestimate Chabrol since he is so jolly in real life
and occasionally even dismisses his own films: "But Chabrol poses real
problems of film *écriture*, each camera movement is carefully planned
out. . . . It is too easy to say that his cinema is simple and straightforward."[42]
Chabrol, much more subtly than Godard or Chris Marker, hops from one tradition to another, from one mood to another, just enough to mix genres,
styles, and themes into exaggerated and biting exercises in social satire,
generic parody, and narrative parataxis or formal play. Thus, the ending of
Le beau Serge should not simply be interpreted as happy or mournful but
should be accepted as an active parody of the problem of ending fiction
films, be they realistic, melodramatic, or romantic.

The Cousins: The City Rat Hosts the Country Rat

Chabrol's second feature became a poster child for the New Wave, thanks to its story, style, and financial success. *The Cousins* is one of the central films, along with *The 400 Blows, Breathless,* and *Hiroshima, mon amour,* typically regarded as "launching" the popular concept of a New Wave in 1959 and 1960, and its healthy box office brought great attention to Chabrol's tactics. According to Antoine de Baecque, "Chabrol and *The Cousins* most directly illustrate a portrait of youth that springs directly from the popular surveys and public opinion polls."[43] This story offers a loose chronicle of the country cousin, Charles (Gerard Blain), who comes to Paris to room with his city cousin, Paul (Jean-Claude Brialy), both of whom are preparing for their law exams. Reversing *Le beau Serge,* it is now the provincial who arrives in Paris. There, Charles is introduced to the world of bohemian wealth and decadence by Paul, as they alternate between his "club" in the Latin Quarter and his lavish apartment in the trendy neighborhood of Neuilly, on the edge of Paris.

The timid and earnest Charles feels more comfortable writing letters to his mother than drinking and dancing with Paul and his often rude friends. Nonetheless, Charles falls for one young woman in Paul's group, Florence (Juliette Maynial), but then loses her to Paul before he can go on a single real date with her. Paul, with the help of his older friend, a disgusting fascist leech named Clovis (Claude Cerval), convinces Florence that she is much too sexually active ever to be able to settle down with the domestic Charles. She seems to agree but is sad to forfeit what may be her one chance to fall in love with a nice, serious young man. Yet, while Charles is awaiting her at the law school, she decides to have sex with Paul. Later, she moves into their apartment, which makes for an uncomfortable household, with Charles moping around the couple or sitting in the next room studying his law books while Florence and Paul romp and giggle in the shower together. Finally, Paul passes his law exams (apparently with the underhanded help of Clovis) while the hardworking, straight-laced Charles, who has been warning Paul to work harder, fails. It is as if Chabrol decided to reverse La Fontaine and make the diligent ant die while the dancing, good-for-nothing grasshopper survives the winter. In desperation, the depressed Charles loads one of the many pistols in the apartment, points it at the sleeping Paul, and pulls the trigger. It only clicks with an empty chamber. But later Paul finds the same pistol lying about and tries to cheer up Charles by imitating one of their recent party guests. Paul accidentally kills Charles with the bullet Charles had loaded in the gun to kill Paul. The final shot presents a stunned Paul sitting with the pistol, looking at his dead cousin's body while the doorbell rings.

In several of the many interviews Chabrol granted upon release of the film, he stated that the overall theme was "the suffocation of purity in the modern world," but as in most statements by this playful director, such a summary can be accepted only partly as a key to the story's structure and functions. Paul, whose wealthy uncle is in New York on a junket, accompanied by two young women, does represent a rich, immoral end of the political spectrum. He is an extreme caricature of a new, right-wing youth, and Chabrol's camera spends a great amount of time gliding across rows of liquor bottles, toy soldiers, animal pelts, and guns to establish the oppressive environment of the family apartment. Paul lives in a world full of British sports cars, seasonal girlfriends (his "winter" girl, Geneviève, needs an abortion, his "spring" girl will be Charles's Florence), and orgiastic parties and recitations from Wagner. These characters never show any compassion for one another, and the city is a sort of concrete playground. Chabrol often presents this claustrophobic world with elegant deep-space framing and camera mobility, however, offering yet another modern French tale trying to borrow some of the flamboyant tactics of Renoir's *Rules of the Game*. Poor Charles is caught up in a network of urban forces he can never navigate, and he spends most of his time hiding in his room, with only occasional trips to buy his law notes or stop at the local bookstore, where the owner (Guy Decomble) recognizes him immediately as a naive provincial and offers him a free copy of Balzac's *Lost Illusions*. Paris oppresses rather than liberates Charles, and even Paul's city friends, including the defeated Geneviève (Geneviève Cluny), seem to go through the motions of their daily excesses with no hint of hope or purpose. By the end, everyone has lost something.

One big influence on the dialogue and characters of *The Cousins* was surely Chabrol's friend and collaborator Paul Gégauff. These two had met in 1950 at a *ciné-club* called Le Celtic. Chabrol was in the audience watching a British war film, when Gégauff, dressed in a Nazi uniform, stood up to disrupt the screening, announcing that showing a movie about defeating the Germans was in bad taste! According to Guy Austin, "This anecdote encapsulates Gégauff's dangerous appeal: a dandy and a joker, a Germanophile, a scourge of bad taste, of bourgeois manners and morals."[44] Chabrol espoused leftist politics; yet he became good buddies with this strange, anti-Semitic, but somehow appealing figure, who would not only collaborate on a score of Chabrol's movies but also assisted with dialogue on scripts for Eric Rohmer, among others. Chabrol regularly defended Gégauff against charges of fascism, arguing that his friend was simply "very anarchistic" and liked to startle people by speaking suddenly in German, as Paul does when he awakens a drunken Jewish friend in *The Cousins*.[45] Nonetheless, Gégauff's contrast to Chabrol motivated many people to see that the Charles and Paul of *The Cousins* were based in part on the writers, Claude and Paul.

The real cynicism in *The Cousins*, which is typical of so many subsequent Chabrol stories, arises not simply in that the city grinds up the provincial Charles nor from the fact that the urban dwellers are revealed to be empty and pathetic. The brutal pessimism, which led one reviewer to call *The Cousins* "poisonous, but beautiful," results initially from the fact that Paul is both fascist and sympathetic.[46] Chabrol explains that in person Brialy is amazingly appealing, even when he is being a brute: "[Brialy's Paul] is supposed to be like Le Pen [the right-wing, racist politician], but Brialy always maintains such elegance and 'class,' while Le Pen is closer to a cattle driver. Brialy was so nice during filming that I couldn't make him a creep."[47] But the second cynical element is embedded in the character of Charles himself, who is established as pitifully naive and even dull. If the country cousin were a bright, rising star with solid morals who was duped and destroyed by the corrupt city cousin and his friends, one would have a sad but moral tale. Rather, Chabrol establishes one of his auteurist story traits with *The Cousins*, creating a perceptive and cruel mockery of all the characters and the worlds in which they live. As in *Le beau Serge*, Chabrol's narration reveals an absurdity in every member of the diegetic world, but even more than in that first film, he now undercuts and divides the male protagonists' ability to accomplish anything of value. While Balzac allowed readers to identify with and mourn the decline of the optimistic Rastignac, Chabrol presents the audience with two lead characters, neither of whom warrants its allegiance.

While *The Cousins* opens with the arrival of Charles at a Paris train station and closes with his death rather than with the consequences of his death for Paul, the range of story information alternates between the cousins, so that the audience almost always has more information than the pitifully naive Charles. The audience sees Clovis and Paul hand Geneviève money for an abortion, while Charles, in the next room, writes to his mother about what he ate on the train trip to Paris. Later, the viewer sees Clovis, then Paul, convincing Florence that she is a sexual creature who could never be happy with the solitary, timid Charles, while the latter waits in futility for her to meet him in town. Both scenes reveal the depth of Paul's depravity—he apparently even shows 16 mm porno films to Florence as part of his seduction; Charles will turn off the projector, spinning an empty reel, when he gets home later—and these scenes provide information that Charles will never fathom. He never understands why Geneviève is so upset with Paul, nor why Florence slept with Paul rather than meeting Charles as planned. He is as helpless and ignorant about the daily life going on in his apartment as he is about the content of his law courses.

Since the plot does not show what Charles's life was like in the country, the narration also denies the viewer even the thematic conclusion that Charles should have stayed home where he was better off. All the audience knows is that his family is poor, and he is his mother's only hope. But it is also clear that Charles's mother has had a too cautionary influence on him; if Paul's father is a poor influence on Paul, Charles's mother has gone to the other extreme in protecting her son from the world. Charles seems ill equipped for any world. For instance, on the night of one of Paul's parties, before Charles has lost Florence, he leads her out into the street for some privacy in hopes of learning if she could be interested in him, even though, as he acknowledges, he is ridiculous and less attractive than Paul. When she protests, he admits he is a mama's boy and whispers into Florence's ear what one can only assume is the revelation that he has never had a date. The bold Florence is very sensitive with Charles but does confess that she, by contrast, has been in love often. Charles tells her that his mother warned him against women; he nonetheless seems to decide to pursue Florence anyway, though Paul interrupts them and takes off with Florence in his sports car. This scene presents Charles as pathetic: he speaks of love with a glazed, ridiculous look on his face, which is made all the more repulsive with the low camera position, harsh lighting, and unflattering close-up on his mooning face. Charles may be earnest, but he has no other appealing qualities; he is not so much humble as he is uncomfortable, uninformed, and a helpless victim. Moreover, none of the women characters in *The Cousins* has any redeeming character traits: Florence is easily convinced that she is nothing more than a sexual toy, Geneviève returns to Paul's parties even after her abortion, the party-girl friends, Martine (Françoise Vatel) and Françoise (Stéphane Audran), leave their boyfriends and are then insensitive to the pain they cause, and even the lower-class concierge fails to see that the haughty Paul is a cruel villain. If there is any sympathy created for any character, it might actually be that for Paul, sitting alone at the end with a smoking gun in his hand. This is Chabrol's wicked sense of humor at its best.

But beyond its cruel, ironic thematic structure, *The Cousins* presents a brilliant example of Chabrol's New Wave stylistic palette. Chabrol, and especially cinematographer Henri Decae, build upon more than neorealism and Bazinian duration in this film, as they construct a narrative space that owes as much to Renoir as to Rossellini. While Louis Malle's *The Lovers* offers overt tributes to *Rules of the Game*, Chabrol's *The Cousins* updates Renoir's highly metaphoric spatial configurations, exploring Paul's apartment and student club in particular via a very mobile camera that yields deep space and planes of action. *The Cousins*, with an average shot length of eighteen seconds, combines elegantly fluid camera movement with intricate character blocking, both for the studio set of Paul's apartment as well as for the location shooting, at the student club or on the streets. The division of fictional space into significant planes of action that are then further complicated by a rich lateral space revealed by tracks and pans provides for a functional, Bazinian duration and complexity. For instance, moments after Charles has first arrived at Paul's apartment, Clovis answers the telephone. Geneviève is calling, upset and demanding to speak with Paul. The shot lasts seventy seconds, beginning with Clovis answering the phone in close-up in the foreground. When he calls for Paul, his head shifts frame left, revealing the great depth of a hallway that leads back to the room where Paul and Charles are speaking. As Paul emerges from the doorway in a long shot, he approaches the camera. When he reaches the middle ground, however, he learns Geneviève is on the phone and throws his cigarette with disgust on the floor before continuing his path until he stands next to Clovis, who has backed even more to screen left, creating a tight two-shot. While Clovis chews on his sandwich, amused at Paul's rudeness and discomfort on the phone, Charles slowly appears in the hallway and approaches, adding a third character to the shot. Charles, trying to be discrete, wanders into the off-screen space, screen left, just as Clovis, too, withdraws from the frame. Paul continues talking alone in the frame, with Charles dipping into the frame in the distance from time to time, until Paul hangs up and Chabrol cuts at a 90-degree angle for the next shot of all three characters.

This sort of long take, with carefully choreographed acting and blocking of characters, continues the tradition, detailed in David Bordwell's *On the History of Film Style*, of staging in depth to guide and block the audience's attention. In the beginning of the shot, Clovis's head blocks the

Figure 4.1. Clovis, left, and Paul, right; Charles waits in depth (*The Cousins*)

deep hallway so the audience can focus attention on his grotesque joking as he answers the phone in a feigned woman's voice. Next, he moves his head to the side to open up the deep space for Paul to appear, and the camera reframes slightly to keep the shot balanced until Paul walks up for a two-shot. Finally, the crevice between their heads is filled by Charles, for two significant planes of action, until he and Clovis exit the frame nearly simultaneously so that all the viewer's attention can be devoted to Paul as he agrees, with obvious reluctance, to allow the pregnant Geneviève to pay him a visit. This sort of staging will recur over and over in *The Cousins*, especially when Charles is placed as a witness to the increasingly erratic and shameless behavior of his cousin, Paul. Such framing demonstrates Chabrol's new maturity at composition in time and space. Many contemporary reviewers called attention to Chabrol's intriguing "film language," with some even arguing that *The Cousins* was more "cinematic" than *Le beau Serge*. Marc Ruscart in particular sums up this respect of Chabrol's style by arguing that historically too many people have underestimated him: "Claude Chabrol is a great chess player, the pawns are already set up before the shot."[48]

Yet Chabrol does not limit the long takes to a sort of 1939 faith in reality. He also uses very modern devices for punctuation and a fluid shift from shot to shot or scene to scene. Shortly after Paul's phone conversation,

Charles goes to his room to write to his mother. The camera pans left, revolving around his new room as he speaks the words of his letter in a soft subjective voice-over. But the end of the thirty-six-second shot loses focus and dissolves into another out of focus shot of the living room with a bright table lamp, as the door buzzer replaces the soft music and the sound of Charles's voice in his room. The shot comes into focus and begins to dolly forward as first Paul and then Clovis cross the room from offscreen right to welcome the miserable looking Geneviève. The camera reframes several times and then follows Geneviève and Paul as they walk right, behind the table with the bright lamp, until she slumps into a chair, in close-up, with Paul leaning over her. Geneviève's face is lit harshly by the lamp, which now stands just offscreen. The choreography in this single, forty-second shot, from an empty long shot to a tight, uncomfortable close-up of a distraught, pregnant Geneviève, is typical of the actor blocking and narrative space employed in *The Cousins*. It works wonderfully to efficiently, if casually, guide the audience's attention to significant details. It also lends a pessimistic sense of a narrator's control, since by the end of so many long takes, the viewer suddenly can appreciate that Chabrol has it all preplanned, as if these characters have fallen into a trap, set long ago and of which they remain ignorant. Later, when Clovis leads Florence by the hand to Paul as an experiment to prove to her that her body will not let her pass up any attractive man, there is another interplay of heads that block and open space for staging, until the close-up kiss between Florence and Paul masks the devious Clovis watching them in the background.

During party scenes as well the camerawork regularly wanders freely and with great spontaneity, only finally to land on a bit of dialogue or a gesture or a sudden kiss that, in retrospect, provides meaning to the entire sequence of seemingly random events. Thus, unlike the more spontaneous open acting of long takes in some other New Wave films, Chabrol's style displays a careful narration that resembles Renoir's: For example, in *Rules of the Game* the camera seems accidentally to pass Christine just as she drunkenly bursts out to St. Aubin that she wants him to take her away from the party. In similar fashion, the camera in *The Cousins* will suddenly reframe and tilt up ever so slightly to change the composition from a two-shot of a couple alone in the foreground to introduce a whole room full of other characters in the background looming over them in the frame. Chabrol often composes with several planes of action, to introduce the ironic contrast between characters in each plane or to force audience, in a Bazinian sense, actively to scan the film space to follow better the simultaneous, complex action.

Figure 4.2. Geneviève caught between Clovis and Paul (*The Cousins*)

Figure 4.3. Florence is convinced to kiss Paul (*The Cousins*)

When the poor, deceived Charles comes home to turn off the projector upstairs and learn that Florence missed her meeting with him because she was in bed with Paul, the audience actually sees the three characters on two different floors in a cutaway set that is divided into perfect quadrants by the chimney and second-floor beam. That so much of this film is based on voyeurism (Charles watches Florence and Paul dance and even shower together through the smoked glass bathroom wall, Paul watches Charles's reactions to Florence cooking their meals, and jealous men at parties watch their ex-lovers arrive with other men) and exhibitionism (Paul turns out the lights and dons a Nazi SS cap to recite Wagner, Florence lies half-naked sunbathing and asks Charles why they cannot be good friends) all motivates the emphasis on the actively probing camerawork. As the *Image et son* review observed, "Chabrol's vivacious camera . . . observes, accompanies, and describes in flamboyant travelings that always seem necessary, and their seeming effortlessness is the height of visual know-how."[49] Thus, both story and style in *The Cousins* build upon Chabrol's delight in cynical, playful observation of his "bugs" under his cruelly positioned microscope.

Figure 4.4. Charles tries to study (*The Cousins*)

Landru Likes Fresh Meat: Chabrol's New Wave Ends

While *Le beau Serge* and *The Cousins* provide productive and logical Chabrol films to analyze in detail, *Landru* might seem less likely. But since one aim of this history is to investigate less canonical texts, *Landru* becomes a pertinent and valuable test case. Not only is *Landru* a color, international coproduction (by Carlo Ponti and Georges de Beauregard), but in contrast to *Le beau Serge* and *The Cousins*, which announced Chabrol and the New Wave, *Landru* can be considered the last feature of Chabrol's New Wave era. *Landru* was certainly closer to mainstream French cinema than any of Chabrol's first eight features, and it was written in collaboration with the popular, "new generation" novelist Françoise Sagan. Moreover, to secure financing, the producers demanded several stars of the 1950s, settling on Michèle Morgan and Danièlle Darieux, and several gratuitous bedroom scenes with Juliette Maynial. By the time of *Landru*, Chabrol, who had earlier shown everyone else how to be his own financier, was unable to follow his own blueprint.

Even with all its potential drawing power, the film sold only 200,000 tickets in its Paris first-run, which was more than recent Chabrols (*Les bonnes femmes* sold just 84,000 and *Ophelia* just 12,000), but far fewer than other mainstream movies with that kind of "star power," much less a Ponti marketing campaign. *Landru* did only fair business outside France as well; for example, it earned just thirty-eight thousand dollars in its four-week New York run (while Serge Bourguignon's first feature, *Sundays and Cybèle*, was in its twenty-sixth "smash" week there).[50] Chabrol's bold, independent financing maneuvers of his earlier career and his personal projects such *Les bonnes femmes* seemed suddenly quite remote from this strange historical tale about a famous French criminal whose life had also been the subject of Charlie Chaplin's *M. Verdoux* (1947). What might allow reviewers or the audience to label this film New Wave was hard to specify; some wrote that it was made by "ex–New Wave director, Claude Chabrol," and thus it becomes a "last gasp," ending his early period. After *Landru*, Chabrol could not find any willing producers for two years, and then he was forced into even more commercial projects, beginning with *Tiger Loves Fresh Blood*. By testing the narrative strategies at work in the transitional *Landru*, one can get a better sense of Chabrol's radically diverse output, how his career challenges notions of authorship, and even how it forces one to evaluate definitions of the New Wave.

The differences between his earlier films and *Landru* are substantial on every level. While characterization in *Le beau Serge, Les bonnes femmes*, and *L'oeil malin* is often ambiguous, with *Landru* it becomes outrageously theatrical, parodic, and farcical. Moreover, parallels with neorealism or neoromanticism can no longer be made for this bizarre period piece. Nonetheless, Chabrol's ideological function remains as dynamically ambiguous here as in his earlier films. The overall goal of this examination, therefore, is to investigate critically *Landru*'s dominant narrative strategies for how they continue and even exaggerate Chabrol's tactics of ambivalent and playfully experimental storytelling. Not only does the point of view on the characters become more bitterly caricatural in *Landru*, but the primary narrator's attitude toward Landru, his family, and his victims remains an uneven collection of cues, miscues, and, most importantly, mixed messages.

The character Landru, it should be pointed out from the start, has been likened to Chabrol himself by both Robin Wood and Joel Magny. Wood draws parallels between the two men because both present disguised, impersonal natures, but also, like Landru, who resorts to murder to help put food on the table, Chabrol is forced to launch into ever more commercial productions to pay the rent and continue making films.[51] Meanwhile, Magny compares the two men on more general levels: "Chabrol has given Landru a personality very close to his own in terms of cultural and (perversely) logical points of view as well as his pragmatic attitude in regard to society."[52]

The strange combination of criticism and ambivalence in Chabrol's presentation of *Landru*'s characters is quite different from that of his other early films since here there is no longer any trace of spontaneity in either dialogue or character movement. Even the locations, including Luxembourg Gardens, look more like movie sets than real locales, more like the Paris of *Gigi* (Minnelli, 1958) than of *The Cousins* or *Les bonnes femmes*. And everyone in this pastel world is closer to the realm of caricature than ever before in his films, including, perversely enough, the real soldiers dying in the tinted, sped-up World War I newsreels. Landru, like the women who surround him, remains impenetrable in his motives and ridiculous in his behavior. He is a comically stiff character, played by a heavily made-up and restrained Charles Denner, who nonetheless somehow implausibly charms everyone with his poetic quotations, good-humored logic, and romance during an era of war and loss.

The narrative is quite simple: Landru has a wife and four children (each of whom is given a number in his famous ledger so he can keep track

of how much money they receive and when). He deals, rather unscrupu-
lously, in antiques and used furnishings. He does not earn as much as he
would like, however, so he takes out ads in the papers to meet and marry
women. He wins each woman over and then sweeps her off to his rented
villa in Gambais (frugally buying one roundtrip and a single one-way train
ticket each time) where he gets the woman to sign over her possessions,
murders her, and burns her body in the stove. Strangely, Landru never
seems to consider he might be detected in his exploits—he leaves an obvious, predictable trail everywhere he goes, to the point that there is no
suspense about whether he will some day be tracked down. Such naive
abandon is seen over and over in Chabrol's villains throughout his career.

The one major variation to this profitable murder routine is that he
eventually meets Fernande (Stéphane Audran) on the return train, and she
becomes his mistress. Landru must then redouble his killing to pay for his
two households. At one point, however, just as he is stoking up the stove
for another potential victim, he is interrupted by neighbors barging in to
tell him the war is over. With the war's end, his killing, reluctantly, stops
as well: there are now too many men around for women to need him so
much. One day, however, the sister of one of his victims recognizes him,
and the police, led by the ridiculous Inspector Belin, capture him easily.
A long trial follows (which suits President Clemenceau, since it distracts
public opinion away from criticizing national affairs). Finally, an unre-
pentant Landru, protesting his innocence, is guillotined offscreen, but the
audience only hears the "smoosh" of the blade and sees Belin's grimace.
The camera tracks in on a tight shot of the gray prison wall's rough surface:
the end.

From the start, *Landru* plays with several structures that shape the audience's uncertainty about what one is to think of Landru and his exploits.
It opens with a dolly-in on the Landru family seated formally at dinner as
he complains about eating ground meat again. Significantly, the camera
dollies in behind Landru, until it sits just behind his neck, exaggerating
his bald head and certainly prefiguring his death by guillotine with the
camerawork and framing. In addition, this opening jokingly foreshadows
his murderous exploits since it is ground meat rather than something such
as potato soup that he tires of, and he will "cook" his victims in the kitchen
stove at Gambais. The film assumes the moviegoer will be familiar with the
exploits and death of Landru ("the French Bluebeard"), so it profits from
that historical background from the start. In the opening scene, Chabrol
simply makes the famous murderer appear ridiculous, bourgeois, but also

pragmatic rather than gruesome: Landru complains that eating ground meat during wartime is not only tiresome but unpleasant, especially because during an era of food shortages, one can never be sure precisely what is in it.

Herein lies the comic ambiguity of Chabrol's Landru: he is rudely bourgeois (the war is upsetting his menu), and he coldly blames his wife for the disappointing meal while the cook/maid, Mirielle, is crying in the background, not because of his complaints, but because her husband is among those feared dead at Verdun. The connections between eating and death, between the war and Landru's bourgeois routine, are glaringly obvious but also a bit comical—while other men die in the trenches, Landru is unwilling to accept his minor sacrifice of eating ground meat. This "motive" of avoiding cheap meat seems to set off the murder spree, further parodying the average bio-pic of a notorious killer. Rather than reveling in the violence or trying to explain away Landru's murderous misogynist impulses, Sagan and Chabrol create a dapper, businesslike villain whose fuse is lit by eating too much meatloaf! Next, there is a fade to newsreel footage of World War I soldiers, explosions, and images of destroyed cities, all with a yellow green tint and accompanying march music.

Yet this violence is followed by the title sequence, which includes romantic music, with titles written in flowing cursive style and superimposed over an idyllic pond, complete with the sounds of frogs croaking, a fly buzzing, and opera music. The title sequence, like its settings, looks more fitting for a Minnelli musical than for a tale of France's Jack the Ripper. Food, Landru's bourgeois tastes, the war, and a calm romantic setting reinforced with opera music form the opening mixture of contradictory cues and comically significant foreshadowing of narrative events to come. If any intrinsic norms are firmly established from the beginning, they include a plot built from comically juxtaposed images and sounds to create an unsettling narrative parody of several genres.

The entire film develops around pertinent narrative ellipses: the audience never sees Landru engaged in the most questionable or horrible aspects of his life. In keeping with art cinema conventions rather than classical ones, Chabrol obfuscates the very reason for Landru's fame. Yet *Landru* is simultaneously structured by the killer's repetitive back-and-forth patterns of performing some action to obtain money, returning to pay the family, then exiting to perform another "job." As the film advances, these routines will even come to include spending quality time, not with his children, but with his mistress, Fernande, as his crimes begin to produce additional physical rewards beyond eating better meat. Other crucial repetitions the viewer is allowed to witness, beyond the domestic scenes, include his visits to the opera (where he takes some victims and Fernande but never his family).

Chabrol's Landru becomes a complex caricature partly because of gaps and diverse repetitions: he is an unlikely dandy and an even more unlikely murderer; he recites Baudelaire seductively to his victims in his silly voice but then chops them up and burns their bodies, though the audience sees only the smoke pouring from the chimney and never witnesses the crimes. While the strange Landru follows patterns, the narrator also creates discursive patterns that allow diverse counterpoints to the story's actions. For example, the narration will cut to war footage or guide the audience's attention to specific headlines in the paper; it readily cuts to police headquarters, Clemenceau's office, or even the neighbor's house in Gambais, yielding varying effects and providing story information not restricted to Landru's knowledge. The narrative structure, therefore, has two avenues for communicating about the story and society represented in *Landru:* the audience sees one side by following Landru, but it receives myriad dialogical effects as the plot cuts to people, places, and things outside of Landru's realm but which comment on him via their syntagmatic placement.

Landru's routine of meeting, seducing, and disposing of the women is certainly the core of the dark, Hitchcock-inspired humor and troubling ambivalence that distinguish *Landru* and unsettle many of its critics. The comical way this silly businessman locates his victims further reduces any ability to build sympathy for the poor women. After Landru has collected his responses to his newspaper notice, he sits in Luxembourg Gardens, shown in a high angle shot, selecting love letters while a policeman paces in the background and a little boy circles him on a tricycle. He thus begins as a comically unmenacing character. As the audience "hears" the letter he reads via a woman's voice-over the camera cranes up, there is a dissolve to the band playing, and then a crane down on the rose held by the beautiful Celestine Buisson (Michèle Morgan), sitting in front of the bandstand at Luxembourg Gardens. Not only does the crane add continuity and provide the body to the voice, but the band's music (like the church bell in *Le beau Serge*) also covers the temporal shift. Landru approaches her, introduces himself, and they go for a walk. Rather than the beautiful blonde appearing disappointed in this short, bald little man, she surprisingly appears quite taken by the diminutive Landru.

After Landru impresses her with his charm, loneliness, and talk of his fictive factories, there is a dissolve in on another flower, which turns out to be in the hands of a second "date," seated at the same bandstand in Luxembourg Gardens. Landru approaches, introduces himself under another false name, leads her on a romantic promenade where he is charming yet timid, and speaks of his factories. Cut to *another* flower in another woman's hands, with the same band music playing; Landru approaches (while several older women recognize him and comment on the fact that his success must be attributable to the absence of men in Paris these days). Landru and Berthe Heon (Danièlle Darieux) walk, and he speaks of taking her with him to Brazil, where his important work awaits. She becomes the first murder victim at Gambais, establishing his pattern of repeatedly securing the women's trust, taking them to Gambais, and seducing and murdering them. In Gambais, there is generally a close-up of the woman's ecstatic and adoring face, then the image freezes; next there is nondiegetic opera music, and a cut outside to smoke billowing out of the chimney.

The gravity of Landru's murder is undercut by the final vision of the women smiling, and the audience's disgust is also dispersed by the macabre jokes involved. First, instead of the freeze frame serving as a substitute for (censored) sexual activity, Chabrol uses it to replace here (censored) murder and dismemberment. Second, Landru has an elderly, upper-class British couple living next door who complain about the stench: "Don't you notice that awful smell?" the man asks his wife. "Between the war and this abominable odor . . . " she replies. Landru had to endure *boeuf haché* because of the war; for them it brings an awful smell. This exchange is followed by a fade and the rapid sequence of smoke still coming out of the chimney at night, Landru working noisily to push something into the stove, and a pan to Berthe's clothes lying on the floor. Landru's pattern of seduction-murder is packed into visits to Gambais (one round-trip, one one-way), the freeze frame on a beautifully happy face, the smoke, and the old British couple closing their windows ("stinks again") to signal the deaths of each victim with, one assumes, a resulting financial gain.

The repetition becomes so efficient that the victims start vanishing faster at certain points when Landru needs money, which minimizes further any real empathy and allows greater humor at the women's expense. The deaths become so routine that at one point he kills four older women in a forty-five-second montage that begins with a tracking shot that zips past a woman, victim number ten, standing in Luxembourg Gardens and ends with victim number thirteen (and her dog) watching Landru stoke up his stove. The montage includes shots of train cars, the kitchen stove at Gambais, and the fuming smokestack. Ironically, Landru's killing spree ends with the war. At this point, he is living a stable bourgeois existence, supporting his wife and children while he lives with his loving Fernande in a tasteful apartment, which echoes the living quarters Kane provided Susan Alexander, complete with piano teacher.[53] Interestingly, once Landru moves in with Fernande, the women he kills become less consistently young and beautiful and more old and ridiculous. He now apparently only needs their money, where before he required sex as well from his victims.

Once the war ends, the alternation newsreels/Landru changes to police (Clemenceau)/Landru. The audience's range of information allows it to learn not only that Inspector Belin is concentrating on finding the man described by a number of the relatives of Landru's victims, but that Clemenceau needs some cause to distract the populace. A government trap is indeed being set. But the narration undercuts rather than builds suspense by mocking the police as latter-day Keystone Kops (Belin, after receiving the final tip in a phone call, misses replacing the phone on the receiver; his matching crowd of bowler-hatted cops file out the door like a chorus line, but then Belin opens the wrong door and runs literally into a brick wall). There is no sympathy for "justice" since those in power, Belin, Clemenceau, and the judges, are shown to be silly and stupid by comparison to the cultured, sensitive, and rigorous Landru.

Even the long trial continues Chabrol's mocking distance by providing no clues to clarify how one is to feel toward anyone, save Fernande, the only person who seems to suffer with Landru. Fernande is isolated from the other witnesses in the waiting room, as a corner splits the wide-screen image in two, with her in front of a white wall in her half of the frame, while everyone else is crammed into the other half, with a blue wall. So it is only at the trial that the audience feels truly sorry for anyone in this film, and it is the faithful, loving mistress, not the victims' relatives, or Landru's obnoxious, complaining family, who receives the viewer's sympathy. During it all, Landru cleverly entertains the court with his wit and intelligence as he logically demands evidence, but unknowingly he is serving Clemenceau's plans by distracting the newspapers for what seems to be all of three years. There are repeated shots to front pages featuring Landru's exploits in banner headlines while stuck off in a corner is mention of the government's dealings. But finally Landru dies without even telling his defense attorney whether he really killed the ten women and one boy he is accused of murdering. Strangely, the audience has seen thirteen women (and one dog) die at Gambais, but no boys, which further complicates the whole project of defining the parameters of Landru's crimes.

This narrative is structured around oppositions of Landru to others (family, various women, Belin, Clemenceau, and judges) on every level, from gesture to dress to dialogue. Nonetheless, while the film does not look or sound like more typical New Wave Chabrol films such as *Le beau Serge* or *The Cousins,* it does continue his auteurist tendency of presenting a troubling perspective on the action via the highly ironic and cynical primary narrator. The ambivalence toward Landru, his victims, and finally his society (where everyone seems to be conniving for something) resembles the point of view on François and Serge and Marie in *Le beau Serge.* Moreover, an additional authorial touch is the constant reference to other filmic traditions.

In *Landru,* rather than calling on and undermining neorealist and romantic conventions, Chabrol plays with silent-film conventions. Here, not only do characters seem to have learned to act in the silent era (especially Landru and Belin), but the film stock, with its sped up and tinted silent newsreel footage, also recalls and parodies how the 1910s were represented at the time and how they look today. Furthermore, other sections and characters seem to have fallen out of a 1940s musical (especially the overly backlit Celestine Buisson and the stuffy Mme. Landru) while others (Andrée and Fernande) are freewheeling, modern "New Wave" characters right out of *Les bonnes femmes.* Thus, just as the soundtrack, editing, and acting were often overly coded in *Le beau Serge* to call attention to the production process and the puzzling, cynical, and ambiguous narrative voice, here, too, Chabrol narrates with a mixture of cues, none of which finally settle key questions regarding conclusive interpretations of characters, motives, or even themes.

Chabrol is a cynical joker in real life, and that quality continues, playfully, in his films. While critics try to decipher exactly how these films attack or reinforce bourgeois norms, they might be better off admitting that, as Tom Milne warns, Chabrol is not to be taken too seriously. Rather, one must reactivate analysis of each Chabrol film in order to test the ambivalence of a primary narrator who presents an entire film that seems to mock every character while destroying any ability to sympathize with their suffering. When one privileged character does seem to rise above the unflattering stereotypes that surround him or her (Yvette in *Le beau Serge,* Charles in *The Cousins,* Jacqueline in *Les bonnes femmes,* Leda in *A double tour,* Fernande in *Landru*), that character is either punished or lost by the end of the film, and any central lessons are thrown back into doubt. Nothing is solid, lasting, or even particularly respectable in these worlds. Guy Austin even writes that while Chabrol is said to write "psychological thrillers," that label is not quite appropriate since the films offer few concrete psychological motivations ultimately for the characters' actions, and Chabrol likes to quip that one of his greatest pleasures is "to reveal opacity."[54]

More interesting, however, are the stylistic markers of Chabrol's mixed generic cues, overcoded textual strategies, and flamboyant camera movements. His stylistic flourishes, rather than being random interruptions, as some reviewers charge, are typically tied to diverse intertextual narrative traditions. Chabrol's style, if it can be summarized in relation to New Wave tendencies, is not only self-conscious but springs from past film traditions as he mixes genres, authorial and intertextual reference, and competing production periods to create a new mixture for film language. And that is certainly one central aesthetic trait for defining a New Wave film.

Le beau Serge and *Landru* mark the beginning and the ending of Chabrol's contributions to the New Wave proper. *Landru*, admittedly, is more interesting as an example of Chabrol's auteurist tendencies than as an exemplar of the New Wave. Chabrol's New Wave, which started off in such dramatically promising fashion and may actually have reached its aesthetic zenith with *L'oeil du malin* and *Les bonnes femmes*, was no longer paying all his bills by 1962. Chabrol had lost most of his capital as a result of the divorce, and, a bit like Landru, he was living in an apartment with Audran rather than in his suburban home with his young family. Guy Austin considers the early and mid-1960s to be Chabrol's wilderness years: "He was rejected by *Cahiers du Cinéma* and generally held to be the disgrace of the New Wave."[55] Beyond the critical fall, the change in his financial position shows how important self-financing had been to his career; in the future, films by many of the *Cahiers* directors would be financed by companies chaired by Barbet Schroeder and François Truffaut, who learned a great deal from Chabrol and his AJYM. Nonetheless, these were tough times for Chabrol, who, like Truffaut, never wanted simply to make films for himself and a small group; he wanted to remake the French cinema. His first eight films helped make a New Wave, but film enthusiasts had to wait five years, until *Les biches* and *La femme infidèle* (both 1968), for Chabrol to help truly remake the commercial French cinema.

5

François Truffaut:
The New Wave's Ringleader

We have to film other things, in another spirit. We've got to get out of the
over-expensive studios. . . . Sunshine costs less than Klieg lights and
generators. We should do our shooting in the streets and even in real
apartments. Instead of, like Clouzot, spreading artificial dirt over the sets.
—FRANÇOIS TRUFFAUT, *Truffaut by Truffaut*

T H E   T W O most universally recognized, iconic images of the New Wave
would have to be Jean-Pierre Léaud's face in a freeze frame at the close of
The 400 Blows and Jean-Paul Belmondo sauntering along the Champs
Élyseés with Jean Seberg in *Breathless.* Not only were Truffaut and Godard
among the initial core of the *Cahiers* critics-turned-directors, they have
become the New Wave's most dominant figures historically. Strangely,
however, even though they began their careers so closely allied, their films
have the least in common of any two New Wave–era directors. The names
Truffaut and Godard, taken together, denote for many cinema students today the essence of the New Wave while also suggesting its broad spectrum
of stories and styles. Thus, like the fictional friends in Truffaut's *Jules and
Jim* (1961), who look nothing alike, do not share a common nationality, and
even compete with one another on several levels, Truffaut and Godard
function today as a strange team who share a great deal historically but
very little in terms of their personal lives or individual styles.

Since both Truffaut and Godard had worked side by side at *Cahiers
du cinéma,* along with André Bazin, Jacques Doniol-Valcroze, Claude
Chabrol, and Eric Rohmer, among others, their beginnings in filmmaking
are closely intertwined and tightly connected with the spirit of auteurism
they had championed. Both these young Turks wanted to storm French cinema's production world as they had done its critical world, proving that they,
too, could display personal stories and styles that fit within their own calls
for a "cinema in first person" in opposition to the cold and calculating

"tradition of quality." Yet, these two highly motivated individualists soon took off in very different directions: "Truffaut and Godard usefully define the poles of the New Wave. One proved that the young cinema could rejuvenate mainstream filmmaking; the other that the new generation could be hostile to the comfort and pleasure of ordinary cinema."[1] Film historians have repeatedly reaffirmed the vital roles of both directors, and their criticism and production have become central to trends in film studies. Many of their movies are deeply embedded in canonical definitions of the New Wave as well as of the modern European cinema so that these two young cinephiles of the early 1950s eventually eclipsed many of their own favorite auteurs in stature and significance. As this chapter and the next demonstrate, these two former friends distinguished themselves quickly. Their modes of production owed much to their predecessors, while their stories and styles brought them more attention than any of their colleagues, as their combined output helped redefine French cinema of the New Wave and beyond. But of the two, it was Truffaut who struck the first blow against the mainstream French cinema critically and again Truffaut who managed to shoot *The 400 Blows* and win acclaim before helping Godard get *Breathless* off the ground. The two would learn from and compete with each other for years to come.

Truffaut, "Le Miston"

The boom in scholarly, critical, and popular press publications on the New Wave during the past forty years has given incredible amounts of attention to the public and private life of François Truffaut. Right from the start, publicity surrounding Truffaut's first short film, *Les mistons* (*The Brats*, 1957) and first feature, *The 400 Blows* (1959), concentrated on the connection between his own childhood and his movies. In addition, Truffaut's interviews and articles usually stressed the parallels between his artistic output and his personal insight, further fueling a fascination with Truffaut the individual and making his private life highly pertinent to the critical understanding of his films. After Truffaut's death from cancer in 1984, there was renewed interest in summing up his career but also in plumbing the details of his amazing life. More than any other recent French director, Truffaut's private life is somehow felt to be essential background material for appreciating and interpreting his films. Only Jean Renoir and Alfred Hitchcock have received the same degree of detailed biographical research, often bordering on blatant hero worship, that Truffaut has garnered. A surprising number of books have been devoted to his oeuvre and his early critical writings, including the nearly six-hundred-page *Correspondence: 1945–1984,* a collection of letters he wrote. In addition, Anne Gillain's *Le cinéma selon François Truffaut* synthesizes three hundred different interviews and edits and reorders the questions and answers into chronological order. Most recently, *Cahiers du cinéma* critics Antoine de Baecque and Serge Toubiana published what will certainly prove to be the definitive, if not final, biography, the 660-page *François Truffaut.*[2] This vast body of literature offers testimony to the depth of adoration felt for Truffaut but also demonstrates the faith people have in the ability of his life to explain his films. There is no such corresponding fascination with the life and times of Claude Chabrol, Eric Rohmer, Jean-Luc Godard, or even André Bazin. Truffaut has come to personify the complex New Wave auteur par excellence.

Admittedly, some major events in Truffaut's personal life can be directly relevant to understanding his role in cinema history. As a young cinephile, Truffaut attended and even organized *ciné-clubs,* where he met André Bazin, Jean Cocteau, Alexandre Astruc, and Eric Rohmer, among others. As a rebellious son from an unhappy family setting, Truffaut escaped into the world of film criticism, where he learned early on the power inherent in his own brand of fanaticism when it was backed up with concrete evidence from his encyclopedic knowledge of international cinema. Truffaut capitalized on confounding his own autobiography with the cinema, encouraging critics reviewing his movies to see him as a truly obsessive child of the cinema, since his own real-world family was so dysfunctional. For instance, he liked to quip that André and Janine Bazin were his true parents and that the only real education he ever received was from the movies: "When I say I never had any schooling, well, I did have. . . . Everything I know I learned through the cinema, out of films . . . at the Cinémathèque!"[3] Moreover, it was André Bazin who, like a surrogate father as well as a good mentor, introduced the young Truffaut to important figures in French cinema, helped Truffaut with his legal problems when he went AWOL from the military, let Truffaut stay in Bazin's home, and vouched for him in his first jobs.

Throughout his career, Truffaut encouraged everyone to see him through this mythical version of his life, in which he was a foster child raised by the great figures in post–World War II cinema, with Bazin, Roberto Rossellini, and Jean Cocteau as his protective father or uncle figures and Henri Langlois's Cinémathèque as his boarding school. He said of

Rossellini, for whom he worked as an assistant reading scripts in the early 1950s, "I learned a lot from him; he took over from Bazin a little, [helping] the transition between the phase of criticism and the phase of creation."[4] French historian Jean-Michel Frodon refers to most of Truffaut's early experiences in the cinema as substitutions for a lack of home life, with *ciné-clubs* and even meetings at *Cahiers* replacing family get-togethers: "Truffaut found his true family in the cinema."[5] Later, as he became successful in the mid-1960s, he even justified his expensive home near Trocadero by claiming he moved to the wealthy neighborhood so he could walk easily to the screenings at the Cinémathèque at the Palais de Chaillot. It thus proves quite fitting that Truffaut, who presents himself as a child of the cinema, creates one of the few great fictional children of the cinema, Antoine Doinel, and then plots out the major events of Antoine's life over the course of twenty years, in four features and one short. Antoine's plot lines mirrored much in Truffaut's own life, and strangely, as actor Jean-Pierre Léaud matured, he even took on an almost haunting physical resemblance to his director. Truffaut always encouraged this blurring of the lines between his real world and his cinematic world, and their interrelations become a motif in both his films and his own historical reception.

For auteurists seeking a rich text to represent the truest kernel of his oeuvre, *Les mistons* should be their starting point, not simply because it is the first extant short film by the young Truffaut but also because it contains so many of the story and style points one will come to expect of his very best films. While Truffaut had already experimented with directing a short film in 1954, that movie, *A Visit,* was left incomplete, though Alain Resnais subsequently tried to reedit it. Truffaut dismissed it as an embarrassment, and apparently no definitive print exists today. Nonetheless, it was a blueprint for the subsequent New Wave since it was filmed in Jacques Doniol-Valcroze's apartment, featured his young daughter, and used Jacques Rivette as camera operator. It was an inexpensive, 16 mm project made by a crew of friends. The second short, *Les mistons,* was filmed during an era of great changes and productive output in Truffaut's life. During the mid-1950s, he was writing more and more film reviews and critical articles at both *Cahiers du cinéma* and *Arts.* At *Cahiers,* Truffaut and Rivette even introduced the practice of publishing leisurely interviews with directors when, in 1954, they tape recorded a long conversation with Jacques Becker so as better "to become intimately acquainted with a filmmaker by inviting the auteur to talk freely about himself."[6] The Grundig portable magnetic tape recorder made a new sort of film scholarship possible, just

as lightweight sound equipment such as the Nagra was about to revolu-
tionize film production as well. Most of the motion picture reviews in *Arts*
had been published anonymously, but gradually Truffaut began to demand
more recognition for his columns; by 1957 the editorial board agreed to his
demands, including a byline for all reviews. They also agreed to his suggestion that they institute a policy of rating movies with a system of stars
printed with each review to denote the films' relative quality. His additions
moved film criticism closer to a professionalism that subsequently became
the norm throughout the world.

The two historical factors that were most instrumental in his shift into
production with *Les mistons* were Jacques Rivette's encouragement and
Madeleine Morgenstern Truffaut's father's business. Truffaut credits
Rivette, who had just made his own highly influential short, *Le coup du
berger* in 1956, for inspiration: "It was Rivette who told us all we had to
make movies. . . . [*Le coup de berger*] was exemplary as much for the way
it was made as for its production style and ambitions. It was produced by
Chabrol, shot in Chabrol's apartment in only two weeks by Rivette on a
borrowed camera with just enough money to cover the film stock, and featured friends such as Jean-Claude Brialy and Doniol-Valcroze as actors."[7]
It is quite clear that by the mid-1950s, there were already many models in
France for shooting cheap alternatives to mainstream commercial cinema,
from Melville, Astruc, and Varda, to Truffaut's own *A Visit*, which precedes
Rivette's *Le coup de berger*. But Rivette's personality, friendship, and success motivated Truffaut in ways the other filmmakers had not.

The second big factor, however, was the financial and production help
Truffaut received from his then future father-in-law, Ignace Morgenstern.
While Truffaut's childhood buddy Robert Lachenay had inherited a small
amount of money in 1957 and wanted to help Truffaut make a short film,
it was Madeleine's father who really made the production possible.
Morgenstern owned a small production company, SEDIF, and the large
distribution company Cocinor Films, which distributed major European
films. Morgenstern asked his director at Cocinor, Marcel Berbert, to make
sure the young Truffaut managed to find the financing to shoot *Les mistons*.
While some accounts of Truffaut's career suggest there was a sort of duel
between the young rogue critic and the older distributor of mainstream
fiction, no evidence suggests that Morgenstern loaned Truffaut money as
a dare or so Truffaut could embarrass himself.[8] Rather, Berbert and
Morgenstern secretly guaranteed loans and lab fees to help Madeleine's
ambitious young boyfriend move from criticism to production. With a four-

thousand-dollar initial loan Truffaut formed his own tiny company, named
Les Films du Carrosse as a tribute to Jean Renoir's *Carrosse d'or* (*The
Golden Coach,* 1952). Between completion of filming in September 1957
and the November premiere, Truffaut married Madeleine Morgenstern,
with André Bazin and Roberto Rossellini as their witnesses. Soon after,
Les mistons proved a triumph, winning the best director prize for short films
at the Brussels Festival of World Cinema in early 1958. Thus, 1957 was
the pivotal year for Truffaut as his private and professional lives both advanced in synchronization, and he moved into a nice apartment, offered by
Madeleine's father, near the Arc de Triomphe. The angry, perceptive young
film critic was rapidly becoming a minor celebrity in Paris film circles for
his many articles, but he was simultaneously setting the stage for his subsequent career in production.

Les mistons was not an original story by Truffaut; in keeping with his critical notions of authorship, he selected an existing short story to adapt himself
for the screen, as he tried to avoid the pitfalls he had cited in other recent
French adaptations. Truffaut had met the young Maurice Pons, who had recently published a collection of short stories concerning youth, titled *Vir-
ginales.* Truffaut read and reread the book, initially planning to shoot a collection of five of the stories: "If I began with 'Les mistons' it was simply
because it was the most economical. It needed little money, there were no interior scenes—all I needed was a little film stock."[9] As Michel Marie notes,
the writers at *Cahiers du cinéma,* like most New Wave critics and directors,
never denounced literary adaptation per se; they just attacked adaptations
that tried to substitute visual "equivalences" for literary devices or aspects
considered "anti-cinematic." Here again, Jean-Pierre Melville and Alexandre Astruc had already pointed the way: "Truffaut remained faithful to the
same strategy . . . throughout the length of this radiant short, the external narrator's voice comments on the brats' escapades in an elegant yet literary manner, since it is the same text written by the novelist. *Les mistons*'s richness
resides precisely in the relation established between this nostalgic text,
enunciated after the fact, and the various bits shown in the image or heard as
shreds of spontaneous dialogue spoken in the region's own accent."[10]

But Truffaut had also recently made the acquaintance of two young actors, Gerard Blain and his stunning, nineteen-year old wife, Bernadette Lafont. Blain had so impressed Truffaut in a small role alongside Jean Gabin in
Julien Duvivier's *Voici le temps des assassins* (*Deadlier than the Male,* 1956)
that when Blain read the flattering review in *Arts,* he immediately wrote to
Truffaut asking for a meeting. At dinner, Truffaut met Lafont; even though she

had never acted, he offered the couple the lead roles for *Les mistons,* which they then decided to shoot in Lafont's hometown, Nîmes, in southern France. What began as a fun group project, however, would end with a great deal of tension between Blain and Truffaut, with the former quite jealous of all the attention the flirtatious young director lavished on Bernadette Lafont.

Les mistons is a twenty-minute film, told after the fact in voice-over, of a young couple, Gerard and Bernadette, hounded by a pack of bored and mischievous young boys during their summer vacation. Bernadette is the object of desire for the boys, who torment her since they are not yet old enough to understand their mixture of love and hate for her. Gerard is a slightly older gym teacher; as he courts Bernadette, and they play tennis, walk in the woods, or ride bicycles through the streets, the boys spy on them and disrupt their embraces whenever possible. Eventually, Gerard goes away for a three-month mountain-climbing expedition but promises, by humming the wedding march, to marry Bernadette on his return. However, a newspaper insert and the voice-over inform the audience that Gerard dies in a climbing accident. Bernadette, in mourning, now walks the streets alone. The voice-over is that of a middle-aged man (Michel François) recalling his experiences as one of the boys who followed Bernadette during this important summer of his youth, but it is never clear from the image which of the boys represents the narrator. They are a group that plays, badgers, and learns a bit about love and loss, nothing more.

Michel Marie notes that Blain and Lafont were significant members of the new generation of actors who brought a striking new range of acting styles to French cinema. While Blain would go on to star in Chabrol's *Le beau Serge* and *The Cousins,* Lafont became "the first feminine model of the New Wave," acting in Doniol-Valcroze's *L'eau à la bouche (A Game for Six Lovers,* 1959), *Le beau Serge,* and *Les bonnes femmes,* among others: "This young actress was the closest to a Renoir-inspired character that the New Wave would have. . . . In the late 1950s, Bernadette Lafont brought with her a more modern image of the young southern French woman who is comfortable with her full figure as well as natural, spontaneous, and popular rather than elitist."[11] Truffaut also preferred Lafont's acting style to Blain's; writing to Charles Bitsch during filming, Truffaut claimed the two were complete opposites: "She's better on the first take without any rehearsal, she's stimulated by the indications I give her once the camera is running, etc. Gérard's taste runs more to chalk marks on the ground."[12] Auteurist studies of Truffaut are quick to point out that Lafont (who returned later in *Such a Gorgeous Kid Like Me,* 1972) is the first in a long line of beautiful and inaccessible women who populate Truffaut's fictional worlds.[13] The very loose, anecdotal script, in which dialogue is minimal, was propelled forward by the relaxed performances of Blain and Lafont, who often communicate simply by waving and calling "Ay-o" from a distance or grinning and kissing rather than chatting. In part, the lack of detailed, diegetic dialogue is motivated by the past-tense narration; a child would not pay as much attention to the couple's verbal exchanges as to the way Bernadette's skirt flew up as she pedaled her bicycle, nor could a man recall accurately words overheard years ago. But Truffaut also recut the film several years after its initial release, reducing the dialogue further and shortening its running time by nearly five minutes. Regardless, Truffaut's direction allowed for a strikingly low-key acting style that, in contrast to Vadim's or Astruc's movies, does not look outdated forty years later.

Les mistons was filmed by a local camera operator, Jean Malige, in 35 mm, shot wild, with no synchronized sound and only three sun reflectors for help with lighting in the natural settings. As in most neorealist productions, all sound, whether diegetic or not, was added later. While the film has a very rapid pace by New Wave standards, with an ASL of 7.6 seconds, it nonetheless contains some wonderfully long takes that exploit the camera's mobility and the deep focus possible with outdoor shooting. In fact, *Les mistons* begins the New Wave trend of including overt intertextual references, or homages, to earlier film practice; Truffaut's most obvious examples are to Lumière and Rossellini, and he often combines these references with stunning shot compositions. For instance, while the film's story structure follows closely Pons's narration in the past tense, a number of scenes inserted in the film did not exist in the original tale. One day, for instance, before the audience learns that the boys go regularly to watch the couple play tennis, there is a recreation of Lumière's famous *L'arroseur arrosée (The Waterer Watered,* 1895), in which a young boy steps on the older gardener's hose, the gardener looks at the end of the hose, and then the boy lifts his foot, spraying the gardener. Truffaut's version, however, unlike Lumière's, is edited into eight shots, but ends with the gardener in the background spraying the boy in revenge while Bernadette, in her short tennis outfit, walks into the foreground, looking on in amusement. This sequence provides a loving tribute to Lumière, and by the final shot provides a pastiche of Lumière's own shot composition, with several planes of action in a single take, unifying two actions. Another reference to Lumière can be seen when Gerard leaves on the train, and the camera position on the quay recreates the diagonal angle from Lumière's *Arrival of a Train.*

Figure 5.1. Gardener and water (*Les mistons*)

Figure 5.2. Bernadette looks on (*Les mistons*)

Figure 5.3. Train leaving (*Les mistons*)

Similarly, a Rossellini-influenced shot occurs when the boys are seated on the ground behind a fence watching Bernadette play tennis with Gerard. The camera dollies slowly across the faces of the boys behind the chain-link fence as they pass a cigarette and look longingly toward the camera, ostensibly at Bernadette's short skirt and legs. This shot recalls the shot composition of the boys in *Rome Open City* (1946) when they witness the horrifying scene of the priest executed in a field. There, too, the young boys are shown in medium shot, resembling older men.

Further, Truffaut's narrative space is typically constructed to yield both depth and several actions, often with the boys occupying one edge of the frame. Usually in *Les mistons* the characters are framed in several planes of action or move in arcs, beginning, for instance, with a long shot of a rider on a bicycle, then the rider turns a corner as the camera pans, and the rider approaches the camera position, dismounting the bike in a medium close-up. Truffaut and Malige block the action repeatedly in longer takes for transitions into and out of scenes, and these shots often recall the shot sequences and intricate figure-to-camera interplay of Truffaut's favorite directors. In addition, Truffaut often composes from lower camera positions both to mimic the boys' short vantage point and to allow the frame to reveal two different planes of action in the top and bottom

Figure 5.4. Boys behind the fence (*Les mistons*)

Figure 5.5. Bernadette's skirt (*Les mistons*)

of the frame, as in the scene when the boys spy on Gerard meeting Bernadette at her home.

Truffaut also allows self-conscious references to the filmmaking process when the characters all go to a movie theater, and the film they watch,
Le coup du berger, has a scene of Jean-Claude Brialy kissing a young
woman; Gerard immediately turns to kiss Bernadette. *Les mistons* repeatedly reminds the viewer it is made by a young man who loves movies and
is not afraid to call attention to his world of *cinéphilia*.

Truffaut also experiments with style in *Les mistons*. He is not afraid to
create discontinuity at significant story moments, such as two of the more
eroticized events. First, when Gerard approaches Bernadette atop the
steps of the stadium and kisses her, in medium close-up he is frame-right,
but in the subsequent close-up shot he is screen-left; the breaking of
screen direction is further reinforced by the shift from a high angle to an
eye-level shot.

Later, screen direction is again disrupted when a boy runs out to return
a tennis ball that Bernadette had lost over the fence. Initially, he runs out
from the right side, but in the cut to a medium-close-up, he is suddenly
facing screen-right, with the other boys in the background grimacing and
a bit jealous that he is the one so close to the lovely, perspiring Bernadette.

Figure 5.6. Boys spy from behind stone wall (*Les mistons*)

Figure 5.7. The kiss (*Les mistons*)

Figure 5.8. The kiss: Changing screen direction (*Les mistons*)

Figure 5.9. Boy runs toward left (*Les mistons*)

Figure 5.10. Screen direction is changed (*Les mistons*)

One other jarring manipulation of the image occurs at the moment when one of the boys leans over to kiss the leather seat of Bernadette's bicycle while she is swimming alone in the river. Truffaut combines this simple act of bowing down and kissing the seat with a dolly in and step printing, causing the camera to move in fits and starts when projected, emphasizing the dreamlike aspect of this moment in the boy's life.

These stylistic traits of shooting minimally on location, employing natural acting rhythms, and alternating long takes with short, self-conscious stylistic flourishes will prove typical throughout Truffaut's career. But there are many other storytelling tactics as well, beyond the use of a beautiful, magical young woman, that are consistently important in his cinema. *Les mistons* switches quickly, even in its brief running time, from one tone to another, in a very casual and, some might say, uneven manner. For instance, just after the boys have frightened Bernadette and Gerard in the stadium, they play a silly game, pretending to be in a gunfight. Not only does the scene recall the exaggerated violence and acting of American gangster films such as *Scarface* (Hawks, 1932), but it also could be a reference to *Top Hat* (Sandrich, 1932), in which the Fred Astaire character elegantly pretends to mow down his rivals, using his cane for a gun. Like the scene of kissing in the movie theater, it also provides

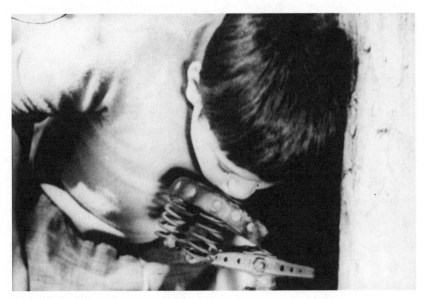

Figure 5.11. The bike kiss (*Les mistons*)

another example of people imitating their favorite film scenes. Moreover, Truffaut foregrounds further the cinematic apparatus when one boy falls but then in reverse action rises back up, recalling the Lumière "trick" film, *Demolition of a Wall* (1895). The next shot, following this noisy scene of the boys screaming and imitating gunshot sounds, dissolves into the gardener with the hose gag, which not only has no connection to the boys in the stadium but is accompanied by a lyrical, nostalgic "silent movie" piano score.

This mix of tones permeates the movie, creating a casual, comic style that defies narrative unity. The overall narrative style, with time devoted simply to following the characters on their bicycles or watching Gerard ask strangers for a light, accumulates into an open, anecdotal story structure. By the end, it seems that the boys have really learned nothing; the events are simply recounted years later as part of one man's somewhat unsettling memory. In fact, the open end of this story anticipates the famous final image of Antoine alone on the beach in *The 400 Blows:* as the narrator explains that one day in autumn, the mourning Bernadette passed the boys by without even seeing them, the camera tracks back in front of her, framing her in a low angle, medium close-up, but then tilts up to the sky, leaving her out of the frame altogether for the end titles. Bernadette has simply lost her interest for the boys now that she wears a long black dress instead of her short white skirts fluttering in the air. The story stops rather than resolving itself, and Bernadette is last seen looking vaguely into the distance, isolated from her world.

One final story trait that will recur in Truffaut's oeuvre is the good-natured way he places children at the center of his narratives. As Annette Insdorf notes, Truffaut's films "constitute a vision of childhood unequaled in the history of the cinema for sensitivity, humor, poignancy, and respect for children themselves. With neither sentimentality nor condescension, Truffaut captures the need for freedom and tenderness, the spontaneity and the frustrations of being a child in a society made by and for adults."[14] The children in *Les mistons,* like those in subsequent Truffaut movies, can simultaneously be intelligent kids and playful brats—here they not only disrupt the movie screening but also rip down a sign for the "tradition of quality" movie *Chiens perdus sans collier* (*Lost Dogs without Collars,* 1958), which, significantly, had been written by Truffaut's enemies Aurenche and Bost but was distributed by his father-in-law's Cocinor. Later in the woods, the boys are irritating when they pester Bernadette and Gerard but more sympathetic when one of them is caught and slapped by

Gerard for the prank. This rich treatment of children and their world begins in *Les mistons* but reaches its first real peak with *The 400 Blows*.

Thus, *Les mistons* clearly demonstrates many of the stylistic and storytelling techniques that will help make Truffaut a highly influential member of the upcoming New Wave and help launch him as one of the most popular French directors of all time. The rough-hewn, casual narrative style of this successful short provides a formative influence on his own subsequent feature films and helps determine the direction for his amazingly resilient career. The *mistons*' games, Bernadette's short skirt, and Gerard's untimely death will all reverberate throughout the best of Truffaut's subsequent films, while appearing here as new options for a new cinema. *Cinéma 59* even cited *Les mistons* along with Malle's *The Lovers* as two films displaying an authenticity that was "one hundred miles beyond the vapid costume dramas that typify our era."[15] And the short film's success boosted Truffaut's confidence, paving the way for his first feature.

The 400 Blows, Antoine Doinel, and Cannes 1959

The 400 Blows is one of the most written about motion pictures in history; the freeze frame of Antoine's face at the end is now as famous as the Odessa steps in *Battleship Potemkin* or the snow globe from *Citizen Kane,* and Antoine's ambivalent look to the camera now symbolizes a whole new sort of film practice.

But *The 400 Blows,* which would go on to win Truffaut the best director prize at Cannes in 1959, was not supposed to be his next project after *Les mistons*. During the spring of 1958, while the short film was garnering

Figure 5.12. Antoine in the final image (*The 400 Blows*)

increased attention on the festival circuit, Truffaut entered into negotiations to direct a film produced by the mainstream Paul Graetz, starring Yves Montand and written in part by Jean Aurenche, the "tradition of quality" scriptwriter Truffaut had so brutally attacked in "A Certain Tendency of the French Cinema." As de Baecque and Toubiana point out, "As an apprentice director Truffaut was prepared to seize any opportunity."[16] As negotiations dragged on for the Aurenche project, however, the anxious Truffaut signed a new contract to serve as assistant director on a Belgian feature. But he broke that contract when Pierre Braunberger offered him instead the opportunity to adapt a novel by Jacques Cousseau, *Days of Heat,* and direct it in southern France. That third project was delayed as well when Bernadette Lafont, the intended star, was injured. These three failed productions illustrate a significant point about New Wave filmmakers: while the mythical version has it that the brash, independent young directors were too proud to attend IDHEC or start their careers conventionally as assistant directors on commercial productions, in reality many, like Truffaut, were quite willing and eager to get a foot in the industry any way they could. If Truffaut never served as an assistant director or collaborated with "tradition of quality" writers such as Jean Aurenche, it was because of chance rather than any pure philosophical determination.

The big break that helped Truffaut avoid these commercial options and instead realize his dream of writing and directing his own first feature came via Ignace Morgenstern. During the spring of 1958, Truffaut's father-in-law was considering buying the rights to a Soviet film, *The Cranes Are Flying* (Kaltozov), and it was apparently Truffaut who finally convinced him to make the deal. Morgenstern's new acquisition went on to win the Palme d'or at Cannes just a few weeks later, guaranteeing a great return on his investment for Cocinor. Morgenstern then agreed to coproduce Truffaut's first feature, which at the time was only an idea for a short film titled "Antoine's Fugue," which Truffaut could now expand into *The 400 Blows.* According to Madeleine Truffaut, "My father respected François and found him intelligent, but he hadn't particularly liked *Les mistons.* So, he produced *The 400 Blows* to help our marriage, to give his daughter's husband the opportunity to prove he could make films."[17] Despite the unexpected windfall from *The Cranes Are Flying,* Morgenstern's SEDIF agreed only to coproduce *The 400 Blows,* whose budget, which is cited as either $50,000 or $75,000, depending on the source, was well below the $250,000 average budget for 1958 features. At the same time,

Morgenstern sold his distribution company Cocinor to Edward Tenoudji, who had recently distributed Chabrol's first two features.

With the financing guaranteed, Truffaut began expanding his short, semiautobiographic script about Antoine Doinel. (He selected the name Doinel in part as a tribute to Renoir's assistant Ginette Doynel and partly as a play on the name of his *Cahiers* friend, Jacques Doniol-Valcroze.) Next he hired screenwriter and novelist Marcel Moussy to help with dialogue and narrative continuity. Moussy had once been a schoolteacher, so while Truffaut and his old friend Robert Lachenay provided many details from their own childhood, Moussy added material from his past experiences with school children and parents. From the start, Truffaut acknowledged his debt to Moussy, which is often overlooked today: "If I had wanted only to put my adolescence into images, I would not have asked Marcel Moussy to come and collaborate on the screenplay. . . . It was not only the television writer I admired in Moussy, but also the novelist of *Sang chaud* [*Warm Blood*], which is the story of a little Algerian boy."[18] Both writers were interested in representing children in a more honest fashion. With a working script finished by August, Truffaut was ready to assemble a crew. A newspaper ad he placed in *France Soir* elicited over two hundred applicants for the children's acting roles, one hundred of whom were asked to appear for 16 mm screen tests. Truffaut also wanted a young, flexible, but professional cinematographer, so he chose Henri Decae, who had already proven his versatility working with Melville, Malle, and Chabrol. As noted earlier, Decae worked well under the unconventional conditions of low-budget productions, using mobile equipment, available light, and shooting few retakes. Truffaut ended up putting Decae's talents to the test, shooting in a small, borrowed apartment, in a real school over Christmas vacation, and even in Morgenstern's SEDIF offices for the stolen typewriter scene. But by 1959 Decae's track record was already impressive enough for him to demand higher wages, and his fee, still a modest three thousand dollars, was the highest single cost for *The 400 Blows*. Truffaut and Moussy received two-thousand-dollar salaries.[19] In addition to hiring Melville's cinematographer, Truffaut engaged Guy Decomble, who portrayed the inspector in *Bob le flambeur*, as the schoolteacher. Friend Philippe de Broca became assistant director. Albert Rémy, who would play the father, was said to have been selected in part because he bore a striking resemblance to Truffaut's father, Roland, which led to bitter accusations afterward that François was seeking to humiliate his parents via this semiautobiographical tale.

After a long, melancholy title sequence, shot from the window of a car driving near Chaillot Palace and the Eiffel Tower, and ending with a dedication to André Bazin, who had died on the first day of filming, *The 400 Blows* begins in a classroom. Twelve-year-old Antoine Doinel (Jean-Pierre Léaud) is caught by the teacher with a postcard of a scantily clad woman being passed around the room. This scene recalls the French postcard used in *Les mistons,* but it also evokes the opening scene of Professor Unrath's classroom in *The Blue Angel* (von Sternberg, 1930). Antoine is forced to stand in the corner while the other children go to recess, but then he is reprimanded for complaining, in writing, on the wall about his being unjustly punished. This opening, beginning with a seemingly lost and wandering camera followed by the claustrophobic space of the classroom, establishes the pattern for the film, as young Antoine moves between an aimless liberty in the streets and an often oppressive world of confinement in small, social spaces.

The overall story line remains restricted to the trials and tribulations of "being" Antoine Doinel. Antoine lives in a small Parisian apartment with his mother (Claire Maurier) and stepfather (Rémy), but whenever possible he spends time with his buddy René (Patrick Auffay). During the course of the film, they skip school, and after one afternoon of movies and carnival rides, they bump into Antoine's mother kissing another man on the street. The next day when Antoine returns to school with no excuse, he lies that his mother died. Once his parents find out, Antoine is slapped by his father in front of the entire class, so he decides never to return home. He spends the evening wandering about, even crossing the paths of walk-on actors Jean-Claude Brialy and Jeanne Moreau, and sleeps alone in an old printing press. Eventually, his mother fetches him home, and the family tries to return to normal. But one final act prevents this from ever happening: Antoine and René steal a typewriter from M. Doinel's company, and when they realize their escapade is ridiculous and try to return it, Antoine gets caught.

Once Antoine becomes involved in such serious trouble, his father takes him directly to the police station. It is decided that he must go to a juvenile detention center, though Mme. Doinel eventually asks whether it can be near the ocean. There, Antoine explains to a psychiatrist that he knows his mother was unmarried when she became pregnant and that she wanted an abortion, but his maternal grandmother made sure he was born and helped raise him. Finally, the unhappy Antoine escapes from the center by darting under a fence one day during a soccer match and running to the ocean shore. Once on the beach, he turns toward the land, and the film ends with a freeze frame of his face; Antoine's journey is unresolved, ending in a sort of tribute to Italian neorealist story ambiguity.[20]

Much has been made about the autobiographical aspects of *The 400 Blows*. Unlike *Les mistons*, which allowed some personal touches but was ultimately based on Pons's short story, *The 400 Blows* includes a great deal of biographical material from Truffaut and Moussy. There are many close connections between Antoine and François in this and subsequent Doinel films. Truffaut's mother, at age nineteen, gave birth to François Roland, "father unknown," on February 6, 1932, and rarely saw him before the age of three. Like Antoine's fictional mother, she had considered an abortion, and her own mother reportedly talked her out of it. Antoine was raised in a foster home, even after his mother married Roland Truffaut late in 1933. That François was initially given the surname Roland implies Roland Truffaut may have been the natural father, but evidence suggests that this was probably not the case, or at least that Roland doubted he was François's true father. At age three, François, who was a sickly child and never ate well, was taken in by his maternal grandmother until she died in 1942. Only at this point, at age ten, did François finally live full-time with the Truffauts. They had another son, René, in 1934, but that baby died at the age of two months, so in order to avoid embarrassment about Antoine's bastard birth, they often used René's birth date for François, who was forced to share the birthday of the dead brother he never met. That Truffaut used "René" for the friend in *The 400 Blows* is significant, adding more ammunition to charges that he was using his first feature for rather cruel revenge against his parents. Further, Mme. Truffaut, like Mme. Doinel, was a secretary. M. and Mme. Truffaut also spent a great deal of time off on excursions with their alpinist club, though in *The 400 Blows* it is an auto club, not mountain climbing, that distracts the father from his family; nonetheless, their real-world hobby may also lend a new perspective on Gerard's mountaineering death in *Les mistons*.

Truffaut's best friend, Robert Lachenay, also lived with parents who were apparently very much like the fictional family created for René in *The 400 Blows*. The two friends often played pranks on Lachenay's parents and stole food and money from them. Their huge, bizarre home was a refuge for François, who often slept over. Another real-life parallel was that once during the occupation, when François had skipped school, he excused himself by telling his teacher that his father had been arrested by the SS, which, according to Truffaut, is the real source for Antoine's lie about his mother dying. When Roland learned of his son's trick, he did, in fact, burst into school to slap François in front of his classmates.

Later, after many schemes such as stealing and pawning a typewriter, losing money to failed *ciné-club* screenings, and other scams that cost Roland dearly, François fell in debt to film distributors, so Roland forcefully took the sixteen-year-old to the police station, leaving Lachenay standing alone watching his buddy being dragged off. "I spent two nights at the police station, like in my movie."[21] Under French law, a father could ask that unruly sons be legally detained for up to six months at a time. François was sent off to an observation center for minors, which he later explained was half jail, half mental institution.[22] It was André Bazin, rather than any escape, that got Truffaut out of the detention center, but François even wrote a heartfelt letter to his father trying to explain his feelings as a bastard child, just as Antoine does in the movie. Thus, much of the backbone of *The 400 Blows* springs from the real-life experiences of François Truffaut filtered through the universe of Antoine Doinel. Nonetheless, there are also anecdotes and dialogue from Moussy and even young Léaud as well as contributions from other actors that help make this a universal and mature tale of childhood rather than just a veiled autobiography. As Truffaut explains, Jean Renoir told him, "This is sad; *The 400 Blows* is really a portrait of France."[23] According to Truffaut, though, his parents felt very insulted by the movie and divorced soon after its release; their marriage ended just as their son became an amazing success.

The story of *The 400 Blows* continues in the loose, anecdotal style of *Les mistons*. Like the earlier short, this feature was initially intended to be a collection of shorter films, with the original script built around Antoine's skipping school and lying about his mother's death and the consequences that resulted. But once the funding was assured for a longer work, it was built, scene by scene, into a chronicle of several months in Antoine's life. The literal "slice of life" scripting, which owes much to Jean Vigo's and Roberto Rossellini's storytelling tactics, sets scene after scene to maintain an accumulation of motifs and events rather than constructing the highly efficient action codes of more classical narrative cinema. For instance, scene nine, in which Mme. Doinel bathes Antoine and promises him a reward if he gets good grades, is followed by scene ten, of the school children jogging down the streets as part of the physical education class. This latter segment pastiches *Zero for Conduct* (Vigo, 1933), but it also shows Antoine and René skipping out on the teacher, proving perhaps that Antoine is not likely to change his attitude toward school, despite his mother's concerns. But the segment does not really advance the plot. This scene could arguably be inserted anywhere in the first three-fourths of the film without disturbing anything.

But then scene eleven reveals Antoine at his desk at school, writing a composition about Balzac; later that evening he lights a candle to Balzac, which nearly burns down the house, but the family goes to a movie anyway (and Rivette's as yet unfinished *Paris nous appartient* is listed on the marquee). Only the next day does the audience discover that rather than earning a good grade on his composition, Antoine has been discovered to have plagiarized Balzac by quoting him from memory. Truffaut's pastiche of Vigo seems to suggest that copying is the best form of appreciation, but in Antoine's school, copying from memory and love is instead interpreted as laziness and deception. Rather than using these scenes to anchor the new attempts at a relationship between Antoine and his mother, they lead to a new problem for Antoine, who now leaves school with René and goes to spend the night on his own. The effect of what amounts to an almost chance ordering of scenes and events decreases any audience expectation for tight cause-effect story construction. Without resolution of the various segments or even clearly defined desires and goals from scene to scene, the narrative structure undercuts any expectation on the part of the audience for complete and total resolution of this open-story film. It is even unclear in these simple scenes whether Antoine is at all worried about his grades when he skips out on gym class, whether he wants to do well on his Balzac assignment to please his mother or simply to earn money, or, indeed, whether he knows he is copying Balzac and that doing so is wrong.

But unlike *Les mistons, The 400 Blows* does, indeed, limit the range of information around a central protagonist, and much of the movie's emotional power is produced by audience identification with Antoine. Since nearly all the scenes revolve around Antoine's presence and perception— the viewer sees his mother on the streets when he does, sees the guard about to nab him with the typewriter just before he does, and so on— this narrative establishes a very engaging structure of sympathy around Antoine. Even though the segments that compose *The 400 Blows* are loosely constructed, they consistently involve a narrative space that revolves around Antoine. Even when the spectator is present for an event when Antoine is absent, as in the scene when the schoolmate Mauricet snitches on Antoine to his parents, the information affects the audience's sympathy for him. Because the story aligns the audience with Antoine's motives, traits, and even perception of the diegetic world, it is relatively easy to understand, appreciate, and feel a degree of allegiance for his character, responding emotionally to his actions and characteristics.[24]

Yet, unlike conventional melodrama, *The 400 Blows* complicates the spectator's understanding of Antoine by providing him with some unsettling traits. For instance, during the famous interview with the psychiatrist (which involved a great deal of spontaneity on the part of Léaud), when viewers learn that Antoine knows he was nearly aborted and was only born thanks to his grandmother, they can feel enough sympathy for him to excuse some of his past mistakes of judgment. Antoine is obviously troubled by the circumstances of his birth and his mother's selfishness. Yet, soon afterward he mentions that he robbed his grandmother occasionally since she was old and did not need much money. Suddenly, the audience is faced with recalibrating their opinion of this thankless little boy who robs the older woman to whom he owes his life. That impression is then further qualified, however, by his admission that his mother in turn stole from him. Mme. Doinel is returned as the object of disgust but only after the plot reveals Antoine's own troubling motivations and emotions. Antoine, like the other characters in the film, becomes impressively complex and alive. The reviewer at *Cinéma 60* was so struck with *The 400 Blows* that he took time to summarize each of the central characters and then reprinted a large section of the dialogue from the psychiatrists' interrogation of Antoine "because it is one of the most amazing scenes in cinema history."[25] It is precisely because Antoine is never reduced to being a simple or weak victim that he is a fascinating and unusual young character. As *Amis du film* wrote in its review, the real novelty of *The 400 Blows* was that Antoine is not a tearful, fearful child but rather a real person and a survivor: "It takes enormous respect, love and intelligence for a director to create such a spontaneous and complex character . . . who is lost and abandoned but knows just how to take care of himself, naturally."[26]

Stylistically, *The 400 Blows* is much more elegant than the informal *Les mistons*. The acting styles are just as natural as in the short film, but the addition of Moussy's dialogue turns the characters into more ambiguous, developed people than those in *Les mistons*. The father may seem a weak, shallow, and finally silly man (a bit like the father in *Rebel without a Cause*, [Ray, 1955]), but he is also credited with marrying Antoine's mother despite her illegitimate son, and he is clearly pained by suspicions that she is regularly deceiving him. Similarly, the mother is presented as shameless, yet her guilt in all things is tempered by her obvious lack of intelligence: she explains that doing well in French class is important because

Figure 5.13. Antoine evaluated by the psychiatrist (*The 400 Blows*)

one always has to write letters. Antoine, who memorizes Balzac, is far beyond both his parents intellectually. The subtle acting style of each major member of the cast ensures the story a naturalism that never slips into parody or stylization. Even the guard at the detention center who asks Antoine which hand he wishes to be struck with is not portrayed as an ogre but rather as an average, pathetic fellow doing his daily task. As James Monaco notes, "What Truffaut loves best about cinema is its ability to capture the poetry of *la vie quotidienne*," and the relaxed, naturalistic, almost nonacting style displayed in *The 400 Blows* helps present that daily life as honestly significant.[27] In contrast to Hollywood's exaggeratedly natural Method style of James Dean or Marlon Brando or the theatricality of Jean Gabin and "tradition of quality" actors, Truffaut's films merged the subtle past traits of Vigo, Renoir, and Rossellini with contemporary gestures from Louis Malle and Claude Chabrol.

Truffaut's visual style also gains a great deal from the practiced hand of Henri Decae, as the fluid camerawork combines a modern mobility with classical depth in many of the location shots. One of the most significant sequences for understanding Truffaut's distinctive plot and mise-en-scène tactics is the series of shots that make up the day when Antoine and René play hooky, ride the rotor, and run across Antoine's mother kissing the other man (played by Truffaut's friend, critic Jean Douchet). This scene displays Truffaut's versatility, with sudden shifts in Jean Constantine's jaunty jazz themes, a mix of camera and editing techniques, and a loose sequencing of shots, often placed end-to-end rather than building classical unity.[28] The scene begins with a thirty-second shot of Antoine, late for school, running out of his front door, only to be hailed in the distance by René, who slows him down, convinces him the teacher will not allow

Antoine to return to class without an excuse, and then leads him off. The camera work begins with a rapid pan of Antoine, then follows the boys, and finally concludes with them wandering off as Antoine says, "So what'll we do now?" The next shot shows the boys in depth walking toward the camera and hiding their book bags. The next five shots comprise a montage of the boys walking, crossing streets, entering a movie theater, and playing pinball, before cutting to the rotor ride sequence.

Throughout this entire scene, Truffaut and Decae maintain a near documentary objectivity, observing the boys in depth, on location, and celebrating their childish freedom. The freedom of the cinema itself is also privileged once Antoine (along with Truffaut) rides the rotor. The music is replaced with spontaneous squeals of pleasure, Antoine struggles to turn upside down, and the camera delivers amazing blurred point-of-view shots from inside the rotor, lending zoetrope-like visuals that allow the audience to marvel at the beauty and power of the wide-screen black-and-white image.

In the wandering montage the camera tilts up to frame the word "Cine"; with the rotor ride, Truffaut really is offering a tribute to the cinema as apparatus. But by the end of this loose scene, built of nearly random events, long takes combined with rapid cuts, and a shift from all nondiegetic music to all diegetic sounds, Truffaut pulls a stunning twist by inserting a narrative jolt to Antoine and the audience: Antoine sees his mother kissing the strange man. Their encounter is broken down analytically into revealing a blonde kissing a man, closer shots to help identify her, and then medium close-ups of Antoine looking offscreen and cut to the mother looking off at Antoine. But the continuity is disrupted, much like the kissing in *Les mistons,* with Antoine's mother facing different directions in some shots, which further signifies everyone's confusion.

The transition from a hurried Antoine on his way to school, to a relaxed, playful Antoine, to a stunned Antoine, rushing off in shock with René in tow, brilliantly illustrates Truffaut's novel mode of storytelling. *The 400 Blows* stages action by manipulating a full range of stylistic options and then circles back to use that striking arsenal of techniques to reinforce the thematics, trapping Antoine now in an even worse situation than he was in before his carefree day of playing hooky. Just before he left for school, his parents were quarreling over money; by the end of the sequence, his mother is with a different man, and Antoine has to return to eat dinner alone with his father. Thus, this scene interweaves unity and disunity, distracting the viewers, like Antoine, away from his school and

Figure 5.14. Antoine in the rotor ride (*The 400 Blows*)

Figure 5.15. Mme. Doinel sees Antoine (*The 400 Blows*)

family problems and then returning them to those difficulties in a scene built around changing pairs of characters: M. and Mme. Doinel, Antoine and René, Mme. Doinel and the strange man, and finally Antoine and M. Doinel.

A second significant scene illustrating Truffaut's investigation of new storytelling options for staging problems is the sequence of Antoine being interviewed by the psychologist at the detention center. This scene is famous both for its elimination of any reaction shots of the female psychologist and for the impressive, often spontaneous performance by Jean-Pierre Léaud sitting alone in a dark room at a barren table. Truffaut had an actress signed to play the psychologist, but she was not available yet, so he and Decae decided to shoot the scene with Léaud and simply add the reverse shots of the psychologist asking the questions later. Truffaut asked the questions himself: "I gave Léaud complete freedom in his responses because I wanted his expressions, hesitations, and a total spontaneity. . . .

He even introduced the whole notion of a grandmother."²⁹ Later, when Decae and Truffaut watched the rushes, they decided to retain the images of the boy alone and simply dub in the questions with the actress's voice. The result is a haunting variation on cinéma vérité practice since they take one or more very long interview shots and condense the footage down to three minutes, using lap dissolves to shorten it into a series of six almost dreamlike responses. This practice, so radical for narrative filmmaking at the time, has since become commonplace on television news shows that want to edit a long quotation without always cutting to a shot of the interviewer looking intrigued as punctuation or a cover for the edited ellipses. In *The 400 Blows* there is also a strange tension between the wide range of attitudes and vocal tones displayed by Antoine and the cold, disinterested professional questions posed by the psychologist, with the only sound other than dialogue being the distant marching sounds outside in the detention center. The interview thus becomes all the stranger, alternating between a trip to the guidance counselor and a death-row confession.

As these sample analyses reveal, *The 400 Blows* continues to elaborate on many of the story and style tactics begun in *Les mistons*. The auteurist Truffaut continued to refer to and give homage to his favorite directors in each of his films, and he claims often to have asked himself how Vigo, Renoir, Rossellini, and Hitchcock in particular would solve certain staging problems he encountered. But in the end, the mix of Bazinian long takes with Hitchcock-style manipulation (creating an ASL of 14 seconds) fit well with the norms of other *jeune cinéma* directors who were also struggling to forge a modern, new style. And to many observers' surprise, this first feature proved a huge hit. Truffaut won the best director prize at Cannes, though Marcel Camus's first feature, *Black Orpheus*, captured the Palme d'or as well as the Academy Award for best foreign film. But Truffaut's movie did, strangely enough, win the Roman Catholic Church's film award for his touching portrayal of Antoine's life. The tone and subject matter of Truffaut's film startled many of his contemporaries, as the review in *Amis du film* noted, "As a critic Truffaut was cruel; as a director he is tender."³⁰

This sensitive New Wave tale generated great interest internationally, earning Truffaut and Morgenstern's firms a windfall. The advance loan from the CNC's *prime à qualité*, which Truffaut had in turn lent to Jean Cocteau, was quickly paid off, since *The 400 Blows* made back its production cost several times over before it had played in a single theater. The American rights alone paid fifty thousand dollars according to Marcel

Berbert, though most other sources, including Truffaut, claim they paid one hundred thousand dollars. Regardless, the immediate success, which angered many of his old enemies, helped spur renewed interest in the *jeune cinéma* and its new stories, styles, and production modes. *The 400 Blows* had the fifth largest grossing run in France that year. As Truffaut explained to *Cinéma 61,* "The success of *The 400 Blows* was a total surprise, and I attribute it to a series of extraordinary coincidences: its selection for the Cannes Film Festival (what would have happened to the film if it had been finished in November of the preceding year?), the birth of the New Wave (I benefited from *The Lovers, Hiroshima, mon amour,* and *The Cousins*), that year's crisis in French production, and so on."[31] Thus, Truffaut had now shifted from being the most influential young film critic in France to being one of its most important young directors. But his most daring early movie was certainly *Shoot the Piano Player,* which followed quickly on the heels of his first two triumphs. Yet, despite its superior qualities, it received some harsh criticism from mainstream reviewers and a very low box office performance.

Authorship and Adaptation

With *Shoot the Piano Player,* Truffaut returned to an adaptation but added many personal touches and reworked its style. Truffaut selected the David Goodis novel, *Down There,* which had been published in France under the title *Tirez sur le pianiste.* The idea of shooting an American-style, B-series thriller appealed to Truffaut: "When we talk about the attraction that hard-boiled detective novels have for French people we have to remember that it is not only the American material in which we find a certain poetry, but, because this material has been transformed by the translation, we get an almost perverse pleasure out of it. For instance, I believe the version of *Johnny Guitar* dubbed in French is more poetic than the original."[32] Truffaut claimed the bizarre story and style in *Johnny Guitar* (Ray, 1954) influenced his second feature; *Shoot the Piano Player* would distort film noir, just as Nick Ray's film distorted, poetically, the Western. And Goodis was one of Truffaut's favorite 1950s American writers: "A single image made me decide to make the film. It was in the book. A sloping road in the snow, the car running down it with no noise from the motor. That's it. That image of a car gliding through the snow. . . . It's an admirable intersection of crime story and fairy tale."[33] Truffaut convinced Pierre Braunberger to buy the rights and produce the movie, and Braunberger obliged, giving

Shoot the Piano Player a $150,000 budget, roughly double that of *The 400 Blows.*

With the budget guaranteed, Truffaut set about gathering a cast and crew, selecting immediately his new friend Charles Aznavour to play the lead role. For cinematographer he hired Raoul Coutard, based on the strength of Godard's recently completed *Breathless:* "What attracted me to him was the originality of his camerawork." Coutard was more direct: "I like quick, candid work. . . . I started by eliminating from my films all the so-called artistic effects, all those things cameramen thrive on. . . . We shot fifteen times more quickly for ten times less money."[34] Truffaut also signed Marcel Moussy again to help write the screenplay. Truffaut, Moussy, Léaud, and Truffaut's current mistress, Liliane David, set off for three weeks in southern France to get the script started. In late November they began filming and wrapped up in the snowy mountains near Grenoble in mid-January after barely seven weeks of production. Truffaut then delayed postproduction work to fly to the United States to receive the New York Film Critics Best Foreign Film award for *The 400 Blows.* At the ceremony he got to meet many of his idols, including Jimmy Stewart and Audrey Hepburn. He also met David Goodis on that trip.

During the completion of *Shoot the Piano Player,* Truffaut was already aware that his second feature was not going to be as well received as *The 400 Blows;* early reactions to the rushes and rough cuts from friends and colleagues suggested this was a more jarring film. But these professional tensions were reinforced by political problems. During postproduction his editor, Cécile Decugis, was arrested for allowing her apartment to be used by the Algerian resistance. Furious, Truffaut used several thousand dollars from his production budget to aid in her defense. By fall he also was invited to sign the famous "Manifesto of the 121," which urged French soldiers to desert rather than fight in the ongoing Algerian War. The manifesto was begun by several intellectuals, including Marguerite Duras, and signed initially by 121 well-known figures, including Jean-Paul Sartre, before the prematurely named 121 swelled to 400 signatures. The French government dealt harshly with any antiwar activity, and the 400 people encouraging desertion risked the wrath of nationalist public opinion and even imprisonment. In an effort to suppress the manifesto's potential cultural power, the government forbade anyone to publicize the names of those who had signed it, but the state-owned media also prohibited any radio or television appearances by those 400 signees, which ironically helped indicate by their absence from national media who had or had not signed. Truffaut, himself a deserter who refused to go to Indochina, signed the manifesto, along with Resnais, Doniol-Valcroze, Pierre Kast, and even Maurice Pons. He signed it in September, just six weeks before the opening of *Shoot the Piano Player,* which further limited his options for publicity, since he was now banned from French airwaves. Television and radio interview shows had proven a strong forum for New Wave personalities to champion their latest films. Truffaut was also attacked as anti-French by his old, conservative friends at *Arts,* but his brave stance did earn him a new respect from his former enemies at the leftist film journal *Positif.*

Shoot the Piano Player is the tale of a shy piano player, Charlie Kohler (Aznavour), who was once a celebrated concert pianist named Edouard Saroyan. One night at the café where he plays piano, one of his brothers, Chico (Albert Rémy), a thug on the run for double-crossing some fellow thieves, happens to see his brother playing and stops in to talk and ask for help. This chance meeting reverberates throughout the movie since the pursuing thieves will repeatedly pester Charlie to find Chico and his accomplice, their brother Richard (Jean-Jacques Aslanian). Later that night, Charlie walks home with a waitress, Lena (Marie Dubois), who secretly idolizes the quiet piano player; they are followed by the thieves but elude them. Just as Charlie is building the courage to ask Lena for a date, she disappears from his side. At home, it turns out that Charlie is raising his youngest brother, Fido (played by Richard Kanayan, who appeared as Antoine's messy classmate in *The 400 Blows*), and that Clarisse, a friendly prostitute across the hall (Michele Mercier), helps watch out for Fido and spends some nights with Charlie. During this scene Truffaut had Clarisse hold up her panties to the camera and bare her breasts while Charlie wraps a sheet around her and explains, "No, this is the way it has to be done in the movies." This scene, along with several others that were later trimmed, like one of a cat being deliberately run over in the street, earned the film an "eighteen or older" rating in France.

The next morning the gangsters, Ernest and Momo, kidnap Charlie and Lena, in an effort to find out where Chico is hiding. But when Lena stomps on the gas and they get pulled over for speeding, Charlie and Lena escape. Lena then takes Charlie to her apartment, which is covered with posters and newspaper clippings of his past as Edouard. At this point a lengthy flashback begins of Edouard's rise from a piano teacher to a famous concert pianist, but whether it is supposed to be Charlie's or Lena's mental, subjective vision is left unclear. During the flashback, it becomes evident that Edouard's wife, Thérèse (Nicole Berger), helped jumpstart his piano

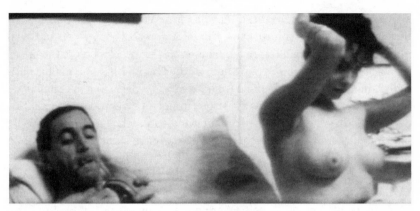

Figure 5.16. Charlie and Clarisse in bed (*Shoot the Piano Player*)

career by sleeping with the agent Lars Schmeel, although it is unclear how long this relationship was going on, since the viewer's first glimpse of the couple begins with Edouard offering her a diamond ring, but Lars is already in the café behind him. Unhappy about her sexual betrayal, Thérèse eventually confesses to Edouard, who initially runs out of their hotel room in disgust but then returns seconds later to find she has hurled herself out a window to her death. The flashback ends with Lena and Charlie in bed, punctuated by a number of lap dissolves. Lena then announces that she and Charlie must quit their jobs so she can help him become Edouard Saroyan again. In the meantime, the gangsters have tricked Clarisse and kidnapped Fido, who is leading them to Chico and Richard's mountain home hideout. In the café, Plyne, the owner, insults Lena, leading to a fight in which Charlie is forced to stab Plyne; hurt and catatonic, Charlie is driven by Lena to the brothers' mountain hideout. Once there, a final shoot-out occurs between Charlie's brothers and the gangsters. Ernest the gangster guns down Lena just before he and his sidekick take off in their car chasing Chico and Richard, leaving Fido, Charlie, and the dying Lena in the snow. The final scene shows Charlie back at the café as the owner introduces him to the new, young waitress, who gives Charlie a shy smile.

Shoot the Piano Player's loose, rather convoluted story was accompanied with a quirky, uneven, almost tongue-in-cheek style that left many reviewers puzzled, though René Lefevre wrote an insightful review: "Unlike *The 400 Blows*, *Shoot the Piano Player* is not and never will be a prestige film, and that is why it is so pleasant. . . . With this tale Truffaut breaks elegantly yet offhandedly all the norms of academic style that still rule a certain sort of French cinema."[35] But others were less impressed by its unconventional touches. In interview after interview, Truffaut was asked why he chose this story and whether it had a central theme and whether he had really intended its wild, chaotic mix of tones. Truffaut, who at first was quite adamant in championing *Shoot the Piano Player* as a radical reworking of cinematic conventions that forces the audience to move "from surprise to surprise," gradually began to show an uncomfortable strain, finally claiming that this movie was just a diversion, meant to amuse, nothing more. Its first run in Paris only sold 70,000 tickets, as opposed to the 260,000 for *The 400 Blows*. Furthermore, this second feature did not find a cluster of distributors clamoring for the rights: it was not even released in the United States until 1962, where it was much less successful than *The 400 Blows*, bringing in forty-five thousand dollars in New York City's first-run, or one-fourth the box office of his first feature. Truffaut took much of the criticism personally as an attack by the "old wave" to discredit the New Wave, especially since many mainstream critics repeated the charge that it was an "unprofessional" film, which was also what many had just said of *Breathless*.

The simultaneous poor box-office showings by other New Wave films, including the latest Chabrols, motivated Truffaut to speak up for the movement as a whole and to write rave reviews of his colleagues' films such as *Paris nous appartient* (*Paris Belongs to Us*, Rivette, 1960) and *Adieu Philippine* (Rozier, 1960–62) to try to bolster excitement over his cherished *jeune cinéma*. But while 1959 had been the year of the New Wave, 1960's top hits in France were made by the "tradition of quality's" old guard, Godard's *A Woman Is a Woman* (1961) was doing poorly, and *Le Petit soldat* (1963) was banned outright, so many in the press, including the critics with *Arts*, began wondering whether the young cinema "had its future behind it."[36] Moreover, La Patellière's *Rue des prairies* was released in 1960 with the ad slogan "Jean Gabin gets even with the nouvelle vague." Truffaut was going through a tough transition; instead of fighting his way to the top he was now trying to stay there, and as soon as his own second feature began to flounder, he fought back in the press, while he also began planning for a rebound with his next film, *Jules and Jim*.

Yet *Shoot the Piano Player* can now be considered one of Truffaut's great stylistic triumphs and one of the freshest, loosest, and even funniest films of his career. Here, instead of poor Antoine Doinel stealing milk bottles to survive, one has the plucky Fido (a character not in Goodis's novel) dropping milk onto the gangster's windshield to distract them. Kidnappings are ruined by speeding tickets and running out of gas, Momo swears on his mother's life and suddenly there is a cut to a woman falling dead, Bobby Lapointe's song is so full of slang and sexual double entendres that it has to be subtitled even for the French, and the timid Charlie turns out to be quite the contrary in bed with beautiful women. Every character is both absurd and sympathetic, and the shifts in tone from a comic-book shootout to the tragically silly death scene of Lena tumbling down a snowy slope become representative of this movie inspired by the mock-tragedy of *Johnny Guitar.*

But it is really the stylistic experimentation, partly motivated by Godard's daring work on *Breathless,* that makes *Shoot the Piano Player* such a lively example of the New Wave spirit. *Cinéma 61* published a review acknowledging that, while Truffaut's second feature would be less popular than *The 400 Blows,* it was nonetheless his best work yet: "It is a sort of manifesto against the dominant, passive cinema. On an aesthetic level . . . it truly is liberated cinema."[37] In terms of camerawork, not only does Coutard shoot with available light when possible, which causes "errors" such as a camera reflected on Lena's jacket in one scene, but his hectic mobility and location shooting turn the characters into specters moving in and out of shadow.

During the opening scene when the fleeing Chico has a long conversation about love with a middle-aged husband and stranger, both characters move in and out of light depending upon the spacing of the streetlights and their faces are barely lit enough to make them recognizable, much less to display their emotions. This encounter, which is not in Goodis's novel, is also filmed in a single, two-minute-twenty-two-second shot before Chico runs off again. The gritty look of Coutard's night scenes lacks the natural beauty seen in Decae's Paris, and the mix of editing and sound strategies at work in *Shoot the Piano Player* also defy the smooth polish of Truffaut's previous work.

Unlike the conventional, literary voice-over in *Les mistons* or the brief mental, subjective words of Antoine Doinel in *The 400 Blows,* the voice-overs in *Shoot the Piano Player* challenge narrative norms. When these daring sound strategies are combined with other unusual stylistic devices, Truffaut's second feature can truly dazzle the viewer. The most representative example of these unique techniques coming together is in the long flashback scene of Charlie/Edouard's life with Thérèse. The scene opens with Charlie climbing the stairs to Lena's apartment, in a mental, subjective conversation with himself about not looking at her legs, but as soon as the door opens and

Figure 5.17. Camera shadow on Lena's jacket (*Shoot the Piano Player*)

Charlie sees the posters of his earlier musical career, the nondiegetic flute music ends and a majestic piano begins. Lena in voice-off speaks to Charlie about his past and her words, "Isn't that right Edouard, once . . . ," repeat with an echo effect into a series of dissolves, several of which show concerned close-ups of Charlie/Edouard's face. Thus, the entire eighteen-minute-long flashback sequence begins with Lena's voice triggering the segment, which includes many scenes only he could know; yet at the end it is again Lena's voice-off that seems to control the images, "You disappeared, you started your life over. . . . You went back to your brothers in the snow and asked them to let you have Fido." She fills in additional narrative information, but there is a blurring of diegetic and nondiegetic elements as well as a confusion about the source of these flashback images: Have they all been in Charlie's memory, or has Lena been helping guide the selection of images? Peter Brunette breaks it a bit too neatly into "Charlie's vision" followed by hers: "Lena takes over the film the second after the flashback ends."[38] Admittedly, she continues narrating the more recent past, explaining that she had watched him in the café for some time, and then there is the dreamy love scene full of panning shots and lap-dissolves to ease the viewer back into the present. But the entire sequence seems to be a shared memory with the characters sharing the role of secondary character-narrator, as this segment destroys the conventions for presenting past narrative information. This is a complete reworking of subjective memory, as Truffaut breaks away from classical conventions such as Gabin's François remembering how he got into his present situation in *Le jour se lève* (Carné, 1939) or Rick remembering Paris in *Casablanca* (Curtiz, 1943).

In *Shoot the Piano Player*, Truffaut's editing again alternates between long, Bazinian takes and discontinuous montages, creating a final wide-screen print with 566 shots, for an ASL of barely nine seconds. During the flashback, the timid Edouard chickens out on ringing the doorbell for his au-dition with Lars Schmeel, and this action is broken into eight shots, includ-ing an extreme close-up of his fingertip poised before the buzzer. Not only is this a strong use of montage to extend time and suggest Edouard's lack of confidence without dialogue, but it provides another scene in which women's actions propel him forward: the door only opens because a young woman is leaving, and, of course, Edouard is only at Schmeel's office because his wife slept with Lars to advance her husband's career. But the most amazing edit-ing sequence, worthy of a Godard scene, is the shoot-out at the family home in the snowy hills. Lena has just told Charlie he is not going to be charged with Plyne's murder, and she has come to take him back to Paris. He goes into the house to tell his brothers he is leaving. But suddenly the gangsters show up with Fido, and space and time get completely confused as Truffaut abandons the long takes and begins to cut from a wide variety of angles, in many different shot scales. Sometimes Lena is in medium close-up watch-ing the gangsters; other times she is barely visible in brief long shots.

When Fido escapes and runs screen right and the camera pans to the right, there is a cut to Lena turning her head from left to right as well, as if it has been her perceptual point of view. This series is then interrupted by Chico firing from an upstairs window, a shot that is broken further with a tiny jump cut; as he and then Richard shoot toward the offscreen left, there is a cut to the gangsters returning fire *also* by shooting off left. Screen di-rection has been broken. Suddenly, Lena spins around, but just where she is positioned is unclear; she cries out "Charlie" and begins running to the right as ominous nondiegetic music starts and the panning camera tries to keep her in focus as she runs. Next, there is a shot of Ernest looking off *right* and twirling his pistol, two more shots of Lena running, but then a shot of Ernest looking and shooting *up left* at Lena, who falls on the top of a ridge. A flash pan and tilt down to a close-up of Charlie at the house reveals him running out to find her, as the flute music returns and Lena slides and tumbles, like a child at play, down the snowy hill.

The bravado mix of sound, camera, editing techniques, and narrative

Figure 5.18. Ernest shoots Lena (*Shoot the Piano Player*)

Figure 5.19. Ernest shoots Lena (*Shoot the Piano Player*)

Figure 5.20. Ernest shoots Lena (*Shoot the Piano Player*)

traditions goes beyond simple parody to create a truly modern (or, as Brunette prefers, postmodern) text that plays with bits and pieces of genre filmmaking while it celebrates the freedom of storytelling in the New Wave era. Like a jazz score, the film has its own unique structure, and it is not unusual for first-time viewers to be simultaneously impressed and confused by its meandering narrative and ironic tone. It seems to call out for subsequent viewings in order for the audience to learn, follow, and appreciate its unique rhythm and charm, and in many ways, its narrative traits (noir source, shared flashback, death of one lover) and stylistic strategies (discontinuous editing, excessive acting styles, contrapuntal music) bring *Shoot the Piano Player* much closer to *Breathless* than to *The 400 Blows*. Thus, Truffaut's second feature synthesizes his own auteurist tendencies with the more radical experimentation that he saw in contemporary Resnais and Godard movies. Critics, expecting another sensitive portrayal of contemporary France, were quite puzzled. Bosley Crowther at the *New York Times*, who had loved *The 400 Blows*, wrote that Truffaut had "gone haywire" with this second feature, creating a "nuttiness . . . that does not hang together."[39] And despite the fact that a number of review articles began to rally round Truffaut and praise this new mixture of narrative devices and techniques, *Shoot the Piano Player* earned very little in its first run and never went on to win any major film festival awards, which were major disappointments to Truffaut, who would have to wait for his next feature, *Jules and Jim*, to return him to the world's spotlight as the top young director from France.

From the beginning stages of preproduction, *Jules and Jim* was a transitional film for Truffaut, who wanted to maintain a personal style and yet, now more than ever, was determined to make another critical and commercial success. While he defended valiantly *Shoot the Piano Player*, he wanted his next film to convince everyone that *The 400 Blows* was not a fluke and he was not a flash in the pan. Truffaut continued to get advice and financial support from Marcel Berbert, but Ignace Morgenstern died during the production of *Jules and Jim*, leaving Truffaut and Les Films du Carrosse increasingly vulnerable, with no guaranteed distributor, so they decided to shoot inexpensively again on borrowed locations and with a tight crew of fifteen. Nonetheless, the budget became high by New Wave standards before the film was finished, at a total of $280,000, including $40,000 completion money from their eventual distributor, Cinédis. Truffaut selected Henri Pierre Roché's novel to adapt, securing the rights from producer Raoul Levy just after Roché died. As early as 1953, when Roché's novel appeared, Truffaut became a big fan of it, even mentioning it as part of his review of an American movie. Roché saw Truffaut's reference and wrote to thank him, which began another of those valuable friendships Truffaut forged with older, influential male friends.

Once he had secured the rights, Truffaut began the adaptation project himself in September 1960, but by January he hired Jean Gruault, who had recently worked with Rivette on *Paris Belongs to Us*. He retained Georges Delerue and Raoul Coutard and again decided to film in widescreen, black-and-white. The unknown actor Henri Serre was selected for Jim, partly because he resembled Roché, and German Oscar Werner for Jules (after Truffaut considered Marcello Mastroianni); Werner had impressed Truffaut in *Lola Montes* (Ophuls, 1955). The choice of Jeanne Moreau for Catherine had been made early, and Truffaut had even given her a copy of the novel when she came on the set of *The 400 Blows* for her walk-on role with Brialy. In the meantime, Truffaut had become fascinated with her and even spent time at her country home as he adapted the project. This sojourn apparently took on traits from the novel and movie since Moreau maintained very open relations with Truffaut as well as her ex-husband, actor Jean-Louis Richard. Her neighbor Boris Bassiak ended up being recruited to write the song "Le Tourbillon" for the movie and appears as Moreau's singing suitor, Albert; he and his wife even lent their home for filming. By the end of the production, Henri Serre, Truffaut, and the producer, Raoul Levy, were all three reportedly in love with Moreau, which led to unpleasant tensions on the close-knit set, repeating some of the problems experienced with *Les mistons*.

Roché's partially autobiographical novel is set in the years 1912–1930 and told in the first-person, much like Pons's *Les mistons* and Goodis's *Shoot the Piano Player*. The film retains some voice-over from the novel, and while Truffaut and Gruault simplified the plot in some spots and embellished it in others, they tried to respect the original. As Colin Crisp points out, "This film contains fewer asides, in-jokes, and other personal notations not directly connected with the central theme than do Truffaut's previous films."[40] Truffaut reined in his loose, anecdotal storytelling style this time.

The story begins as the French writer Jim meets the Austrian Jules in the Paris café and art scene, and they become great friends immediately. Jim is involved with a woman named Gilberte but pursues other women, and Jules meets several women, including the anarchist Thérèse (Marie DuBois), who promptly leaves him for another man. But when Jules and Jim watch their friend Albert's slide show of statues and become fascinated with one, the two friends run off to the Adriatic Sea to contemplate the original. Some time later, they meet Catherine (Moreau), and both Jules and Jim are struck by her resemblance to that stone bust. For one month she lives exclusively with Jules, but finally the three friends begin to spend time together, though Jules warns Jim not to steal "this one." The three leave on a vacation to southern France, where they rent an isolated villa. Jules considers asking Catherine to marry him, but Jim warns him that she may not be content with one man, much less as a wife and mother. Reinvigorated, they all return to Paris, where Catherine decides to marry Jules.

Just after their marriage World War I erupts, however, and the men must fight on opposing sides. At the end of the war, Jim goes to visit Jules and Catherine, who now live in a cottage on the Rhine with their daughter, Sabine; he discovers that their family is unhappy. Jules distracts himself, writing books about insects, but Catherine takes lovers, including their old friend Albert, now a neighbor in Germany. Jim is attracted to her as well; Jules gives him permission to pursue her but also asks that he be allowed to see her from time to time. Once Jim moves in, their *ménage à trois* creates intense pleasures for all; but after one month Jim has to return to Paris, hoping to come back later to marry Catherine. In Paris,

Jim has trouble leaving his long-time lover, Gilberte (Vanna Urbino). When he returns to Germany, Jim and the indecisive Catherine quickly become frustrated with each other, and Jim rushes back to Gilberte in Paris, where he falls ill. Upset and doubting the seriousness of his illness, Catherine writes to the bedridden Jim that she is pregnant with his child. Jim heads back to Germany, but just before their reunion, she suffers a miscarriage, ending any hope of reconciliation. Some time later, Jules, Catherine, and Sabine move to France. When Jules invites Jim to visit them, he warns that Catherine is very fragile mentally and perhaps suicidal. When Catherine drives them to dine, it turns out that she does so to be with Albert, who has apparently followed them back to France, and she spends the night with him. The next day, Catherine tries to get Jim back, but he finally tells her he is going to marry Gilberte. Catherine pulls a gun on him, but he escapes. Later, while watching sound newsreels on the rise of Nazism at the Studio Ursulines movie theater, the three principals meet again. Catherine drives the men to a café on the banks of the Seine, then invites Jim into the car so she can tell him something. Instead, she drives off a bridge into the river, killing them both. Jules follows their ashes to the burial vault and descends the cemetery hill alone back into Paris.

The characters in *Jules and Jim* all seem strangely frozen in time; even after the war, when years have passed since their bohemian early days in Paris, they comment on the fact that "no one has changed," and Truffaut even includes a brief freeze frame of their amazing reunion to reinforce the miracle of their timeless friendship. The girl, Sabine, remains constantly a toddler, though she disappears visually by the final segment in France and is only mentioned in dialogue. This notion of presenting a world where real events such as a war are mere backdrops to the central characters' unfaltering concerns for love and happiness, lends a fairy-tale-like quality to the story as a whole, turning it into a universal fable that somehow remains very contemporary in its cavalier attitudes toward friendship, sex, and devotion. This mix of nostalgia and modern themes is reflected in Truffaut's prepared statement for the press package sent out for the premiere: "With this film I wanted to get back to the 'tone' of *The 400 Blows;* a story recounted in half-tints, sad in its line, but droll in its details."[41] This New Wave historical melodrama provided just the boost Truffaut needed, as *Jules and Jim* won the Best French Film prize from the French Film Critics (though the award for best film overall went to Luis Buñuel's *Viridiana*) and ended up as the sixteenth highest box office hit in France that year and the sixth best French film (Robert Dhery's *La belle Américaine* was the most popular French film that year).

The story of two artistic men who share everything, including the war experience and their mad love for Catherine, appealed to a wider range of ages than many of the contemporary New Wave films. Jeanne Moreau's name, along with the amoral tale, lent marketing power both at home and abroad, even though the Catholic Church condemned the movie. It was also banned by the American Legion of Decency, which cited Truffaut's moral ambiguity as one of the leading factors for their disapproval: "This story about an unconventional 'household of three' arrangement is developed in a context alien to Christian and traditional natural morality. . . . If the director has a definite moral viewpoint to express, it is so obscure that the visual amorality and immorality of the film are predominant and consequently pose a serious problem for a mass medium of entertainment."[42] In the United States, the fledgling distributor, Janus Films, took full advantage of the Legion condemnation in its advertisements to attack the Legion as "endangering freedom of expression." Janus set the Legion quotes about the alien morality alongside positive reviews of *Jules and Jim* from *Time* and *Saturday Review*.[43] The film's youthful, sexy aspect reinforced international stereotypes for the New Wave (after all, even *The 400 Blows* was advertised with a publicity still of Antoine's father grasping his wife's breasts), which helped market *Jules and Jim* as very modern and even risqué despite its 1910s and 1920s time frame.

It was precisely the brazen amorality of Moreau's Catherine (echoing her roles in Louis Malle's films), reinforced by the passive acquiescence of the men, that triggered initial thematic discussions of Truffaut's film. The Legion of Decency is correct in noting the ambiguity of tone. As René Prédal comments, "Truffaut shows characters who try to live as honestly as possible, in its most literal sense, leaving the spectator to draw any lessons."[44] Just what "lessons" could be learned from watching two men drawn against their better judgment to devote so much of their lives to a woman who is obviously incapable of living with only one man were, indeed, left up in the air. Near the end, Jim does make the half-hearted decision to marry the eternally devoted Gilberte and refuses Catherine's offer to try again to have children with her. Nonetheless, he remains so fascinated with Jules and Catherine that he agrees to get in the car with her and sits confusedly, as if stuck in his seat by the magnetic power of her presence, allowing her simply to drive off the pier to their death. That the "good" Gilberte and the weak Jules, to say nothing of the innocent daughter Sabine, are all left alone because of Catherine's actions hardly provides a concrete moral for the story. *Shoot the Piano Player*, a bit like a reversal of *Breathless*, ends with one dead lover (Lena) and one lonely survivor (Charlie); now *Jules and Jim* pushes that formula one step further, with two dead lovers and Jules left behind. The melancholy closure device, of Catherine's tune playing as Jules walks off alone, further reinforces the stunning pointlessness of her actions, even as the power of her personality continues to haunt Jules after her death. The story's overall structure, of tagging scene to scene in a chronological order, remains unified and classical in its continuing saga of these three unhappy lovers, yet, much like *The 400 Blows*, its coherent story organization builds complex characters with intricate, vague motives and finally obscure collections of desires.

But if most of its story traits remained close to classical literary norms, the stylistic strategies employed in *Jules and Jim* marked it as a sophisticated example of New Wave filmmaking. As in his previous films, Truffaut alternates between scenes preserving time and space via Bazinian long takes, and sequences that rely on discontinuous devices; in the end the ASL is a rapid ten seconds, despite the many longer takes. While Truffaut reserved the freeze frame for the final shot of *The 400 Blows*, here he employs it within scenes to stop the action, much like a photographer's camera would, helping foreground the emotion of his characters while isolating specific moments in time. One of the most daring and successful uses of the freeze frame occurs during the scene in southern France when Jules and Jim are playing dominoes and a bored Catherine tries to win their attention. After Catherine has asked them to scratch her back and Jules replies comically that the Lord scratches those who scratch themselves, she slaps him and they all laugh. Not only does this sort of behavior epitomize Jules and Catherine's relationship—no matter how poorly she treats him, he cannot resist her—it also motivates her to explain that before she met them, she was often sad. Catherine frowns to demonstrate her previous and new moods; Truffaut freezes several poses for a second or so each, while the diegetic sounds of everyone chuckling continue throughout the still frames. These poses echo the sequence of photographs of men in various moods from *Shoot the Piano Player* when Edouard/Charlie considers taking courses to end his timidity. In *Jules and Jim*, this tactic also recalls the earlier slide show to connect the "previous" stone Catherine with the new lively Catherine, and it further makes mythic her attitude and gestures.

Many reviewers claimed that *Jules and Jim* was indeed Truffaut's tribute to Jeanne Moreau's amazing presence. However, the freeze frame is not reserved for her alone. Later, when Jim first visits the couple in Germany and Jules looks at him, exclaiming that he has not changed a bit, there is another brief freeze frame. Such cinematic touches, along with the inserted 1910s documentary footage of Paris for transitions, the World War I montages to present the war, and the beautiful handheld wide-screen shots and 360-degree pans all open up the literary aspect of the film and escape the "tradition of quality" conventions of historical melodramas. Truffaut continued struggling to put a personal auteurist and cinematic mark on his adaptations. Moreover, by situating this love triangle between 1912 silent-film footage and 1930s newsreels of the rise of Nazism, Truffaut connects personal and political history with the cinema, reinforcing his recurring motif of the potential for movies to help the viewer understand his or her own real-world life.

Jules and Jim has a rich polish to its style that moves it beyond the rougher, cheaper, and, for some, more vibrant look and sound of his earlier work; after all, the bicycle rides here are shot with smooth tracking shots and not from the trunk of a borrowed car, as they were in *Les mistons.* But *Jules and Jim* nonetheless retains some experimentation and even a mixture of tones and genres, though in a much more subtle fashion than in *Shoot the Piano Player.* There are still playful references to early film practice, as when Catherine dresses like a man, or more correctly, like a pastiche of Charlie Chaplin's tramp. The film refers several times to slapstick comedy, Jules and Sabine play together framed like a Lumière short, and there is the musical scene when Catherine and Albert perform "her" song. Yet the most jarring scene may be when Catherine, saddened that Jim is going to marry Gilberte, suddenly pulls a pistol on Jim. That scene bursts forth as a parody of melodramatic excess, complete with swelling music, exaggerated gestures, rapidly zooming and reframing camerawork, and Jim's heroic leap out the window as he runs away. As the triumphant music fades, Truffaut even cuts to a shot of storm clouds gathering, to suggest Catherine's sinister machinations are not over. The very next scene includes footage of Germans burning books, so the inserted shot of a clouded sky provides a bridge between both dramas. The combination of comedy, history, and generic parody creates a text whose overall tactics still seem fairly loosely motivated, at least by classical standards, yet they remain more muted than the fragmentation and dissonance of *Shoot the Piano Player.*

Finally, with *Jules and Jim,* Truffaut's mise-en-scène reaches a plateau that further proves it is a transitional film for him, leading him away from the rapid, spontaneous staging of his earlier work toward a more refined and pictorial visual style. The large budget not only allowed more lighting units, costuming, and additional postproduction work on the soundtrack; it also seems to have granted him more preproduction time to rework the script with increased attention to detail, both literary and cinematic. The result is a very mannered style, in contrast to his previous work. A perfect example of this new, "reformist" Truffaut may be seen in the simple scene set in the German cottage of Jim and Catherine's first night together. In a sequence reminiscent in tone of the almost religious treatment of infidelity in Malle's *The Lovers,* Jim and Catherine stand in her room in very soft, low-key lighting, accompanied by slow, romantic orchestral music as he caresses her face. The interesting aspect is that there is a dimly lit window in the background, and despite the shallow focus, the viewer can see a large insect crawling about on the windowpane as Jim and Catherine face each other just before their first night of lovemaking. Her husband, Jules, has been writing books about insects and is even planning a novel in which insects are the characters. But here, just before Jim decides to kiss Catherine, he steps back, leaving Catherine in silhouette and profile on the right; his movement allows much of the left side of the wide-screen frame to be empty, except for the bug, which crawls over toward her side of the frame, disappearing behind her mouth at the very instant that Jim finally leans in to kiss her. Not only does the insect's presence compete with the viewer's attention for Catherine's gestures, but it makes sure that the audience cannot forget the absent husband, Jules, who is willing to allow Jim to marry Catherine as long as he can continue to be a part of her life. This sort of attention to detail in the mise-en-scène, along with the careful studio lighting effects, does not exist in the any of Truffaut's previous films.[45]

Jules and Jim, called "Truffaut's masterpiece" by many reviewers at the time, proved that this movie brat was now situated securely within French cinema. Even *Variety* noted in 1962 that Truffaut was now part of the industry he had so recently assaulted. Yet he did not simply slip into the traps of commercial cinema, even though he had moved closer to many mainstream French cinema narrative techniques: "Truffaut built a unique place for himself within French cinema by practicing a balancing act that became more and more complex between his long-held critical ideals and the rules of the system. To a certain extent, *Jules and Jim* announced this evolution which would carry him away from the New Wave's 'hard core.'"[46] David Nicholls, too, sees this film as a sign of a changing Truffaut: "Watching *Jules and Jim* we are also watching the end of the New Wave. The first half of the film, set between 1900 and 1914, moves at a cracking pace; the full panoply of cinematic devices is used, and the camera seems to be as liberated and carefree as the characters on screen. After 1918, as the story becomes more somber . . . Truffaut's direction becomes more conventional, more 'classical.'"[47] And despite the fact that Truffaut's next film, the short *Antoine and Colette* (1962), continued the Doinel series, it looked much more like the smoothly fluid *Jules and Jim* than the spontaneous and choppy *The 400 Blows*.

Yet, by the time his second installment of the Antoine Doinel saga appeared in 1962, the author of "A Certain Tendency of the French Cinema" was only thirty years old. He had successfully revitalized film criticism in the 1950s, thanks in part to André Bazin's mentoring and faith, and then he had made the leap, like Alexandre Astruc and Claude Chabrol before him, to writing and directing his own films. Moreover, he became one of the most popular directors of post–World War II France, serving as a role model for young critics and directors around the world. Even when he moved to more commercial projects in his career, he would always be celebrated by critics and historians alike as one of the most influential of the "wave boys," a tough, self-educated street kid who, like Antoine Doinel, was confident and practical. In addition, he became a great advocate and spokesperson for French cinema and its cultural significance. Unfortunately, Truffaut, who had directed twenty-one features, succumbed to brain cancer in 1984, at age fifty-two, but even in his last months he surrounded himself with his favorite actors, such as Jean-Pierre Léaud and Marie DuBois. His role as a representative of the New Wave cannot be overstated, and Truffaut has become an almost mythical icon of the impatient, idealistic young director who, frustrated with the state of cinema, could muster enough determination, spunk, and creativity to revitalize world cinema. This image is perhaps the condensed, lasting legacy of the term "New Wave," and he personifies it best.

6

Jean-Luc Godard:
Le Petit Soldat

Criticism has taught us to love both Rouch and Eisenstein and that we must
not neglect one sort of cinema in the name of some other mode. A young
writer today is aware of Molière and Shakespeare. Well, we are the first
directors to be aware of D. W. Griffith. Even Marcel Carné, Louis Delluc,
and René Clair had no real critical or historical background.
    —JEAN-LUC GODARD, "Entretien avec Jean-Luc Godard"

GODARD, LIKE Truffaut, was a confident, often brash critic. Even before he began shooting his first feature, he proudly and loudly proclaimed
himself a member of the *jeune cinéma,* taking part in the famous discussion
in May 1959 at the La Napoule colloquium outside Cannes, as one of the
"seventeen young directors" of the New Wave who discussed the future of
French cinema. Yet, while he has earned an incredible amount of attention
from film critics, historians, and theorists, Godard never received the sort
of adoration lavished on Truffaut. In person, Godard could be combative
and obscure. As demonstrated in the opening epigraph, in which he claims
the New Wave was the first cluster of directors to be aware of film history,
Godard readily made ridiculous claims, often making it sound as if they
were the only directors ever to have seen many movies or cared about film
history. Unlike the romantic Truffaut, jokingly endearing Chabrol, or eva-
sive Rohmer, Godard made sure that he was always a force to be reckoned
with and even feared. Moreover, while Truffaut intertwined cinema history
with his own personal history, Godard saw film history as a series of modes
of discourse rather than merely mise-en-scène options. He concentrated on
the relationship between various filmmakers, industrial systems, and ideological functions of the cinema, seeing every shot as more than a potential
homage to a favorite director: each cinematic device was a signifier with
multiple cultural effects. The cinema was more than a personal means of
expression; it was the principal means of culture formation.

Godard also differed from Truffaut in his personal background. Born in Paris in 1930, Godard was raised mostly in Nyons, Switzerland, in great luxury. Godard's father, Paul-Jean, was a distinguished doctor, licensed to practice in France, England, and Switzerland. His mother, Odile Monod, was the daughter of the founder of the Banque de Paris et des Pay-Bas. Her family owned a vast estate just across Lake Geneva on the French side, where Jean-Luc spent many summers. Thus, while young Truffaut was denied a happy, stable family setting and often found himself scrounging for refuge, Godard had a lavish childhood, shuffling between Nyons, Paris, and Lake Geneva. In 1940, with the Nazi victories, the Godards retreated to Switzerland, secured Swiss citizenship for Jean-Luc, and enrolled him in school, though he returned to Paris to study immediately after its liberation in 1945. By the late 1940s, he began regularly attending the Cinémathèque, where he met Rivette, Rohmer, Chabrol, Resnais, Truffaut, and Bazin, though he also pursued a degree in ethnology from the Sorbonne. Like Truffaut, Godard credited Henri Langlois and the daily screenings at the Cinémathèque with providing him an education in film history. He also attended the booming *ciné-clubs,* and by March of 1951, was writing review articles, first for Rohmer's *Gazette du cinéma* and then for *Cahiers du cinéma,* typically under the pseudonym Hans Lucas. As Colin MacCabe writes, even from the beginning with his first long article in *Cahiers,* which confronted classical decoupage and storytelling, "Godard was always trying to push a genre to the moment it would break down to reveal the operations of the cinema."[1]

But while Truffaut and others had to grapple with the mandatory draft during the Indochina escalation in the 1950s, Godard, with his Swiss passport, could avoid service. During 1952 and 1953, he even followed his recently divorced father to Jamaica, before touring South America on his own, visiting distant relatives. Upon his return, Godard's life became more turbulent as he stole small amounts of money from family members, was cut off by his father, and reportedly jailed briefly in Switzerland and even sent to a clinic for psychological evaluation.[2] But in 1954, Godard's mother got him a job on the construction of a massive dam in Switzerland, and he used his earnings to make a documentary about it, the 35 mm short *Opération Béton* (*Operation Cement*), which the company purchased from him to use for publicity. Shot silent, with sound added in postproduction, it is a very conventional document that clearly demonstrates the stages of the massive construction project. This experience and his earnings motivated him to return to Paris and leap back into the cinema culture he had abandoned for several years. There he wrote for *Cahiers* and *Arts* and even replaced Chabrol at his job in the publicity department at Twentieth-Century Fox. He also continued to shoot short films, including his first New Wave–era film, *Tous les garçons s'appellent Patrick* (*All the Boys Are Called Patrick*, 1957), shot in 35 mm, based on a script by Rohmer, featuring Jean-Claude Brialy and Nicole Berger, and produced by Pierre Braunberger.

Godard went on to shoot two more Paris shorts, *Une histoire d'eau* (*A Story of Water*, 1958), which is a strange muddle of a film, codirected with Truffaut, and then *Charlotte et son Jules* (*Charlotte and Her Jules*, 1959), both of which were produced by Braunberger and his Films de la Pléiade. He tried to interest producers in feature-length projects, but it was finally Chabrol's and Truffaut's initial successes that helped him convince Georges de Beauregard to produce Godard's first feature. Truffaut had once discussed an idea for a film about a young French man who steals a car and shoots a police officer on his way to Paris to see his American girlfriend, which was the basic idea for *Breathless,* so Godard asked if Truffaut could sketch out the story line to test on Beauregard. Based on Truffaut's name, the short script idea, plus the fact that Claude Chabrol had agreed to serve as "technical advisor," Beauregard agreed to take on the project. Truffaut sold Beauregard and Godard his scenario for only two thousand dollars and agreed to read the final script for them; the producer wrote back, "I know it's out of friendship for Jean-Luc, but believe me, a producer doesn't often have the opportunity to encounter such disinterestedness. Therefore, thank you."[3] While Godard did make many additions and a few fundamental changes to Truffaut's scenario, such as adding its tragic ending, he nonetheless retained quite a few of the original details. The budget was roughly eighty-five thousand dollars, requiring Godard, like all his filmmaking friends, to cut corners whenever possible. According to Truffaut, Godard himself was so poor during the production, "he didn't have enough money in his pocket to buy a metro ticket, he was as destitute as the character he was filming."[4] He continues, "The miracle of *Breathless* is that it was made at a time in the life of a man in which he normally would not make a film. One doesn't make a film when one is sad and destitute."[5]

Yet, Godard had been ready for years for his first chance at a feature film. He was very aware of the production strategies of his predecessors, and he had already been referring to himself as a member of the French *jeune cinema* even before he knew what his first feature would be. When André Malraux's office announced that France's submissions to the 1959 Cannes Festival would be the three first features by Marcel Camus, Alain

Resnais, and Truffaut, Godard wrote proudly in *Arts,* "Today it seems that we have won the battle. It will be our films that go to Cannes, proving that France has a pretty face, cinematically speaking. And next year the same thing will happen. Fifteen new, courageous, sincere, lucid, beautiful films will again take the road over, blocking out conventional productions."[6] He was correct, of course, and *Breathless,* which won the Prix Jean Vigo in 1960, was most prominent among those courageous next films. Thus, when he got his chance, he had a long list of feisty claims to live up to.

For his actors, Godard began with Jean-Paul Belmondo in the lead role. Godard had praised Belmondo in a review of *Les tricheurs* (Carné, 1958), and the two had become friends, with Belmondo acting in his short *Charlotte et son Jules.* For the leading woman, Patricia, Godard persuaded Beauregard to hire Jean Seberg, whose salary was the highest part of the budget. She had starred in Otto Preminger's *Saint Joan* (1957) and the Françoise Sagan tale *Bonjour tristesse* (1958). Godard considered the role of Patricia to be a continuation of her character in *Bonjour tristesse,* and with her presence he could make reference to one of his favorite American directors while creating a connection to the popularity of "New Wave generation" writer Sagan. Most importantly though, he used her to forge a hybrid acting style that seems to owe as much to film history as to the casual, contemporary spontaneity of the New Wave proper.

Since most of *Breathless* was shot silent, its technical team was reduced to a bare bones crew, with cinematographer Raoul Coutard proving to be the only other individual allowed much creative input, especially before composer-sound director Jacques Maumont and Truffaut's editor, Cécile Decugis, joined Godard in postproduction. Coutard, who had previously shot only three quick films with Pierre Schoendoeffer, forged his quick, quirky signature style while improvising with Godard, who was not always clear or certain just what he wanted. "From day to day, as the details of his screenplay became more precise, he explained his conception: no [tripod] for the camera, no light if possible, traveling without rails . . . little by little we discovered a need to escape from convention and even run counter to the rules of 'cinematographic grammar.' The shooting plan was devised as we went along, as was the dialogue."[7] Thus, from the beginning, the mode of production for *Breathless* was more unconventional and "personal" even than most of its contemporaries, as the shooting method and scripting and improvisation affected every aspect of the mise-en-scène as well as the dialogue. Moreover, Godard and Coutard settled on a fast Ilford film stock that was not available commercially for motion-picture cameras, so they purchased spools of the still-camera film and spliced it together into adequate rolls for their 35mm Cameflex. They decided also that Coutard should use the camera hand-held, perched on his shoulder, while seated in wheelchairs and even a mail pushcart or in the backseat of a car, rather than placing it on conventional camera mounts. The goal was to capture a rough documentary quality, following the characters as if Coutard were a reporter out to get a story. Godard's procedure with the actors was very similar; he often showed up in the morning with sketchy notes for the actors, who were expected to improvise as the camera shot them from various angles, experimenting in order better to capture their loose performances. Seberg and Belmondo, however, became quite discouraged during production, feeling as if Godard had no idea what he was doing and that he had come to despise them. According to Godard, "Belmondo never invented his own dialogue. It was written. But the actors didn't learn it: the film was shot silent and I cued the lines."[8] The result would prove stunningly "unprofessional" to some critics but historically monumental to others.

Breathless, whose opening titles simply announce the name, *A bout de souffle* and the dedication to Monogram Pictures, tells the tale of Michel Poiccard (Belmondo), who steals an American military officer's car in Marseilles, with the help of a young woman he then abandons, and heads to Paris. His goals are clear, as bits of dialogue, spoken to himself as he drives, reveal: he needs to get some money owed him, pick up Patricia, and head for Italy with the cash. But along the way, he is chased by two motorcycle cops for a traffic violation; in a disorienting scene, Michel uses a pistol he found in the car to kill one of the officers. Michel flees to Paris, where he visits and robs one old girlfriend (played by Truffaut's mistress, Liliane David), before locating the American college student, Patricia, who had spent part of a vacation recently with Michel before returning to Paris to register at the Sorbonne and sell *Herald Tribunes*. Over the course of several days, Michel alternates between pursuing his two goals: seducing the reluctant Patricia to come with him and locating the money through his friends Tolmatchoff and Berruti. But Patricia struggles to remain independent and pursue her interest in writing; she even spends the night with her editor in order to get an interview with a famous novelist, played by Jean-Pierre Melville, but she also discovers she is pregnant, probably with Michel's child. In the meantime, the police detectives connect Michel with the crime and begin to track him via Patricia, warning her that they can take away her visa and work permit if she does not cooperate. But she and Michel evade the police, even ducking into movie theaters to lose the agent tailing them.

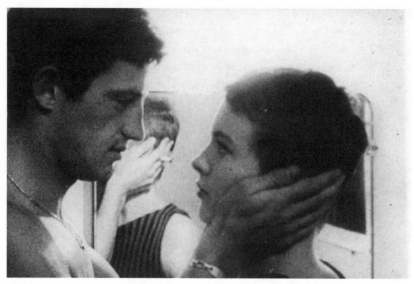

Figure 6.1. Michel and Patricia chat in her apartment (*Breathless*)

Figure 6.2. Inspector Vital warns Patricia (*Breathless*)

On the last day, as Berruti is on his way with an escape car and the cash, Patricia goes out for a newspaper and suddenly calls the police to tell them where Michel is hiding. She quickly warns Michel to leave, arguing that this was her test: if she could turn him in, then she must not be in love with him. But Michel, contrary to everything he has done and said up to this point, decides not to drive off to Italy and that he will stay and go to prison. He runs outside to warn Berruti that the cops are coming. Berruti tosses him a pistol from his glove compartment as the police arrive; the police shoot Michel on the street as Berruti drives off alone. Patricia runs to Michel in time to hear his dying words, "C'est vraiment dégueulasse." ["That's really disgusting."] She looks confusedly as the police alter his final words: "Il a dit, 'vous êtes vraiment dégueulasse.'" ["He said, 'You really are a bitch.'"] She turns toward the camera in a shot strangely reminiscent of Antoine Doinel's freeze frame. Patricia seems not to understand what has happened. The original script by Truffaut provides the same basic outline for the action but concludes differently, with Michel, spurned by Patricia, driving off to Italy: "Out of the car he hurls insults at Patricia. The last shot shows Patricia watching Lucien [changed to Michel by Godard] leave and not understanding him because her French is still not very good."[9] Thus Godard's ending preserves aspects of Truffaut's conclusion while going further with Michel dead on the street and the malicious police victorious; Godard even wanted to include dialogue from Inspector Vital telling his men to shoot Michel in the spine, but Truffaut vetoed that cruel touch.

As James Monaco points out, *Breathless* was hailed as a landmark film right from the start, and even though a summary of its story line sounds rather generic, or at least a bit like a tale by Melville, its overall style and attitude made it amazing: "*Les 400 coups* was fresh and new but it was also perceived to exist essentially within certain broad traditions. *Breathless*, on the other hand, was clearly revolutionary."[10] The overall story structure is chronological, yet has large scene-to-scene gaps that, mirrored by the discontinuous jump cuts, leave out some information. For instance, after Michel shoots the police officer and runs across a field, the audience next sees him in Paris riding in a car. No attempt is made to explain how much time has passed, whether he hitchhiked the whole way, or whether the police have even discovered the crime yet. Similarly, when Michel enters a café, checks for money, orders breakfast, and runs out to buy a paper, the viewer never knows whether he returns for the food. Moreover, the spectator is left pondering whether this scene is in anyway significant to the story.

Thus, while Truffaut sets complete scenes end to end, more in the fashion of a neorealist film, Godard presents incomplete shards of action and often reduces the most significant narrative events, such as Michel shooting the officer or Inspector Vital shooting Michel, to brief and confusing scenes, while lavishing longer shots and more screen time on other events, such as watching Patricia brush her hair or seeing Michel walk around in a travel agent office, that do not significantly advance the action.

Godard's story construction remains more fragmented than that of many of his contemporaries, with time and space simultaneously concrete and subjective. The central characters come to the audience in bits and pieces as well. The audience slowly learns more about Michel's past and Patricia's concerns, but there is never a scene like Truffaut's flashback in *Shoot the Piano Player* that explains character motivations and clarifies the attraction of the lovely young woman for the "wrong" man. It is unclear why Patricia even bothers with Michel, and she becomes a satirical representative of the American college woman abroad, who is excited by the exotic and dangerous French male but in the end pulls back to a safe distance. Nonetheless, Patricia remains a complicated art-film character full of contradictions: She loves art and literature, but spends time with an uneducated thug; she wants to remain independent of men but seems happy to depend upon and please men (her boss, Michel, the police) and her family to get by. She tells Michel she is pregnant, curious to see his reaction, but she never uses the pregnancy, or his reaction, as a motive for any of her subsequent actions. But the strangest twist is that she finally tells Michel that she loves him only late in the movie when she is driving in the stolen Cadillac and learns from the newspaper that he is a cop killer and married to boot. Nonetheless, she will spend the night with him only to squeal to the police the next day to chase him out of her life. And it is never clarified why Michel, who has had no qualms about exploiting other women, is suddenly ready to give up money and a sure escape to Italy for a chance to stay and talk more with Patricia, who just betrayed him. The characters remain fascinatingly complex and incomplete.

Breathless, like Truffaut's films, includes many intertextual references to other movies and also to painting, music, and literature. Here, too, Godard's storytelling is a bit more extreme. The differences between Patricia and Michel are partly defined by their taste in art: he likes Bogart and only one Mozart violin concerto; she likes Brahms, Renoir paintings, and William Faulkner novels. At one point she even hangs up a poster of a Renoir painting and asks Michel what he thinks. He rubs her bottom and replies, "Not bad." They rarely speak about the same things with the same meanings. This scene anticipates the scene with the musical parody in *Pierrot le fou* (1965), in which the Belmondo character sings about the Anna Karina character's "thigh line" while she tries to sing about chance and eternal love. Among the scenes that best reveal that these two young people literally live in different worlds is the one in which Patricia asks if Michel knows Faulkner and he assumes she means some guy she has slept with. Many of the movie references are already inscribed in Truffaut's script, including Michel's pause before a picture of Bogart outside a theater showing *The Harder They Fall* (Robson, 1956) and the fact that Michel and Patricia hide out in a movie theater that is showing an American Western. So, while references to other arts help delineate character differences, the many movie references establish a generic milieu for Michel and Patricia's saga and place the final death scene, in which Michel is gunned down in the street, in relation to those other texts: his death is a duel gone wrong—it is broad daylight, but Michel refuses to shoot and is shot in the back—as if film noir rules perverted a classic shoot-out. Yet it all seems to have been predetermined when Michel passed a movie poster proclaiming, "Live dangerously to the very end!" As David Bordwell and Kristin Thompson point out, "Michel's behavior is presented as driven *by* the very movies *Breathless* imitates," right down to rubbing his thumb across his face à la Bogart.[11] The Paris of *Breathless* is thus a modern patchwork and an allegorical setting that looks nothing like the city of *The Cousins* or *The 400 Blows*. But as in those films, Paris is continually signifying; New Wave mise-en-scène is ever conscious of the locations selected and the ongoing fictionalization of the real worlds explored.

Beyond mode of production and story, *Breathless* is most famous for its narrative style. While the jump cut is the most obvious device that rendered Godard's first feature new and strange, a host of other strategies function alongside that one editing tactic. *Breathless* opens with twelve shots of Michel stealing an American officer's car with the help of an anonymous young woman. This sequence immediately establishes a number of patterns for the film's overall style: the hand-held camera makes the medium close-ups vibrate, the eyelines do not match, continuity editing is rejected in favor of discontinuity, and the soundtrack is emphasized as an artificial construction, with the boat and fog horns coming and going, even though the sounds and dialogue are exclusively diegetic. The opening shot shows Michel behind a girlie magazine, *Paris Flirt*, but his very first words are ambiguous in both source and meaning: "Après tout, je suis con. S'il faut, il faut!" ["All in all, I'm a dumb bastard. All in all, if you've got to, you've got to."] Not only is the audience unsure what has to be done, but since his face is obscured by the paper, the close-miked words could be those of Michel or of a voice-over, and just who is being addressed or why is left unclear. *Breathless* begins as if in midscene, and later, at the film's end, Michel's final words will be just as enigmatic: "C'est vraiment dégueulasse." ["That's really disgusting."] The beginning and end remain vague: What, precisely, is he talking about? Does he intend for anyone but himself to hear it? Camera and sound selection, especially in the opening scene, obscure the character, disrupting any clear exposition, and this recurs at the end, undercutting clear resolution. Style disrupts rather than clarifies Godard's story.

The dysnarrative function of Godard's style brings the viewer back to the jump cut as one key device since it is emblematic of the film's overall radical nature. For instance, when a jump cut occurs, even on a simple event like Michel's perceptual point of view of the road as he drives north to Paris, the soundtrack remains constant, while time is missing in the image. The resulting contradiction between Michel singing Patricia's name continuously, while the images show time is cut out of the visuals, creates an impossible situation: either there is a gap of distance on the road or there is not; time cannot flow smoothly in the sound space while it is fragmented in the visual space. As David Bordwell points out, the jump cut was born with the in-camera tricks of Georges Méliès, exploited by a number of internationally famous directors in the 1920s, and then returned with New Wave directors such as Malle and Truffaut, but especially Godard, who helps make the jump cut a recognized stylistic option, albeit a disruptive one.[12] Interestingly, Godard would never again use this technique as consistently as in his first feature, yet he is often identified with the jump cut nonetheless. Like his entire arsenal of narrative tactics, however, the jump cut is highly significant since it calls attention to the constructed reality of the filmic text, to the spectator's on-going labor of generating a fictional world out of often contradictory stylistic cues, and to Godard's own expressive, auteur presence.

The use of temporal and spatial ellipses, which characterizes the overall visual style in *Breathless*, recurs in multiple ways beyond the repeated jump cuts. Discontinuity editing tactics abound throughout, though some continuity conventions do recur, such as occasional "correct" eyeline matches, matches on action, and analytical editing with consistent screen direction. But the instances of discontinuity, combined with some very long takes, distinguish *Breathless,* as the narrator disrupts or undercuts both mundane and highly significant story events, in contrast to Truffaut's *Shoot the Piano Player,* which reserves discontinuity for the most significant moments in Charlie's chronicle. The editing rhythm is unusual in *Breathless,* even though the thirteen-second ASL sounds fairly conventional. One rich example of Godard's dysnarrative style can be seen in the scene when Michel has to steal a car as Patricia waits at a café for her ride to interview the writer Parvelesco (played by Jean-Pierre Melville). In this ninety-seven-second montage, alternating between the impatient Patricia (who even looks at her wrist as if checking a watch she does not have) and Michel trying car doors, there are seventeen shots, most of which systematically violate basic continuity rules. Michel begins to run left in one shot and the next shot shows him moving right, but more interestingly, actions are begun with no consequences. In one shot Michel is leaning into a silver sports car when a man arrives in the background and strikes an indignant pose, but there is never any shot to show whether the man confronts Michel. Instead the next shot shows Michel passing a man getting out of the Thunderbird convertible Michel will eventually steal. But here, too, the dysnarration denies more information than it delivers: Michel, in several shots, checks out the car and quickly runs to follow the athletic, T-shirted man into his building and up in the elevator. The elevator shot is a thirty-two-second long medium close-up of both men as they move in and out of darkness, rising to the fifth floor where Michel announces he was mistaken about his floor and pushes the down button. The next shot shows him running out of the building; five shots later he picks up Patricia in the Thunderbird.

The representative significance of this sequence is that it displays an array of story fragments, none of which are finally completed, and several possible outcomes can be assumed, though none is definite. For instance, perhaps Michel had a brief confrontation with the first sports-car owner and, having learned his lesson about the risks of stealing a car in broad daylight, decides that next time he will make sure the owner is at a safe distance indoors before hot-wiring the car. Hence, he follows the Thunderbird's owner all the way to his door before risking a theft. But since the viewer never sees just how Michel starts the Thunderbird, one could also hypothesize that Godard is showing the audience a slick pickpocket job, where Michel, passing in and out of the light, steals the man's keys while they share the cramped elevator. If so, then the sequence could be a tribute

Figure 6.3. Michel is seen snooping around a car (*Breathless*)

to Bresson, who regularly denies the audience the very shot it needs to see to understand the event fully. The fact that the seemingly uneventful elevator ride is the longest continuous shot in this scene motivates the audience to ask, "Why is he showing us all this when he cut out the confrontation with the first car owner?" There is, of course, no answer; the entire sequence calls attention once more, like most every scene in the movie, to the personal style of a filmmaker unwilling to follow conventions and unwilling to allow the audience to create passively the world of his characters. Similarly, Godard never clarifies whether the impatient Patricia looking at her watchless wrist is meant to serve as a joke on the subjectivity of time in this world, or whether the audience is to surmise that she just realized that her watch is missing, and perhaps Michel, who has robbed most everyone he has met in the movie, may have pinched it, just as he is pinching another car while she waits.

Thus, this typical scene contains many strategies that reappear in scene after scene, as the visual style complicates rather than clarifies cause-effect events or the worlds of the characters. Dysnarration is a strategy that does more than employ discontinuous devices; it emphasizes the arbitrariness of story construction, creates permanent complexity and ambiguity, and calls the viewer's attention abruptly to the labor of signification. The overall stylistic arsenal in *Breathless* does all of this with a fresh flourish.[13] Nearly every scene, such as the conversation between Patricia and her editor, the detective's shadowing of Patricia, and the final circular explanation by Patricia to Michel of her reasons for turning him in to the police, is constructed from an intriguing menu of disruptive images and sounds. Most telling of the dysnarrative qualities of *Breathless* is the shooting of the police officer and finally Michel's death; in both scenes it is impossible to reconstruct the actions into a logical space and time. For the death scene, Berruti's car travels to the right in one shot, left in the next, yet there is classical match on action as Michel begins to explain to Berruti why he will stay behind, though the next two-shot again breaks screen direction. Once Michel is shot, Patricia, running to him as he lies in the street, is obviously holding up drivers who just want to get through the street, and no police or police car are visible. Yet the detectives seem somehow to get to Michel, who has now rolled over on his back, before she can. The soundtrack is also a jumble, with the music coming and going, crescendoing and dropping out altogether, and occasional diegetic sounds such as audible running footsteps but no traffic noises.

Much has been made about the use of unflattering lighting, harsh images, wildly mobile camera work, and other significant aspects of *Breathless,* but one of the most radical strategies was its reconceptualization of the soundtrack. Michel Marie claims the dialogue alone "constitutes the most revolutionary use of language since the coming of sound. . . . Poiccard was the first film character to violate the refined sound conventions of 1959 French cinema by using popular slang and the most trivial spoken French," producing a totally new linguistic texture.[14] Marie's hypothesis is that Godard's interest in Jean Rouch's groundbreaking ethnographic filmmaking, and especially *Moi, un noir* (1958), helped him rethink sound-to-image relations here. *Breathless* stood as a complex text, exploiting and expanding many cinematic devices simultaneously. Godard's combination of a hand-held camera, Michel's dialogue with asides, quotations, onomatopoeic outbursts, and vulgar whisperings, plus a nondiegetic music track that can boom parodically and then disappear, and discontinuity between time and space on the visual versus audio tracks owed something to nearly every form of world cinema. But *Breathless* also provided a unique New Wave experiment, against which all others would quickly be judged. Godard, who liked to quip afterward that he made the movie as if cinematic conventions had not yet been invented, nonetheless also liked to acknowledge that the *Cahiers* directors were the only ones truly aware of film history; thus, in typical Godardian fashion, he offered bold contradictions in his interviewed statements just as he did in his narratives. *Breathless* at once broke new ground while it acknowledged its debt to film history, and Michel and Patricia became the ultimate New Wave couple, at once exemplary icons and unique works in progress.

By contrast, Godard's second film, *Le petit soldat* (*The Little Soldier,* 1961), became more a *cause célèbre* than an important or canonical New Wave film, because it was banned outright for several years. This movie, funded again by Georges de Beauregard, with Raoul Coutard as cine-matographer, was shot on the fly, with Godard often failing to have any di-alogue or action sketched out until each morning before shooting, though the actors did have to rehearse most scenes repeatedly. Rather than film-ing in two weeks, as hoped, it took most of April and May 1960, just as *Breathless* was opening to rave reviews in its first run. For the leads he cast newcomer Michel Subor along with Danish Anna Karina, who had just appeared in Michel Deville's *Ce soir ou jamais* (*Tonight, or Never,* 1960). While *Le petit soldat* would prove neither a financial nor a critical success, it did firmly establish Godard as a more combative and esoteric filmmaker and set up a crew, including editor Agnès Guillemot, that would go on to help him establish many production practices and aesthetic traits that continue into his subsequent works.

The story of *Le Petit soldat* is at once simple and confusing. It is told in flashback by its protagonist. Bruno Forestier (Subor), a photojournalist and member of a pro-French, antiterrorist commando group is ordered to kill a man named Palivoda, who is opposed to France's Algerian War. Strangely, Bruno is a French Army deserter living in Geneva who pretends to have no political ideals. Bruno's colleagues Jacques and Paul in the Organization of the Secret Army (OAS) suspect he may be a double agent, so they want him to prove himself by killing the pacifist Palivoda, who encourages desertion and supports the Algerian Front de Libération Na-tionale (FLN). Bruno, who would rather discuss Paul Klee's paintings than kill people, meets and quickly falls in love with Veronica Dreyer (Karina), who turns out to be slightly involved as well with the outlawed FLN. Bruno fails initially to kill Palivoda and is captured by FLN members, who tor-ture him in their hotel room until he leaps through a window and escapes to Veronica's apartment. In long monologues Bruno tries to explain the dif-ficulty of living with no ideals; he even reverses Patricia's thought from *Breathless,* pondering whether he is happy because he is free or free be-cause he is happy. Hoping to please the OAS and in turn get visas to es-

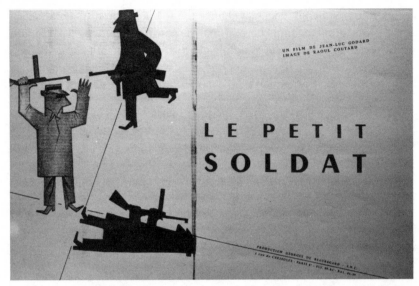

Figure 6.4. Ad for *Le petit soldat*

cape with Veronica to Brazil, Bruno calls Jacques to say he will kill Pa-livoda, but while he pursues and finally shoots his target, Jacques and Bruno decide to kidnap, torture, and murder Veronica. As Jacques puts it, "A woman on her own is either a whore or an informant." The film ends with Bruno in voice-over explaining that he has to learn not to be bitter; luckily he is still relatively young and has time.

Since the French government banned any mention of the Manifesto of 121, it should have been no surprise to Godard and Beauregard that *Le petit soldat* would face harsh treatment, though during postproduction Godard, in an interview with *L'Express*, showed no such concern: "Will my film be censored? I doubt it. It's an adventure film. I could just as well have invented a story based on the theft of Sophia Loren's jewels. But why not choose something current?"[15] But this movie proved a bit too current: it not only demonstrated a French government–supported underground group assassinating political enemies in a neutral country; it also showed in de-tail how the FLN and the OAS French commandos practiced torture and espionage. French Minister of Information Louis Terrenoire banned *Le pe-tit soldat* outright, proclaiming, "At a time when every young Frenchman is being called upon to serve and fight in Algeria, it seems quite impossible to allow this oppositional conduct to be exposed, presented, and finally justified. The fact that [Bruno Forestier] is paradoxically engaged in a

counterterrorist action does not change the fundamental problem."[16] That
the censors found the film "paradoxical" is not surprising. Even as Godard
tried to justify the convoluted politics in his film, many of the motifs from
later in his career, such as posing problems without solutions and offering
bits and pieces of truth rather than concrete analysis, are already hinted at:

> Politics are talked about in Le Petit soldat, but it has no political bias. My
> way of engaging myself was to say: the nouvelle vague is accused of show-
> ing nothing but people in bed; my characters will be active in politics and
> have no time for bed. . . . So I showed a man who poses himself a lot of
> problems. He can't resolve them, but to pose them, even confusedly, is al-
> ready an attempt at a solution. . . . Since it is a film about confusion I had
> to show it. It appears throughout, and it is experienced by the hero, who
> discovers that both the OAS and FLN quote Lenin. . . . The events are
> confused because that's how it is. My characters don't like it either.[17]

Seen in light of *Breathless, Le petit soldat* looks like an amateurish,
undisciplined, chaotic, and even ugly film. But many of the most frustrating aspects of this second feature will reverberate throughout Godard's career, most immediately in *Les carabiniers*. The story, while playing with
parodic moments from film noir, political thrillers, and even Jean Rouch
ethnography, presents a jumble of ideological issues that have to be considered in relation to personal politics. Just as hitchhikers in *Weekend* will
be asked whether they would prefer to have sex with Lyndon Johnson or
Mao Tse-tung, characters here have to decide whether they have ideals
and whether they should violate those ideals for love, friendship, or even
blackmail. As Bruno proclaims, "Even soldiers cannot be forced to kill,"
but by the end of the film he proves his own statement wrong. Godard also
sprinkles more references to the arts throughout the text, with Bruno trying to decide whether Veronica, named after director Dreyer, has eyes that
are closer to Velázquez or Renoir gray, and the pair debate what time of day
is best for listening to Mozart versus Haydn. Bruno even quotes Rousseau's
Confessions "because he is passing near the Iles Rousseau in Geneva."[18]
When Bruno plans to leave alone, he echoes Johnny Guitar, asking Veronica to lie to him about whether she will miss him. The rabid transtextual-
ity, discussed by David Bordwell in relation to Godard's work as a whole,
is everywhere here; further, high art, love, and torture are all intertwined
in an unpleasant mixture that forces the audience, in this overtly Brechtian
text, to judge every aspect of daily routine and cultural representation for
potential significance. Thus, while the story concerns generic bits and

pieces tied to current events, the overall themes have more to do with abstract Godardian concerns than with whether France should be fighting to retain its colony, Algeria. It is also significant to note that Godard never did sign the manifesto urging soldiers to desert and thus perhaps really did have no political bias at this point; he may even have been critiquing himself as a "man with no ideals."

Thus, on thematic levels, *Le petit soldat* returns to and expands upon some auteurist aspects already seen in *Breathless:* The male character is wandering and indecisive, one member of the romantic couple will die at the end, there are long, seemingly spontaneous and unnecessary conversations (with Bruno proclaiming at one point, "We never know what is important"), and American cars and pistols are featured prominently. Godard even shows up in a scene to stand self-consciously next to Bruno, as if he were again an informant, as in *Breathless.* But this loose story construction, told in flashback from an uncertain time and place, raises new narrative style issues that build upon the experimentation begun in *Breathless.* For instance, the soundtrack here is less playful and more seriously experimental. Bruno's voice-over often overlaps with spoken diegetic dialogue, but it can also intervene, further blurring the lines between subjective and objective depth. He begins the film by announcing that for him the time of action has passed and the time for reflection has arrived but also that three days earlier several battling nations engaged in mortal combat in neutral Switzerland. *Le petit soldat* seems then to be a reconstruction of events that occurred within the past week; yet whether his words are always coming from outside or from within the diegetic space and time is often confusing, a confusion reinforced by the postsynchronized dialogue.

Bruno's voice intervenes in the action in bizarre ways. At one point while Bruno is photographing Veronica and, with his camera held high, covering his mouth, he mentions that Russians are always studying; she asks, "What?" The second time he repeats his statement, his voice has a slightly different quality, suggesting that perhaps the first line was mental subjective but Veronica somehow sensed it, and the second time it is spoken dialogue. (Of course, the disparity could also result from a poor dubbing job in the postproduction recording session.) Next, Bruno says, "I find it funny you want to be an actress," while Veronica, seated, reaches for her cigarettes. And he adds in voice-over, "She lit a cigarette and asked why." The only diegetic sound is her striking of the match, as she then tosses the match aside and asks "Why?" to which he responds that he finds actors stupid because they do whatever they are told. This experimentation with the narrative functions of dialogue undercuts any sense of an absolute fictional time and space and reminds the spectator that, as in *Double Indemnity*–like films noir, everything the viewer sees and hears comes from Bruno's mind and memory, so on one level every word is "his" and there is little difference between story and narration. But *Le petit soldat* also lacks the visual or narrative charm of the conversations between Michel and Patricia. If Michel complained about an actor or artist, the audience, nonetheless, was intrigued by his opinions, in part because he had a sense of humor. But when Bruno complains about actors and Veronica responds by showing him a photo of Paul Klee's painting *An Actor*, it seems artificial and cold rather than narratively significant. The drab style and experimentation here do not lend qualities to the characters since the characters seem more like the actors Bruno is condemning: they have no freedom and simply stand there doing what they are told, whereas in *Breathless* there was an open spontaneity, as if the filmmakers were trying to follow their characters. Here the actors simply follow direction in a cynical and lifeless, overly rehearsed performance.

Visually, *Le petit soldat* is a dreary experience, far from the lively and fragmented world of *Breathless*. The time and space Bruno inhabits reinforce his comment that for men, death is more important than life, and Godard's mise-en-scène repeats over and over that this is a world of death, loss, and confusion. Characters move in and out of shadow, and despite the thematic content of torture and murder, everything is shot as if it were a mundane observation of events, producing a Geneva composed of dull, flat narrative spaces in contrast to the Paris of *Breathless*. Godard even employs conventional continuity eyeline matching often, as in the scene when Bruno, set up by his fellow commandos and in trouble with the police, exchanges looks with them to nod that, yes, if they get him out of this scrape, he will kill for them. The ASL is twelve seconds, and there are only a few jump cuts in this film, as Godard selects whip pans instead as a constant punctuation device. Sometimes the camera swings to one side of the street to reveal one character and then swings back to the other side to catch another action. At other times the camera work is used to blur events or simply as a transition; for example, when Bruno arrives at Veronica's apartment, there is a whip tilt up her building and a cut to him inside chatting with her. But unlike the jump cut, these whip pans and tilts merely provide a striking device to suggest a rapid narrative perspective, while the action itself rarely feels vibrant, as the characters plod heavily, as if already doomed, through the streets and hallways of *Le petit soldat*.

Because of the exhibition and export ban, *Le petit soldat* provided no potential for income. Nonetheless, Godard, who to a certain extent still owed Georges Beauregard a movie, began his third feature in fourteen months, getting Beauregard and his new coproducer at Rome-Paris Films, Carlo Ponti, to fund a wide-screen, color musical comedy, *Une femme est une femme* (*A Woman Is a Woman*, 1961), starring Godard's new wife, Anna Karina. *Le petit soldat* would not be released in France until 1963 and then only after a few additional cuts for the censors, such as Veronica being tortured by the French OAS; it did not play internationally in markets such as the United States until 1965. That Beauregard took another risk on Godard proves his dedication to the young director who had earned him a great deal with *Breathless,* but it also reveals just how bold and unconventional a producer Beauregard was, traits that allowed him to become one of the major New Wave producers. Godard's third feature was based on a script he had already written and even published in part in *Cahiers du cinéma* in 1959, based on an idea from actress Geneviève Cluny.[19] In a slightly different form, the same story had just been filmed by Philippe de Broca as *Les jeux de l'amour* (*Games of Love,* 1960), starring Cluny.

Godard began shooting *A Woman Is a Woman* in November 1960, with a five-week production schedule; its commercial premiere was in September 1961, six months after Jacques Demy's *Lola,* which shared some similar dialogue and story events and was also shot by Raoul Coutard. This was Godard's first film to be shot partly in a studio, though he did have ceilings built on many sets to make sure the lighting set-ups did not mimic conventional high-angle studio light grids. He also insisted on direct sound recording for the first time, a documentary/newsreel tactic that seems to contradict the control of moving into a studio. For a few scenes, Godard used his own apartment on rue du Faubourg Saint-Denis, and some scenes were filmed on the street or in real shops and cafés. Since Godard had already published the original scenario, he not only possessed a basic script to show Beauregard and Ponti, but he had, as with Truffaut's outline for *Breathless,* more of a structure than with *Le petit soldat.* Nonetheless, he continued writing dialogue and action up to the last moment, claiming often to have finished the day's script while the principal actors, Karina, Jean-Claude Brialy, and Jean-Paul Belmondo, were in make-up.

This would be the second Godard feature seen by the public, and, as James Monaco points out, it, like Truffaut's *Shoot the Piano Player,* would also be a surprising and disappointing second film for many critics,

especially since *A Woman Is a Woman* reworked the musical even more
radically than *Shoot the Piano Player* did film noir, and neither film resembled Truffaut's or Godard's first, more popular, features.[20] Despite
color, wide-screen, the success of *Breathless,* added marketing from
Rome-Paris Films, and a first prize at Berlin's film festival, *A Woman Is a
Woman,* sold only sixty-five thousand tickets in Paris, which was a little
worse than *Shoot the Piano Player.* Today, however, *A Woman Is a Woman*
can be seen to exhibit many of the personal story and style traits audiences
have come to expect of Godard, though by the 1970s he himself would dismiss it as a bourgeois experiment.

After a brilliant title sequence of one-second-long blue, white, and red
flashing words and names, such as "Once Upon a Time," "Beauregard,"
"Eastmancolor," "Comedy," and "Lubitsch," but also "Musical" followed
with composer "Legrand," and "Theatrical" followed by the name of art director "Evein," there are three rapid shots of Karina, Brialy, and Belmondo
along with their superimposed names. This opening, accompanied as it is
with crew sounds and the discordant sounds of tuning instruments and
Karina's voice yelling, "Lights, camera, action," playfully begins the film
with a series of discursive reminders of the artifice and process of filmmaking. Such overt references to personnel and context will become the
norm for the rest of Godard's career. *A Woman Is a Woman* tells the tale of
Angela (Karina), a stripper at the crummy Zodiac club, who suddenly decides that she wants to become pregnant. Although she has a device to cal-
culate "scientifically" the precise moment for successful impregnation,
and it has indicated that December 10, 1961, is the day, her live-in
boyfriend, Emile Récamier (Brialy), thinks this is not the time to start a
family. He wants to wait until they are married in the near future, but she
insists she wants to make a baby within twenty-four hours. Emile has a
bike race on Sunday and uses that as an excuse: he wants to rest, so refuses
to have sex with her. He is baffled as to why she wants a child now, and her
only explanation is "because," though she then presents a circular argument that since she thought Emile loved her she wanted a child, but since
he does not want a child, he must not love her. This explanation resembles
Patricia's explanation for why she turned Michel in to the police in *Breathless:* it was to test her love.

Disappointed, Angela promises to ask the first man she sees to im-
pregnate her, at which point the police arrive at the door, looking for an escaped suspect. She chickens out. But Emile calls out the window for their
friend Alfred Lubitsch (Belmondo), who is also in love with her, to come

up to the apartment. While the couple waits for Alfred to climb the stairs, they sit in silence, and superimposed titles announce that it is precisely *because* they love each other that things will go badly for Angela and Emile. Alfred, who is in a hurry because he wants to get home to see *Breathless* on television, is bemused when Emile tells him Angela wants a baby; Alfred even asks whether this is a comedy or a tragedy. Alfred and Angela flirt and joke in the bathroom for a few moments under red-and-blue flashing lights, but finally the men decide to go out for a drink together. As Angela announces to the audience, it is now the end of the third act, so, in the tradition of great tragedies the heroine must hesitate as her fate hangs in the balance.

In bed that night, Emile and Angela argue in silence by showing each other titles from books that replace their dialogue, and the next day she makes a date with Alfred. But progression toward some resolution is delayed with chance meetings and anecdotal events. In a café Alfred sees Jeanne Moreau and asks her how things worked out with Jules and Jim, but she simply replies, "Moderato!" (she had just completed filming Peter Brooks's *Moderato Cantabile* along with Belmondo).

Before Angela meets Alfred, she runs into her friend Suzanne (Marie Dubois), who mimes out the title for *Shoot the Piano Player*, and Angela tells her how much she liked the movie and especially Charles Aznavour. When Angela and Alfred meet for a drink, Alfred tells her the story of a woman who has two lovers and sends them each a letter; she thinks she put

Figure 6.5. Alfred caught between Emile and Angela (*A Woman Is a Woman*)

Figure 6.6. Jeanne Moreau in a café (*A Woman Is a Woman*)

the letters in the wrong envelopes and apologizes to each man. However, she had *not* mixed up the letters, but her explanation cost her both men. This, of course, will be the story Godard films for his episode of *Paris vu par* (1964). As Alfred and Angela try to decide what to do, he shows Angela a photo of Emile with another woman; in pain, she asks to hear a sad Aznavour song on the jukebox.

Meanwhile, Emile searches for Angela, but finally goes with a prostitute, which undercuts his entire defense to Angela that he cannot make love for fear of weakening his performance in the bike race the next day. At the same time, Angela and Alfred make love at his apartment. Back at home, Angela and Emile decide the only way to remedy the unfortunate situation is for them to have sex together right away so that if she does become pregnant there is a chance Emile will be the father. Finally, Emile tells her she is *infame,* or shameful, but she plays on the word's pronunciation and says "Non, je suis *une* femme" ["No, I am a woman"]. The tale ends with a wink to the camera from Angela and a musical crescendo, then the sound of studio lights being turned off: click.

The story construction for this light-hearted parody of a sex comedy is just as loose as it is linear. It opens with a classical Hollywood-like motivation: Angela wants to become pregnant and has roughly twenty-four hours in which to accomplish her goal. Her desire is, in fact, met doubly, as she ends up in bed with both Alfred and Emile. Many scenes are devoted to helping and/or hindering Angela in her pursuit: Emile tries to understand her concern but then makes fun of her, Alfred shows up but then goes out for drinks with Emile and two other women, Angela reads baby books and speaks with her women colleagues at the Zodiac about pregnancy, and so on. But like *Breathless,* this film also has many seemingly inconsequential scenes and conversations: Alfred encounters a hotel landlord who proves he skipped out without paying; Angela has a long chat with Emile about what he wants for dinner despite the fact that she's already overcooked a beef roast; Emile searches for Angela to win her away from Alfred but then goes with the prostitute; and the women at the Zodiac repeat lines of dialogue from *Lola* in which they discuss who will go off on a striptease tour to southern France. But none of this affects Angela, so the scenes are merely important for providing background information, standing in as pleasant individual mininarratives or as intertextual connections with Demy's movie. Godard provides a loose, artificial story that appears both as a reference to Doris Day–Rock Hudson color romantic comedies and as a good-natured comment on love, sex, and contemporary New Wave youth. It also continues the New Wave plot device, already worked out in *Le beau Serge, The Cousins,* and *Jules and Jim,* of peering into contemporary morality by placing one woman in relationships with two males. In the end, however, the tone of *A Woman Is a Woman* is comically contradictory; as Brialy explains, "[Godard] made us play false situations in a realistic way, and realistic situations in a false way. The phonier it was, the more it had to seem natural."[21]

But Godard's style here is certainly what makes *A Woman Is a Woman* such an unusual film, or as *Cahiers* wrote, "Cinema in its pure state. It's both spectacle and the charm of spectacle. It's Lumière in 1961."[22] It is indeed a stunning exercise in mise-en-scène, sound-to-image relations, and narration. The characters talk to the camera, superimposed titles provide narrative commentary to the audience, there are mismatches and tiny jump cuts alternating with perfectly classical eyeline matches, the music drops out just when Angela sings or speeds up like a calliope out of control in other scenes, characters repeat lines, and the camera occasionally pans away from the characters to cross the room, pause, and pan back, elegantly ignoring the characters for a moment of nothingness while they decide what to do or say next. The intertextual references, including Godard's suggestion that *A Woman Is a Woman* is an updating of Ernst Lubitsch's *Design for Living* (1933) crossed with Jean Rouch, all make this another fascinating variation on Godard's narrative experimentation and motifs. At one point Angela even tells Alfred what she really wants is to be in a musical comedy with Cyd Charisse and Gene Kelly, choreographed by Bob Fosse. But its most striking innovation is its use of color; it not only prefigures Godard's own life-long fascination with how to use color anew, but it also points the way for other 1960s art films to update their arsenal of cinematic tricks with the bold semiotics of color.

Godard and Color

Today one associates the low-budgets and often grainy black-and-white images of movies such as *Breathless* and *Le petit soldat*, as well as *Shoot the Piano Player* and *The Cousins*, with the essence of art film production in the late 1950s and early 1960s. But not all of these young directors, including Godard, shot in black-and-white simply out of aesthetic choice. The *Cahiers du cinéma* directors in particular display a long fascination with color aesthetics, as they did with wide-screen framing. Color in particular could provide the New Wave a more contemporary "look" and a chance to rethink color codes, paralleling their ongoing challenges to editing and sound conventions. But color doubled the cost of production, and its slow speed limited the sorts of locations they could use. Thus, when Godard did manage to shoot in color with *A Woman Is a Woman*, he immediately engaged its radical narrative potential, exploiting color systematically to fit his own personal aesthetics, which had been a long time in critical preparation.

For New Wave directors, color posed unique challenges. On the one hand, black-and-white allowed them to shoot on location with low budgets. On the other hand, the New Wave obviously identified with the vibrant postwar youth culture. Their stories reveled in the novelty of American cars, whiskey, and jazz, but also glossy magazines, neon lights, and billboards. As Alain Bergala observes, "Strangely, the most contemporary, youthful films, the ones reflecting major changes in French society and cinema, were still using the oldest technology—black-and-white film— precisely at the moment when color film was on the rise in France."[23] In 1959 only 15 French films were in color, while by 1961 there were 54 (of 105). But for the most part, the New Wave had to abandon color to their enemy—the big-budget "cinema of quality."

For New Wave directors trying to shoot quickly and cheaply, color offered a host of practical problems. Most importantly, color 35 mm raw stock, laboratory fees, and release prints were much more expensive. A few people followed Jean Rouch's example and tried shooting color in

16 mm, which was roughly one-fourth the cost of 35 mm color. But even that option was expensive: in 1960, 16 mm Kodachrome had an ASA of only 16 (versus 50 for 35 mm Eastmancolor or 250 for black-and-white XX) and thus required extensive lighting set-ups for interiors. Such a slow speed also inhibited spontaneous shooting on location. But 16 mm also provided another economic hardship: the CNC did not recognize 16 mm as a professional standard and thus could not give Film Aid to 16 mm features, even if they were going to be blown up to 35 mm for exhibition (a format required in all Art et essai theaters).

For aesthetic reasons, too, a few New Wave directors did not see color as fitting their needs or desires. François Truffaut was one of the more outspoken advocates of black-and-white during the 1950s: "The proliferation of color has pushed backwards the average quality of images, making our perception of films simpler and less spellbinding."[24] Truffaut represents the sort of critic for whom black-and-white possesses a distinct nostalgic value but also a richness of visual parameters that help define the essential artistry of the cinematic image. Noel Benoit explains, "In Truffaut's eyes color is hideous because it contents itself with recording reality without transforming it . . . [and] it also destroys fiction by carrying the image ineluctably toward documentary."[25] Truffaut did make effective use of black-and-white in scenes such as the opening of *The 400 Blows* with the spilled black ink on the white paper or the scene in *Shoot the Piano Player* in which Fido drops the "milk bomb" onto the windshield of the would-be kidnappers. In contrast to Truffaut, however, the bulk of young French filmmakers of this era were, indeed, fascinated with color as one more creative parameter for film language. Jacques Rivette wrote in 1954 that color was even more important to film history than the advent of sound: "It is no longer from the shadow of things that the filmmaker will draw substance, but from the most alive and striking forms. . . . For us the history of Technicolor is synonymous with films of Jean Renoir, Alfred Hitchcock, and Howard Hawks."[26] Similarly, Eric Rohmer, who would not shoot a color short until 1964 or a feature until 1966, wrote as early as 1949 that color has great potential but only a handful of filmmakers use it productively. In subsequent articles, he divided color films into those that exploit it as an ornament versus those concerned with its power as an emotional motif. For him, the best color is seen in Hitchcock's use of the green dress for Miss Lonelyheart in *Rear Window* (1954). He wrote, "Do not use color like a painter, use it in a more cinematic way."[27]

Godard later echoed this sentiment when he wrote that filmmakers should not search the Louvre for lessons on how to use color. Instead, he looked both to film history and contemporary pop culture, including comic books and op art, when he finally got to add color to his palette. But many historians trying to explain how color burst upon the scene in 1960s art films still fail to acknowledge fully the amazing contributions by Godard and his colleagues. Alain Bergala, for instance, locates the pivotal moment in the art cinema's transition to color as the 1964 *Cahiers* interview of Antonioni by Godard. In that interview, Antonioni agrees with Rohmer's claim that color can help reveal the beauty in things such as factories and even barren landscapes, and Antonioni and Godard both refer to the bright metal and plastic objects that have begun to dominate modern landscapes. For Bergala, once Antonioni and others like him decided color film can best represent their world, modern European cinema was changed forever. Yet, by this 1964 interview concerning *Red Desert*, Godard, Malle, Chabrol, and Demy have already shot in color. It is, indeed, the French New Wave directors that establish new color norms in the cinema precisely by combining their interest in certain theorists and directors with their desire to further their own personal experimentation. Most likely, Antonioni rethought how to use color, thanks to them. The New Wave directors first carried color beyond the Technicolor stylists Vincente Minnelli, Douglas Sirk, and Alfred Hitchcock by combining it with more formal manipulation right out of Eisenstein's theories and their own practical criticism.

Of the *Cahiers* filmmakers, Godard is certainly the most important in his novel use of color for its thematic as well as formal qualities. *A Woman Is a Woman*, even more than Chabrol's *A double tour* (1959) or Malle's *Zazie dans le métro* (1960), forcefully established the narrative power of color for the New Wave. Godard offered *A Woman Is a Woman* as a tribute to his new "toy," color, but also in homage to the sort of films Hollywood would never make again, especially the 1950s musical. But he also exploited color as one more strategy that could parallel his interest in other devices such as the iris and direct sound, all of which were present in *Singin' in the Rain* (Kelly, Donan, 1952). Thus, *A Woman Is a Woman* is central to understanding how New Wave color films borrowed some of Hollywood's most daring color strategies but carried them further according to intricate and personal color systems.

Godard had already praised color in his critical articles, including his 1958 review of *Pajama Game:* "Robert Fosse has managed to coax a maximum of bright and graceful effects from the austere Warnercolor, juggling red lipstick, blue jeans, green grass, yellow flags, and white skirts, to compose a wild and ravishing kaleidoscope."[28] For Godard the objects filmed are inseparable from their color (it might seem redundant to say red lipstick or green grass, but for Godard their color comes first). Moreover, Godard, like Truffaut, regularly praises a certain sort of American cinema but always a cinema that he admits can never be made again, such as *Singin' in the Rain* (which was "number five" on Godard's Best Hollywood Movies list). But Godard develops a more modernist response to the challenge of color and bases it in part on his experimentation with representational challenges that also face modern painters. Jacques Aumont argues that *A Woman Is a Woman* announces Godard's early fascination with op art, collage, and cubism's potential to confuse and fragment space. "Godard's references to artists, especially Picasso and Klee, connect his own work to their lively experimentation; but rather than identifying with artists, Godard identifies with their pictorial problems."[29] Noel Benoit writes, "Godard never lost sight of the weight, power, and potential of color and especially the possibility that color could be used to disguise reality . . . and undo whatever it was coloring."[30] Godard grapples with color within the context of past film practice, the history of modern art, and theories of representation from Eisenstein to Brecht.

Godard's color scheme in *A Woman Is a Woman* establishes many of the traits that his later films will continue to develop: First, he uses uniform interior lighting levels to create homogeneous and pure colors. By contrast, Technicolor's Natalie Kalmus, who is responsible for the Technicolor style that dominated Hollywood of the 1930s into the 1950s, had argued against maintaining equal light levels in interiors since "unimportant" bright objects such as a painting in the background would compete for attention with the actors. Second, Godard plants his camera directly in front of highly saturated primary colors, producing a very flat, pop art space, resembling modern paintings or collages that destroy depth cues. Third, Godard's color echoes Eisenstein's call for color selection that is textually determined for a limited color palette specific to the world of each film. Godard does not rely on traditional cultural connotations or even thematic development so much as recurring formal patterns. In *A Woman Is a Woman* all three of these strategies are already at work, and his standard color range is established with the recurring blue, white, and red that he will use throughout his career.

A Woman Is a Woman's intertextual references to Hollywood color are also quite striking. First, there are dialogue references to *Singin' in the Rain* and Bob Fosse; second, are the exaggerated formal color patterns that

recall the most transgressive moments in 1950s American cinema. For in-
stance, movies such as *Johnny Guitar, Singin' in the Rain,* Sirk's *All That
Heaven Allows* (1955), and Tashlin's *Will Success Spoil Rock Hunter* (1957)
were already breaking away from the functional pastel harmonies of
Natalie Kalmus and the Technicolor style. When Rock Hunter (Tony
Randall) tries to confront his test of success by keeping his pipe lit, Tashlin flashes red-and-blue lights on his face, much like Godard's lights on
Angela when she sings her "I'm so beautiful" song or when she and Alfred
joke in the bathroom. Where Godard exceeds the artificial 1950s models
is in narrowing the range of options on his palette, rejecting wholeheart-
edly the use of color as "natural" or simply thematic in any single scene.
Color for him is rediscovered and purified partly by discarding any appeal
to realism or reducing color to thematic function.

Godard's color reveals just how deep his debt to Sergei Eisenstein
runs. Eisenstein preferred that color create new emotional significance
without relying on previous cultural symbols, which, of course, is the exact opposite of Natalie Kalmus's color theories. In David Bordwell's summary of Eisenstein's color theories, one can see how closely they anticipate
Godard's cinema: "There is no universal psychological correspondence
between a specific color and a certain feeling. . . . Color is, like graphic
contour, detachable from specific objects. Pure color can suggest concepts. . . . The filmmaker can start by exposing the film's palette, associat-
ing certain colors with particular narrative elements, and then building
each episode around a dominant color or color combination. . . . It
[thereby] maximizes the interaction of color motifs within the film's
polyphony . . . and reinforces the inner unity of picture and sound."[31] Now
the changing reds and blues on Angela's face during her striptease not only
parallel her red and blue stockings, or recall Rock Hunter's frightened
face, but they also pastiche Vladimir's horror in *Ivan the Terrible, Part II*
(Eisenstein, 1946). And unlike Tashlin's musical comedy, the color palette
in *A Woman Is a Woman* continues to be narrowly defined and controlled,
creating a very limited, textually specific menu that is all Godard's. Even
for Godard's short, "Montparnasse et Levallois," in *Paris vu par,* the red
and blue recur, helping distinguish these characters from the drab grays of
their traditional Parisian setting, but the colors never seem thematically
significant. Initially, the woman seems tied to red, as she always wears a
red sweater, and the first man wears a blue jacket. But Roger, the second
man, wears blue *and* red, is working on the pope's red car, and has a shop
full of red automobile posters. Red is not thematically limited to the

woman in the space of this short film, and thus the color leans more toward formal patterns (character number one wears red, number two wears blue, number three wears red and blue, and so on) than characterization.

Godard's Paris, like that of Louis Malle's *Zazie dans le metro,* is full of modern color accents among the drab city colors. The world is changing, and the color announces those changes in the modern urban terrain, where red fire trucks, blue billboards, and intense neon lights lash the wild world of commercialism and pop art onto gray Paris. Jacques Aumont labels Godard "the next-to-last painter of the cinema," claiming Godard's investigation of pictorial problems and his defamiliarization of color composition make him the ultimate film theorist.[32] Thus, when Angela, wearing her red sweater, walks into her white kitchen, surrounded by blue pots and pans, while Emile, in his dark blue blazer, stands in the white living room next to white and red flowers and a red lamp shade, the viewer is witnessing a bold modern portraiture that owes as much to advertising posters and Mondrian's formal patterns as to Eisenstein and Tashlin's color compositions. Right from the beginning this novelty is announced: the opening blue, white, and red titles proclaim that *A Woman Is a Woman* won a special jury prize at the Berlin Film Festival "for originality, youthfulness, audacity, impertinence in shaking off the norms of the classical film comedy." Color is part of the medium communicating to the audience, yet it can never be reduced to simple monological connotations—this movie does not reward a facile attempt to read the triple color motif as representing France or the United States—any more than the colors in a Paul Klee can be narrativized. Color, for Godard, had become a central, formal parameter, like editing, music, and camerawork. But he would have to follow this expensive failure with two more black-and-white features, *Vivre sa vie* (*My Life to Live,* 1962) and *Bande à part* (*Band of Outsiders,* 1963), before returning to color experimentation with *Le mepris* (*Contempt,* 1963).

Dysnarration and Godard

By the time of *Vivre sa vie,* Godard's distinct narrative strategies for investigating the cinema's modes of storytelling were fully in place. While he varied the specific tactics of experimentation in each text, he nonetheless had staked out a set terrain, exploring sounds and images in fairly consistent ways. *Vivre sa vie* proves exemplary in that it shows him pushing even further the limits of what is, or is not, appropriate in a feature film's content and style. As V. F. Perkins observes, "As a filmmaker, Godard remains a critic speculating on the nature of film and the possibilities of direction. One of his concerns, here as elsewhere, is to test the relative strengths of language and the movie image as media for various forms of communication."[33] Hence, by the early 1960s, Godard's career was veering off a bit from simply telling new stories in casual new ways. His niche was rapidly becoming what at the time was labeled an "anti-cinema" that paralleled more extreme work in the New Novel as well as trends in the academic fields of philosophy, semiotics, and art theory. He may have learned to love the cinema from watching Renoir, Hawks, and Hitchcock, but his own films began to owe as much or more to theories of capitalism's inherent alienation effects or Bertolt Brecht's applicability for forging a nonbourgeois film style. Every mode of film practice and critical perspective could now pop into his films, lending them a forbidding quality that would eventually force friends like Truffaut to complain that Godard no longer made movies that people like Truffaut, who had never attended college, could understand. The irony was that much of Godard's antibourgeois cinema was incredibly elitist, requiring more than just an apprenticeship at the Cinémathèque.

Vivre sa vie would again be shot in an unorthodox manner, with Godard making many decisions during the production stage while working from a brief scenario and increasingly chaotic notes to himself as well as a source book on prostitution by sociologist Marcel Sacotte. The shooting schedule was only four weeks, but the second week saw almost no shooting. Godard had promised with each new project to begin working differently, relying more on an established script, but by *Vivre sa vie* he seems to have accepted that production to him was a personal process involving last minute decisions or long pauses so he could further reflect on just what he wanted next: "The big difficulty is that I need people who can be at my disposal the whole time. . . . The terrible thing is that in the cinema it is so difficult to do what a painter does quite naturally: he stops, steps back, gets discouraged, starts again."[34] *Vivre sa vie* is composed of twelve scenes, each capped off with its own introductory title, such as "The Record Shop," "Two Thousand Francs," "Nana Lives Her Life." Each scene is set in linear order, though there are sizeable temporal gaps between some of them. The film was shot mostly in sequence, and according to Godard, there was little postproduction editing: "What the crew saw at the rushes is more or less what the public sees. . . . The film is a series of blocks. You just take them and set them side by side. . . . I obtained a theatrical realism."[35] The result is a stunning film, again shot by Raoul Coutard, whose static shots, filmed with the bulky, studio Mitchell camera, lent a very polished and stable look to what was in fact a very improvisational project. Moreover, its ASL was a leisurely twenty-two seconds, as opposed to the ten-second ASL for the wide-screen *A Woman Is a Woman.*

Vivre sa vie opens with white titles on a black background announcing its Special Jury Prize at the Venice Film Festival; the second title provides the visa number and copyright date, adding "conceived, written, shot, edited, in brief: directed by J.-L. Godard." Next the white title and cast are superimposed over a dark profile, the silhouette of Nana (Anna Karina). In the first scene, or tableau, Nana, an aspiring actress, chats with her ex-husband Paul (critic André S. Labarthe) in a scene that hides their faces, shooting each separately from behind, occasionally with their faces visible in the café mirror. They have a son, raised by Paul now, and she works at a record store. In scene two, made up mostly of a three-minute-and-fifteen-second shot sequence, Nana is bored at work, and she tries to borrow two thousand francs from her female coworkers, in an episode that recalls the demoralized shop women in Chabrol's *Les bonnes femmes.* In the third scene it becomes clear why Nana needs money: her landlady will not let her back into her apartment until she pays the overdue rent. Chased away from her apartment, she meets Paul to see photos of her son, then goes to Dreyer's *Passion of Joan of Arc* (1928); Godard includes an entire scene from that film, in silence, intercut with Nana's teary face. After the movie, she brushes off one man and meets another who wants to take nude photos of her for a potential film acting job, and as Patricia did with her editor in *Breathless,* she spends the night with him to further her possible career.

By the fourth scene, "Police, Nana Is Questioned," Nana in silhouette admits that she tried to steal one thousand francs that a woman had dropped; since she had failed, she argues, she should not be arrested. Scene five depicts Nana having decided to prostitute herself and shows her servicing her first client. In tableau six, she encounters a prostitute friend, Yvette (Guylaine Schlumberger), who explains that her husband had left her with several children, so she slipped into prostitution. Nana claims that everyone is responsible for his or her own actions. Yvette then introduces her to Raoul (Sady Rebbot), her pimp, but machine-gun shots and a huge police raid send her running away. Scene number seven reveals Nana writing a letter to a madam in another town, asking if she can work in her brothel. Raoul finds her, however, and she asks him whether he finds her "special" (she had complained to Paul in the first scene that she left him because he never saw her that way). With scene eight, Nana learns the "business" of prostitution from Raoul. On the soundtrack, she asks questions concerning rates, numbers of clients, and rules, and he answers matter of factly; the image offers a montage of Nana at work, especially entering hotel rooms and exchanging money.

Scene nine does not, at first sight, seem to advance the plot: Raoul meets with his friend Luigi, so the bored Nana, waiting for him to finish, dances to the jukebox and flirts with another young man (Peter Kassowitz). During tableau ten, Nana secures a client and then procures a second woman for him as well. In scene eleven, Nana strikes up a conversation with Sorbonne professor (Brice Parrain) in a café near Châtelet (where Nana claims once to have acted on stage). The professor tells her the story of a Dumas character who killed himself accidentally the first time he bothered to think deeply. The pair discuss the value of words and thought, with references to Hegel and the centrality of contradiction in one's life. This scene, like Patricia's interview of Melville in *Breathless,* relates tangentially to issues in both the story and the film's style, but the interview also has a more polemical motivation. Filmologist Gabriel Marcel had once written that placing a Sorbonne professor in a film to discuss Kant and philosophy would be "a ridiculous abuse of film, from an aesthetic viewpoint." As V. F. Perkins points out, much of the force and value of *Vivre sa vie* resides in Godard's direct attack on such preconceived notions of any fixed "nature of the cinema."[36]

The final scene, number twelve, finds Nana with the young man from scene nine; he reads Poe's tale of the oval portrait for her (although the voice is actually Godard's). Parts of their conversation are delivered only in subtitles, including the final line stating that she will move in with this man and tell Raoul she is finished with prostitution. But the next shot shows Raoul pushing Nana out of her old apartment and into his car with three other men. Raoul is angry with Nana for refusing to take certain clients, so he intends to sell her to these other pimps. He drives them past a long line of people waiting to see *Jules and Jim* as well as a sign for "Enfer et ses fils" (Hell and sons). When he stops to transfer her to the men's car, the men argue over money. In a tragic-comic exchange, one man clicks his gun, then tells his partner, "You shoot, I forgot to load." One of the men shoots Nana, then Raoul does too. Raoul drives off, pursued by the other men, leaving Nana lying crumpled on the street in a shot that recalls Lena's death in *Shoot the Piano Player:* an innocent woman is killed, and the incompetent gangsters take off on a chase that the audience never sees to its end.

Figure 6.7. Nana in a café (*My Life to Live*)

Figure 6.8. The philosophy professor (*My Life to Live*)

Figure 6.9. Nana is killed (*My Life to Live*)

The story construction in *Vivre sa vie* is fascinating in its mix of linearity and ellipses. While the twelve tableaux are summarized in their chapter headings and placed in sequence to produce the "theatrical realism" Godard mentions, they nonetheless leave huge gaps between one another. The viewer never learns, for instance, how much time has passed between Nana's first customer and her meeting with Yvette, who already seems like a long-time acquaintance. Moreover, the audience is given no cue that the young man playing billiards and watching Nana dance around him in scene ten has become her lover and, by scene twelve, her willing protector. Rather than using intertitles to clarify the missing story action, such as "Over the next two months, Nana secretly met with this young man and fell in love," the film leaps from Nana in the café with the professor to her presence in an apartment with the young man. Storytelling here offers concrete sections of time and space within chapters but communicates little about what is not shown in the scenes. Arguing, as many critics have, that *Vivre sa vie* is an essay about or a study of Nana, prostitution, or even contemporary French culture is unconvincing since the narrative provides so little background or context for the characters or their actions. What minimal information the audience does receive—Nana had a family, Yvette too has children, the young man likes Poe—is undercut by large gaps of space, time, and causality. The result is an aggressively open-story film that is simultaneously a brave and distancing formal experiment, though some critics, such as Wheeler Winston Dixon, insist the narration is "brutally realistic," lending the portrayal of Nana, "considerable depth and humanity."[37] But for most viewers, it offers a shallow though fascinating presentation of bits of a tiny piece of Nana's life; neorealism it is not.

Visually, *Vivre sa vie* avoids jump cuts, replacing them with fades as the most obvious and privileged form of punctuation. Each fade further emphasizes the narrator's denial of information, with the blackness on the screen representing physically the ellipses. In addition to the many experiments with direct sound and the resulting range of image-to-sound relations (diegetic sounds crossing to become nondiegetic, subtitles replacing dialogue, Godard reading from the offscreen space, characters offering lecturelike tracts, and so on), *Vivre sa vie* was striking for its formal strategy of varying the means of staging conversations. Perkins and Bordwell have both outlined how Godard organized the framing of each scene around variations on "how one *might* shoot a conversation."[38] As Bordwell points out, the opening title sequence and first scene shoot Nana from 45-degree angles, beginning with a left profile and ending by filming her from the rear, which "announces this 'theme' of varying camera/figure orientations."[39] The rest of the scenes explore other options, including laterally tracking, arcing, and panning shots; 180-degree line variations, and even the shot/reverse shot sequence of Dreyer's film intercut with Nana's point/glance. For Godard, "one should feel that the characters here are constantly avoiding the camera."[40] Thus, like his previous films, *Vivre sa vie* continues to provide a vibrant example of a text that is as much about variations on cinematic storytelling alternatives as it is about young characters wrestling with romantic and career options in their lives. It quickly became a canonical 1960s art film, celebrated by a wide range of critics and historians in a way that neither *Le petit soldat* nor *A Woman Is a Woman* would be. It also bolstered Godard's reputation as a highly significant cinematic renegade and genius; in *A Woman Is a Woman*, Brialy's Emile declares that he does not know whether the movie he inhabits is a comedy or a tragedy, but regardless it is a "masterpiece." But many reviewers were now eager to declare *Vivre sa vie* Godard's masterpiece, his best work to date, prompting some to call him the French Ingmar Bergman.

Godard's next project, *Les carabiniers* (*The Soldiers*, 1963), was less fortunate, critically and at the box office. The story outline was based on a play by Benjamin Joppolo but then revised by Roberto Rossellini and Jean Gruault, who provided a typed script for Godard, who revised it further, cutting parts he liked out of the original and taping them into a notebook alongside his own handwritten additions. The short scenario was summarized in four acts (Nature, War, Paradise, The World) and is reprinted in *Avant-Scène Cinéma* (August–September 1976), along with a description of the final film. In his famous *Cahiers du cinéma* interview, taped before filming began in 1963, Godard claimed that the scenario was so good that he would simply film it with few complications or decisions; it would be like making an old Rossellini movie.[41] The initial written script, however, was rejected by the CNC's censorship board.

Once again, Godard worked with the producers Beauregard and Ponti and with the usual crew of Coutard, Guillemot, and camera operator Claude Beausoleil, among others. While Godard hoped to film in color, his budget was too low, so he switched to shooting in Kodak XX, printing it onto high-contrast stock for a stark, grainy look; sometimes he even had the footage duplicated several times to make it look, at least in his eyes, like the orthochromatic stock used by Charlie Chaplin. Jean Douchet celebrates the result: "He worked with [high-contrast stock] as a form of Art Brut, the way Dubuffet treated paint and canvas. He extracted from it a chalk-colored world of immense sorrow."[42] He also included newsreel footage, following Truffaut's model in *Jules and Jim*, though here the images are not so aesthetically moving: they are ugly, sometimes even banal, images of warfare.

The story for *Les carabiniers*, even more than that of *Le petit soldat*, belongs to political theater and allegory. A cluster of comical and unpleasant peasants, living in a shack in a field, are visited by two carabiniers, who, by command of the king, order the two men, Ulysses (Marino Mase) and his younger brother, Michelangelo (Albert Juross), to join the army. The soldiers also threaten Ulysses's wife, Cleopatra (Catherine Ribeiro), and apparent daughter Venus (Geneviève Galéa). But soon everyone is excited by the promise of travel and riches as the soldiers explain they can take anything from the enemy: their land, their sheep, their palaces, their cities, their cinemas, their cigar factories, their Maserati automobiles. Michelangelo is suspicious and asks whether he could smash an old man's eyeglasses, leave restaurants without paying, massacre innocent women and children, and steal designer slacks. Finally convinced that all is permitted, the men sign their contracts, and the women urge them to go to war; Cleopatra wants a washing machine, while Venus asks Michelangelo to bring her back a bikini.

The war, introduced with stock newsreel footage of cannons firing and tanks in battle, is punctuated with title cards handwritten by Godard, such as "We saw infantrymen and generals die without a whimper, their stomachs ripped open, uniforms soaked in blood, and eyes gouged out," "A nice summer nonetheless." The progression of the war is shown in bits and pieces and intertitles; Cleopatra and Venus receive postcards recounting the soldiers' adventures, and the audience sees Ulysses and Michelangelo accost civilians, execute hostages, and eventually take over apartment buildings and kill the concierges. Godard makes comical use of the Kuleshov effect and his own creative geography, alternating shots of the men looking with cuts to the Sphinx or the Statue of Liberty. Michelangelo also interrupts a movie he sees in a theater, supposedly in Mexico, by trying to peek into the offscreen space and join a naked woman taking a bath in the projected film. Later, after being injured and denied a Maserati, the men turn up at home, where Cleopatra must kick out her new lover as Ulysses arrives. The men claim to have the riches of the world in their suitcase, but it is only postcards and photographs of all the objects and places they now claim to own, such as monuments, animals, automobiles, Tiffany's, and the planets. More soldiers show up, however, to announce that no one can claim any riches unless the king wins the war. Soon afterward, loudspeakers announce the war is over, but the king's faction has lost. Chaos reigns as the resistance and the soldiers try to kill each other off in the streets and Venus and Cleopatra are attacked and have their hair cut by the victorious enemy. Finally, a soldier explains to Ulysses and Michelangelo that the defeated king has agreed to execute all war criminals; he ushers the men into a building, then machine-guns them down before driving off alone in a jeep. The final handwritten card informs the audience that these brothers, sleeping now through eternity, thought their dreams were really paradise.

Les carabiniers was immediately attacked by a wide range of critics who found it bizarre, a dull mess, distasteful, and/or pretentious. According to Douchet, during the film's first run, a Champs Élysées theater simply closed its doors one night since there was no audience. *Les carabiniers* was nearly as big a financial failure as the banned *Le petit soldat*. Only twenty-eight hundred tickets were sold, or roughly 1 percent of the Paris attendance for *Breathless*! Some critics found the opening dedication to Jean Vigo pompous and insulting, while others tried to find parallels between the casual vitality of Vigo and the challenging political theater offered here by Godard. A number of reviewers cited one or two comical or even invigorating scenes, but Jacques Siclier's review of *Les carabiniers* was fairly typical: Siclier wrote that while some scenes were truly admirable, they simply did not add up to "a film."[43]

By this point in Godard's career, all his motion pictures were radical experiments, but they were uneven since he was testing various cinematic options in story and style with each new project. Nonetheless, similar motifs can be discerned from film to film, and, contrary to the argument of historians such as Wheeler Winston Dixon, there is no implicit pattern in Godard's alternating commercial and noncommercial projects.[44] Rather, Godard's dysnarrative strategies, which reveal the arbitrariness of narrative forms and concentrate the audience's attention on the practice of signification, have led him to create texts that try to incorporate Bertolt Brecht, Roland Barthes, and Marxism into a single text without necessarily attempting a culminating synthesis. Characters have long been open, dialogical constructs for Godard, but by *Les carabiniers*, Venus, Michelangelo and the others, including the murdered concierges, are mere representations on an equal footing with other elements of the mise-en-scène, such as the postcards, intertitles, documentary footage, and underwear ads. Godard's cinema is already struggling on the "two fronts" of signifier/signified, offering up collages of images and sounds and variations on cinematic figures and exploiting simultaneously codified tactics from documentary and the most abstract fiction. It therefore comes as no surprise that someone actively investigating and attacking the norms of storytelling should elicit such strongly divided reactions from his contemporary reviewers. *Les carabiniers* is not an essay on war (it has no argument), nor a tract on exploitation of the working class, nor a study of consumerism; it is a cluster of experiments barely held together by a linear, fablelike tale of some weakly defined characters going off to a ridiculous semblance of war and then dying. As David Bordwell writes, "Those who dislike Godard's films may well find the works' resistance to large-scale coherence intolerably frustrating; those who admire the films have probably learned to savor a movie as a string of vivid, somewhat isolated effects."[45] *Les carabiniers* was the least popular of Godard's New Wave–era films, but it was hardly atypical in terms of its general narrative strategies.

Godard finished shooting *Les carabiniers* in January 1963; by April he was fast at work, shooting *Le mepris* (*Contempt*) in Italy, one month before the former film premiered in France. Thus, by this early point in his career, he was already filming his sixth feature in three and a half years; plus he had shot three shorts: "Sloth," for *The Seven Capital Sins* (1961); "The New World," for *RoGoPaG* (1962); "Le grand escroc" ("The Big Swindle"), for

The World's Biggest Swindles (shot in January 1963 in Marrakech as soon as *Les carabiniers* was complete). In December 1963, as *Contempt* was premiering, he filmed his episode of *Paris vu par.* He had thus managed, despite the financial failures of every feature since *Breathless,* to shoot constantly; only Chabrol had made more movies by then, but Chabrol was rapidly losing the financial clout to continue. Godard began *Bande à part* in February 1964, followed closely by *A Married Woman* in June 1964 and then *Alphaville* in January 1965. If he had a master plan or production pattern, it was to be at work shooting his *next* film as his *previous* film was appearing in its first run. Each of these subsequent films continues Godard's experimentation; while they belong to the New Wave, their director was no longer "new," and they began to have less and less in common with the work of his contemporaries from *Cahiers.* Thus, they were increasingly seen as "Godard" films rather than as "New Wave" films, and for the purposes of this study at least, analysis of his first four features proves his centrality to the history and narrative tactics of the French New Wave, tactics that will continue to be explored in his subsequent films.

As a director, Godard managed always to be in pre- and postproduction almost simultaneously, a pattern that was helped along by his unconventional and spontaneous shooting strategies as well as by the continued support of his producers. Unlike Malle, Chabrol, or Truffaut, during these early days, Godard never produced his own movies.

By 1964, Truffaut and Godard began to move in very separate directions in every aspect of their lives. Truffaut, who was also considered a "man of cinema" like Godard, obsessed for all things cinematic, readily blurring the lines between the personal and professional worlds, but by the mid-1960s, he was working at a more leisurely pace, premiering a new film every other year, which ensured a high level of technical polish, narrative purpose, and consistent, auteurist results. These two friends, who had argued side by side for a new auteurist cinema in France, had each won his own battles in his own way by that time. Both directors had become spokesmen for the *jeune cinéma* and the New Wave in particular. But most important, each had offered a unified body of work that pointed out the options open to 1960s world cinema.

Of all the new directors, Truffaut and Godard represented the extremes of the New Wave to contemporary critics. While Chabrol initially helped define the New Wave and motivate its sensational reception, and Rohmer and Rivette would be recognized later as highly significant, Truffaut and Godard were the core of the *Cahiers* directors at this point, and despite their incredible differences, they were proof of the New Wave's vitality and versatility, but most of all its victory over the so-called tradition of quality. They had indeed altered the image of French cinema, its directors, and its stars, changed its direction, and expanded the arsenal of contemporary film style at a time when the popular press was constantly asking whether the New Wave had perhaps just been a temporary phenomenon, a media creation, or a great joke. Amazingly, Truffaut and Godard kept proving over and over that they were here to stay, and they also kept helping their friends continue to move into production; at the same time, they provided a model for directors in other nations, motivating them to rethink cinematic stories, styles, and modes of production. Both Godard and Truffaut have received some of the most thorough critical and historical attention of any filmmakers in history. Thus, it seems fitting to close this chapter with two celebratory quotations:

> The secret of great storytellers is perhaps to be able to unite in their work ingenuity and generosity. Truffaut understood this secret. He put it to practice in each of his films.[46]

> If God (or Henri Langlois) could edit Lumière and Méliès together, mightn't he get something like Godard?[47]

7

The *Cahiers du cinéma* Cohort:
Eric Rohmer, Jacques Rivette, Jacques
Doniol-Valcroze, and Pierre Kast

BY 1960, Claude Chabrol, François Truffaut, and Jean-Luc Godard had made the biggest impressions among the *Cahiers du cinéma* critics-turned-directors, yet many of their friends and coworkers had also been active in writing and directing shorts and even features. But while Eric Rohmer has now come to be considered a major New Wave force, in the late 1950s and early 1960s he was known more for his editorial work at *Cahiers* than for his filmmaking. During the New Wave era, he never rivaled "the big three" in significance. Similarly, Jacques Rivette has earned New Wave status, and for English-language film students, his name is often included on even the shortest lists of core New Wave members, though he made no film that received wide distribution before the late 1960s. In contrast to Rohmer and Rivette, Jacques Doniol-Valcroze has generally been excluded by historians from the inner circle of New Wave directors even though he cofounded *Cahiers du cinéma* along with Bazin and shot a stylish, Renoir-influenced feature, *L'eau à la bouche* (*A Game for Six Lovers,* 1959). He even acted in several New Wave films. Finally, Pierre Kast, who had written criticism with Bazin at *L'Ecran français* and was one of the most leftist of the *Cahiers* critics in the 1950s, is rarely mentioned in reference to the New Wave even though his *Le bel âge* (1959) was praised by *Cahiers* and starred Doniol-Valcroze. Kast and Doniol-Valcroze also joined François Truffaut and Alain Resnais in signing the "Manifesto of 121" encouraging desertion during the Algerian War. This chapter investigates the historical place and narrative strategies of these four important *Cahiers* directors, for they, too, helped revitalize French cinema with new stories and styles, even if their final products were not as numerous nor as immediately popular as those of their three more successful *Cahiers* friends and colleagues.

Eric Rohmer: The Humble Moralist

When I think about it, Bazin had ideas; the rest of us just had opinions.
Bazin's ideas were all good, but opinions are always debatable.

—ERIC ROHMER, "Entretien avec Eric Rohmer"

Of all the New Wave directors, Rohmer is without a doubt the one to have
worked out the most coherent systems and managed to maintain the most
finicky sort of rigor.

—JEAN-MICHEL FRODON, *L'age moderne du cinéma français*

Eric Rohmer (b. 1920) was a decade older than his more immediately
successful filmmaking friends from *Cahiers*—Chabrol, Truffaut, and
Godard—and only two years younger than their mentor, André Bazin. And
as Colin Crisp points out, Rohmer, along with Rivette, actually began
shooting short films five years before most of their *Cahiers* colleagues,
though both men would end up five years behind the others in gaining any
real attention from the public.[1] By the late 1960s, when *La collectioneuse*
(*The Collector,* 1967) and *My nuit chez Maude* (*My Night at Maud's,* 1969)
finally brought international attention, Rohmer had become a major figure
in French film, but during the New Wave era he was known almost exclusively for his critical work at *Cahiers,* and even that ended unhappily. By
1964, Eric Rohmer was working in television, watching from the distance
as *Cahiers du cinéma* and the filmmaking careers of his former friends
there took off without him. Another difference between Rohmer and his
three more famous colleagues is that he has been obsessively private about
his personal life, denying any connection between his own life and his
films. As Joel Magny writes, "There is a radical separation between his
private and professional lives. Rare are the friends who have passed
through the door of his home or met his wife and two sons." Moreover,
Rohmer sees a sort of purity of spirit in being an auteur who hides in the
shadows, warning that critics "too often awarded auteur status to what are
in reality just megalomaniacs."[2] While Chabrol, Truffaut, and Godard often lived as if their whole existence sprang from their film lives, Rohmer
offered a refreshing, if almost unsettling, alternative to the stereotype of
the brash, outspoken New Wave directors who exposed their private lives
for all to witness.

But Rohmer's professional life proves exemplary at revealing the
power wielded by this new generation of cinephiles in determining the direction for French film culture. Born Jean-Marie Maurice Schérer, Rohmer

was initially a French teacher in a lycée, writing short stories in his spare time. He continued teaching in order to have steady income, right up until 1958. He also published a novel, *Elizabeth,* in 1946, under a different pseudonym, Gilbert Cordier. But like Godard, Rohmer began spending a great deal of time watching movies, especially admiring the constant stream of backlogged American films from the World War II era, as well as attending *ciné-clubs,* where he met Bazin, Godard, and the others. He published two seminal articles in 1948: "Cinema, the Art of Space," in *Revue du cinéma,* and "For a Talking Cinema," in *Les temps modernes.* Each article set down clear aesthetic foundations for evaluating contemporary cinema in light of the other arts and clarified its specificity for realistic representation. These articles not only established theoretical assumptions that would guide Rohmer's subsequent criticism and production, they also proved highly influential among the new generation of cinephiles, helping define the cinema as the new art of the "real."[3] By the late 1940s, he established his own Latin Quarter *ciné-club,* which met Thursdays, and a bulletin of the Latin Quarter *ciné-club,* which turned into the short-lived *Gazette du cinéma* in 1950.

Part of Rohmer's significance resides in his consistent aesthetic arguments, which soon affected the way in which a whole constellation of critics conceptualized the cinema. He based many of his critical arguments on his love of Alfred Hitchcock, Howard Hawks, Jean Renoir, and Roberto Rossellini, praising long takes and static camerawork that did not interfere with the presentation of events. Colin Crisp summarizes Rohmer's position as less subtle than Bazin's, since Rohmer calls for a self-effacing director: "The cinema is a privileged art form because it most faithfully transcribes the beauty of the real world. Art can never improve on reality."[4] Rohmer also shaped French film criticism by encouraging the cadre of critic friends he brought on board with him. Already in *Gazette du cinéma,* he published reviews by Rivette, Truffaut, and Godard alongside Alexandre Astruc and Jacques Doniol-Valcroze. When Doniol-Valcroze at the new *Cahiers du cinéma* asked him to come write for him, Rohmer was thrilled; he started with their third issue, in 1951, and he brought some of his young friends along. At *Cahiers,* Rohmer (initially signing articles as "M. Schérer") joined forces with Truffaut and celebrated an auteurism and love for what he called the "modern classicism" of the best of Hollywood cinema. He wrote forty articles and reviews, including his five-part "Celluloid and Marble," which Antoine de Baecque claims is the most important theoretical article published by *Cahiers* in the 1950s. That series centered on the realistic specificity of the cinema; while praising many contemporary forms of popular cinema, it also looked to the past for archetypes of cinematic beauty. His review articles continually praised contemporary American cinema, locating a lively, accessible modernity in movies such as Fritz Lang's *The Big Heat* (1953), Howard Hawks's *Monkey Business* (1952), and Frank Tashlin's *Will Success Spoil Rock Hunter?* (1957), as well as recent films by Roberto Rossellini and Jean Renoir. He even argued that Tashlin's film, which reminded him of Emile Cohl's fantastic caricatures, was the first true comedy of the sound era, and that Tony Randall's Rock Hunter would prove just as memorable as Chaplin's tramp. His celebration of popular American cinema proved quite controversial for many of his more politicized or avant-garde colleagues at *Cahiers*, but his articles helped set a new tone there nonetheless, encouraging Godard, Chabrol, Rivette, and Truffaut to pursue their own bold brands of film criticism as well.

Soon, Rohmer (called "big Momo" by Truffaut and the others because of his age, height, and serious nature) was leading a group referred to as the "young Turks" by senior *Cahiers* critics, including Bazin. Rohmer quickly built a power base from among these demanding young critics until he had worked his way onto the editorial board alongside Doniol-Valcroze and Bazin in 1957. Rohmer and Chabrol also firmly established their aesthetic positions with their exemplary book on Alfred Hitchcock, published in 1957. Their *Hitchcock* became a model of auteur criticism, which combined detailed narrative analysis with great attention to mise-en-scène. The book became an important tribute to Hitchcock's films up to that point, as well as an exciting example of *Cahiers du cinéma*'s burgeoning critical methodology. When Bazin died in 1958, and Doniol-Valcroze decided he was more interested in shooting a film than in watching the daily operations of the journal, Rohmer took over as editor-in-chief. He had shaped the critical agenda for the world's most influential film journal and now, from 1958 to 1963, during the height of the New Wave, he was in almost complete control, assisted faithfully by friend Jean Douchet. Together they worked hard to present their own theoretical slant as central to *Cahiers* and its mission. As a result, Rohmer managed to guide the journal through its most consistent critical and economic stage, though some soon warned that the journal was perhaps too obsessed with its focus on auteurism and realism during an era of revolutionary change and renewal in French cinema.

Rohmer's role at *Cahiers* began to deteriorate as Rivette, Doniol-Valcroze, and Truffaut in particular began to pressure him to open up the critical range of the journal. His refusals surprised them. Many recent New Wave films were being attacked by *Positif* as well as by many mainstream publications, and Truffaut, for one, complained that *Cahiers* was too busy praising commercial American movies. He charged that *Cahiers* was turning its back on new French films such as *Shoot the Piano Player, Les carabiniers,* Rivette's *Paris Belongs to Us,* and Jacques Demy's *Lola,* all of which desperately needed close attention and vigorous support. Moreover, Doniol-Valcroze begged Rohmer to allow more direct political commentary and take advantage of the journal's steady sales and solid economic footing to expand the range of films reviewed, including documentaries and Third World cinema. But Rohmer refused to revise his aesthetic range and frugal financial policies, both of which he credited with providing the recent prosperity. By 1963, however, Rivette and Doniol-Valcroze, along with young critics such as André S. Labarthe, were impatient with Rohmer and his team at *Cahiers,* which now included future filmmaker Bertrand Tavernier, for ignoring new cultural and critical trends. Rivette and Doniol-Valcroze were reading structuralists such as Claude Lévi-Strauss and cultural theorists such as Roland Barthes and asking *Cahiers* to reevaluate classic texts from modern critical perspectives. Even Truffaut had begun handing out copies of Barthes's *Mythologies* and *On Racine* to friends, claiming Barthes's ideas opened up the field of criticism, allowing new and important avenues of inquiry. But Rohmer dug in his heels, rejecting their pleas; at one point, while trying to stop his inevitable ouster, he actually began sleeping in his office at *Cahiers* to defend his position by physically occupying the premises.

Nonetheless, in June 1963, Doniol-Valcroze, who controlled the money and had rallied most of the staff behind him, forced Rohmer out of *Cahiers du cinéma,* arguing that a more modernist slant to the journal was long overdue. Rohmer was devastated. A modest family man, without the financial resources of Chabrol, Doniol-Valcroze, or Truffaut, Rohmer suddenly needed a job. Fortunately, friends and admirers helped him secure a vague and flexible position in educational television at ORTF, the national radio and television unit. Rohmer felt obligated to justify his new post: "The only real hope for the young cinema seems to be television—not as it is now, but as it could be if the right people took an interest in it."[5] So Rohmer, who had written passionately about the cinema for twenty-five years, found himself producing and directing for state-run television at the very moment when most of his *Cahiers* friends, current and former, were successfully positioned as the New Wave of French film.

Yet if Rohmer was not known as one of the New Wave directors at that point, it was not for lack of trying. Even before he shot his first short film in 1950, he had written short stories meant to serve as the bases for eventual film adaptations. While his novel *Elizabeth* was never turned into a film, other early stories became the outlines for his much later movies: the 1969 hit *My Night at Maud's* was based on a 1947 short story, while *Le genou de Claire* (*Claire's Knee*, 1970) was first written in 1950. As Rohmer wrote short stories and edited his *Gazette du cinéma,* he also shot his first short, *Journal d'un scélèrat* (*A Villain's Diary,* 1950). That movie, like many of his earliest shorts, was never fully completed. But during this era he was already shooting in collaboration with his cinephile buddies, including Paul Gégauff, Jean-Luc Godard, Jacques Rivette, and editor Agnès Guillemot. In 1952, Rohmer also began filming *Les petites filles modèles* (*Perfect Little Girls*), based on a story by Madame la Comtesse de Ségur. As Claude Chabrol recalls, "Rohmer looked like a fake Nosferatu. . . . It seemed logical to him to search for his actresses in the Parc Monceau. Imagine the scene: This long brown silhouette (did I mention he typically wore a cape?) gliding silently along the garden's paths. . . . When he saw a pretty girl who pleased him, he would motion to her and say, 'Come here, little girl. I would like to tell you a beautiful story.' After three or four hours of this game, he was stopped by the park's guards."[6] Unfortunately, this film, too, was shot but never finished.

Of the seven short projects to which Rohmer contributed between 1950 and 1958, the best known today is surely *Tous les garçons s'appellent Patrick* (*All the Boys Are Called Patrick,* 1957), which was written by Rohmer, directed by Godard, and produced by Pierre Braunberger. The plot structure in this short also most closely parallels later Rohmer stories: it involves one man involved with two women, in a sort of light-hearted morality play. Patrick was played by Jean-Claude Brialy, as "a fast-talking seducer, one of Rohmer's prototype Don Juans."[7] Patrick has been involved with two different blonde women friends; the women are initially oblivious to the fact that they have each been dating and bragging about the same man, until together they see "their" Patrick, now arm-in-arm with a third blonde. Godard's playful directing infuses more cinematic references and in-jokes than is the case in the films directed by Rohmer, so *All the Boys Are Called Patrick* provides an insightful glimpse into both of their future careers. At the time, it was the only movie that Rohmer had written but not also directed. His next short, *Véronique et son cancre* (*Véronique and Her Dunce,* 1958), and his first feature, *Le signe du lion*

(*Sign of Leo*, 1959), were both produced by Claude Chabrol through his AJYM productions.

Thus, by 1960, Rohmer would seem to have helped define the shape and direction of New Wave film production: he was a critic who simultaneously filmed, he worked closely with a small group of friends, also associated with *Cahiers du cinéma*, he shot simple tales on location, with small crews, in both 16 mm and 35 mm, and he even employed later New Wave regulars such as Brialy, Gégauff, and Guillemot. Yet, his decade of filmmaking left him with surprisingly few projectable works and very little critical attention for those he did complete. The biggest problem for Rohmer as a director in 1960, however, was the failure of *Le signe du lion*. Unlike Chabrol, Truffaut, or Godard's first features, Rohmer's introductory work never found an appreciative audience, hence his continued presence as editor for *Cahiers* while his comrades were leaving criticism for careers in filmmaking.

Rohmer filmed *Le sign du lion* in seven weeks, with a budget of sixty thousand dollars. Shot on location in and around Paris, it features many of his friends, including Godard and Stéphane Audran, in small roles; it was such a low-budget group project that Truffaut even lent Rohmer a clapperboard.[8] It is the tale of Pierre Wesserlin (Jess Hahn), a thirty-year-old foreign composer, who lives a reckless, bohemian life in Paris. Down to his last money in the month of June, Pierre hears of his rich aunt's death and expects to split her fortune with his cousin, Christian, so he borrows money from his reporter friend, Jean-François (Van Doude), for a drunken night on the town. The next morning, Pierre reads in his horoscope that he will have a difficult period followed by unexpected happiness in August. He figures the stars are off by two months. But weeks later, after Jean-François returns from abroad, he learns that Pierre has been kicked out of his hotel and is broke, because his aunt had disinherited him. But now none of his friends can find the wandering Pierre, who sinks lower and lower into homeless poverty. He finally befriends another tramp (Jean Le Poulain), and they play music for handouts. Eventually, in August, Jean-François learns that Pierre's cousin, Christian, has died in a car accident, leaving all the inheritance now to the vanished Pierre. When Jean-François recognizes Pierre in his ragged clothes, he chases him to tell of his good fortune. The horoscope had not lied: it is now August, and Pierre, now a wealthy man, leaves his clochard friend to return to his previous life.

Le signe du lion, with Pierre's long slide into misery and final redemption, in many ways fits the structure of a parable more than the later films of his Six Moral Tales series. The sense of fate, which often influences Rohmer's stories, is dominant and heavy-handed here. Moreover, while later Rohmer male characters spend much of their time thinking and debating, Pierre seems to have no real mind of his own. The first private screenings of *Le signe du lion* were very disappointing, and its distribution was further complicated by financial problems at Chabrol's AJYM. Completed in October 1959, though later recut and rescored, it was not shown commercially until 1962 at the Pagoda in Paris, selling only five thousand tickets. *Le signe du lion* never earned any money, though it garnered a few sympathetic reviews. Magny points out that the biggest problems for the film were that it offered a thin story line, an unappealing protagonist, repetitive music, and insignificant details that were nonetheless granted excessive screen time.[9] Magny does acknowledge that Rohmer's first feature fits the New Wave spirit in many ways, however, especially in its documentation of a Paris that is very different from the commercial cinema's stereotypical city of romance and monuments. Here, Paris in August is presented as a hostile place, and many images preserve Pierre's heavy boredom and emptiness via the aimless duration of time and cavernous deep space in striking long takes. Jean Collet praises Rohmer's city, arguing that Rohmer's first feature proves right away that he is as much an architect as a director: "*Le signe du lion* is nothing if not a meditation on the city, the indifference its inhabitants show for one another and the distance established, as in *Rear Window,* between the characters and the spectator-tourists."[10]

Certainly *Le signe du lion* should be seen today as an interesting but failed experiment; some of its traits, such as the connection between appearances, setting, and character, will be worked out more elegantly in Rohmer's later Moral Tales. Here, the obsessive documentary-like observance of the decline of Pierre and the hard, cruel space of the unforgiving Paris around him become a bit too obvious and even preachy. Frodon, however, praises Rohmer's fascination with the concrete: "The mise-en-scène belongs firmly to the material side, granting a striking physical presence to the building walls, pavement, and cobblestones that surround this character, who could not have been named anything other than Pierre [stone]."[11] But Crisp effectively sums up the problems: "The New Wave had accustomed the public to all sorts of frenzied and unpredictable outbursts, but not to the austerity and understatement of this film . . . [much less to] being told that men were drab, slack, and uninteresting."[12]

The presence of fate, a fascination with spatial arrangements, and a strict story structure that nonetheless result in some ambiguity are all present in *Le signe du lion* and will typify Rohmer's later work as well. But here the audience is left unsure whether to sympathize with Pierre, much less consider him worthy of an inheritance that depends upon two people's deaths. Even Crisp complains that the movie "makes the Finger of God look a little sadistic, like a cat idly teasing a sullen and uncooperative mouse."[13] There is no evidence that Pierre's new riches will make him rethink falling back into the excessive life he used to lead or the way he looks upon the less fortunate around him. Reviewers such as Claude Beylie, who praised *Le signe du lion* as a great work and tried to rally more attention for Rohmer's feature, were rare indeed. Beylie liked its predestined tragic structure ("like all great works it follows the plight of the individual") as well as its stunningly realistic cinematography, which he compared to *Cléo de 5 à 7* (Varda, 1961).[14] Some of those traits and the carefully crafted story logic would recur in later Rohmer films, though the Six Moral Tales improve on the formula by exploring more interesting characters who are involved with more erotic concerns and cannot always see fate hard at work around them. But with the commercial failure of his first feature and Chabrol's concurrent financial problems, by 1962 Rohmer was forced to condense his next film back to a 16 mm, short-film format.

The twenty-minute-long *La boulangère de Monceau* (*The Girl at the Monceau Bakery*) launched the Six Moral Tales series for Rohmer in 1962. He had already conceived of and mapped out the six stories, which all revolved around a similar schema: A male protagonist is interested in or committed to one woman, becomes distracted by a second woman, but finally takes stock of his life and returns to his original plans. Much of each story is preoccupied with this "digression" to another woman, so the movies concentrate on what could be considered the time wasted by an indecisive man. Rohmer was interested in revisiting and reworking this sort of plot device, which he had discovered in one of his favorite movies, F. W. Murnau's *Sunrise* (1927). Significantly, *The Girl at the Monceau Bakery* brought Rohmer into a vital partnership with Barbet Schroeder and his new, small production company, Les Films du Losange. The twenty-one-year-old Schroeder founded his company in 1961. He had gotten to know Rohmer at the Cinémathèque and agreed to produce and act in *The Girl at the Monceau Bakery.*

Barbet Schroeder typified the engaged young cinephile who, seeing the nouvelle vague begin around him, wanted immediately to learn as much as possible about every aspect of filmmaking so as to get involved.

Fortunately, he was also wealthy, and his mother allowed him to mortgage one of her paintings by Emil Nolde to finance the start of his company. Not only did Schroeder agree to produce Rohmer's first two short Moral Tales, but he allowed Rohmer to shoot the second short, *La carrière de Suzanne* (*Suzanne's Career*, 1963), in his family's apartment, filming many scenes in Barbet's own room, which doubled in real life for the offices of Les Films du Losange. Rohmer then donated both shorts to the production company, earning him a large share in the venture, which would eventually go on to help produce nearly every feature film Rohmer would make. According to Jean Douchet, Les Films du Losange became "the most important independent production company in France. In his own way, Rohmer became even better at financing than Truffaut."[15] But Rohmer would never earn much money from his filmmaking until the late 1960s, and these first two Moral Tales, at twenty-six- and fifty-two-minute lengths, defied conventional exhibition formats.

With *The Girl at the Monceau Bakery*, Rohmer established many of the traits that would define his stories and style throughout his career. The film begins with a voice-over narrator (Bertrand Tavernier), who provides the dialogue for the actor (Schroeder). Tavernier explains the accompanying images of the precise intersection where the story will unfold, naming streets (boulevard de Courcelles) and the Métro station (Villiers), presenting the gates to Parc Monceau, and showing the student cafeteria, which was being demolished, disrupting the life of the main character, a law student. Every day the main character walks the same stretch of street on his way to study, and he often sees an attractive young woman, Sylvie (Michèle Girardon), walk through the neighborhood. The narrator is timid, but his friend Schmidt (Fred Junk) urges him to speak with her. But as the narrator explains, "She was not the type to let herself be picked up. And it was hardly my style to try." Finally, one day he physically bumps into her, which allows him to speak, and Sylvie agrees to join him at a café the next time they meet. But the next day he does not find her. She seems to have disappeared; day after day she does not pass as usual, and he grows more frustrated. "My good luck was followed by equally bad luck."

The narrator continues to walk the neighborhood every day looking for her, even sacrificing his dinner since that is his only free time away from his studies. Then, one day he enters a new bakery (*boulangerie*). He is a man of routine, or as he says, "ritual"; day after day, he returns to the bakery to purchase a cookie, until gradually he begins to flirt with the working-class bakery clerk, Jacqueline (Claudine Soubrier), buying more

Figure 7.1. Narrator bumps into Sylvie (*The Girl from the Monceau Bakery*)

pastries on each successive visit. Eventually, almost as a game, he decides to seduce her, justifying it as a sort of revenge on both women. He becomes more comfortable with the idea, eating in the store and finally rubbing her neck, before he makes a date to meet her the next night for dinner.

The following day he passes his law exams, but then just before his rendezvous with Jacqueline, he meets Sylvie again; her foot is in a cast. She had sprained her ankle and was restricted to her apartment for three weeks, which happens to be across the street from his bakery. She also explains that she had passed him on the street the day before, but he was lost in thought and never noticed her. He invites her to dinner; as he waits in the street while she goes into her apartment to prepare for the occasion, the narrator decides his rash decision to ask Sylvie out and stand up Jacqueline is, indeed, a proper "moral" decision since to put Sylvie off one more day and meet Jacqueline tonight would now be a "vice." He walks Sylvie past the bakery but is unsure if Jacqueline sees or whether she is already waiting for him at the restaurant. That evening, Sylvie admits to seeing him repeatedly enter the bakery and jokes that she is a bit disappointed that his concern for her could so easily be placated by sweets. She even mentions that by watching him, she now knows all his vices. The final scene shows Sylvie and the narrator entering the bakery as he explains in voice-over, "We married six months later." The older woman who owns the bakery waits on them; Jacqueline has moved on to a different sales job.

This short, while it never received any real commercial distribution until the 1970s, is one of Rohmer's most successful examples of a "moral tale." Since Rohmer's realist aesthetic demands that he seem to present things as they are yet also offer them in a strict, "moral" structure, he must strike a careful balance between documentary narrative techniques and predestined story events. Rohmer had criticized Louis Malle's and Claude Chabrol's early features for being too transparent in their morality lessons. As Crisp explains, for Rohmer, "The moral must seem to flow naturally and inevitably from an objective observation of the world, rather than being imposed on that world."[16] *The Girl at the Monceau Bakery*, with its location shooting, careful observation of time and geography, and random passersby on the streets, offers itself as a sort of good-humored science project, observing the narrator and his romantic antics, and thus it becomes the exemplary Moral Tale. Frodon agrees that *The Girl at the Monceau Bakery* fits perfectly the Moral Tales' goals: "These stories are less about what people do than about what happens in their mind as they do it. It is a cinema that paints the movements of the soul. . . . *La boulangère de Monceau* already establishes the bases for Rohmer's circulations of seduction where chance and fate, plotting and spatial disposition, personal maneuvers and social forces all lend their relative weight in pushing the action to its logical outcome."[17] *Le signe du lion,* which limited itself to watching Pierre rather than to understanding anything about his life, is the opposite of *The Girl at the Monceau Bakery* or the other Moral Tales.

The rigorous story structure still offers some of the ambiguity of *Le signe du lion,* but now instead of a character stuck passively alternating between poverty and wealth, one has a naive, modest, and yet strangely confident narrator stuck between patiently waiting for the potential love of his life to resurface and testing his chances with the more available Jacqueline. The opposition between the elegantly beautiful Sylvie, who works in an art gallery, and the sensual, animated Jacqueline, is also a typical Rohmer device. Often Rohmer's male protagonist is preoccupied with contemplating beauty and love and his own motives. Moreover, once this narrator rubs Jacqueline's arm and neck, anticipating Jerome's touch of young Claire's knee years later, he seems to feel some disrespect for her. Obtaining the cold beauty, Sylvie, is his eventual goal, though it remains unclear just what she knows of his flirtations with Jacqueline. It is equally unclear whether Rohmer is offering a tale to show how the narrator's free will is put to a test or whether fate was in control all along. Even the initial "accidental" meeting between the narrator and Sylvie is left ambiguous since the audience has seen that both characters are interested in each other. The range of information never reveals whether Sylvie may have seen him before bumping into him and perhaps helped that fateful encounter along. Moreover, *The Girl at the Monceau Bakery* echoes the end of *Le signe du lion;* the audience is still left to ponder what, if anything, the "moral" was: If this was a test, did the narrator pass or fail? Was Sylvie just a passive prize at the end of the rainbow for the protagonist, or did she come down from her apartment because she realized that if she remained away any longer she might lose the narrator to Jacqueline?

Stylistically, too, *The Girl at the Monceau Bakery* provides a wonderful summary of Rohmer's distinctive narrative patterns. One might expect this strict realist to employ consistently long takes of the narrator in his concrete neighborhood, yet the ASL is a brisk eight seconds, and the short is punctuated with many rapid panning shots and zooms, taking full advantage of the lightweight 16 mm camera. This Moral Tale owes more to Jean Rouch's camera work than to Jean Renoir's. It also reinforces the repetition of the narrator's trajectory by including occasional jump cuts on him as he searches the streets. It then cuts on the 180-degree line, so that as he walks directly toward the camera, explaining in voice-over that Schmidt is gone so he has to search for Sylvie alone, there is a jump cut; the next shot shows him walking directly away from the camera toward the end of the block. There is a jump cut in this walking away as well, but as he reaches the corner, the camera zooms in to observe him; he stops, then walks directly back toward the camera. There is another cut on the 180-degree line just as he is again about to bump into the camera, but the shot of him walking away shows he is now on a different street. Rohmer and cinematographer Jean-Michel Meurice reinforce the rigor of his search but playfully expose the ridiculousness of the narrator's obsessive rituals, using tactics from cinéma vérité as well as from Godard to show him walking his rounds.

Rohmer is nonetheless famous for a concrete, realistic mise-en-scène that takes on metaphorical significance gradually and naturally. The confined space of *The Girl at the Monceau Bakery* is motivated by the protagonist's obsessive, narrow concerns. Rohmer shoots almost compulsively with natural lighting, and the difference in shots (sunlit, cloudy, in the rain) in this film is justified by the overall structure, which presents snap shots of the narrator's actions over a period of

Figure 7.2. Narrator walks toward the camera (*The Girl from the Monceau Bakery*)

weeks. His gestures, clothes, and setting remain the same; only days
and weather change. But most revealing of Rohmer's sparse style, which
avoids close-ups and expressionistic lighting, is that he frames the shots
from unusual angles only if motivated by the narrative. For instance, the
first time the narrator exits the bakery, there is a high angle shot of him
as he eats the cookie in the street. The change at first seems motivated
by the fact that he has broken his rigid routine and given in to hun-
ger; of course, with the title implying a bakery girl will be important, it
also seems to announce a change in events. Only at the film's end, however, is another justification for this high-angle shot provided: Sylvie
explains she lives across the street and watched him eat pastries. In retrospect, this earlier shot becomes her perceptual point of view, though
no one could guess it on a first viewing since Rohmer does not insert a
shot of her looking.

Subsequent shots reinforce this hypothesis that Rohmer's framing
changes to suggest that the narrator is being observed and that windows
and buildings now matter in a new way: increasingly, he is shot from low
angles, with second-floor windows in the top of the frame and the narrator's
head cut off at the bottom.

The camera work suggests already the importance of the surrounding
buildings and windows around the narrator, though he and first-time viewers

Figure 7.3. High angle on narrator (*The Girl from the Monceau Bakery*)

Figure 7.4. Narrator low in the frame (*The Girl from the Monceau Bakery*)

are not consciously aware that the setting may hold the recuperating, observing Sylvie. The framing also comments upon Jacqueline, often isolating her breasts and hands as she wraps the cookies. The camera regularly places other pastry delights in the frame with her, equating her with the sugary trifles that surround her.

Rohmer's shots are never overtly charged with significance—this is not the cinema of his hero Alfred Hitchcock—but they are incredibly efficient and functional. Thus, when he cuts from a shot of the narrator leaving the bakery, he may follow it with a rare close-up of the street sign that was in the distant background of the previous shot. As the viewer will learn later, he is on Sylvie's street without knowing it, but the audience cannot yet read the clue so it must initially accept this unusual inserted close-up as more evidence of the geographical rigor of a director who wants to be sure his audience knows exactly where the story unfolds.

The Girl at the Monceau Bakery thus encapsulates many of the best and most impressive traits of Rohmer's cinema. His range of information is carefully built around the central male protagonist, but it also provides many banal details that slowly accumulate to create the character and his world. Yet, the plot structure is also highly manipulative rather than merely plausible; for instance, it denies the viewer not only Sylvie's whereabouts but key events as well, such as how she hurt herself and the scene in which the narrator apparently walked right past her, oblivious, the night before he finally finds her again. Sylvie mentions that he seemed lost in thought, but the audience knows that he had just come from asking Jacqueline on a date. Similarly, the next night, as the narrator and Sylvie walk off to dinner and his voice-over tells the audience he will never know just what Jacqueline did or saw that evening, Rohmer makes a point of refusing to tell the audience either. What can one conclude about the story's "moral"? It should make a big difference to the viewer whether Jacqueline was humiliated by sitting at the restaurant waiting for the narrator, who never arrived, or whether she saw him passing arm-in-arm with Sylvie and so witnessed his betrayal. That the Moral Tales are about characters and situations rather than lessons is made quite clear here, but if the characters have, indeed, learned anything important, they are never going to let on.

The second, longer Moral Tale, *Suzanne's Career,* lacks some of the charm and subtle humor of *The Girl at the Monceau Bakery* but continues many of its strategies as well as the theme of searching for truth and beauty. In particular, this film again presents a rather timid young student as the

Figure 7.5. Jacqueline serves the narrator (*The Girl from the Monceau Bakery*)

central male, here Bertrand, an eighteen-year-old pharmacy student living near the Sorbonne, who introduces the film in voice-over and sets up the locale. *Suzanne's Career* revolves around the space of bourgeois Parisian students. Bertrand (Philippe Beuzin) has a friend Guillaume (Christian Charrière), who is much more sexually active than Bertrand. Right away, Guillaume meets Suzanne (Catherine Sée) and invites her to a party that evening. There, Guillaume flirts instead with the more elegant Sophie (Diane Wilkinson), in part to make Suzanne jealous and thus more willing to do anything for him. But the cad Guillaume also knows that Bertrand is timidly interested in Sophie as well, so he seems to be punishing both Bertrand and Suzanne with his behavior. Guillaume ends the night seducing Suzanne. Their relationship continues for a while, with Bertrand, who is not wild about her, often accompanying them out on the town. Neither man respects Suzanne, so they exploit her, letting her pay for most of their fun in nightclubs.

When both Guillaume and Suzanne are broke, their relationship ends, and Suzanne begins to flirt a bit with Bertrand. He resists and then learns that someone has stolen money from his room. The earnest Sophie is convinced it must have been Guillaume, but Bertrand prefers to believe it was Suzanne.

Figure 7.6. Sophie confers with Bertrand (*Suzanne's Career*)

Regardless, Bertrand learns there is no chance that Sophie will fall for him; at the end, he discovers that Suzanne is about to marry another very nice young man. On an outing with Sophie, Suzanne, and her fiancé at the swimming pool, he looks longingly at both his platonic friend Sophie and at Suzanne. He finally realizes he should have pursued Suzanne when he had a chance, since she turns out to be nice, interesting, and even lovely after all. The film ends with Bertrand watching Suzanne's fiancé rub suntan lotion on her, while Sophie puts hers on herself and he is left on his own. He explains in voice-over that he is flunking his exams and losing Sophie. He feels as if Suzanne's happiness were mocking him and that everything she had done no longer mattered, except that she made Guillaume and him look like children.

Suzanne's Career ends abruptly and even seems to undercut its own sense of purpose since the narrator proves himself more inept than naive. He is left looking foolish, as if he has wasted his time these last few months, which in turn risks making the audience feel it has been wasting its time as well these past fifty minutes. The narrative strategies also undercut Bertrand's conclusion, however, since the audience has no idea why Suzanne is suddenly getting married; it could be a very poor choice or even from financial desperation. The viewer has seen no evidence up to this point of her doing anything very intelligent. Yet, for Bertrand, this unexpected engagement somehow marks her superior maturity. Crisp points out that Rohmer reveals many of his signature traits in *Suzanne's Career*, such as the opposition between one less-respectable but more seducible woman and a more elegant but distant one. Rohmer has nonetheless lost some narrative clarity by shifting away from love triangles to a less precise romantic formula that includes the unappealing Guillaume.[18] Interestingly, because Rohmer returns to a narrow, manipulative range of information mirroring that of *The Girl at the Monceau Bakery*, the audience will never know who stole Bertrand's money and has no insight into the women's daily routines or thoughts, except for what they tell Bertrand. The viewer is almost as clueless about the women as is poor Bertrand. Nonetheless, as Ginette Vincendeau writes of Rohmer in general, "Even when focusing on the dilemmas of male protagonists, Rohmer's films give women a prominent place."[19]

Regardless, *Suzanne's Career* remains the weakest of the Six Moral Tales and far less accomplished than its predecessor. Because of the film's extremely low budget, the dialogue is often out of sync with the image, and the film lacks the lively editing and documentary clarity found in *The Girl at the Monceau Bakery*. There are also many underexposed shots that lend an amateurish quality to the project, with none of the engaging freedom one might hope from such unconventional techniques. The many murky shots also reveal that Rohmer's obsessive naturalistic tactics can occasionally backfire. Visually, this Moral Tale reveals little of the formal beauty one comes to expect of later Rohmer films.

Rohmer's first films were thus quite modest in contrast to those of Chabrol, Truffaut, and Godard. Rohmer and his young friend, producer, and occasional actor, Barbet Schroeder, were anxious to expand the range of their projects. Schroeder could hardly be considered an active producer with only two short films with no commercial distribution, so he needed a project to help launch Les Films du Losange. He came up with the idea for *Paris vu par* (*Six in Paris*, 1964) for both aesthetic and practical reasons. The young Schroeder hoped to help encourage a new film style that combined Italian neorealist naturalism with the documentary quality of contemporary television production. That Rohmer was now working for ORTF may have helped him define his artistic goals. But the practical consideration was actually something of a daring ploy. Schroeder planned out a collection of six short films, each telling a story set in a different district of Paris and written and shot by six different young directors. That way, each director could apply for Film Aid from the CNC based on a short film

Figure 7.7. Suzanne and Bertrand meet in a café (*Suzanne's Career*)

proposal. Schroeder could then use those six quality grants to produce and market a single feature-length compilation. The project raised eighty thousand dollars, allowing Schroeder to test his new ideals by producing a low-budget group project under New Wave conditions. In addition to Rohmer's contribution, the project included work by Chabrol, Godard, Jean Rouch, Jean Douchet, and Jean-Daniel Pollet.

According to Douchet, Schroeder fully exploited new techniques, using 16 mm cameras and equipment developed for television to shoot in color and blow it up later to 35 mm. "The goal was to prove that films could be made under amateur conditions yet yield a product in a professional format, which could be commercially distributed."[20] The result proved successful but remained Les Films du Losange's only real asset until Rohmer's *La collectionneuse* in 1967. For *Paris vu par,* Schroeder insisted on a set of consistent guidelines for the directors to follow. Everything had to be shot on location, interiors as well as exteriors; the crews were to be small, with only a camera operator, assistant, and sound engineer, and an occasional electrician to provide a bit of fill lighting. Whenever possible Schroeder wanted the actors to be nonprofessional, reinforcing both the neorealist connection and the New Wave celebration of youth and novelty: "I think of the modern cinema as in color with direct sound. And 16 mm . . . allows a great mobility for filming and recording sounds—allowing considerable economy—but also providing total freedom of inspiration for the auteur directors."[21] The result, while a bit uneven—the episodes by Rouch, Godard, and Rohmer are the most inspired—proved impressive nonetheless, though its final premiere did not arrive until October 1965. Michel Marie notes that *Paris vu par* was important in pushing further the New Wave tactic of breaking down barriers between fiction and documentary while it also was one of the New Wave movies most dedicated to the significance of its concrete settings.[22] Douchet even sees Schroeder's collection as marking the end of the era: "Today, *Paris vu par* appears as both the New Wave's manifesto and testament, for it marked the end of the movement." For Douchet this is the last time New Wave directors would truly work together, with their different personalities all moving in the same direction.[23]

Rohmer's contribution to *Paris vu par* is one of his most clever and perhaps most personal movies ever. Set near the Arc de Triomphe de l'Étoile, "Place de l'Étoile" presents the tale of Jean-Marc (Jean-Michel Rouzière), a meek salesman in an upscale men's clothing store. Rohmer's film opens with his own voice-over explaining the geography of place de l'Étoile, where twelve grand avenues converge; each morning, at precisely 9:25, Jean-Marc climbs up from the Métro and navigates the many intersections to get halfway around the square to his store. The fastidious clerk takes great pleasure in this harrowing trek, as if it were an epic journey full of danger and suspense. On the second morning in the film, Jean-Marc is accosted by a drunken stranger and clumsily knocks the man down with his umbrella. Fearing the man is dead, Jean-Marc dashes the rest of the way to his job. From that day forward, the frightened clerk checks the paper, searching for news of his attack on the clochard, a bit like a rattled Michel Poiccard, but he finds nothing. Nonetheless, he changes his precious daily routine and walks to work from a different Métro station, avoiding Place de l'Étoile all together. Finally, months later, he recognizes his "victim" harassing people on the Métro; once the clochard sees Jean-Marc, however, he calms down and moves away. The anonymous riders seem to admire Jean-Marc, and he appears relieved and somewhat proud. Elated, he exits the Métro at his old stop. On his way up the stairs, however, he bumps a woman with his umbrella; he apologizes profusely, recognizing that she could easily have been injured.

Joel Magny declares "Place de l'Étoile" a perfect example of Rohmer's fiction: there are two worlds, the objective realm, described in documentary fashion by the camera and sync sound, and the world of Jean-Marc's imagination, suggested in his voice-over as well as his concrete gestures. The audience clearly sees that Jean-Marc's scuffle is an accident, but the clerk himself cannot picture it that innocently, proving he lives with an inherent sense of guilt. Moreover, after he knocks the man down and begins to run, crossing each of the streets against the walk light, there are distant sounds of dogs barking and police whistles. Once he gets to work and buys himself a new umbrella, having left his old one at the scene of the crime, a siren can be heard, but whether these are all objective, diegetic sounds or reflections of Jean-Marc's mental, subjective fear remains unclear, further displaying the wonderful mix of real and fantasy worlds.[24] The use of the voice-over as well as occasional intertitles to address the audience adds further distancing effects. Rohmer also breaks up the fictional world with a comical photomontage. Jean-Marc checks the newspaper again for potential stories about his own crime, and there is a series of close-up shots of various newspaper headlines describing silly crimes, including one about the umbrella as a potential weapon, followed by still photographs of a woman attacking a man with her umbrella in a photojournalist's recreation. Whether Jean-Marc is imagining articles on umbrella violence or whether there is some strange contemporary case that indeed warrants a photomontage is left comically ambiguous.

By contrast to the Moral Tales, women are only important to the protagonist of "Place de l'Étoile" as witnesses and potential judges of his character. In the first scene when a woman on the Métro accidentally pokes his foot hard with her pointed high heel, it not only anticipates Jean-Marc's upcoming umbrella battle, but it also reveals that he feels uncomfortable as the object of female attention. Later, after having dashed across six major intersections, fleeing the scene of his crime, he again meets the same woman from the Métro, and she seems amused to see him self-consciously trying to hide from her. When in his own small store, he seems relieved, perhaps because there he only has to deal with men (including customers played by Rohmer's friends Jean Douchet and Philippe Sollers). By the end, therefore, when Jean-Marc seems to have the power to strike fear into the clochard with his glance of recognition, Jean-Marc's value increases in his own eyes specifically because it also increases in the eyes of an anonymous woman near him. When he confidently emerges from the Métro, heading to Place de l'Étoile, and bumps into a woman with his umbrella, he is not only careful to apologize, but he seems stronger now as he addresses her directly without hiding his eyes as he would have at the film's beginning. Jean-Marc's tiny "victory" is all the more humorous when considered in contrast to the opening narration in which Rohmer explains that the Arc de Triomphe was built to celebrate Napoleon's military conquests.

Stylistically, "Place de l'Étoile" is also a great success for Rohmer. The nearly maniacal fascination with location, time, and space he displayed in *The Girl at the Monceau Bakery* comes back with a vengeance here, so much so in fact that the title is not "The Clerk of l'Étoile" but instead the place itself. Rohmer knew this spot particularly well since the *Cahiers* offices were nearby. The geometry and the unsynchronized stoplights set up and finally motivate the drama. Rohmer's voice-over explains, during shots of tourists, that real Parisians never come here, except for the president of France. In a quick flurry of shots that resemble the Champs Élyseés sequence in *Breathless,* there are disjointed shots of crowds and motorcycle police, but finally at least the audience does see De Gaulle riding past in his limousine. The overall visual style resembles cinéma vérité with handheld cameras shooting often with pans and zooms and using only unflattering, greenish available light in the Métro. The ASL is also the shortest of all Rohmer's films, at a rapid 5.1 seconds. This is not the slow, Bazinian style of some of his later films. Rather, Rohmer and cinematographer Nestor Almendros seem to have taken Schroeder's plans to heart, creating a fast-paced, lively film that owes much to the brisk editing of the location footage. As in his later films, Rohmer makes no use of nondiegetic music in "Place de l'Étoile"; unlike his other Moral Tales, however, this one relies much more on physical action and editing than on dialogue. Moreover, while it would be quite impossible to imagine the later *My Night at Maud's* or *Claire's Knee* without the long, talky dialogue scenes, Jean-Marc's drama would lose almost nothing if presented as a silent film; after all, it even includes parodic intertitles. Thus, the style in "Place de l'Étoile" fits many of Rohmer's narrative traits, while also distinguishing this film in other ways.

But it is the use of color that further signals the efficient and rigorous Rohmer style here. As mentioned in chapter 5, Rohmer had long praised color as a narrative device, and in his own cinema he manages to pare it down to be just as functional as his other strategies. Rohmer combined his penchant for the meticulous recreation of reality with careful attention to the rare instances of bright color highlights in his compositions. Since Rohmer likes to remain faithful to reality and its presentation, he is not willing to repaint houses or whole blocks as Jean-Luc Godard and Jacques Demy do. Rather he cautiously adds color motifs through object selection (clothes, furniture, signs in the street, and so on). Yet, colors are so important to Rohmer's conceptions of each diegetic world that he wrote the script for each of his color films in notebooks whose covers were chosen to match whatever color would dominate that project. If one looks to "Place de l'Étoile," one might be surprised at the restraint and subtlety of color choice in the hands of someone who had written fifteen years earlier that feature films should dare to use flat, primary colors the ways cartoons do: "You can't shoot a film in violent tones, the painters say. . . . [But] what does it matter if a shot disobeys the rules of painting? A film does not hang on a picture hook. . . . We must learn to think of cinema and its colors as separate from painting or reality and look for a new angle."[25] Rohmer claims that he limited his basic hues in "Place de l'Étoile" to red, green, and yellow, in part because the Italian president was in town and there were already Italian flags flying on the Champs Elysées. The greenish fluorescent lights of the Métro are used to cast a sickly tint on the skittish Jean-Marc's face, which is also in keeping with Rohmer's argument, advanced in articles in *Arts* from 1956, that thanks to color, "[t]he moralist will be better able to scrutinize faces, washed of their wan masks, even if he cannot detect every fleeting blush or passing pallor."[26] The overall composition privileges the green-and-red traffic lights as Jean-Marc initially follows their orders slavishly, but, when rattled, he runs wildly around Place de l'Étoile, violating the traffic warnings and the giant yellow signs pointing for pedestrians to go in the opposite direction.

The overall exterior Paris palette is muted except for those red, green, and yellow accents, such as the bright red winter coat of the woman in the Métro who stepped on Jean-Marc's foot. In his shop, where Jean-Marc is most comfortable, Rohmer condenses the color range further to characterize Jean-Marc with cool, bland, but tasteful blues. Even the wall of shirt boxes behind him at the store counter match the pale blue of his tie. Unlike the gaudy umbrella store in *Umbrellas of Cherbourg* (1964), where Demy takes full advantage of the array of colors one might expect with so many products for sale, Rohmer reduces Jean-Marc's store to a mundane, muted space. This is a world where color is repressed, paralleling Jean-Marc's own personality, and when he has to confront the brighter patches of color, it is in the more dangerous world of intersections.

It would be several years before Eric Rohmer's second feature, *La collectionneuse*, would help jumpstart the Moral Tales again and launch his own international reputation along with the financial success of Les Films du Losange. In the meantime, Rohmer continued to work at ORTF, producing and directing educational films, including several tributes to directors such as Carl Dreyer as well as two more shorts for Films du Losange. Only after *My Night at Maud's* would he be able to earn a living as a filmmaker, catching up with his younger friends from the *Cahiers du cinéma* days. Yet even with his continued importance, his old journal often criticized his cinema as quaint and apolitical, before it chose to ignore him altogether for a number of years in the early 1970s. Rohmer's unusual progression, however, from 1950 to 1965 proves essential for understanding his cinema in particular and the New Wave in general. Not every *Cahiers* critic who made a movie in 1959 was catapulted to fame, and just because historians by the late 1960s heralded Rohmer as a major figure of the New Wave does not mean he was a vital member during its core years. Rather, even though Rohmer helped establish the critical climate of the 1950s and helped launch the careers of Chabrol, Rivette, Truffaut, and Godard, his own production trajectory remained unusual and exceedingly marginal. A bit like Robert Bresson, however, Rohmer remained true to his own aesthetic concerns and gradually proved that working on the margins can produce a truly original and important personal cinema.

Jacques Rivette: Representation and Mise-en-Scène

> The only possibility left for French cinema would be in films which,
> although not exactly social (I'm not happy with that word) at least take up a
> position, analogous to Italian post-war cinema.
> —JACQUES RIVETTE, "Six Characters in Search of *Auteurs*"

Jacques Rivette (b. 1928) was another New Wave *Cahiers* critic who never earned much success as a director during the 1958–1964 period. Rivette had served as assistant director to Jean Renoir and Jacques Becker and as camera operator for shorts by Eric Rohmer and other directors, and he had inspired his friends with his own short, *Le coup du berger;* however, he made only one feature during the New Wave period (as opposed to Chabrol's and Godard's total of eight each). He began *Paris nous appartient* (*Paris Belongs to Us*) in the summer of 1958, even before Chabrol started shooting *Le beau Serge,* initially borrowing eighty thousand old francs, or roughly one hundred and fifty dollars, from *Cahiers* to begin production. To economize, Rivette shot the entire movie silent, an oddity since the film is about the theater and live performance. "Script girl" Suzanne Schiffman literally filled her role by acting as a stenographer on the set, jotting down the spoken dialogue so the actors could more easily dub in their own voices later during postproduction. Rivette managed to complete the film in 1960 only after Chabrol and Truffaut helped with supplies and money, though some sources set the final budget for *Paris Belongs to Us* at a surprisingly high $140,000.

The nearly mythical accounts of Rivette's long struggle to finish his personal project typically ignore one factor beyond finances, however: he was slow and obsessive in postproduction. His editor, Denise de Casabianca, explains: "He never let me make a single splice without his presence. The problem was that we edited *Paris Belongs to Us* for a whole year; he never wanted to see the film projected. It was an endless editing process, reworking sequences in detail. . . . He had a very passionate relationship with the film stock."[27] During an era identified with shooting on the run and quick turnarounds between shooting and exhibition, Rivette's mode of production was a slow, methodical, labor of love that showed no need or desire for rapid critical or financial feedback. *Paris Belongs to Us* played in a very limited run.

Not until 1966 and the censorship battle over *La religieuse* (*The Nun*, released in 1971 in the United States) was Rivette considered as a major figure of the New Wave. At *Cahiers du cinéma* during the 1950s, he had written a number of reviews and was known as the most extreme cinephile since he not only spent incredibly long hours in the Cinémathèque and other movie theaters, but he was famous for wanting to discuss films with almost anyone who was willing to spend the time. According to Casabianca, what set Rivette apart was not so much his critical past as his detailed knowledge of so many movies: "His entire notion of culture came from the repeated vision of certain films. He loved very diverse films."[28] Rivette, like Rohmer, was a shy fellow who seemed uninterested in the blatant self-promotion that helped many of his colleagues from *Cahiers* launch themselves into the limelight. Chabrol describes him as resembling the Cheshire cat in *Alice in Wonderland:* "He was a little fellow you hardly noticed. When he smiled, he disappeared entirely behind his superb teeth. But he was no less ferocious a critic than the rest of us."[29] Rivette began his critical career in 1950, writing for Rohmer's *Gazette du cinéma*, where he violently attacked the older generation of critics, including his friends Bazin and Doniol-Valcroze, for ignoring the new aesthetic standards in mise-en-scène criticism. Rivette championed Hitchcock rather than Welles as the model for a modern director. He joined *Cahiers du cinéma* in 1953, where he continued his campaign for praise of American auteurs such as "the genius Howard Hawks" and Nicholas Ray. In his review of *Lusty Men* (1952), he even admitted that admiring this Ray film requires "a little love": "Far from wishing to excuse it, you must love this lack of artifice, this very pleasing indifference to decors, plasticity, evenness of light."[30]

Later in the 1950s, Rivette became known for his impatience with imitation genre films, or movies that repeated generic conventions while lacking "roots" in the genre. For instance, he attacked British films for trying to use American genres, which could not work outside their national context, and charged that French films were now following suit, turning into weak imitations of British films that were weak imitations of American films. In the famous *Cahiers* roundtable discussion of contemporary French cinema, "Six Characters in Search of *Auteurs*," in 1957, Bazin even asked Rivette to initiate the discussion: "In my view Rivette should begin. He's the one with the most radical and decided opinions on the subject."[31] His auteurism was nearly as extreme as Rohmer's during this period. In 1955 Rivette claimed that a revolution was afoot in Hollywood, when he noted that great, young (forty-year-old) directors in Hollywood were stressing consistent story and style markers across generic boundaries, proving that mise-en-scène criticism was more pertinent for this era than was genre criticism, which could only account for the less creative American directors who followed generic rules rather than forging a personal style. By 1960, however, he was praising the modernism of Antonioni over the classicism of the usual American auteurs. Rivette replaced Rohmer as editor of *Cahiers du cinéma* from 1963 to 1965, and he continued to contribute articles and reviews until 1969. It was precisely during his conversion to a new sort of modernist criticism in the late 1950s that Rivette was experimenting with the complex, mock-theatrical story of *Paris Belongs to Us*.

Rivette's 140-minute feature takes place in June 1957. It tells the story of a young student, Anne Goupil (Betty Schneider), who is indifferent to her upcoming exams and lives next door to a woman who knows Anne's brother, Pierre (François Maistre), and is convinced several friends have been murdered. Later, Anne runs into Pierre, who invites her to a party, which ends up being more like a wake. A friend, Juan, has died of a knife wound, but no one is sure whether it was suicide or murder. At the party Anne meets a drunken, paranoid American, Philip Kaufman (Daniel Crohem), who has fled the McCarthy hearings but now fears he cannot escape the clever network of fascists who are out to conquer the world. Philip's friend Terry (Françoise Prevost) has been dating Juan and is upset over his death. Several people warn Anne to stay away from Philip and

Terry, hinting that their depressing fears led to Juan's death. Throughout the film, however, Anne is drawn, rather inexplicably, toward this creepy pair, believing their paranoia to be real and that several people, including her brother, may be in some danger. One night, Philip and Anne see a man get hit by a car and die in the street; Philip seems to recognize the man and remarks to Anne, "Another one." He begins a wild run through Paris to escape his unseen enemies, pulling Anne along with him.

A second, intertwined plot line involves Anne's old friend Jean-Marc (Jean-Claude Brialy). Jean-Marc introduces her to his acting circle, organized around the unstable director Gerard Lenz (Gianni Esposito), who, although he has no money, is staging a production of Shakespeare's *Pericles*. Gerard is trying to locate an audiotape of guitar music Juan had made for the show. Anne agrees to join the troupe, partly because she is attracted to Gerard, even though he suddenly begins to date the moody Terry, who seems to appear magically in her sports car at any time or place. Gerard explains to Anne that he likes *Pericles* because it is a difficult collection of "rags and patches" that nonetheless holds together because of a vague, global concept behind it. This statement has often been cited by reviewers as evidence that Rivette was conscious of the loose, halting logic of *Paris Belongs to Us* and that he also meant audiences to see parallels between the poor, obsessive stage director and Rivette, laboring against the odds to complete successfully this unwieldy first feature.

Because of strange, prophetic statements by the unbalanced Philip, Anne begins to fear for Gerard's safety: "Either I'm crazy or Gerard is doomed," she tells her brother, Pierre, in a delivery style that reminds one of an intertitle in a silent Murnau or Lang film. Once Gerard gets a big break to present *Pericles* in a real theater, Terry suddenly leaves him, so he turns to the lovesick Anne. Strangely, even though this is just what Anne has been hoping for, she tells him she cannot be his new lover. She is also disappointed in him for making compromises with the new producer, who has cut her out of the show.

The last third of the film continues to build suspicions among the characters that some of their friends may be in jeopardy. Paranoia and madness gradually increase for each character. Gerard writes to Anne that he will follow Juan's lead and kill himself if she does not come to him, which ironically upsets her and drives her away further, though later Gerard denies writing that note. As Anne is watching Fritz Lang's *Metropolis* (1926) later, however, Philip calls to tell her Gerard is, indeed, dead, apparently a suicide, though the audience never sees or hears any evidence about what happened. Terry and Philip blame Anne's brother, Pierre, for having caused Gerard's death, and a zombielike Anne seems to believe them. Terry goes to pick up Pierre in her two-seater car and Anne hails a taxi, supposedly to meet them, along with Philip and some others, at a country hideout. When she is the first to arrive at their destination, however, she has a mental, subjective vision of Terry shooting Pierre in a clearing. After Terry arrives alone and admits that Pierre is dead, Philip cries out suddenly that they were wrong, Pierre was not guilty. Meanwhile, Terry recites as if in a dream that the organization they have been fighting only exists in Philip's imagination but then claims, "Money, police, political parties are all part of it: different forms of fascism," and adds that Pierre is dead because Anne wanted too much: "the sublime." Philip and Terry drive off in her sports car, and an actor in the background tells Anne he will just go on with *Pericles*. The final shots are of Anne looking out over a lake, watching geese fly past.

This convoluted story line is built from a highly restricted range of information, generally centered around Anne and her fragmented comings and goings. Some characters, such as the neurotic neighbor from the first scene, disappear mysteriously, and those who presumably die, Juan, Gerard, and Pierre, are never fully explained: Did Juan compose guitar music that communicated a critical message to someone and motivated his being driven to his death by an organization, or is the sad Spanish music just a symptom of a deep depression that many of this friends now share? As one friend says, "The guitar is all we have left." Did Gerard die at his own hand, and if so, was his suicide motivated by Terry and Philip and/or his severe debts and/or the coldness of Anne, who would not help him when he needed it most? Finally, are the images of Terry shooting Pierre to be read as Anne somehow seeing exactly what happened or as mad imaginings? Even the reasons for Philip to charge that Pierre belonged to the organization and killed Gerard are never explained, much less why Philip then screams that he and Terry were all wrong about Pierre. As far as the audience can tell, Philip has received no new information regarding anyone. Thus, Rivette's end to the story verges on the absurd, especially with Terry proclaiming there was no organization, yet charging Anne helped kill her own brother by hounding Terry with questions.

Every level of the story in *Paris Belongs to Us* is built upon unverifiable bits and pieces of action that can never be reorganized into a logical, coherent diegetic world. The story is open on the level of character and action, creating a modern story in the process of becoming a story. The editors at *Positif* praised Rivette, claiming *Paris Belongs to Us* "displays an excessive desire to be inconclusive," and that it proved Rivette, unlike his friends at *Cahiers,* was not a right-wing director.[32] Much as in a tale by Robbe-Grillet in which it may simultaneously be a hot day and a cold night, the film has characters such as Pierre who are both guilty and innocent and dead men such as Juan who are both murder victims and suicides. The paranoia of the characters is so pervasive as to infect and undermine the audience's ability to understand them or their world.

Because Rivette makes it impossible to understand character traits and motivations, he undercuts the possibility for unity of action or concept to lend cohesiveness to his fiction. After its premiere, Rivette claimed that *Paris Belongs to Us* was an incomplete adventure, or the story of an idea: "But no idea can pretend to explain the world . . . because the real world's contradictions will always thwart it. And yes, we might believe at the age of twenty or thirty that we will discover the meaning of the universe and that Paris belongs to us . . . but Paris belongs to no one."[33] These statements sound a bit like something one might expect from Godard, as in the latter's claim that in order to show confused characters one must be confusing. Rivette, who had praised the clean, efficient mise-en-scène of Hitchcock, did surprise many New Wave critics with this very *nouveau roman*–influenced tale that was such a jumble of conflicting character statements and actions. But for James Monaco it seemed almost predictable that Rivette would make such a film: "*Paris nous appartient* seemed to be exactly the kind of film one would expect a critic to make, full of what seemed like forced, false, intellectual mystery: thin, monotonous, and lacking resonance."[34] Similarly, Roy Armes complains that *Paris Belongs to Us* is completely uncompromising, as it avoids clever dialogue or striking images; he concludes, "The film's major defect is its failure to create any sort of dramatic tension."[35] But *Paris Belongs to Us* should not be reduced to a failed experiment that taught Rivette which problems to avoid in his later films. Rather, it should be investigated for its striking, erratic stylistic flourishes, which foreground the narration of an impossibly obscure story that weaves together "the threat of fascism, the fantasmagoria of Feuillade, seduction and paranoia, plus humor and cruelty," according to Jean-Michel Frodon.[36]

Rivette is famous for an obsessive belief in mise-en-scène's centrality to cinematic production; François Truffaut even told him that he had the most "directed style" of all the *Cahiers* directors. But the average spectator may be hard pressed to isolate the precise stylistic markers that distinguish the visuals of *Paris Belong to Us.* On the broadest level, however, the baffling, ominous vision of these obscure characters seemingly trapped in Paris is created by Rivette's unflattering portrayal of the city, in which every building seems to hold a secret, alternative purpose. The characters' ongoing dialogue about who may or may not be in danger is spoken in cafés, on street corners, or in gloomy apartment locations that seem to reinforce their suspicions and desperation. Michel Marie identifies this use of the city as one of the film's important aspects, building as it does on the mise-en-scène of Louis Feuillade, René Clair, and Fritz Lang of the 1910s and 1920s: "Rivette provides a singular survey of Paris. . . . The countless stairways and jam-packed buildings help accentuate the labyrinthine aspects of the story. Rivette's Paris is a dark maze where intricate plots are underway. . . . All the characters feel threatened. The climate evokes the McCarthy-era witch hunts in the United States or Prague's rebellion crushed by the tanks, while it also provides a remarkable account of the intellectual mood at the end of the Fourth Republic in France, with all its military and political plots surrounding the Algerian War."[37] Much like the Paris of early Rohmer, Rivette's city takes on subtle connotations that reflect on the characters but also suggest what may have made them the way they are.

Rivette's interior scenes also provide carefully crafted locations that are both functional and significant. At the first night's party, for instance, the camera work generates part of the oppressive atmosphere, panning and re-framing across the many people milling about in the room like so many prisoners pacing in their cells. But in addition to the often disruptive editing, the set, lighting, and gestures all generate a harsh room for people who look and act miserable. Even Anne wants to leave right away, asking, "What's going on here?" The party's host is a painter, but his painting of Juan has just been sold; everyone is disappointed that the picture is now gone, for they now seem to have no purpose for being there. The party participants, including a gangly young Claude Chabrol, cast perverse shadows on the walls, dangle their arms at their sides, stare blankly at their cigarettes in their hands, and seem simply to clutter the frame. When they mention Juan's death, the camera position even shifts to a lower position, so characters loom in a distorted way toward the low-key ceiling, which seems to hold in the cigarette smoke and absorb what little light is available. There is even a stairway that appears to lead nowhere. The mise-en-scène combines German expressionism and film noir with a claustrophobic documentary feel. By the end of the scene, Philip tosses his glass of wine across a blank canvas in this painter's loft; this pointless gesture further reinforces the emptiness of the characters' lives. Rivette's painful party scene ends with Terry's arrival; Philip slaps her and blames her for helping get Juan killed, and he warns Pierre to stay away from her if he wants to live. The entire evening and its location create almost unbearable angst for these characters, as Anne gets pulled inexorably into their plots and illusions of plots.

The settings for every character tend toward the tawdry, and the location shooting combined with Charles Bitsch's cinematography, shot with available light when possible, give the film a grim, rather unprofessional look, not unlike parts of Rohmer's *Suzanne's Career*. During one of Gerard's rehearsals, however, when Pierre has followed along with Anne, Rivette stages Gerard's angry outburst and scuffle on three planes of action, à la Renoir, but this is a rare composition for him. Rivette prefers short, abrupt shots to long takes; *Paris Belongs to Us* has nearly seven hundred shots for an ASL of twelve seconds. Typically, Rivette packs the frame to reinforce everyone's discomfort at being trapped by his or her paranoia; he even covers the walls of Philip's room with grotesque, childish black sketches of a monster-face icon. When Anne visits the young Finnish woman who lives in Philip's building, a bizarre photo montage of her in various modeling poses seems to suggest that everything the audience needs to know about her is communicated in these staged photographs, while this inserted montage shatters the diegetic space. And later, when Anne visits a woman who knew Juan, that woman walks around her apartment with a board tied to her back, claiming the end of the world is upon them. The madness of each character is generated visually in very different ways, some bluntly, others subtly, but it is this obsessive accumulation of specific visual signifiers that distinguishes Rivette's glum but fascinating style. *Positif* even went so far as to suggest that *Paris Belongs to Us* evokes Plato's cave: "With decor and gestures, Rivette presents that section of the cave where some of us are still watching the dance of our shadows on some dark surface."[38]

The final product combines New Wave realism with themes of contemporary alienation, references to favorite directors and their styles, and touches of science fiction mixed with bits of a modern thriller. The result lacks the formal rigor and elegantly composed images of Antonioni, but it offers a good synthesis of New Wave and contemporary art-film modes. Rivette's distinct auteurist traits would be established gradually over the next decade, but Claire Clouzot effectively summarizes his contribution: his rigorous style is in perfect conformity with his scripts, which is always about "complex, serious, and profoundly pessimistic subjects."[39] Rivette investigates his nightmarish diegetic worlds further by introducing the themes of representation and especially theatricality; this device provides an escape from the real world and attempts to come to terms with the struggle between truth and illusion. Even his stunning and successful *La belle noiseuse* (1991), which deals with a painter and his model, grapples with the relationship between the real, the imagined, and the represented. The uncomfortable collage of theatrical, bizarre, and realistic tactics at work in *Paris Belongs to Us* can account for its poor reception, but one should recognize in it a rare example of a difficult film that nonetheless puts into practice the very production experiments and narrative strategies that the New Wave encouraged its new directors to explore as they challenged how and why to tell stories in the modern French cinema. Rivette's answer is one very distinctive option.

Jacques Doniol-Valcroze and Pierre Kast: Toward a Nouvelle Vague Comedy of Manners

Jacques Doniol-Valcroze (b. 1920) was a contemporary of André Bazin, a cofounder of both the *ciné-club* Objectif 49 and *Cahiers du cinema,* and a very active film reviewer, one who especially enjoyed writing the summaries of film festivals. He was greatly influenced by his fellow cinephiles; thus his critical ideas were often less distinctive than those of Bazin, Rohmer, or Truffaut, though he wrote lively, engaging review articles. In the 1950s he was firmly auteurist, but, along with Jacques Rivette, he also called for more attention to a wider range of international cinema and, eventually, social issues in *Cahiers.* He wrote the lead article in the first issue of *Cahiers* as a tribute to Edward Dmytryk, "Dmytryk ou les arêtes vives" ("Dmytryk or the sharp edges"), and then wrote the second article in the second *Cahiers* on another American figure, "All about Mankiewicz." He is an important, often overlooked figure in French film culture, who was nonetheless as actively involved in the auteurist aesthetics of *Cahiers du cinéma* as any critic there. In the famous "Six Characters in Search of *Auteurs,*" it was Doniol-Valcroze who praised Alexandre Astruc's *Les mauvaises rencontres* and Roger Vadim's *And God Created Woman* for going beyond conventional French cinema to show the specific social and historical context for their characters: "The greatest possibility of doing good work that is open to young filmmakers is to continue in the manner of Astruc and Vadim."[40] He was actively engaged in helping define and promote *le jeune cinéma français,* and *Cinéma 60* considered his contributions in establishing 1950s film culture, his helpful advice, and his contacts invaluable in launching the New Wave.[41] But Doniol-Valcroze also wanted to participate in its production; thus, he moderated the famous La Napoule colloquium outside Cannes in 1959, appearing alongside

Chabrol, Malle, Godard, and Truffaut. He was also one of the twenty-four first-time directors to complete a feature that year in France.

With his own film, *L'eau à la bouche,* which means "mouth watering," Doniol-Valcroze offers a social satire that owes more to the Renoir of *Rules of the Game* than to any of his contemporaries. Michel Marie sees *L'eau à la bouche* as sharing, along with Pierre Kast's *Le bel âge* (1960), "a common theme of networks of seduction between intellectuals and pretty women, set in the sophisticated style of Marivaux."[42] *Le Film français* was among the first to notice that *L'eau à la bouche* combined aspects of Renoir's masterpiece with Bergman's *Smiles of a Summer's Night* (1955); it concluded that the film proved Doniol-Valcroze was a distinctive director displaying "an inspired, poetic style."[43] Doniol-Valcroze's story builds off class and gender divisions and intrigues that hark back to French comedies of manners, yet the characters inhabit the France of 1959 in their social customs, with sex used more as a weapon and a distraction than it was for Renoir in the 1930s. Doniol-Valcroze made no attempt to hide his love of and fascination with beautiful women, foregrounding beauty and desire as motivators for his characters' actions.

L'eau à la bouche was the first New Wave feature produced by Pierre Braunberger, who had just completed Jean Rouch's *Moi, un noir* (1958). Doniol-Valcroze hired veteran 1950s cinematographer Roger Fellous, who had worked with commercial directors such as Marc Allégret and later went on to work with Luis Buñuel on *Diary of a Chamber Maid* before slipping into a career of filming pornography. One of the most impressive crew positions was occupied by the thirty-year-old Serge Gainsbourg, making his debut as a film composer; his contributions also helped add a hip, young angle to the production. Nonetheless, what finally distinguishes *L'eau à la bouche* is the collection of fine actors, many of whom were close friends of Doniol-Valcroze and so already felt they were part of his entourage before filming began.

L'eau à la bouche is an elegant treatment of a melodramatic tale that begins by establishing that the château at Roussillon in which the action takes place is as essential to the story as are the characters. Surprisingly, this sumptuous château, complete with turrets, a swimming pool, and an extravagant park, was an inexpensive location set for Doniol-Valcroze since it belonged to his wealthy family. The plot begins in the present when a beautiful young woman, Milena (Françoise Brion), discovers that her American cousin, Fifine (Alexandra Stewart), is missing and fears that she has committed suicide.

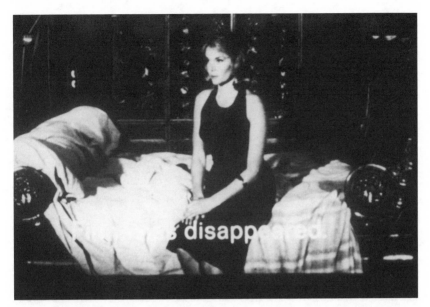

Figure 7.8. Fifine on the bed (*L'eau à la bouche*)

The camera dollies in and the time shifts back to a flashback set in the recent past when the handsome notary, Miguel (Gérard Barray), tells Milena that he has located her two cousins, Fifine and Jean-Paul, and that they will arrive on Friday. Their grandmother has died, and the three distant cousins stand to inherit the amazing château and the family business and must be present for the reading of the will. Milena is in residence, as are the head of the household staff, César (Michel Galabru), and the new maid, Prudence (Bernadette Lafont), the cook, and her young granddaughter, Rosa. Fifine arrives, but in the company of her boyfriend, Robert Godard (Jacques Riberolles), who is mistaken for cousin Jean-Paul; Robert finds Fifine's cousin Milena stunning and decides to play along and pretend to be the other absent cousin, Jean-Paul, who has apparently been delayed until Monday.

With the arrival of Fifine and Robert at the château, which is filled with romantic paintings and sculptures of nudes and has an excessively exotic decor, the characters begin to size up one another and flirt, often under the watchful eye of Rosa. The jealous Fifine warns Robert to stay away from her cousin; she knows he has a long history of seducing women and worries that his lies will destroy their relationship and lead to a bad end. Nonetheless, she cannot bring herself to tell everyone that Robert is her boyfriend and not her cousin.

Figure 7.9. Lafont title card (*L'eau à la bouche*)

Meanwhile, César actively pursues the new maid, Prudence, mostly be-cause he is bored and likes the challenge. In a scene that recalls moments be-tween the marquis and the poacher in *Rules of the Game,* he discusses women and seduction with Robert, who is also attracted to the maid, Prudence, as well as to her employer, Milena. But the wily Prudence steals Robert's pass-port, thus becoming the only person there other than Fifine to know that he is not the rich cousin Jean-Paul. The naive Milena begins to take strolls with Robert and explains that she used to be involved with Miguel but suddenly had to break off their relationship; at this point, Doniol-Valcroze inserts a brief flashback shot of Milena slapping Miguel. Meanwhile, Miguel has be-gun pursuing Fifine. The Saturday night ends with Miguel and Robert chat-ting as Miguel plays "Jesu, Joy of Man's Desiring" on the château's pipe organ, and César tries unsuccessfully to force his way into Prudence's room.

But on Sunday all the plot lines begin to accelerate: Prudence is quite animated and goes to Robert's room with his breakfast tray to confront him by saying, "Bonjour, M. Godard," revealing she knows his true identity. In-trigued, Robert asks Prudence to meet him at midnight. Meanwhile, the disgusting César gets to take Fifine her tray and watches her bathe. In the late afternoon, it rains, so the couples dance, with Fifine and Miguel now a pair like Robert and Milena.

Figure 7.10. Milena on stairs watches Robert (*L'eau à la bouche*)

Figure 7.11. Fifine confronts Robert (*L'eau à la bouche*)

Figure 7.12. Dancing couples (*L'eau à la bouche*)

That night, Fifine swims nude in the pool, with Miguel looking on, while César chases Prudence to her room, ripping off her clothes as they go. Safe in her room, Prudence eventually unlocks the door, assuming Robert will come to her, but he heads for Milena's room instead, providing César the chance he has been waiting for to enter Prudence's room. Thus, all three women end up in bed with a new partner at the same moment, with Miguel explaining to the distraught but romantic Fifine that he will tell her the next day whether he loves her, while the music returns.

On Monday, the jealous Prudence walks into Milena's room and drops Robert's passport papers to show who he really is, while Fifine wants to know whether Miguel really loves her. On the terrace, Robert tries to explain himself to an angry Milena, claiming that while it "seems like a melodrama" at the moment, he really is planning to leave Fifine; Milena adds that Miguel is untrustworthy and will undoubtedly drop Fifine soon as well. But Fifine overhears Robert and Milena discussing her fate, and the camera zooms in to register her shock; she runs off, leaving everyone to worry about her.

The time of the flashback has now caught up with the present. The real cousin Jean-Paul (Paul Guers) arrives, further complicating the mix-up, and only the observant child, Rosa, can locate Fifine, who is huddled on

Figure 7.13. César chases Prudence (*L'eau à la bouche*)

Figure 7.14. Fifine sleeps as Michel dresses (*L'eau à la bouche*)

Figure 7.15. Robert and Milena: "It's like in melodramas" (*L'eau à la bouche*)

the roof like a scared child, apparently contemplating whether to leap from the tower. Rosa leads her safely back to the group. At this point, Fifine explains that she has lost everything. The film concludes with Robert and Milena as a happy couple, César and Prudence as a feisty, romantically involved pair, but Miguel and Fifine sad and alone. And little Rosa goes on playing with her yo-yo and wandering around the château as the camera meanders about after her.

Doniol-Valcroze provides an elegant combination of comedy-of-manners predicaments with references to past and recent films. There are not only the obvious connections with *Rules of the Game,* including the exotic Asian settings that equate Fifine with Renoir's Genevieve, but also more recent references to the convoluted sexual games of Louis Malle's *The Lovers* and Kast's *Le bel âge. L'eau à la bouche* becomes a modernized Marivaux-like game for six lovers that satirizes the upper class while exploiting the new sexual sensibilities pioneered by Vadim and Malle as well as the by New Wave as a whole. Stylistically too, *L'eau à la bouche* borrows from a number of fine influences, but the result is a highly polished, luxurious mainstream-looking movie that lacks any strong markers of a personal style. Doniol-Valcroze, like a number of good French directors of this period, including Pierre Kast and Michel Deville, suffered at the hands of

Figure 7.16. Fifine hiding on the château roof (*L'eau à la bouche*)

Figure 7.17. Rosa walks off (*L'eau à la bouche*)

most critics who, during an era obsessed with auteurism, recognized few individualistic traits in his films. Doniol-Valcroze provides a great synthesis of traditions without forging a personal alternative in the way that Godard, Truffaut, or Alain Resnais did.

L'eau à la bouche can nonetheless be seen as a tribute to many of the aesthetic ideals celebrated in *Cahiers du cinéma* throughout the 1950s. On the level of acting, Françoise Brion recalls that Doniol-Valcroze gave his actors great freedom for improvisation; he set up the beginnings and endings of shots but allowed them liberty in dialogue and movement between those moments.[44] The result is a nice combination of a tightly scripted world that flows very naturally with many significant but spontaneous gestures and touches by the actors. Thus, this film presents its action via many long takes that stage the action both laterally across the screen and in deep space. Character mobility is matched by fluid camera work that dollies, tracks, and pans along the halls. The camera work does more than pastiche Renoir's *Rules of the Game;* it creates a diegesis that breaks away from theatrical constraints while cinematically linking space and time with characterization. For instance, Doniol-Valcroze stages the important confrontation between Prudence and Robert in a shot that echoes the deep space and long takes of William Wyler. Prudence insists upon delivering breakfast to Robert and enters his room as he is performing his morning push-ups on the floor. The camera rests in a low position just behind Robert, to reveal him falling to the floor as Prudence enters and exclaims, "Bonjour, M. Godard." Stunned that she knows he is not the rich cousin, Robert calls her over to him. In the same shot, Robert confronts Prudence, trying to learn what she intends to do with her information, and he ends up pulling her to him to kiss her, using his seductive powers to "buy" her silence. The clarity and unity of action, with Prudence testing Robert's reactions to her news and moving gradually from her safe perch behind the table to kneel on the floor with him, is interrupted only when the phone rings, forcing them to postpone their passionate encounter. Doniol-Valcroze's diegetic time and space are highly functional and fluid, and the characters' emotions are delivered as much by the careful shot composition and polished mise-en-scène as by the musical accompaniment and dialogue, which itself comes off as natural and contemporary, despite the classical influences from past French literature and cinema.

Surprisingly, Doniol-Valcroze's sexy, eloquent comic drama proved only moderately successful at the box office, though some sources claim it did quite well. Because of its brief nudity and sexual subjects, *L'eau à la*

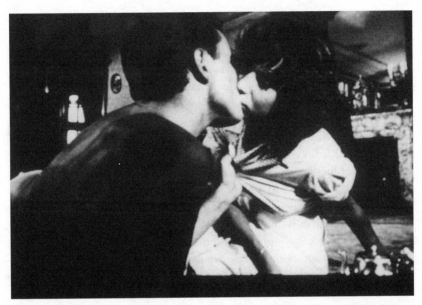

Figure 7.18. Prudence is pulled into the foreground to join Robert (*L'eau à la bouche*)

bouche was restricted to audiences age sixteen and older. According to *Le Film français*, it only sold 71,000 tickets in its six-week run in Paris, which was even lower than Chabrol's *Les bonnes femmes*, which sold 84,000 tickets in three weeks at roughly the same time. But other sources cite its sales at 150,000, which may be the total for the entire nation.[45] Either way, it made money for Pierre Braunberger, especially since it was popular abroad.

The film was celebrated by *Cahiers* in a review that proclaimed that Doniol-Valcroze proved his faith in cinema to adapt literature onto the world, which was the opposite of Alain Resnais and his *Hiroshima, mon amour*. *Cahiers* reviewer Louis Marcorelles even compared the presentation of space and time here to Proust's notion of "lost time" as well as to the themes and style of Virginia Woolf, which was high praise indeed.[46] For contemporary audiences seeking New Wave films with radical styles or audacity to their stories, however, *L'eau à la bouche* was less than revolutionary, while critics hostile to *Cahiers* and the New Wave proper, attacked its failure to engage serious social issues. *Positif* and others would interpret it as just another example of bourgeois cinema by a bourgeois fellow pretending to be new and exciting. The fact that the movie displays Doniol-Valcroze's vast personal and family wealth, placing him on a financial par with Louis Malle, did not help him with leftist critics either. Freddy Buache provides a satirical summary that is representative of the scorn that politicized reviewers had for *L'eau à la bouche:* "Four characters (two women, two men), young, attractive, and rich, search for one another, tease and chase one another in the moonlight, in a universe full of seductive touching, languid looks, mussed beds, and an overly comfortable interior of a château. At midnight, one plays 'Jesu, Joy of Man's Desiring'; in the afternoon another reads Kafka aloud on the patio. They also play jazz records, drink whiskey, and dance in the rain while the valet courts the tease of a kitchen maid."[47] Marcorelles tried to counter this sort of attack by congratulating the leftist Doniol-Valcroze for being honest enough not to hide his origins: "he even offers it as an homage to the beauty and grace of an artistic style of living."[48]

Doniol-Valcroze would continue to act and direct, following *L'eau la bouche* with *Le coeur battant* (*The French Game*, 1960), produced by Cocinor, and *La denonciation* (1961), produced by Pierre Braunberger. Both films starred his new wife, Françoise Brion, but none of these first three films proved sufficient to catapult Doniol-Valcroze to a status equal to that granted his younger colleagues from *Cahiers*. All his features nevertheless verify his love of cinema and strong sense of visual storytelling.

Pierre Kast (b. 1920) was the same age as Doniol-Valcroze but had been active in an even wider variety of film-related activities from a younger age. A clandestine secretary for the communist student group during the occupation, Kast was hired by Henri Langlois in 1945 as his assistant for two years at the Cinémathèque. Antoine de Baecque argues that only Truffaut may have been familiar with more movies than Kast, who watched thousands of reels of film as an employee and constant spectator at the Cinémathèque.[49] But Kast also wrote scores of critical film reviews for *L'Ecran, Revue du cinéma, Cahiers du cinéma,* and even *Positif,* among others. He combined his political interests with surrealism and was a close friend of Boris Vian, Jean Cocteau, and Raymond Queneau. A very independent spirit, Kast argued he was an intellectual dandy, meaning someone above the fray who is no one's accomplice; in criticism he argued for an intellectual, biting, formalist cinema to attack bourgeois norms with a refined style. He was an elegant and provocative critic who regularly defended directors out of favor at *Cahiers,* such as René Clément, Federico Fellini, and Luis Buñuel. During the 1950s, he became an assistant to his friend Jean Grémillon as well as to Jean Renoir on *French Can-Can* (1955). He also made a large number of shorts, such as educational films for Pathé, and shot a first feature, *Amour de poche* (*A Girl in His Pocket,* 1957), which was a goofy adaptation of a science-fiction script, done in the style of Preston Sturges, whom Kast had met and even worked with briefly. Kast was later embarrassed by this first attempt at a mainstream film, which was a terrible flop. He claims he had compromised too much and argues that if it had been a success, it would have sent him off in a commercial but unproductive direction.[50] His second feature, *Le bel âge* (*Love Is When You Make It*), which took nearly two years to complete during 1958 and 1959 before its premiere in February 1960, serves as his first true nouvelle vague movie.

Kast found an unusual way to produce *Le bel âge* that anticipates Barbet Schroeder's scheme for *Paris vu par*. He was working for Pathé, making shorts, and decided to propose three short films that could be released as a feature-length compilation. By pretending only to be making three separate short films, he could avoid CNC permits and restrictions required of feature-length productions. Pathé agreed to help fund the project, but Kast also found outside backers among his friends, including Doniol-Valcroze.

The story follows a small cluster of men and women, beginning in Paris during springtime in the first episode, to Saint-Tropez during August in the second, before finally shifting from the beach to the Alps for the concluding skiing tale. Filming began in May 1958 and continued on and off throughout the year. The cast included an ensemble of actors who mostly knew one another and worked as a group of friends more than as coworkers. The men included Jean-Claude Brialy, Jacques Doniol-Valcroze, Gianni Esposito, and Hubert Noel. The women were Françoise Prévost, Françoise Brion, Ursula Kubler, and Alexandra Stewart. For music, Kast brought back Georges Delerue, who had begun his career composing the film music for Kast's short, *Un amour de poche,* in 1957 and was now working on *Hiroshima, mon amour* as well. Kast's cinematographers included newcomers Ghislain Cloquet and Sacha Vierny, who had both gotten started in the industry with *Un amour de poche* and then worked on Alain Resnais projects as well. Despite their youth, these crew members gave *Le bel âge* a playfully mature look and sound, aided by Noel Burch as assistant director.

Kast's feature opens with a montage of the actors dressed in hunting outfits out in the woods, many pointing their rifles off screen. When asked what they were firing at, Kast told an interviewer, "Some shoot at Aristotle, others at Kant."[51] These hunting scenes recur between each of the three short-story episodes, helping establish a general theme: "There is always a hunter and a prey." Each story involves optional approaches for romantic "hunting" available in late 1950s upper-class culture; where *L'eau à la bouche* gave homage to the interior château scenes of *Rules of the Game*, *Le bel âge* refers instantly to Renoir's exterior and hunting and poaching sequences. One organizing principle behind the action is that various characters select some romantic strategy; if it works, they try it again on another object of desire, but if it fails they adopt and test a new tactic. Several of these romantic experiments in pursuit and seduction are played out across the course of the three stories while others are limited to one or two episodes. But the related theme is that women are driven to struggle for parity with men, which must finally involve taking over and controlling the seduction process, which actually proves less certain and decisive than the women had hoped. In many ways, Kast's *Le bel âge* looks to Laclos's novel *Dangerous Liaisons* for its inspiration and action. The result was a critical success: *Cahiers du cinéma* selected it as the best film of the month during its premiere, while *L'eau à la bouche* came in third in that issue.

Kast's first episode, which was loosely adapted from Alberto Moravia's "Un vieil imbécile" (An old fool) and cowritten with Moravia, takes place in Paris and is built around a group of men, including the central narrating character, Jacques (Doniol-Valcroze). The narrator attracts and basks in women's attention on his morning stroll to work: "Every morning I would go for a walk; I felt a bit like a fisherman: I always had a fish on my hook." In this first episode, the men, including Steph (Hubert Noel) and Jean-Claude (Jean-Claude Brialy), are all equally interested in women but try to avoid any jealousy or drama. Jacques explains, in his dandy's voice-over banter, "We were sporting, but not competitive. . . . We all agreed that just as there are types of wine—cheap, Bordeaux, Burgundy—there are specific types of girls in Paris." When an attractive woman, whether a new secretary or a potential client, enters their art book shop, which is arranged "scientifically" for seduction, with its many little levels, stairs, and tiny passageways, the men decide who gets to try, and each has different seduction methods to deploy. But once the newest secretary, Alexandra (Alexandra Stewart), arrives, their tried and true rituals of seduction begin to crumble, and all three men begin to compete for her attention. When the old pro Steph fails, Jean-Claude and Jacques are stunned but eager to try their turn. Finally, Jacques persuades Alexandra to agree to go to the shore at Deauville with him. He becomes melancholy, however, losing his confi-

Figure 7.19. Françoise firing (*Le bel âge*)

dence; rather than seduce her, he takes her back to Paris where he looks at himself in his three mirrors: "I have one joy in life—girls—and now all that is over." This episode ends when, three weeks later, it turns out that Alexandra is engaged after all to old Steph, which gives Jacques hope again; a new beautiful young woman enters the shop, Françoise (Françoise Prévost), and the newly revived Jacques takes her out of a walk.

This episode, which reveals how fragile the men's feigned sexist superiority actually can be, is followed by a short hunting scene in which the men discuss Françoise, who is now with Claude (Gianni Esposito). They are breaking up, however, and she is leaving the château. Claude is also tired of the relationship, but he asks her what will become of him now, to which she replies, "I'll be gone in one and a half minutes, you'll be lost in three, in five you'll have a drink, in seven you'll be on the phone, and in ten minutes you'll be off on vacation." And after Françoise drives off in her big American car, Claude does just as she predicted, heading to Saint-Tropez.

This concluding segment sets the stage for the second episode, which shows a more relaxed and open sexuality than in the first one. Jacques and Alexandra appear in it, without Steph, whom she seems to have abandoned ("It is just like ping-pong," explains Jacques). This episode does seem to be heaven on earth to the men, with Jacques explaining to Claude, who despite

Figure 7.20. Jacques in mirrors (*Le bel âge*)

his good looks and money somehow turns off all the women he tries to seduce: "If you don't think like a child, you'll never enter God's kingdom."
Claude does think he is on "another planet where the men and women have
abandoned themselves to a natural state of love." But he nonetheless has
problems seducing women, until his "guide" in love, Barbara (Barbara
Aptekman), proves to be "good medicine," giving him confidence. When he
falls for a newcomer, Anne (Anne Collette), he tries relentlessly to win her
over, but in the end she rejects him after she overhears Jacques and Claude
discussing her: "I saw you both looking at me; you were like two men buying
a horse." She leaves with another man, proving once again that the men's insensitive plans can occasionally lead to failure.

During the next transitional hunting scene, Jacques discusses
Claude's mistaken belief in a universal method of seduction but asserts
that women have a mysterious quality that cannot be underestimated. but
several women hunters, including Françoise, overhear the men and ponder whether there really is a feminine mystique and how they can use it to
their advantage.

This dilemma sets up the final episode in which the women, Françoise,
Alexandra, and new friends Carla (Françoise Brion) and Ursula (Ursula
Kubler), go to the Alps for a skiing vacation but then learn that Jacques,

Figure 7.21. Claude and Jacques discuss seduction (*Le bel âge*)

Steph, and Claude are coming to join them. Françoise decides that it is time for the women to exploit their mysterious powers, so she gathers the women around the chalkboard and designs their romantic couples "scientifically," giving Carla to Claude, for instance. But the new blonde, Virginie (Virginie Vitry), tries to horn in on all the men. After enduring a number of flirtatious games led by the women, Jacques discovers their master plan on the chalkboard and tries to modify it a bit. In the meantime, Carla is hurt by Claude's attention to Ursula and ends up saddened by the whole affair, complaining it is no longer an organized game; it becomes clear everyone is on his or her own now. Carla even cuts up one of her favorite photos of Claude. By the end of the episode, another friend, Roger (Boris Vian), has joined in. He is curious about a plot point in a story he is trying to write, so he asks whether a very beautiful woman can ever have a desperate love affair. Carla replies, no.

Le bel âge ends with a final hunting scene that sets up three happy couples—Alexandra with Jacques, Ursula with Claude, and Françoise with Steph. As for Carla, she is trying to forget the desperate love she pretends not to believe in by dating Roger. During the Alps episode, Jacques's voice-over had announced that he felt as if he were in a "pre–World War II play"; however, the film's comedy-of-manners antics combine with very

Figure 7.22. Carla cuts up photo (*Le bel âge*)

contemporary issues of seduction, gender, and a lost postwar generation to lend *Le bel âge* a modern, youthful feel. *Le bel âge* thus becomes a tribute to Renoir, but also to Luis Buñuel, Françoise Sagan, and Louis Malle. In the end, however, it is as much a Doniol-Valcroze production as a Kast film, which proves the camaraderie of the New Wave era, where personal productions can come out of a shared creative connection between director, writers, and producers, and an ensemble of actors, who are almost all friends of the director. Though Doniol-Valcroze helped write most of it, *Le bel âge* is a group project in every sense of the word.

Stylistically, *Le bel âge* is also quite interesting in that it ends up offering a collection of tactics for mocking the characters and their ridiculous obsessions. The mise-en-scène typically comments on the characters, so that while the troubled Jacques's face is reflected back at him from three mirrors when he has lost confidence and mopes, at his peak of strength paintings of naked women adorn the walls behind him. Similarly, when the men observe and comment upon a woman's character, they are often isolated in the frame, staged in depth, with some vertical barrier between them and their "prey." The world of these characters is adorned with expensive artwork, flashy sports cars, good wine and whiskey, as well as handsome clothes and furnishings. If this is a new generation, it is a spoiled consumer culture as well; the characters flaunt their buying power and exquisite taste, which carry over into their personal relationships in which women, and later men, are trophies to be acquired.

The time and space are also organized around the narrative moments; long takes preserve the duration in some scenes, while discontinuous editing is used for montages of women's legs or the moment when the rattled Jacques runs his Alfa Romeo into a moped while he is trying to look smooth and impressive in front of Alexandra. But Kast fails to adopt either the formal rigor or the radical experimentation of many of his contemporary New Wave–era colleagues. Michel Marie complains that *Le bel âge* is an inadequate attempt at moralizing: "Kast's ambition is huge since he wants to propose new relations between the sexes where women can take the initiative in seduction just as much as men. But, his project falls flat because of his impoverished direction of the actors and the weakness of the dialogue."[52] Frodon enjoyed the project more: "It was shrewd, pleasant, yet awkward."[53] Kast does rely too heavily on Doniol-Valcroze's voice-over dialogue to add the dandified observations of Jacques, who comes to resemble a heterosexually active version of an Oscar Wilde character. By contrast, the women often come off speaking like representatives of a certain "type" of female, just as the narrow-minded men of the story might have envisioned them. But Kast's late addition of Boris Vian as Roger, a character who happens to be writing a story, hints that perhaps he is also attempting a *mise-en-abyme* narrative structure here: The narrative is not entirely provided from Jacques's stilted point of view but comes perhaps from the observing Roger as well. There does seem to be a split function for the narration, in which the diegetic narration by Jacques is both reinforced and mocked by the primary narration's manipulation of the camera work, mise-en-scène, and the jazz music score. In the end, *Le bel âge* is an engaging, if not groundbreaking exercise in storytelling that foregrounds sexy themes rather than an engaging visual style. As Jean-Michel Frodon summarizes it, "*Le bel âge* highlights Kast's and Doniol-Valcroze's penchant for great literature and pretty women and a world where men and women both have the single goal of pleasure."[54]

While Pierre Kast's and Jacques Doniol-Valcroze's pedigree with *Cahiers du cinéma* would seem to place them firmly at the core of the New Wave, their narrative strategies have led historians to situate them on the fringes of the New Wave at best. Several historians have even argued that they both fit most logically within the subset known as the Left Bank Group. Antoine de Baecque for one argues that these two share more with

Agnès Varda and Alain Resnais than they do with Godard and Chabrol. Having connections to *Cahiers* does not prevent a director from being defined as belonging to the allied Left Bank Group.[55] Similarly, Jean-Michel Frodon argues that Doniol-Valcroze and Kast share both political convictions, like the Left Bank Group, and similar film styles, which move them each to be historicized on the immediate edge of the New Wave: "Doniol-Valcroze and Kast shared a culture, an aesthetic taste, and a talent for pushing their ideas forward. They also shared an elegant film language, with references to Choderlos de Laclos and eighteenth-century libertines," and those references were embedded in very modern frameworks.[56] For Frodon, like de Baecque, these two directors are highly modern and interesting, but their subsequent films become increasingly tangential to most of the central concerns and strategies of their New Wave comrades. Michel Marie, too, argues that Doniol-Valcroze and Kast are symptoms of renewal in France rather than key participants in the New Wave.

However, minimizing these directors as somehow "less New Wave" than others hardly helps one understand the breadth and depth of French filmmaking during this era. Doniol-Valcroze and Kast were successful critics-turned-filmmakers who managed to shoot feature films in 1959, with low budgets and casts made up of lesser-known young actors and friends, including New Wave icons Jean-Claude Brialy and Bernadette Lafont. Taking into consideration their themes of youthful indiscretion, sexual experimentation, and consumerism, plus their references to film history and fresh performance styles, one may productively praise their slightly mannered mise-en-scène as evidence of active and creative participation in the ongoing renewal in French cinema. In these ways, they fit perfectly the exuberant spirit and tactics of the French New Wave and should not be overlooked anymore than the earliest films by Eric Rohmer and Jacques Rivette should be ignored in deference to their later, more commercially successful films. All four of these directors help reveal the diversity of stories, styles, and production techniques explored not only by the New Wave directors in general but by *Cahiers* critics-turned-directors in particular.

8

On the New Wave's Left Bank: Alain Resnais and Agnès Varda

THE FRIENDS and cohorts of *Cahiers du cinéma* may occupy the core niche within the New Wave, but there was also another subgroup of new French film practice during the late 1950s and early 1960s, known as the Left Bank Group. Definitions of this active cluster of young directors often concentrate on their differences from the *Cahiers* critics-turned-filmmakers and stress their deeper involvement in aesthetic experimentation, their connections to documentary practice, overt political themes, and increased interest in other arts beyond cinema. Typically, they are seen as working in the shadow of Jean Rouch and *cinéma vérité*, as well as the New Novel, and as early as 1960 some French critics were labeling them *"nouvelle vague* 2."[1] The principal participants include Alain Resnais, Agnès Varda, Chris Marker, Henri Colpi, and Jacques Demy, among a few others. If I concentrate on just two directors, Resnais and Varda, as representative of this fascinating array of people and films, it is in part because they created some of the most distinctive and successful features of the Left Bank tendency, yet they are also most closely tied to the New Wave. Moreover, though Resnais and Varda were and are close friends and collaborators, they demonstrate the stunning variety of movies to come out of this era.

Alain Resnais (b. 1922) had distinguished himself with a series of highly influential documentaries, especially *Nuit et brouillard* (*Night and Fog*, 1955), before directing his first feature, *Hiroshima, mon amour.* That film, which premiered out of competition at the infamous 1959 Cannes Film Festival, created a sensation and allowed most observers to hail him alongside Truffaut and Chabrol as a founding member of the New Wave. Yet, quite rapidly critics began to separate Resnais and his rigorous formal experimentation from the more playful, genre-influenced filmmaking that typified much of the French New Wave. *l'Année dernière à Marienbad* (*Last Year at Marienbad*, 1961), written by Alain Robbe-Grillet, and then *Muriel* (1963), written by Jean Cayrol, revealed Resnais to be advancing along a very unique auteurist path, as he explored sound-image relations, modes of adaptation, and themes of isolation and reflection. His work also parallels productively the formal rigor and alienation effects seen in other modern European directors, such as Michelangelo Antonioni and Pier Paolo Pasolini. Resnais worked closely with a faithful band of friends, as did the *Cahiers* directors, but his collaborators were mostly outside the *Cahiers* circles, including Chris Marker, Agnès Varda, Jean Cayrol, cinematographer Sacha Vierny, and producer Anatole Dauman. Resnais' thematic interests, radical aesthetics, and productive friendships make him typical of this new generation of young French filmmakers working to renew the modern cinema from very personal vantage points.

Agnès Varda had written and directed three documentary shorts of her own since completing *La Pointe Courte*. She then managed to synthesize many of her distinctive strategies and discursive tactics into the very important *Cléo de 5 à 7* (*Cleo from 5 to 7*, 1962). Cleo, who wanders through Paris for ninety minutes, agonizing over a probable illness, became one of the most interesting female protagonists of the New Wave era. Varda followed with *Le bonheur* (*Happiness*, 1965), an unsettling domestic melodrama. These two films offer startlingly different treatments of contemporary sexual politics that continue to figure prominently in debates over the representation of women in cinema. Thanks to an amazingly productive career making both documentary and fiction films, Varda has solidified her position as the world's most important woman filmmaker of the past fifty years. Significantly, while Resnais and Varda were each products of the same social and aesthetic conditions that gave rise to other young French directors, they can also be studied as a distinctive pair overtly exploring the very boundaries of cinematic language during the New Wave era. Their work proves the vitality of the young French cinema's impulse to tell new stories in new ways to a new audience.

Alain Resnais: Montage Revisited

> *Hiroshima mon amour* proved to be as masterly and revolutionary as Orson Welles's *Citizen Kane* eighteen years earlier.
>
> —ROY ARMES, *French Cinema*

Among New Wave filmmakers, only Truffaut and Godard have received more critical and historical attention than Alain Resnais. His career is also the longest of any New Wave director. His parents gave him a much prized

8mm camera early on, so that by the time he was thirteen, in 1935, he was already filming. Resnais' film career began in earnest in 1948 with his first 35mm short film, *Van Gogh*, which won an Academy Award. He has been directing and editing movies ever since, earning hundreds of international awards, scores of France's César awards, and seven best director awards from the French Syndicate of Cinema Critics for films as varied as *La Guerre est finie* (*The War Is Over*, 1966), *Providence* (1977), and *Mon oncle d'Amérique* (*My American Uncle*, 1980). Moreover, in 1997, *On connaît la chanson* (*Same Old Song*), a joyous musical comedy, was a critical and financial success, followed in 2003 by the eighty-one-year-old director's stylish *Pas sur la bouche* (*Not on the Lips*). His *Coeurs* (*Private Fears in Public Places*, 2006) won two awards at the Venice Film Festival, including the Silver Lion for best director. For sixty years, Resnais enriched the cinema, challenged its conventions, and provided a remarkably diverse oeuvre of films concerned with art, literature, memory, and love. During the 1950s and early 1960s, he exploited daring narrative strategies in adapting original scripts by New Novelists, rapidly becoming a much respected giant of the international art cinema. In 1962, *Variety* called him the most controversial of the new French directors: His next film "will be awaited by film buffs, vied for by film fests, and haggled over by foreign film buyers."[2]

Resnais was born in Vannes, Brittany, and suffered bouts of asthma as a child. As a teenager, he had to be home schooled by his mother for part of his lycée education. He read a great deal of material, including art books and comic books, but also Marcel Proust's *Remembrance of Things Past*. Given the importance of memory and the blurring of objective and subjective depth of information in Resnais' subsequent films, the Proust reference has been emphasized by many biographers. Resnais has protested that though he read Proust, he does not believe *Remembrance of Things Past* overtly influenced his own work. He prefers to mention the time he spent as a youth watching films by Sacha Guitry, Abel Gance, Louis Feuillade, Harold Lloyd, and Jean Renoir.[3] After lycée, Resnais moved to Paris to pursue his passion for live theater, and by 1941, during World War II, he was studying acting with René Simon, before giving it up in 1943 to enter the new I.D.H.E.C. film school, created by the Vichy government. Given his later dedication to leftist politics, it is strange that Resnais refers very little to the Occupation or the effects of the war in his own life. Regardless, he entered I.D.H.E.C. where he learned editing in particular. In 1945 he dropped out before his final year, claiming he found the school too theoretical and lacking in real production practice. For one year he performed his required military service, after which he managed to find employment as an editor for *Paris 1900* (Védrès, 1947) and began shooting several shorts, including a mime routine by Marcel Marceau (*La Bague* [*The Ring*, 1947]) and five short documentary "visits" with artists, including Hans Hartung.

Resnais credited these shorts about painting as valuable testing ground for making still images come alive through editing and camera movement. In 1948, after directing two other shorts, *Les Jardins de Paris* (*The Gardens of Paris*) and *Château de France* (*The Chateaux of France*), he made *Van Gogh*, first in 16mm, then re-shot in 35mm, thanks to funding from Pierre Braunberger. *Van Gogh* explores what Resnais calls the "imaginary life" of Van Gogh by selecting paintings and fragments of paintings in a carefully edited and narrated twenty-minute documentary that functions almost as a travelogue. In *Van Gogh*, and again in *Guernica* (1950), Resnais edits together details of painted canvases, filmed with a close, moving camera, accompanied by music, sound effects, and voice-over commentary, to re-present a larger, real world series of events. In both art films, the heavy dependence on short shots of static paintings placed extra weight on the soundtracks. As Resnais explains, "Sound was no longer used to 'accompany' the images, but to create the film's skeleton. Its role was to weld the paintings together into a coherent universe."[4] For instance, Van Gogh's life is narrated, while images from his paintings accompany the words. The narrator explains, "Other horizons called. Leaving Nuenen, one November evening, Van Gogh set out alone toward his destiny," while the simultaneous montage of early paintings includes a pair of old shoes, a snowy field, and a man and his dog wandering off down a country road. Similarly, the grim *Guernica* combines commentary from Paul Eluard's writings and often discordant music by Guy Bernard with a hectic, desperate montage of haunting images. Two other shorts, *Les Statues meurent aussi* (*Statues Die Also*, 1953), co-written with Chris Marker, and his study of the huge Bibliothèque nationale, *Toute la mémoire du monde* (*All the Memory in the World*, 1956), provide rich glimpses into Resnais' themes and formal experimentation that will reappear in his later features as well. Two of his most successful documentaries, the shocking *Night and Fog* and the giddy *Le chant du styrène* (*Song of Styrene*, 1958), prove the value of his mixture of careful documentation, a roving, observant camera, and an increasingly experimental film style.

Night and Fog was commissioned by the Historical Committee of World War II, with the aid of Argos Films. It was shot in both color and black and white, alternating many brutal still photographs from the concentration camps with contemporary color footage of the camps. Jean Cayrol, a camp survivor, provided a mesmerizing voice-over commentary. *Night and Fog* won the prestigious Louis Delluc Award and still stands as one of the most troubling and brilliant cinematic treatments of the Holocaust. Further, while its contemplative pacing builds upon strategies employed in his earlier art films, *Night and Fog* also demonstrates Resnais' new, mature style that would influence a whole generation of documentary filmmakers. *Song of Styrene* is a very different, commercially commissioned project. It is a playful and colorful parody of industrial documentaries, with a clever alexandrine commentary written by Raymond Queneau. Both films exploit eloquent tracking shots, poignant montage editing, and evocative soundtracks, all of which will distinguish Resnais' eventual feature films. As Jean-Luc Godard wrote of Resnais' documentary work,

> If the short film did not already exist, Alain Resnais would surely have invented it. . . . From the unseeing and trembling pans of *Van Gogh* to the majestic tracking shots of *Styrene*, what is it, in effect, that we see? An exploration of the possibilities of cinematographic technique . . . and without which the young French cinema of today would simply not exist. . . . Alain Resnais is the second greatest editor in the world after Eisenstein. Editing, to them, means organizing cinematographically. . . . [Further] Resnais has *invented* the modern tracking shot, its breakneck speed, its abrupt start and slow arrival, or vice versa.[5]

All Resnais' documentaries reveal themes, traits, and discursive strategies that will continually appear and develop across his entire career, from *Hiroshima* right up to *Coeurs*.

But there was another important, formative film project during the 1950s: Resnais' collaboration with Agnès Varda on *La Pointe Courte* proved to be a valuable relationship for both their careers. As Roy Armes points out, *La Pointe Courte*, with its free style, mix of theatrical and documentary tones, and troubled lovers placed in an alien setting, anticipated much of Resnais' later cinema.[6] Varda had already shot the footage when she asked Resnais to edit the project. They worked together for several months, cutting the ten hours of footage down in Varda's home; he worked for free, though Varda was expected to provide lunch. As she recalls, "It was a time of reflection. Like an apprenticeship in the kind of cinema I had to continue. . . . By scrupulously editing my film he allowed me to clarify my own thoughts."[7] All these experiences proved Resnais as a major new presence in French cinema of the 1950s, but by the end of the decade he made the leap to directing his own narrative films.

Unlike most New Wave feature film projects, *Hiroshima, mon amour* did not begin as the director's personal idea. Resnais explained to interviewers in 1959: "All my films so far have been commissioned. . . . I should not be considered a struggling auteur; St. Resnais the martyr does not exist."[8] Rather, Argos Films, his producers from *Night and Fog,* approached him to make another documentary for them, this time on the atomic bomb. Choosing Resnais for such a serious topic seemed logical, based on *Night and Fog,* but also a bit risky, given his parodic *Song of Styrene.* In a way, the origin of *Hiroshima, mon amour* parallels Roberto Rossellini's *Rome Open City* (1945): Both films were initiated as potential WWII documentary topics but grew into startling feature-length fiction films. According to Resnais, "the three gods of Argos Films," Anatole Dauman, Philippe Lifchitz, and Samy Halfon, were heading up an international co-production, which also involved Pathé and Daiei studios. They had funds stuck in Japan that could not be transferred out, so they organized a project to be shot jointly in Japan and France. Argos asked Resnais to make a documentary of roughly forty-five minutes in length. He watched a number of films on the atomic bomb, including Japanese productions, and became increasingly frustrated with how to present the mammoth and troubling topic. He discussed drafts with his friend Chris Marker, and the producers even suggested the popular young novelist Françoise Sagan help write the script, but then they contacted Marguerite Duras.

Resnais and Duras discussed the challenges of a movie on the atomic bomb for hours one afternoon, when Resnais pointed out that during their entire conversation, planes loaded with atomic bombs had been circling the earth, but everyone seemed oblivious. "Our days roll on as before, so maybe the movie that needs to be made is not the one we had in mind. . . . We should shoot a classic love story in which the atomic bomb would be more in the background."[9] Three days later, Duras phoned with a basic concept for a contemporary narrative. Over the next several weeks Duras worked on the scenario, although she apparently had real problems fashioning a love story set against the disaster of Hiroshima. Resnais provided photos and other materials from Japan, and as Duras struggled to find a footing, she claimed to begin to identify with the challenges facing her female character who "saw nothing" in Hiroshima.[10] The final movie would include location shooting, some fragments from other documentaries, and

even some fictional reconstructions, but was anchored around the brief affair between a Japanese man and a French woman on the eve of her return
from Hiroshima to Paris. Many aspects of the story fit themes and situations common to Duras' later novels and films, especially the woman's un-
tenable position, torn between object and subject of love, her near madness, and the role of loss and mourning. While Duras wrote the script,
Resnais encouraged her to forget about the camera and think more along
the lines of an operetta or sung theatrical production, with Hiroshima and
the French town of Nevers as the two lyrical poles for the drama.[11]

Duras and Resnais prepared two different sorts of scripts, a normal
scenario and a "subterranean" version that included detailed biographies
of the main characters. According to Duras, Resnais wanted to intimately
understand the characters, and asked her to explain, as a sort of "pre-
visualization," how the characters *saw* things: How the woman saw Nevers, how she saw the marble that rolled into the cellar one day, and so on.
"So we invented Nevers as she must have seen it from the other side of the
world." Finally, Resnais began to frame and shoot "as if he were taking
over a film that already existed."[12] The result has been hailed as a uniquely
creative product: "The most original aspect may be this: The two authors
said what they wanted simultaneously in images and speech. One cannot
imagine *Hiroshima* silent; the dialogue is never really explicative and it is
a fundamental element of the story."[13] Stage actress Emmanuelle Riva was
chosen by Resnais to play the woman, in part apparently because of the
timbre of her voice, though Duras interviewed her as well. Eiji Okada was
hired to play the Japanese man. Not only did Riva recite many of her lines
as if hypnotized or dreaming, but Okada, whose French was actually quite
poor, post-synchronized all his dialogue back in France, where he memo-
rized his lines phonetically. Early in his career Resnais decided to select
theatrically trained actors who could "give a certain type of intonation, a
certain phrasing more difficult to obtain from actors trained in the cinema."[14] The collaboration between Duras and Resnais made *Hiroshima,
mon amour* fundamental for both their subsequent careers.

Hiroshima, mon amour proves to be an exemplary art film from its first
frames until the end title. The opening scene involves puzzling shots of
two intertwined, anonymous bodies, their arms and legs locked in rather
haunting embraces sequentially filmed with what Duras explains are
"ashes, dew, atomic fallout—and the sweat of completed love," all accompanied by a slow, sad musical score. These shots are soon followed
with voice-off dialogue of the Japanese man telling the French woman that

Figure 8.1. Okada and Riva (*Hiroshima, mon amour*)

she saw nothing while in Hiroshima, and her protests that she saw "every-thing." The rest of the opening includes montages of the places she men-tions, including the hospital and museum, though she is never shown within those images. She mentions seeing melted bottle caps and deformed skin at the museum, while the image track reveals the objects on display. There are also shots from newsreels and reconstructed films, apparently also on exhibit at the museum. These images include disturbing footage of cruelly burned bodies and women's hair fallen out from radiation, shots reminiscent of the horrors depicted in *Night and Fog*. But the man keeps protesting, even though she lists specific sights and the image track offers them up as evidence of their existence, including a map of Hiroshima, and footage of fish killed by atomic rains. Importantly, this opening sequence establishes the unsettling tone for the rest of the film as it mixes sex, death, and even laughter while foregrounding the juxtaposition of sounds and im-ages. It is never proven that the conversation we hear happened simulta-neously with the couple hugging in bed, nor can we be sure whether the images shown are her (or his) mental subjective memories, footage from the peace movie she is making, or simply shots inserted by an intrusive nondiegetic narrator. The status of every sound and image, as well as their resulting narrative time and space, will be continually contested in the course of the film. The opening also establishes him as metonymic with the city. She recites: "How could I know this city was tailor-made for love? How could I know you would fit my body like a glove?"

As dawn arrives and the couple showers and chats, they learn more about each other's past. He was a soldier, away during the war; she grew up in Nevers, but lives in Paris. He becomes intrigued with knowing more about Nevers, the memory of which clearly upsets her. She explains that she is an actress in a peace movie, and will fly back to France the next morning. Disappointed, he insists that they meet again, but she refuses. During the next scene, however, he shows up on her movie set, they watch the staged peace march, then he convinces her to come to his home. Both are married and claim to be happy with their spouses, but his wife is out of town, and her husband is back in France. In bed together, as the afternoon begins to darken, she tells him more about her life. "I'm just beginning to understand you," he tells her, and he knows that her identity today depends upon what happened years ago in Nevers. His persistent questions, calming hands, and steady gaze draw her out, as if he were her analyst. She tells bits and pieces of her love affair with a young German soldier (Bernard Fresson) during the war. She was eighteen, he twenty-three. A series of shots of her riding her bicycle, leaping fences, and running across fields provides a descriptive syntagma of her many secret meetings with the

Figure 8.2. Riva recounts the past (*Hiroshima, mon amour*)

German. Her story, delivered out of order, and told on and off during the afternoon and evening, reveals that the German was shot by a sniper as she was going to meet him on the day before Nevers was liberated. She spent the night lying on his dying body. Her hair was shorn as a collaborator, and she was forced to stay home, where she struggled with grief and madness and was often stuck in the dirt cellar. Then one night, on her twentieth birthday, her parents sent her off to Paris on her bicycle and she never returned. Just after she arrived in Paris, Hiroshima was bombed.

During her reminiscences, the Japanese man mixes himself into her past, as the German: "When you are in the cellar, am I dead?" She increasingly confuses the lovers as well: "I loved blood since I had tasted yours." At the bar that evening, the Japanese man relentlessly pursues her tale, even pouring beer into her mouth as she hypnotically recites events from the past. At one point he slaps her to pull her out of her increasingly hysterical state. When the bar closes, she returns to her hotel, refusing to see him anymore. At her sink and mirror she speaks aloud of herself in third persona and even as her dead lover, "We'll go to Bavaria, my love, and will marry." "She never went to Bavaria." She soon slips into a voice-over as well, "I told our story. I cheated on you tonight." Her experience in Hiroshima, and concerns over forgetting the German's face and voice, increasingly take a toll on her mental condition. Thus, the recounting of her deep and painful memories has not proved to be any sort of deliverance or cure. Rather, her memories produce a mix of positive and negative effects. She leaves the hotel and wanders the street thinking: "You're still destroying me. You're good for me." The images of buildings alternate between Hiroshima and Nevers. The Japanese man follows her during portions of her rambling, and he tries to convince her to stay in Hiroshima a few more days. She explains that staying is even more impossible than leaving. She ends up at a train station waiting room, presumably to catch a train to the airport, but slips away and takes a cab to another bar. Her lover follows her and watches from a separate table as another Japanese man flirts with her in English. But then, after a false end, when the camera cranes up to the skylight to reveal the start of dawn, there is a second final sequence of her standing by her hotel door. The original Japanese man enters, she cries that she is already forgetting him. Finally, she tells him, calmly and sadly, that his name is Hiroshima. He says hers is Nevers, and the film fades to black.

Perhaps one of the more surprising aspects of *Hiroshima* was its international success. It was shown out of competition at Cannes so as not to offend the United States, the "they," mentioned by Riva's character, who had

Figure 8.3. She speaks to her dead lover (*Hiroshima, mon amour*)

dared drop the bomb. *Hiroshima* played for six months in Paris and London, won the Best Foreign Film prize in Brussels, and tied with *The 400 Blows* as the year's best film according to French critics. Even in the United States it did very well; it played both in sub-titled and dubbed versions and was called "a surprise arty sleeper" by *Variety*. In New York City, *Hiroshima* played for twenty-seven weeks at the Fine Arts theater, earning $279,000 in its first run, more than any other New Wave film.[15] It also won the New York Film Critics' award for Best Foreign Film. Review after review, in France and elsewhere, marveled at the mature and complex treatment of character, but also the radical reworking of time, with many critics comparing its strategies to the modern novel, and especially Proust. Godard called it Faulkner plus Stravinsky plus Picasso, while Rohmer added Dos Passos, and Rivette said it returned cinema to the fragmentation of Eisenstein within a narrative labyrinth worthy of Borges.[16] Typical is Jacques Chevalier's review in *Image et son:* "For the first time, cinema achieves 'the remembrance of things past,' creating a temporality that one can call 'novelistic,' mixing the past and present in a dialectic fashion that previously seemed impossible to accomplish in the cinema."[17] Even Alfred Hitchcock acknowledged the importance of Resnais' film when, in the fall of 1959, he claimed that his juxtaposition of the final scenes in *North by Northwest* (1959) was comparable to the montage style of *Hiroshima, mon amour!*[18]

Hiroshima's characterization is minimal, offering sketchy background information on the two protagonists across the course of the day. And, while reviews often referred to the man and woman's shared struggle to deal with the aftermath and loss of World War II, most of their conversations concern her past alone. The range of information also privileges her actions and visions. Despite the condensed plot time, just over twenty-four hours, there are many gaps. The film begins with the couple in bed making love, but we are not shown how they met, nor do we know what they have discussed up to this point. Much like the relations between Michel Poiccard and Patricia in *Breathless,* narrative information is doled out in small bits during intimate moments together, but their initial encounter is suppressed. However, unlike *Breathless* and many other New Wave films, the conversations between lovers here lack any spontaneity. Riva's often monotone revelations about her time in Hiroshima ("I saw the newsreels") or Nevers ("At first we met in barns. Then among the ruins") are spoken as earnest commentary on her own past, but hardly as naturally occurring thoughts. Her memories resemble Lena's summary of Charlie's life in *Tirez sur le pianiste* (*Shoot the Piano Player,* 1960), complete with visual flashbacks, recounted as if they had been practiced many times. Fate hangs heavily in the air during every scene. But even our understanding of her past is fragmentary at best. There are brief images of the German, but we never know anything about him. Similarly, we learn nothing about her current life in Paris. She mentions that she likes men, so apparently she takes many lovers, but whether this is a symptom of her painful loss of the German is unclear. Moreover, we have no idea whether she regularly selects non-French lovers, or whether she often looks at the men lying in her bed and confuses their hand with that of the dying German, as she does the first morning with the Japanese lover. As Christophe Carlier points out, "the Nevers episode is not a simple parenthesis that explains the woman's behavior."[19] It is no wonder so many contemporary reviews referred to *Citizen Kane;* in both, one word, whether "Nevers" or "Rosebud," cannot be expected to sum up a person's life.

If we know little of Riva's modernist character, this French actress played by a French actress, we understand less about her Japanese lover. There are no mental subjective inserts of his experiences during the war. Riva's character asks few questions of him, and never pursues his past in the way he probes her memory. We learn he is an architect and a hopeful politician, but we never hear any explanation of his motivation or goals. Does he hope to rebuild Hiroshima as a curative revenge for not being able to stop its destruction? Rather, in a manner that is strangely echoed in Hitchcock's *Marnie* (1964) a few years later, the bulk of the plot concerns his nearly perverse obsession with plumbing the woman's troubled past, a past into which the Japanese man wants to insert himself. We learn that he too engages in romantic "adventures" fairly regularly, but we do not have enough information to ascribe any significance to his adultery. His wife, like the French husband, is simply elsewhere. The protagonists with no names remain obscure art film characters, which also helps assure the lack of any certain resolution to their tale. Okada's character seems to need more time with her, but what he hopes to gain from her is unclear. *Hiroshima* remains a stubbornly open-ended film.

Alain Resnais and Marguerite Duras were often asked what they thought "happened next" after the final fade to black. Typically, Resnais claims that he is not sure: "Perhaps she'll miss her plane. . . . Yes, she must miss it. . . . Day is dawning. She is in no hurry. But that might last two weeks. Their relation is not over. Nonetheless, it is a new person who will be returning to France."[20] Duras has been less definite, sticking closer to the New Novel notion that the diegesis is a fictional construct and there is no "before or after." She claims that Resnais and she were never really preoccupied with whether Riva's character would break her vow and remain.[21] By contrast, Godard seems convinced she was in Japan to stay and claims that he would only believe that the actress returned to France if Resnais and Duras made another movie to prove it![22] *Hiroshima*'s intriguing ending refuses to close off either the long-term traumas of the characters or the short-term affair. Moreover, neither character seems to have come to any cardinal turning point in their lives. After all, there is no apparent reward for her having told her tale of Nevers. She seems even more distraught upon returning to her hotel room after telling the story. The Japanese lover continues to pursue her, in a pathetic, ineffective manner. He has not learned some "key" to understanding or determining her behavior, which stands in stark contrast to the function of flashback sequences in classical realist films like *Casablanca,* where Rick's memories of better days in Paris help us understand his bitter character today. In *Hiroshima,* the characters go to the Casablanca bar, but find no closure there. They end up in her hotel room, and name each other after their home towns, which only inscribes their sense of alienation all the more. Her rehashed memory has not delivered anyone from anything. Leaving and staying are equally impossible in this circular, mise-en-abyme story in which we never see the characters meet or separate.

Clearly, Resnais reworks every aspect of film style in *Hiroshima*. The camera work and editing complicate notions of perceptual and mental subjective depth of information, while also undercutting conventions for presenting space and time. But the complex relations between sound and image account for much of the film's experimentation. As Pierre Marcabru points out, "*Hiroshima* is miraculous because we are unable to determine where the image begins and the word ends."[23] There is rarely a simple equivalence between dialogue and images, even during the woman's narrated memories of Nevers. For instance, in the Japanese man's apartment, he asks her whether her lover during the war was French. Once she mentions that he was German, a slow dissolve brings the German into the shot. A montage of her riding her bicycle through woods and fields follows with no accompanying dialogue, so the images seem to fit her private memories. She does not mention a bicycle to him, much less the fences she hops across. Similarly, later that night in the bar she tells him, "Then one day I screamed again, so they put me back in the cellar." Rather than the image dissolving to her being moved back into the cellar, the accompanying image is of a marble falling through her basement window. The camera pans to show her crouched on the dirt floor, picking up the marble and rubbing it against her lips. We hear, "It was warm. I think then is when I got over my hate." There is no way her diegetic narratee, the Japanese man, would have any idea what was "warm" from her dialogue. Only the audience sees the tiny marble, yet that image can hardly explain why this moment was her turning point. Her conversation must often be completely incomprehensible from the Japanese listener's perspective, but even the audience, privy to both sound and image, cannot fully comprehend the thoughts and feelings of this traumatized French woman.

Finally, the unusual sound to image relations, combined with the disarming plot structure, create an intricate, modernist text. As Thompson and Bordwell point out, "Often the viewer does not know if the sound track carries real conversations, imaginary dialogues, or commentary spoken by the characters . . . While audiences had seen flashback constructions throughout the 1940s and 1950s, Resnais made such temporal switches sudden and fragmentary. In many cases they remain ambiguously poised between memory and fantasy."[24] The film's earlier mix of documentary photographs, newsreels, and reconstructed movies, as well as disembodied voices and the long, smooth tracking shots down hospital and museum hallways, provide the spectator with a wide array of material that can never be easily sorted out. It is rarely clear whether an image or sound is ob-

Figure 8.4. The warm marble (*Hiroshima, mon amour*)

jective or subjective, past or present, and the often hypnotic acting style fails to prove whether the characters can always tell the difference either. Robert Sklar summarizes *Hiroshima* as, "An allusive film, austere and cryptic, it raises questions about individuality and identity in ways that film theory would pursue in the coming decades: what is human subjectivity, how is it formed? 'The art of seeing has to be learned,' the actress says."[25] These narrative strategies, which blur reality and fantasy, recur throughout Resnais' career and influence much of subsequent international art cinema. Resnais followed up *Hiroshima* with another formally rigorous narrative, *Last Year at Marienbad*, based on a script by another famous New Novelist, Alain Robbe-Grillet.

If the characters in *Hiroshima, mon amour* owe much of their humanity to Duras, the cold, mannequin-like figures in *Last Year at Marienbad* clearly belong to the fictional world of Robbe-Grillet. Moreover, with its labyrinthine plot, *Last Year at Marienbad* fundamentally challenged the entire notion of fiction, and especially narrative discourse, while its refusal to separate past from present, or fact from fiction, motivated some to reconsider *Hiroshima, mon amour* and its characters in light of this subsequent Resnais film. After all, a character in *Marienbad* conjures up a past that may or may not be accurate: Perhaps the French actress in *Hiroshima* was making up the entire tale of Nevers. Susan Sontag summarized their core difference: "As the idea of *Hiroshima* is the weight of the inescapably remembered past, so the idea of *Marienbad* is the openness, the abstractness of memory . . . the past is a fantasy of the present, according to both."[26] *Hiroshima* and *Marienbad* prove the success of Resnais' synthesis of a distinctive novelist's personal script with his own rich cinematic concerns. Robbe-Grillet was much more established in the literary canon in 1960 than Duras had been, yet Resnais' reputation was also rising quickly, so their collaboration on *Marienbad* immediately motivated a great deal of curiosity within international cinema and literary criticism.

Last Year at Marienbad was another project initiated by producers, Raymond Froment and Pierre Courau. During the winter of 1959–1960, Resnais and Alain Robbe-Grillet first met, at the producers' suggestion, to discuss whether they might collaborate. Thanks to Resnais' success with *Hiroshima* and Robbe-Grillet's international reputation, the producers provided $400,000, making this a fairly expensive film by New Wave standards. Robbe-Grillet, by then author of four celebrated New Novels, including *La jalousie* (1957) and *Dans le labyrinthe* (1959), was famous for his precise descriptions and even catalogues of physical details that ultimately composed impossible or dreamlike places. For instance, the first paragraph of *Dans le labryinthe* offers two incongruous introductory sentences; in the first it is cold and rainy, in the second it is bright and sunny. He already had a strong interest in pursuing filmmaking, which he saw as a way to make his nouveau narratives more concrete. Based on conversations with Resnais, Robbe-Grillet spent several days sketching out four project proposals of roughly one-and-a-half pages each. Together, they decided to pursue *Marienbad*, since, as Resnais pointed out to him, it seemed like an extension of *All the Memory in the World*, with its camera probing long dark hallways.[27] *Marienbad* also harkens back to his early films on gardens and chateaux. Robbe-Grillet's scenario, which was subsequently published, was so precise that Resnais claims it took him just over two days to write up the shooting script. Robbe-Grillet had even written in suggestions for camera placement ("the camera movement ends with a close-up of her face"), instructions for the actors ("her face should be calm and empty, only a trifle tense at moments, not at all upset"), and even sound levels ("starting from zero, the sound increases very rapidly, attains normal volume and immediately fades").

Soon after *Marienbad*, Robbe-Grillet would have a chance to write and direct his own film, *l'Immortelle* (1963). Though he was absent during the actual filming of *Marienbad*, the experience with Resnais obviously proved inspiring for him. Many of the puzzling discontinuous editing strategies of *Marienbad* recur in *l'Immortelle,* such as matches on action that cut on characters and their gestures, but insert them into a completely different time, space, or setting. Most of these false match shots were written into the script by Robbe-Grillet: "Abrupt cut: although X and A are still close to each other, evidently in the same place on the screen as in the preceding shot, the scene is now entirely different."[28] Resnais reinforces the discontinuity by changing the costume on both characters; although gesture, dialogue, and editing logic provide an illusion of continuity, there are clear markers of discontinuity in the mise-en-scène. Similarly, basic objects such as mirrors, beds, statues, and even people may be displaced from shot to shot, and scene to scene, so that every element of the diegesis is merely a temporary or potential item of the storytelling. This sort of manipulation of story time and space goes far beyond the subjective memory and occasionally jarring leaps within *Hiroshima,* and makes *Marienbad* more overtly concerned with exploring cinematic language and technique, while undercutting the story's veracity. As Thompson and Bordwell explain, "*Last Year at Marienbad* pushed modernist ambiguity to new extremes."[29]

Last Year at Marienbad involves a triangle of central characters, designated in the script as a woman A (Delphine Seyrig), a man X (Giorgio Albertazzi) who is pursuing her placidly but relentlessly throughout a chateau, and another man, M (Sacha Pitoeff), who is probably her husband (M for "mari") and encounters them on occasion. The filming was done on location at several chateaux near Munich. There are some parallels here with *Hiroshima,* since much of the conversation revolves around a seductive man trying to connect the past with the present, while the somewhat traumatized woman resists. The characters within *Marienbad,* however, are also like characters in a theater of the absurd drama. People have gathered, perhaps like last year, at a vast and luxuriously furnished chateau, with a formal garden, though it is uncertain whether all the exterior shots are supposed to be in one place, or an obviously impossible geography, in the style of Lev Kuleshov's composite locations. The figures in the chateau dress formally and drift uncomfortably from one distraction to another. There is a theatrical performance, joyless dancing, somber card games, and even a shooting gallery, but in *Huis clos* (*No Exit*) fashion, no one ventures outside, except A and X.

X seems to be alone, an outsider, and spends much of the film meeting up with A, trying to convince her that they met last year, either here (wherever that may be) or at Frederiksbad or Marienbad or somewhere similar.

Figure 8.5. A and X dance and remember (*Last Year at Marienbad*)

X's struggle with his memory of this woman is a sort of art cinema reworking of *Vertigo.* The puzzled A denies any connection with this man, even
after he shows her a photo that he claims to have taken of her. However, we
later see she has a drawer full of identical pictures. The dour M often
watches their encounters but never interferes. X acts as A's guide, and they
discuss the meaning of a statue of a man and woman in the garden. X claims
the man has seen danger and is stopping and protecting the woman; A disagrees, claiming the woman has seen something marvelous and is pointing
it out to the man. This sort of discussion, where questions may have two
contradictory answers, is a constant motif throughout the film. No detail
can ever be verified and every image could be subjective, especially since
a conversation may begin next to the statue in the garden but end abruptly
inside the chateau beside a sketch of the garden.

By the middle of the film, the persistent X recounts in detail how he
came to A's room last year, just after M had left her, but she denies it and
disagrees with some of his details, such as owning the white feather dress
he describes. Meanwhile, there are shots of her in a bright white room as
he recalls her movements. She suddenly responds, "I don't know that
room, that ridiculous bed, that fireplace with its mirror . . ." However, he
is quick to point out that he had not mentioned these items. Thus, as with
a number of scenes in *Hiroshima,* the audience cannot be sure whether

what they are seeing is an objective past or mental subjective images from one or both of the characters. Eventually X explains that M is in the room and shoots her, which is followed by a montage of her lying in mock dead positions in her room. But X quickly tells A, "No, this isn't the right ending, I must have you alive," further undercutting the accuracy of any information in the film. This is a mise-en-abyme fiction, built on an unreliable character-narrator, and everything from the lighting shifts, to the poses of the people, to the shooting of A, is presented as coldly artificial and improbable. By the end, however, X may have convinced A to leave with him (or she may have agreed last year, but asked for a one year extension) and the film ends with the two soberly walking away, still within the chateau. The final shot of the chateau's exterior at night recalls the end of *Rules of the Game*, with the music swelling. X's narration ends with his catalogue of the garden (gravel, stone, straight paths, statues) where "you were now already getting lost, forever, in the calm night with me." But there is no sign of the two in the dark garden and the music continues over the fade to black.[30]

Marienbad was another great triumph for Resnais, despite his being barred from state radio and TV interviews in France because he had signed the Manifesto of the 121. The film could only be shown outside competition at the Cannes Film Festival. It went on to win the Venice Golden Lion,

Figure 8.6. M shoots A (*Last Year at Marienbad*)

though one Italian critic complained that rewarding this film could spread "Marienbadism . . . the poison of aestheticism and moral indifference," into Italian cinema, at the expense of human characters and realism.[31] Regardless, *Last Year at Marienbad* proved to be an international sensation and Robbe-Grillet's script was nominated for an Academy Award. In New York, it ran for thirty-two weeks at the small Carnegie Theater art house, earning a record $240,000. *Marienbad* was one of the top ten foreign films playing in the United States in 1961. *Variety* argues that 1961 was a turning point for French films in general, as they stole the thunder from Italian imports, with Vadim's *Les liaisons dangereuses* (*Dangerous Liaisons,* 1959) and *Marienbad* leading the way: "The French have been as thick as flies and twice as articulate."[32] Part of the strength of *Marienbad's* box office came from repeat viewers who returned several times to try to sort out the action. This film, like Robbe-Grillet's New Novels, requires the audience to rethink everything, to hunt for cues of character motivation (Does A actually want X to pursue and convince her?), temporal organization (Are any of the shots supposed to be from "last year"?), and spatial arrangements (Where is the shooting gallery in relation to the garden?). Even repeat viewings cannot provide definitive answers to any or all these questions, but the plot is a labyrinthine game, and the engaged 1960s art film spectator was the perfect player.

The two creative voices behind the film also encouraged viewers to see *Marienbad* as a plurivocal metafiction, and their comments on the story echoed the uncertainty suggested by Resnais and Duras with *Hiroshima, mon amour:* "When you have a difference between the screenwriter ('One must remember that the man is not telling the truth. The couple did not meet the year before') and the director ('I could never have shot this film if I had not been convinced that their meeting had actually taken place'), the viewer is free to decide what, if anything, did occur."[33] *Positif* also pointed out that rarely had a writer and director spent so much time explaining a film, yet even more astonishingly, all that explanation had done almost nothing to end the debates or narrow speculations. Resnais admits to *Positif* that the questions spectators ask him most often are the same questions he still asks himself about the story.[34] Many of those questions are rooted in whether the narrator, X, is reliable or not, and whether A is dead or not. But for Robbe-Grillet there is always ambivalence; narrative is about the selection and ordering of fictional options, so of course it can be dark and sunny at the same time.

Critics have worked very diligently over the years, following textual and intertextual leads with *Marienbad,* comparing the characters to Freudian concepts, with A, the ego, caught between X, the id, and M as the superego, or interpreting it all as an allegory for Europe after World War II with dead souls wandering around a morally vacant world. T. Jefferson Kline connects Lacan's interrupted delivery of a paper on the Mirror Phase in Marienbad in 1936 as an uncanny but productive background for considering the mirrors, gaps, unclear chronology, and crises of identity in Resnais' film.[35] Kline privileges the internal play whose poster we see, Ibsen's *Rosmersholm*, but clearly there are many cinematic references as well. There is a gathering, staged entertainment, and shooting at a chateau as in *Rules of the Game*, floating, dreamy characters from Cocteau's *Orpheus* (1950), the madness and intense stares in an isolated castle as in *Fall of the House of Usher* (Epstein, 1928), and shadows and acting styles right out of *The Cabinet of Dr. Caligari* (Wiene, 1919) and *Nosferatu* (Murnau, 1922). The mysterious game played by M, which he always wins, also figures prominently in many critics' attempts to unify the whole project, though the film finally resists making that game any more or less important than any other motif. The *Positif* review emphasizes the film's openness, pointing out that the audience can "enter" this world from a variety of angles thanks to the theme of parallel universes and the multiple perspectives on the characters and the chateau.[36] Even *Variety* mentioned "the oceans of printers ink spilled" by various critics trying to analyze *Marienbad*.[37]

While critics struggled with sorting out the false leads, repetitions, and obscure citations, André S. Labarthe at *Cahiers* took a more unexpected approach by claiming that *Marienbad* "is the last of the great neo-realist films," since it manages to reinsert the complexity and ambiguity of lived experience into contemporary cinema. *Marienbad* presents the spectator with undigested raw material and the meaning is not imposed on the audience: "In this perspective . . . it fits naturally into the groove dug by neo-realism. The same gaps in the script, the same ambiguity in the events, the same effort demanded of the spectator."[38] This attempt by Labarthe to slip Resnais into the legacy of Renoir, DeSica, and Rossellini was based in part on the director's repeated claim that he wanted to make the film as if it were a documentary on a chateau and even a statue. While *Last Year at Marienbad* does boast deep space and long takes, with an average shot length of sixteen seconds, Labarthe's attempt to exaggerate the realistic elements, which are few and far between, much less compare them to DeSica's *Paisan*, seems a stretch indeed. However, this is a claim that *Cahiers du cinéma* would want to make in 1961, as it tried to adapt its critical, auteurist traditions onto increasingly uncooperative, modernist film practice.

The visual and audio styles of *Last Year at Marienbad* are often as beautifully puzzling as the story. Right from the beginning, with X's haunting, monotonous voice-over, which accompanies the fluid tracking shots through the chateau, the spectator is overwhelmed with the task of processing the two rich signifying layers of sound and image. The dialogue begins during the title sequence, with X's quietly droning voice competing with loud organ music. Then shots from a moving camera seem to present the narrator's vision since the words provide a summary of the images: "I walk on, once again . . . down these silent, deserted corridors overloaded with a dim, cold ornamentation of woodwork, stucco, moldings . . ." These first few shots are immediately disorienting. The gliding camera exploits a ponderous angle that seems to be tilted back while tracking along the ornate molding at the same time. As in many Robbe-Grillet novels, the male narrator is in complete control, delivering precise descriptions of what may turn out to be complete fantasy. But this opening also echoes that of *Hiroshima, mon amour*, when the unassigned voices, heard over images of bodies, museums, and hospitals, replace any establishing shot or introduction to the characters. From its start, *Marienbad* distances us from the fictional world, and the figures within it, complicating the usual hypothesis-making activity of story construction. The spectator, faced with a daunting onslaught of material right from the opening, can hardly decide which images and words are most pertinent for story comprehension.

Even the shot composition adds to our confusion. One of the recurring staging options in *Marienbad* involves placing a character off center, for instance near the left edge of the frame, looking off screen left, away from any figures in the rest of the shot. This is precisely how X is introduced to us in one of the longer shots of the film, and this staging option works to undercut the normal function of preserving a "real" time and space. X is looking off left, but apparently he sees the couple that is also reflected behind him, screen right, in a gigantic mirror. As the couple moves in the mirror the camera pans right to follow them, while the man repeatedly berates the woman about their relationship. The woman begins to walk away from the man until the couple gets larger in the mirror, then walks out of the mirror, past the camera, and down a hall. The camera's pan to the right reveals that X has left his spot, while A, in a black dress, stands to the left of where he had been. Two men in tuxedos steadily approach from the hall and the camera tracks back on their discussion about the cold summer of 1928 or '29, as their bodies block out A. They continue into another room, as their dialogue and the organ music come and go, until X is seen stand-

Figure 8.7. X looks off screen (*Last Year at Marienbad*)

ing in nearly the identical screen position as the beginning of the shot, but now with a map of the garden to his right, instead of the large mirror. X walks right, begins retracing the men's steps back into the previous room, and there to the right is the same couple that began the shot, with the man repeating his same complaints. But A is no longer standing in the other room. This nearly two-minute long shot sequence allows Resnais and Robbe-Grillet to reinforce the fantastic, hypnotic sense of uncertainty that permeates the movie, without resorting to the usual strategies of disruptive editing. They carefully choreograph a long take with deep space that parodies the camera work in Renoir's famous *Rules of the Game* staging, while the use of mirrors, further refracting the figures, reinforces the film's overall mise-en-abyme structure, as viewers discover, then lose, A in mid-shot.

A second long take occurs six minutes later when X's voice-over directly addresses A, who is initially seen alone in a dark gallery. While X describes their encounter in a garden, she turns her head as the camera pulls back slightly to reveal X now standing beside her. Soon the camera pans to the right to show a room full of people in various conversations we cannot hear, but finally it comes to rest on X, standing alone and looking off right. His dialogue has just stopped and is lips are no longer moving. Then the camera follows him walking to the right and tilts up to reveal A, apparently just entering the room and standing above at a railing. This shot, with actors as painstakingly blocked as in the earlier long take, also defies the unity of the usual shot sequence and reinforces the subjective quality of what should be an objective conversation about whether or not his memory of them meeting in a garden is true or false. No certainty can result from such contradictory film style, as it violates the very function of long takes as used by Renoir and the neorealists.

The plot organization is famously difficult to sort out in *Marienbad,* but even the smaller editing tactics within scenes can complicate or at least mock notions of there being any discernible real diegetic time or space. As mentioned earlier, false matches on action foreground the artificiality of cinematic conventions of continuity. After the initial theatrical performance, for instance, when the audience is filmed in various staged poses, one young woman stands alone in the foreground, with a slight scowl and her hands clasped. She seems to be looking for someone, and turns to look over her left shoulder. There is a perfect match on action of her gesture; however, the setting around her changes from empty chairs to the front desk. This disruption on the profilmic level—the change in setting—challenges the logic of a match-on-action's temporal continuity. She is, and is not, turning in the same place and time. Such false matches recur a number of times, including seven minutes later when X raises his arms to offer himself to A as a guide, but as she accepts and raises her hands to meet his there is a cut to them joining hands to dance in another room. On other occasions, A simply turns, much like the woman in our first example, but her dress changes as well as her location. Such discontinuity on the microlevel of editing accumulates with other dysnarrative devices to threaten the coherence of the narrative as a whole. Alain Fleischer points out that it is through editing and découpage that Resnais is most distinguishable as an auteur, but while such disruptive *écriture,* or cinematic language, was already present in *Hiroshima, mon amour, Last Year at Marienbad* also owes a strong debt to Robbe-Grillet's influence on every level.[39]

The sound to image relations are equally unconventional. Often, X's dialogue covers images that contradict it, or at least seem disconnected from it. For instance, when X builds up to the scene of how he entered her room the previous year, he tells A, "You turned to the bed, you sat down on it." The accompanying image is of her wearing her white feather dress in her white room, but she is rolling along the walls, not sitting. X becomes more adamant about the details, insisting the door was closed, while in the accompanying shot, A looks out an open door. The images enter into a dialectic relation with his words; the visuals resist his summary, yet they also seem to provide evidence of something: there was a room, she had a white feather dress, but perhaps he does not remember it all quite right. Neither image nor dialogue can be privileged as more accurate than the other. Moreover, X's memory seems to be able to adapt to changing events. While he is sitting, intently recounting to A how she stood in her room, afraid, M shows up just behind the two in the gallery where X is speaking to her. X and A do not seem to notice him behind them, but X suddenly works M into the tale: "Who is he? Your husband, perhaps . . ." The referents in his narration are unclear: Is the "he" the M we see behind X or another, or the M of last year in her room? A stands as if troubled and the image cuts to her in her white room as X describes it, and she screams there. Next, however, there is a cut to X and A seated in a different place and she disagrees, claiming she never knew him or that room. By the end of the scene she runs out of the door to the formal garden and the camera pans back to show her in a washed out white shot. The space, time, and quality of light are all manipulated to reinforce her mental crisis or at least desperation of denial brought on by his attempts to convince her of their encounter last year.[40]

These creative interactions between what we hear and see fit André Bazin's term "lateral montage," a new image-sound counterpoint that built on Kuleshov's experiments.[41] Resnais believes that audiences are quite competent at unraveling intricate visual and audio language, but commercial sound cinema led to a regression, with dialogue dominating the image. Resnais, by contrast, working from rich, complex scripts, develops a rigorous synthetic film language, overturning conventions that privilege one signifying system or technique over any other, so the result is a constantly shifting set of relations and meanings from scene to scene and film to film.

While critics initially considered Resnais and Robbe-Grillet co-authors of *Marienbad,* with a great deal of praise being heaped on this rare, close creative collaboration during an era otherwise characterized by individualistic writer-directors, subsequent critics tend to minimize the script's importance. According to André Gardies, after 1963, when *l'Immortelle* failed to earn much critical attention, Robbe-Grillet's status declined rapidly among film critics, and *Marienbad's* paternity was forever shifted solely to Resnais.[42] However, clearly the film's success owes to both men, as well as to the unsettling soundtrack, written by Delphine Seyrig's brother, Francis Seyrig, and the exquisite cinematography by Sacha Vierny. While Rémi Lanzoni dismisses *Marienbad* as "more rewarding to talk about than to watch," for many of us it remains one of the most stylistically stunning examples of French cinema, and it rewards repeated viewings perhaps even more than *Hiroshima*.[43] *Last Year at Marienbad* was a fortunate product of many individuals and cultural contexts, and remains an important milestone in French cinema that owes as much to the New Novel as to the New Wave.

Resnais' third feature, *Muriel ou le temps d'un retour (Muriel or the Time of a Return*, 1963), was written by Jean Cayrol, and the locations were filmed at Boulogne-sur-mer. Its title already prepares viewers to connect this film with the themes of time, memory, and even Proustian construction that had figured so strongly in his previous two features. However, *Muriel* is again based on a very complete script from a well-established writer. As Jean Douchet points out, "Resnais pretended to obliterate himself behind these writers and requested that they create a narrative object that he could explore with his camera."[44] Born in 1911, Cayrol was hardly of the New Wave generation. He was a highly respected poet and novelist, as well as editor at Editions du Seuil, where he helped publish important work by Roland Barthes and Philippe Sollers. His detailed script offers a large number of complicated characters, especially in contrast to the limited triangles of *Hiroshima* and *Marienbad*. Cayrol's characters are no longer sketchy figures from a New Novel, designated by pronouns or letters, rather, as James Monaco states, "they are allowed to live."[45] *Muriel*, which may not initially appear as formally startling as the previous two, presents a frenetically fragmented web of action, built around some familiar themes that include traumas from the past, absent figures, and frustrated desire, all set in a gray town marked by the devastating bombardments of the war.

Muriel's story is delivered in a linear plot, which nonetheless confuses time within the script's five acts. The plot time involves two weeks, beginning Saturday, September 29, and ending Sunday, October 14, but it would be difficult for the spectator to know this without the aid of the printed script. A condensed summary of the story hardly does it justice, in part because it proves to be so open-ended, but Hélène (Delphine Seyrig), a fortyish widow, sells antiques out of her apartment in Boulogne, where she lives with her neurotic step-son Bernard (Jean-Baptiste Thierrée), who returned the previous year from fighting in the Algerian War. Recently, Hélène wrote to a former lover, Alphonse (Jean-Pierre Kérien), who arrives with his young mistress, Françoise (Nita Klein). She pretends to be his niece. Alphonse and Françoise are broke, Bernard has not worked since Algeria, and Hélène has a bad gambling habit. Although she sells furniture, she apparently also depends financially on her lover, Roland de Smoke (Claude Sainval). Hélène and Alphonse spend bits of time reminiscing, and Françoise becomes interested in the jumpy Bernard, but Bernard also has a lover, Marie-Do (Martine Vatel), who visits him at his bombed-out studio above a barn on the outskirts of town. Gradually, it becomes clear that Hélène is suffering from anxiety over her wasted life, and Bernard is obsessed with a young Algerian girl named Muriel who was tortured to death during interrogation by his group of soldiers during the war. He now pretends to have a fiancée named Muriel. His former comrade Robert (Philippe Laudenbach) also lives in Boulogne, but Bernard, who watches old home movies of the war, becomes increasingly troubled over their brutal military acts.

Throughout, it is not clear just what Hélène and Alphonse expect from one another. Twenty years earlier, Hélène had avoided Alphonse for a time, apparently to make him appreciate her all the more. She has always wondered why he did not bother to find her. Alphonse tells Hélène that at the beginning of World War II he wrote to ask her to meet him; he planned to propose marriage. Hélène never received the letter. This news brings a new sadness into their relations, and Alphonse becomes more reflective and less attentive to Françoise. Later, an old friend of theirs named Ernest (Jean Champion) shows up, and while explaining to Hélène that Alphonse is married to his sister Simone, he mentions that he never mailed Alphonse's letter. Nonetheless, by the end, it is clear that Alphonse has lied about nearly everything and is trying to avoid his current life, while Hélène is increasingly traumatized by the disappointments in her own life. Perhaps they would both be happy now if things had worked out differently in the past. Further, Bernard shoots Robert and leaves town for good, while the final scene reveals Alphonse's wife Simone wandering through Hélène's empty apartment looking for Alphonse.

Susan Sontag called *Muriel* the most difficult of Resnais' first three features, though thematically it shared their "search for the inexpressible past." "It attempts to deal with the substantive issues—war guilt . . . racism . . . —even as *Hiroshima* dealt with the bomb. . . . But it also, like *Marienbad*, attempts to project a purely abstract drama. The burden of this double intention . . . doubles the technical virtuosity and complexity of the film."[46] The result is a movie that estranges the audience, beginning with a frenetic opening montage and ending with a solemn, mobile camera exploring the remnants of Hélène's life. Because much of the background information only comes to the surface gradually in snippets, or has to be inferred, the spectator is doubly challenged to build any real allegiance with Hélène, much less Bernard or Alphonse. Even the patient Roland, who seems to be the only solid figure in her life, takes up with young Françoise by the end.

Figure 8.8. Bernard films the slowly collapsing building (*Muriel*)

Initially, we are aligned with Hélène, who is a hard worker and has to support the difficult Bernard. But before long we realize that she is obsessed with gambling (we see her enter and leave the casino, although we never see her display any pleasure betting) and is emotionally fragile. We never learn anything about her relationship with Bernard's father, and have to assume she lives in Boulogne in part because she and Alphonse spent a passionate few days in a hotel there many years ago. It is not easy to feel full sympathy or allegiance for anyone else. Further, when Cayrol developed the scenario he wanted a setting that was visually alienating. Boulogne for him was a city with no intimacy, it had been bombed and rebuilt with gray modern structures and empty squares that welcomed no one. The brand new building that Roland points out, perched on a hillside and sliding to its eventual collapse, is typical of this city without a future, where people are "living between two times . . . as if they live there only temporarily."[47]

Hélène is exemplary, she still owns the decaying building outside town where Bernard spends his time, while her own apartment is full of old furniture that is all for sale. Nothing functional really belongs to her. In the prologue to the script Cayrol writes that Hélène is trying to rehabilitate the past since she put all her life into her first love affair with Alphonse; she should look both twenty and forty-five years old in the film. Alphonse, by contrast, is a sort of failed actor, "an old Tristan," who constantly burns bridges and covers his tracks as he improvises his way through an uncertain life. Françoise is with Alphonse because he got her an acting job once. She lives in the present, and speaks without thinking or caring. By contrast, Bernard has no present. Traumatized and guilt-ridden, he is a walking time bomb and a spoiled child, but he is also a tender lover to Marie-Do. Cayrol wrote up extended backgrounds on all the central characters that were much more detailed than those by Duras in *Hiroshima*. For instance, Hélène is given a first love at fourteen, while Alphonse's mother in La Rochelle had an adulterous affair that affected Alphonse's family life! It is almost as if Cayrol had first written a novel about these characters, and then wrote a movie about what became of them since then. His paratextual summaries provide deep background information that may explain some of their character motivations, but the intricate, fragmenting plot structure, and Resnais' editing style, combined with the heavy-handed musical soundtrack, undercut our ability to understand these characters as real people, and they end up modernist, allegorical figures.

Muriel is also the subject of one of the most impressively theoretical and detailed textual analyses of any single film, by Claude Bailblé, Michel Marie, and Marie-Claire Ropars, including an appendix outlining each of the film's 773 shots. Ropars examines in creative detail the film's narrative

Figure 8.9. Hélène's old home has no roof (*Muriel*)

material, especially its multiple strategies for structuring a fluid, complex time and space, and the network of incomplete character relations in this film that begins with the arrival of Alphonse and wraps up with characters dispersing. Michel Marie concentrates on the functions of the surprisingly static camera set-ups but also the productive soundtrack for this "film cantata," which boasts eight interventions by singer Rita Streich, five airs by Hans Werner Henze, and the poetic song "Déjà" by Paul Colline. Claude Bailblé maps out the editing structures in specific scenes, revealing the intricacy of Resnais' brand of *écriture*, while all three join to consider the dialectical aspects of *Muriel* which present a certain reality while denying the ability to represent anything definite. For them, *Muriel* is another of Resnais' textual mise-en-abymes; it acknowledges the impossibility of representing the real, while it strives to find a way to do so. Bernard's film is an important failure, and even Robert tells him, at the end of the third act, "You want to tell about Muriel? Muriel cannot be told." Their immense study reveals the varied strategies exploited by Resnais and Cayrol to systematically subvert the ideological and technical conventions of classical realist cinema.[48] Marie followed up recently with a short but detailed study guide to *Muriel*.[49]

Stylistically, *Muriel* is a model for the study of editing options, with its daring blend of long takes, mismatches, jarring inserts, disorienting cutaways, and occasional conventional point of view shots. For instance, while Hélène, in her apartment, tries to explain to Alphonse that she wrote to him after hearing some man's voice in the street that reminded her of him, Resnais cuts to Françoise, coming out of a movie theater alone and looking at the poster for *Women at the End of the World*. The seemingly unmotivated insert at first appears random and inappropriate, but the lone woman, looking at a poster whose title recalls an earlier line of dialogue, cues us to understand it also as a comment on Hélène's sense of desperation when she wrote to Alphonse. Yet, if the editing rhythm fits what spectators expected of Resnais, the camera work does not. Shot in color by Sacha Vierny, *Muriel* lacks the probing tracking shots that had become Resnais' standard technique for exploring space. While Resnais typically displays Hiroshima from a camera mounted inside a car, and tracks across the halls and gardens in *Marienbad* as if they were a Van Gogh painting, he presents Boulogne in static shots of buildings, streets, and the casino. During conversations, the camera pans and reframes to follow characters, but dinner scenes, wrenching heart-to-heart discussions, and Alphonse's investigation of local bars and restaurants are shot from a static camera. The most consistent mobile shots are found in Bernard's hand-held, grainy home movies from Algeria. This marked difference in style between the static banality of Boulogne and the chaotic images of war recalls *Night and Fog*'s representation of present and past. The use of color, however, reinforces the drab aspects of post–World War II France, with only a few red accents in the shops and cafés. Color also helps guide our attention and reinforce the sense of discontinuity, when, for instance, Françoise is wearing a dark outfit in one shot, but a red dress several shots later. *Marienbad* uses black, white, and silver dresses on A to suggest changes in time; *Muriel* uses color for the same function.

Muriel became a perfect example of the *nouveau cinéma*. *Cahiers du cinéma* featured a bizarre diagram to show that *Muriel* and *Contempt* were the "two poles of modernity," and Truffaut celebrated it as a collection of references to Hitchcock—perhaps because it is permeated with a sense of foreboding within a banal setting. *Cahiers* also devoted a roundtable discussion to the film.[50] With *Muriel*, Resnais offers more avenues to pursue than in his previous two features, so some see it as a detective film with no real object, others as a melodrama in process of deconstructing itself, still others view it as an allegory for modern Europe where no one fits in. For such interpretations, the most peripheral, surreal character, an Australian near the beach who somehow believes Bernard can find a goat for his lonely sheep, becomes a key figure. But *Muriel* also remains another example of the impossibility of telling a conventional story, or offering an authoritative, omniscient, or even coherent narrator. This film too is about the limitations of storytelling, and it refers to all the possible modes of production, from Bernard's doomed attempt to understand the past through documentary, to montage traditions, to the New Novel's experimentation with characters as artificial constructs. But, behind it all, is the devastating war in Algeria, which meets up with the continuing destruction caused by World War II to mark two generations still trying to represent, explain, and understand who they are and what sort of world they have built around themselves. Godard was very fond of *Muriel* and claims it was one of the inspirations behind his *Deux ou trois choses que je sais d'elle* (*Two or Three Things I Know about Her*, 1967), which features a poster from Resnais' film.

Right from the start, Alain Resnais had become a major player in the art cinema, exploiting every narrative device of the modern European cinema and taking advantage of the cultural and economic conditions of his era, especially those established by the New Novel and the New Wave. His shorts, followed by these three feature films, set the central concerns for the rest of his career, and as Jean-Luc Douin points out, "Alain Resnais and his colleagues of the rive gauche would invent much in the realm of editing, never hesitating to abandon conventional punctuation, to reverse shots, juxtapose shots that did not match, and disrupt chronological order."[51] In interviews with the press, Resnais played down the "intellectual" side of his films, claiming he simply had a great respect for the skills of the audience. He said he was amused that critics claimed he owed a debt to Dos Passos and Faulkner, when these were writers influenced by the cinema of Griffith: This showed cinema had indeed come full circle.[52] Nonetheless, Resnais, along with Godard, was one of the New Wave's most daring storytellers, and, like Godard, he continually experimented within the parameters set by his own practice. David Bordwell provides the best summary of Resnais' early years:

> The career of Alain Resnais offers a good instance of how the art cinema as an institution encourages a filmmaker to formulate a discernible "project" running from one film to another. Resnais's recurrent concern has, of course, been the representation of time. In its day, *Hiroshima mon amour* caused considerable surprise for its minimal cuing of flashbacks, and *Last Year at Marienbad* was widely understood as blurring the line between memory and fantasy. *Muriel* contained no flashbacks or hallucination sequences but did exploit a highly elliptical approach to the moment-to-moment unfurling of the syuzhet. . . . The creation of a distinct formal project can lead the filmmaker to innovate fresh intrinsic norms from film to film. No two Resnais films treat the same aspects of narrative time, or handle time in quite the same way.[53]

Agnès Varda: *"Cinécriture"*

My years as a photographer taught me much about the rendering of each lens and every film stock. I learned to work with light, and especially daylight, and to consider white and black as colors. As a filmmaker I strive to bring the spectator into these sensations.

—AGNÈS VARDA, *Varda par Agnès*

Agnès Varda has never been comfortable with being included within the New Wave, much less the Left Bank Group. "It is not my fault I made a movie just before the New Wave. But, I cannot control how histories treat me, as a precursor."[54] Nonetheless, *La Pointe Courte* established Varda as an exemplary young filmmaker and producer, inspiring many to follow her lead. While she continued her career, making three short documentaries

Figure 8.10. Varda at work on *La Pointe Courte* (courtesy of Agnès Varda)

during the remainder of the 1950s, she did not direct her second feature film, *Cleo from 5 to 7*, until 1961. Ironically, while her first feature helped pave the way for the New Wave, it was the critical and economic environment generated by the New Wave that helped her obtain production funds for *Cleo from 5 to 7*. Meanwhile, two of her documentaries had been completed thanks to financing from two of the New Wave's top producers: *Ô saisons, ô châteaux* (Oh Seasons, Oh Castles, 1957) was produced by Pierre Braunberger and *Du côté de la côte* (*The Riviera—Today's Eden*, 1958) was produced by Anatole Dauman's Argos Films. In between, she produced *l'Opéra mouffe* (1958) through her own Ciné-Tamaris. Varda's documentary practice was inspired and informed by a wide range of influences, mixing poetry, art, photography, and elliptical narration into pure cinematic expression, all of which is clearly demonstrated in *La Pointe Courte*. She allows contingency and spontaneity, including chance encounters and sudden inspirations, to affect the final projects. She is often compared to an artist with a sketch pad, observing, capturing, and reworking the world around her. Throughout her career, Varda has continually refined and explored the relations between documentary and fiction, often forging a synthesis with subjective documentaries and authentic fictions.

With *Ô saisons, ô châteaux*, Varda was given an assignment from Braunberger, as part of a national tourism project, which she did not initially relish. However, upon arriving in the Loire Valley in October 1957 to document the famous castles, she was surprised by the beautiful setting: "I stumbled into a sublime late fall, all golden, bathed in sunlight. I was taken with the gentleness of the Loire Valley, and the film became instilled with the melancholy of bygone epochs."[55] The twenty-two-minute film includes an architectural tour of castles in chronological order of their construction, but also scenes with gardeners, voice-over commentary by Danièle Delorme, and sixteenth-century poems read by Antoine Bourseiller. Her second documentary, *l'Opéra mouffe*, is an even more unique, avantgarde film. Varda, then pregnant, made a personal study of a trajectory through one neighborhood in Paris, behind the Pantheon and along rue Mouffetard. She planted herself, and the camera, along the street, observing and occasionally filming the people and places. As Varda explains, pregnancy is a contradictory time of hope and anxiety, and this sensibility affected her vision of the neighborhood, adding special poignancy to shots of the homeless but also happy families working and living there. "After two days no one noticed me, I was just like the merchants selling lemons and bread, I was part of the decor."[56] Many reviewers pointed out the film's parallels with *La Pointe Courte* in its sensitive observation of the locals, but also cited connections to neorealism and other film traditions: "We rediscover somewhat the biting tone of Jean Vigo's *A propos de Nice*, but improved by tender touches and even an admirable, erotic freedom."[57] Varda's resolve and individuality permeate *L'Opéra mouffe*, particularly because she shot almost all the footage herself (cinematographer Sacha Vierny quit after several days). Starting from her "pad of notes by a pregnant woman," Varda filmed, edited, and produced the unique film. Sandy Flitterman-Lewis celebrates *L'Opéra mouffe* as a landmark in feminist cinema, with its emphasis on Varda's subjectivity and perception: "The images generate a variety of reflections both on the life process itself (love, death, birth, old age) and on the gentle absurdity of ordinary daily activities."[58]

The third documentary, *Du côté de la côte,* continues Varda's penchant for loose, picaresque journey structures. Here, too, the film wanders perceptively along a predetermined path, the length of the French Riviera, revealing its alluring and deceptive beauty. For Varda, the Riviera offers a false Garden of Eden, so she concentrates on the strange, even surreal, exoticism of the people and locale. *Du côté de la côte* was dedicated to André Bazin. Unlike *La Pointe Courte,* these documentaries were all released commercially in French movie theaters. *Du côté de la côte* was even shown before *Hiroshima, mon amour* in much of France. But the real tribute to this first phase of Varda's career came at the Palais de Chaillot theater in Paris on June 2, 1959, when the evening screening of her four films attracted an astonishing two thousand people. As Jean Douchet explained to the readers of *Arts,* it had been unjust that during an era when a new generation of filmmakers was being heralded, almost no one was crediting Agnès Varda, who "was the true precursor and promoter of the renewal" in French cinema.[59] Varda's unique path had begun to pay off. In the pages of *Cahiers,* Truffaut had written that Varda's documentary work exhibited five cinematic virtues: "fantasy, taste, intelligence, intuition, and sensitivity," while Godard added that, "Within the French film industry, Agnès Varda's short films shine like real little gems."[60] Varda's earliest films were vital to revising French film language, and her inspiring pregnancy with her daughter Rosalie became symbolic of France giving birth to a new cinema.

For international audiences, however, it was the stunning *Cleo from 5 to 7* that launched Varda's name. This film, shot in chronological order during June and July 1961, had a small budget of $64,000 thanks to Beauregard and Ponti's Rome-Paris Films. With *Cleo from 5 to 7,* Varda had now worked with each of the top three New Wave producers. Varda came to know Beauregard through Jacques Demy. She and Demy had met at the Tours film festival in 1958, and the following year they fell in love and became a couple. In 1960, Demy shot *Lola* for Beauregard, to whom Varda pitched her plans for a color costume drama shot in southern France and Italy. Beauregard suggested she shoot something inexpensive for him instead. She quickly considered ideas set in Paris, and landed on the notion of a study of a woman in a limited period of time, somewhat like *Lola,* but Varda wanted her story to reflect more of the angst of present-day life. Throughout her career, Varda researched her films personally. For *Cleo from 5 to 7,* she developed the idea of a woman who fears she may have cancer and Varda actually made appointments at local cancer hospitals so she could listen to conversations in the waiting rooms, learn more about the anxiety of waiting, and "capture the fear" of real experience. She also inserted real, found individuals, including street entertainers and on-lookers, into the project as she proceeded.

Cleo from 5 to 7 follows a successful pop singer as she nervously waits for cancer test results, between 5 and 6:30 one afternoon. The story unfolds in real time, with chapter intertitles outlining the precise timing of each scene: "Cleo, 5:25–5:31." Gradually it becomes clear that Cleo (Corinne Marchand) has been waiting for two days for the results of her medical exam, though we only see the final slice of that time, the last ninety minutes. The film opens at a fortune-teller's, shot in both color and black and white, where the tarot cards foresee a complete transformation of Cleo, including the prediction that a talkative stranger will enter her life. Disgusted and fearful, especially by the death card, Cleo flees the fortune-teller's apartment, commenting in voice-over that at least she still has her external beauty. Cleo next meets her secretary-assistant, Angèle (Dominique Davray), in a café, where Cleo pouts about her illness. The servile Angèle blows Cleo's nose for her, but dismisses her fears as childish. Angèle and Cleo then stop in a hat store where Cleo buys a black winter hat despite Angèle's warnings against buying new things on Tuesdays. The women take a taxi home, where Cleo feigns embarrassment when the female taxi driver turns on the radio to a station playing one of Cleo's songs. Once home, Cleo takes refuge in her large, empty white loft dominated by her bed, a piano, a swing for exercise, and many kittens. Even her hot water bottle is shaped like a cat.

Cleo's middle-aged lover, the dreamy, calm José (José Luis de Villalonga, who played Raoul in Malle's *The Lovers*), appears briefly, and he too treats her like a child. When he sees the hot water bottle, he wants to know "What is it today?" After José leaves, Bob (Michel Legrand) and his lyricist (Serge Korber) arrive and joke at being doctors examining her. They rehearse several songs, but Cleo is testy, complaining that they never show her any respect. During one striking new song, "Cry of Love," whose lyrics include "I'll have been laid to rest, ashen, pale, alone," Cleo breaks down. She rebels against the somber song, changes from white clothes into black, and leaves the apartment. On her walk, she is disgusted by a street entertainer eating live frogs. Next, she enters Le Dôme café where she nervously orders a cognac, plays one of her own songs on the jukebox, and watches for reactions. No one seems to enjoy the song, so she leaves. But as she stomps along the sidewalk, shots of various people from the film so far are inserted, as if she is haunted by all of them looking at her.

Figure 8.11. Cleo watches the street entertainer (*Cleo from 5 to 7*)

Figure 8.12. The man swallows frogs (*Cleo from 5 to 7*)

Figure 8.13. Dorothée models (*Cleo from 5 to 7*)

In the café Cleo overheard mention of the name Dorothée, so she heads to an art studio where her old friend Dorothée (Dorothée Blank) is a nude model. Cleo admits fears of illness to Dorothée, who tries to distract Cleo, taking her along on a drive to pick up some 35mm movies for her boyfriend, a projectionist. At the cinema, they watch a short silent film in which a young man (Jean-Luc Godard) mistakenly thinks he sees his girlfriend (Anna Karina) fall and die, but his dark glasses are to blame. Finally, Cleo heads into Parc Montsouris where she encounters a soldier, Antoine (Antoine Bourseiller), on his final day of leave before returning to the Algerian War. Antoine flirts with her, pointing out it is the first day of summer and the longest day of the year. She mentions her cancer test and they go together to the hospital. She promises to have dinner with him and see him off on a train later, in exchange for his companionship now. At the film's end, Cleo's doctor drives by and tells her that two months of radiation treatment should put her right again. Cleo, left standing stunned with Antoine, explains that her fear seems suddenly to have left her, and the film ends.

Cleo from 5 to 7, one of the richest works of the "young French cinema," combines techniques from documentary and fantasy, blurring shifts from objective realism to abstract subjectivity. The location shooting, with many elegant long takes and seemingly chance backdrops of funeral parlors and flower shops, is reinforced by cameras shooting from car windows or a high perch, hidden across the street so that Cleo's strolls, like the meanderings of Antoine Doinel in *The 400 Blows,* look spontaneous, reflecting the contemporary honesty of the moment. Other scenes rely on poignant nondiegetic music, disruptive cut-ins, and even tiny jump cuts. Everything is possible in Varda's very personal cinematic style, which she cleverly labels *cinécriture,* or cine-writing, a unifying term meant to avoid the limits of "directing" by designating all aspects of communicating with the cinematic medium. She reminds us that we cannot think of an action without its representation via sound, editing, and camera work, all of which are equally significant narrative tools in her auteurist *écriture.* She also takes advantage of chance events, documents them, and weaves them into her fiction to lend a sense of immediacy and honest poetry to the final film. Like many other rewarding works of the New Wave era, including *Breathless, Adieu Philippine,* and *Jules and Jim,* Varda's *Cleo from 5 to 7* builds upon a wide range of discursive and historically informed stylistic options, offering the spectator a primer in modern cinematic techniques within a seemingly free flowing, personal narrative.

But *Cleo from 5 to 7* also owes directly to the context and personnel of the young French cinema. For the role of Cleo, Varda selected Corinne Marchand, who had played a minor dancer in Demy's *Lola.* Varda acknowledges that in real life Marchand was very different in taste and style from Cleo, but that Marchand became increasingly fascinated with the role. Varda also considered casting Jacques Demy for Antoine, but ended up with Bourseiller, who had done voice-over work for her previously. This production is also important as evidence of the interpersonal and professional camaraderie of the New Wave era. The short "film within a film" boasts Sami Frey, Georges de Beauregard, Eddie Constantine, and Jean-Claude Brialy, in addition to Godard and Karina. According to Varda, "The light that day, and the general good humor remain a memory for me that symbolizes the New Wave as we lived it, with the power of imagination and friendship in action."[61] Further, *Cleo from 5 to 7* was shot by Jean Rabier, Marin Karmitz was assistant director, and Aurore Paquiss (later Chabrol) provided continuity. Demy's friends and collaborators set designer Bernard Evein and composer Michel Legrand were key figures in the production, as well. It is also worth noting that Varda had taken the wedding photos a few months earlier for Godard and Karina's splashy wedding. *Cleo from 5 to 7* is a tribute to a close circle of New Wave–era friends.

Filming began on the longest day of the year, but was shot in chronological sequence, with great attention given to preserving time markers

Figure 8.14. Varda rehearses with Marchand (courtesy of Agnès Varda)

and the appropriate daylight levels within the diegesis. The crew even changed some clocks along the streets as they filmed. While the principal shoot only lasted about five weeks, Marchand constantly lost weight, so that Cleo would look increasingly worried and even stricken, as the time of her potential death sentence ticks away around her. By the final day of shooting, when Cleo and Antoine watch the doctor drive away and try to deal with the immensity of Cleo's impending cancer treatment, and Antoine's impending absence, the actors achieved a great, restrained intensity. However, upon reviewing the rushes, it was clear that the tracks for the camera were visible just over their shoulders. Two months later, Varda re-shot the sequence, but in finding that the actors lacked the emotion and bond she retained the original take and cut quickly to black, hoping the spectators would not as readily notice the rails. The sudden ending adds a succinct, ominous final punctuation mark.

This film by and about a woman, with its sensitive attention to Cleo's growing mental and physical crisis, has justifiably become one of the milestones of feminist cinema. Much of the theoretical interest in *Cleo from 5 to 7* centers on the title character's increasing independence, as she shifts from an objectified, repressed, and suffering body to a subjective, more cognizant being. Agnès Varda's own comments helped shape the critical perception of Cleo's character from the beginning. In often eloquent, always insightful interviews, Varda carefully explained that the objective time of the titles is contradicted by the internal, subjective time of Cleo's perception. But she also acknowledged that Cleo had a chance to change during these ninety minutes, gauge the egotism of those closest to her, and gradually become more aware and sensitive to others: "This struggle between coquettishness and anguish allows Cleo to be truthful for the first time in her life."[62] From the director's perspective, Cleo is not so much a person as a formal problem in a narrative plot. As she explains, "I thought women were themselves victims of being defined by looks from others— father, lover, judge. . . . Women have to wake up, so right in the middle, Cleo does. . . . In the first half she is the princess all the time. . . . Even her lover, the maid, and musicians do not care about her or her fears. She is a doll to everyone. So, she changes to a black dress, like Edith Piaf, and decides to go out. Now *she* looks."[63]

This sort of clarity of feminist purpose has unified many of the critical reactions to *Cleo from 5 to 7*, often condensing Cleo down to an uncomplicated psychoanalytic trajectory, maturing from passive object to an active subject position. As Flitterman-Lewis writes, "The film traces the process by which Cleo, the woman-as-spectacle, becomes transformed into an active social participant, rupturing the oppressive unity of identity and vision and appropriating the gaze for herself." Cleo undergoes a "profound transformation."[64] Alison Smith agrees, arguing that by the time Cleo arrives in Parc Montsouris she has a "confident knowledge" of her own subjective identity.[65] Clearly, *Cleo from 5 to 7* addresses issues of women as image, yet it seems difficult to claim she is a completely different character by the end, much less that she is somehow more socially engaged and aware after forty minutes of wandering. Watching one man eat frogs and another demonstrate a hole in his arm has hardly given her a new respect for humanity or herself. Instead, she still seems afraid and disgusted by much around her. Her desperate glare at the people in the café ignoring or even complaining about her song on the jukebox reinforces her sense of panic. She never seems to find solace or understanding on the streets, though the short comic movie does briefly distract her.

The famous scene of Cleo walking down the sidewalk, intercut with shots of many of the film's characters seemingly looking at her, only reinforces her fragile mental state. Janice Mouton believes *Cleo from 5 to 7* is built on a complete transformation of subjectivity, but adds that Cleo's exit from the café and walk prove "Her first brave steps are only a start; she must continually summon up courage to proceed along her path."[66] Based on the flow of story information and resulting characterizations, Cleo's current crisis is active and ongoing. It is a process understood by the audience from a series of cues available from the start, full of ambiguity and ambivalence. These cues continue right up to the final moment outside the hospital. Cleo may feel a moment of calm at the end, as the doctor pulls away and she chats with the earnest, concerned Antoine. But, given Antoine's imminent departure, and her appointment to meet with the doctor the next day to begin treatment, Cleo's mental health can hardly be summarized as stable, empowering, or socially engaged. For instance, she never makes any connection between the cancer in her body and what the Algerian War is doing to France and young men such as Antoine. Varda's narrative may suggest a parallel, but Cleo never sees it. It is never proven that Cleo begins to see the world through clearer glasses, as the Godard character in the embedded short movie had.

Cleo's degree of self-awareness and maturation is further complicated by what seems to be an ambivalent narrator. In the opening scene, Cleo already believes she is gravely ill, and also suggests to the fortune-teller that her lover is a disappointment. Then, the fortune-teller secretly tells her husband that Cleo is doomed. Varda initially aligns us with Cleo and we feel great sympathy for her. However, as soon as she descends the stairs, in time to the music, and looks into the mirror, it is a disappointingly shallow, vain Cleo we hear in voice-over. Throughout the movie, Cleo alternates between spoiled child and independent woman, a dichotomy the narrator never quite resolves. In parallel, the spectator alternates between sympathy and amusement toward her. Cleo is a contradictory character. Admittedly, she begins the movie in near hysterics, is babied by Angèle, and exploited physically by José, a man who hopes to spend Friday afternoon with her rather than the evening, which she prefers. She is also apparently regularly mocked by the musicians. There is no evidence that she is treated like a queen before leaving her apartment in anger, nor that life for Cleo has been perfect up until this awakening by disease.

When Cleo runs to her old friend Dorothée, it is to tell her troubles to someone who will treat her kindly and sympathetically. Nonetheless, she does not come to some new understanding. We have no evidence that Cleo will now feel more comfortable in her beautiful, if sick, body. She ends up in a state of shock, standing next to a man she has only known for twenty minutes, facing an uncertain fate. Even Varda is not sure what will become of Cleo, though she admits, "I don't think it is good." Varda constructed Cleo from a number of stereotypes, including spoiled pop stars of the 1950s and '60s, but also the nineteenth century's notorious Cléo de Mérode, who "tempted our grandfathers," as Antoine explains. Varda also includes touches from Edith Piaf's persona and Varda's own mother, who loved hats and was highly superstitious, like Angèle and Cleo, all of which helps reinforce the film's inconclusive mix of exasperation and sympathy for Cleo.

Visually, Varda builds upon her observing, restless camera work and poignantly framed shots from her earlier films, but she pushes the punctuating editing style a bit further to reflect the occasional shocks to Cleo's mental state. While the overall average shot length is just over twelve seconds, some chapters are composed of scores of shots, while others average shot lengths of fifty seconds and beyond. Even the choice of lenses is linked to emotional effect: A short 35mm, the "lens of reality" to Varda, is used on Angèle and a longer 90mm on José to reinforce his smoothness. Varda also films the fortune-teller in very sharp focus, to show Cleo's fear, and the saturated color on the Tarot cards is meant to prove how important and memorable the images are to Cleo. Among the most representative long takes are the arcing camera movements in the hat shop, when the camera seemingly takes off on its own but constantly comes to rest on significant reflections and fragmented glimpses of Cleo, the other women, and the military procession outside. Another case involves her initial inquiries at the hospital with Antoine, where the camera shifts from the couple to the staff and back to Cleo and Antoine framed in a window. Locations function like carefully constructed sets, so when Cleo passes a poster for *Don Juan*

Figure 8.15. Cleo and Antoine, carefully framed at the hospital (*Cleo from 5 to 7*)

in the café we are reminded that José said he was too busy to accompany her to its premiere. When a distraught Cleo sits with Antoine on a bench in the hospital's garden, the lawn in the background is overexposed, appearing almost snow-like, once more isolating her from the real world. Varda blurs reality and fiction visually.

The most famous scenes in *Cleo from 5 to 7* prove Varda's versatile mix of styles. When Cleo sings the devastatingly sad "Cry of Love," the 150-second shot begins with an establishing shot of Bob to the left, Angèle in depth, Cleo, dressed all in white behind the black piano, and the lyricist to the right. The blocking and framing gradually obscure Angèle, to concentrate on Cleo and the men. The camera dollies in, arcing to isolate Cleo, changing her backdrop from the pure white walls and beams to a black curtain. After sixty seconds, nondiegetic strings join the piano and Cleo. Isolated and backlit against black, she grows increasingly intense and turns to the camera; suddenly tears stream from her eyes. The quality of her singing voice increasingly changes to a studio mix. At the end, the camera quickly dollies back out while Cleo weeps on the piano. As Claudia Gorbman writes, the everyday world temporarily disappears: "What prevails until the song ends is a deliberately glossy studio effect as in television variety shows: one performer, dramatically illuminated out of any spatio-temporal context, interprets with unmitigated feeling a contemporary tune accompanied by an hidden orchestra."[67] Nonetheless, the reality of Cleo's foreboding intensifies her performance as well as her emotions and those of the audience. This scene, which clearly depends upon Evein's art direction, Legrand's music, and Varda's lyrics, demonstrates Varda's mastery of the graphic potential of black and white, but also a mix of narrative styles, where fantasy seems to sneak into the reality of a rehearsal session filmed in stunning long takes. Moreover, the audience empathizes with Cleo's torment over the beautifully sad song, while her three friends just see it as more evidence of her as a temperamental diva.

A second scene demonstrating Varda's radical approach to time and space can be seen in Chapter 8 ("5:45–5:52"), when Cleo is disappointed by the café response to her song on the jukebox and walks down the street. In contrast to the "Cry of Love" long take, this fifty-second stroll is broken into twenty-seven shots of Cleo and passersby, but also ten inserts of posed characters from elsewhere in the film, including the fortune-teller, José, the frog swallower, and even her abandoned wig. Whether these inserts are signs of Cleo's precise mental perspective, or a summary of the general forces weighing on her mind, or pure intervention of a narrator reminding the audience of the cast of characters Cleo has recently encountered, the scene acts as a highly punctuated representation of the life and concerns

Figure 8.16. Cleo isolated by the camera (*Cleo from 5 to 7*)

Cleo is trying to walk away from and ignore. Objective reality and subjectivity are blurred once again. But the real strength of Varda's *cinécriture* approach can be seen in how she interrelates striking combinations of image, sound, and editing into complex signifying structures. As Claudia Gorbman points out, music in *Cleo from 5 to 7* does not just function to support the visuals, but actually motivates editing rhythms and reinforces the continuity and discontinuity of filmed events, whether it be Cleo descending the stairs from the fortune-teller's apartment in a fragmented series of shots, or Cleo stomping out of her apartment, passing a child in the street banging out notes from "Cry of Love" on a toy piano. Claudine Delvaux summarizes this rich synthesis well: "Simply to be a spectator of Agnès Varda's films is a great pleasure for me—a pleasure of the image and pleasure of the text. It is as if she fills the screen with images, just as a writer fills a page with poetry."[68]

Cleo from 5 to 7 received great critical attention from those interested in the new French cinema. The fact that Varda was not a *Cahiers* director allowed those more suspicious of the New Wave proper to praise it, as well. A 1962 review in *Positif* celebrated Varda's lucidity, intelligence, and instinct, declaring that she might just be "the most complete auteur," while *Cleo from 5 to 7* was considered the best French film since *Hiroshima, mon amour*.[69] Surprisingly, while Varda's gender was often acknowledged in reviews, the fact that she was perhaps the only successful female art film director in the world was largely ignored at the time. Though *Cleo from 5 to 7*'s fame and significance have continually increased since 1962, its initial box office performance was rather uneven. In Paris, its first run sold a respectable 111,000 tickets, more than Resnais' *Muriel,* but less than *Hiroshima, mon amour.* However, in New York, where Bosley Crowther's review in the *New York Times* dismissed it as another in a string of shallow new French films that stress visual style over story,[70] *Cleo from 5 to 7* sold only 22,000 tickets. Today, *Cleo from 5 to 7* is accepted as one of the most important French films of the 1960s, and one of the most significant films in the history of women filmmakers. During the 1980s, Madonna, whose mother had died of cancer in 1963, approached Varda, wanting to star in an American remake of *Cleo from 5 to 7,* though that project eventually fell through.

Varda's next feature, *Le bonheur,* toned down the experimentation in a more subtle, and for many critics, more troubling film. *Le bonheur* was also something of a surprise for Varda. She and producer Mag Bodard had initially planned to make *Les Créatures* (*The Creatures,* 1966) next. However, the CNC commission granting advances on receipts turned down that proposal. Angry, Varda set about writing a new movie for the final CNC deadline, which was only four days away: "I still ask myself where this simple tale of a carpenter came from. . . . Are there stories inside us, waiting in hidden corners?" Jacques Demy helped Varda transcribe her hurried script and they managed to get the new project typed up and the thirty required copies mimeographed just in time.[71] The CNC approved the scenario, and Varda set about choosing actors. For the family, Varda selected a popular television actor, Jean-Claude Drouot, who had just been featured on the cover of *Marie-Claire* magazine, with his beautiful wife Claire and their two children. Varda convinced them all to be in the film, and then hired another blonde, Marie-France Boyer, to play Emilie, the tempting postal worker.

Part of *Le bonheur*'s initial impact was due to its reworking of the "other woman" romantic drama formula, but Varda's version is far from a generic love triangle. François and his loving wife, Thérèse, live with their two small children, Pierrot and Gisou, in the calm town of Fontanay-sur-Rose just outside Paris. He is a carpenter, working in his uncle's friendly shop; Thérèse is a seamstress, making dresses out of their home, and caring for the children. They spend Sundays in the park or at old-fashioned family gatherings and picnics. Their life is ideal, and all are happy and devoted to one another: They have *le bonheur*. However, when François spends several days working in nearby Vincennes, he meets a pretty postal clerk, Emilie. She is about to move to his town, so he offers to help build some shelves when she arrives. On that day, François lies to his wife and goes to meet Emilie, and they begin an affair. François is now doubly happy, which he explains to Emilie; he is always honest with her about loving his wife and family. One clever shot captures this period of his life: During a street festival the camera tracks back and forth as various couples dance and exchange partners. A tree in the foreground occasionally blocks the action. Emilie begins dancing with some friend while an oblivious Thérèse dances with François. During the one hundred-second shot everyone changes partners several times, with François and Emilie eventually dancing happily not far from Thérèse and her new partner. Soon after, Emilie and François share an intimate conversation in her apartment, which is shot in one long take of nearly five minutes. He explains again his double happiness, telling the slightly jealous Emilie that she makes love better than his wife: Thérèse is more like a tender plant, while Emilie is an animal set free. He loves them both.

But this male dream-come-true soon unravels. On their next Sunday outing in the woods, Thérèse carefully puts the children down for a nap in

Figure 8.17. François and wife Thérèse (*Le bonheur*)

Figure 8.18. François and lover Emilie (*Le bonheur*)

a homemade tent, then settles down on a blanket with François, exclaiming that he seems particularly happy this summer. He is glad it shows, and
Emilie's earlier, smiling acceptance of the love triangle motivates him to
reveal the situation to his wife so that she too can be happy for him! During a daring long take that parallels the earlier five-minute shot with Emilie, François explains that there is "another tree" in their family orchard
now. He does not want to miss out on "more life" and hopes Thérèse might
be able to love him even more now, but, "If you ask me to do without her, I
will." Thérèse tells him she may be able to share him, and the two make
love under their blanket in the meadow. However, upon waking up, the
family cannot find Thérèse. With Pierrot and the wimpering Gisou in tow,
François runs off to discover that Thérèse has drowned in a nearby pond,
the same pond where the family picnicked in the opening scene. After the
funeral, the children go briefly to live with François' brother, then they
share a family vacation with the sad François, before he returns to Emilie,
who is a bit hesitant to "take another woman's place." Nonetheless, she
quickly moves in with François, takes over the children, and the story ends
with the four of them enjoying a lovely, sunny fall Sunday in the country.
In a shot that reverses the opening title shot, the four of them walk away
from the camera into the trees. The film fades to orange, and ends.

Figure 8.19. François clutches the drowned Thérèse (*Le bonheur*)

Le bonheur initially garnered more international attention than *Cleo from 5 to 7,* winning the Louis Delluc Award, the Silver Bear at the Berlin Film Festival, and the David O. Selznick Award in the United States. Nonetheless, in Paris *Le bonheur* only attracted 86,000 people. By contrast, it played for eight "splendid" weeks in New York, earning $101,600, despite Bosley Crowther's *New York Times* review in which he complained that it "landed like a cinder in the eye." He found it memorable and exasperating, though "perhaps tongue in cheek."[72] Its critical reception has been just as contradictory. Even Alison Smith dismisses the film as atypical of Varda and based on cliché: "I find it hard to like."[73] Yet *Le bonheur* delivers a surprisingly interesting narrative, full of ambivalence and ambiguity, all built on very rigorous and modern formal structures. Part of the critical confusion may owe a debt to Varda's comments and interviews upon the film's release. She often defended François, and reinforced the themes of happiness. She refused to condemn François or adultery during interviews, and even called him wise: He loved his wife, she died, and François will always love her, just as he does his late father. Varda avoided making large moralizing social statements about the movie or its characters. For her, the film expressed a sort of idyllic freedom in love, a world with "no conscience." It may have also reflected some of the nonconformity in her own personal life.

It should be no surprise that *Le bonheur* puzzled many reviewers. Often, they were looking for a more obviously ironic tone, or harsher narrative judgment of the naively happy François or even Thérèse, who quietly abandons her children and dies, seemingly to make way for the new woman. Georges Sadoul explains that it "would have stirred up less argument or indignation if it had been titled *A Great Misfortune.*"[74] Similarly, Alan Williams argues that in *Le bonheur,* life and patriarchy go unexamined. As he points out, the audience is likely to ask "Has Varda no *feelings* about the dead woman? . . . It is probably dangerous to antagonize one's audience to this extent with unmarked irony."[75] Varda never shows Thérèse's pain. Rather, the narration concentrates on François, the sensitive man who suffers briefly, losing part of his happiness, before returning to his initial state of bliss, now with Emilie. Feminists in particular have been divided over how best to deal with this narrative that does not fit at all what some wanted to see from the world's most interesting woman director. Most extreme may be Claire Johnston's attack on *Le bonheur* as replicating the "facile day-dreams perpetuated by advertising. . . . There is no doubt that Varda's work is reactionary: in her rejection of culture and her placement of woman outside history her films mark a retrograde step in women's cinema."[76] Flitterman-Lewis admits that *Le bonheur* upset many women, but she defends it as "profoundly feminist": "When people left the film they were asking themselves—and each other—questions concerning the nature of happiness, of sexual relations, of social constructs."[77] Moreover, those looking for Varda's authorial commentary on the action believed they found it: "As François makes love to his mistress, shots of his wife shopping with the children provide an ironic commentary on his idea of happiness."[78]

France's influential *Le film français* praised *Le bonheur* and Varda highly: "Agnès Varda does not shy away from the most difficult subjects—she already proved this with *Cleo*—but she also demonstrates an originality and an inspired richness that have no equivalent in French cinema today. The theme developed here—a man's love split equally, purely even, between his wife and his mistress—has never been treated with such directness on the screen. It will surprise and even shock some spectators despite its subtle style." They even labeled it a "hymn to life."[79] Interestingly, Varda's ending, in which François all too contentedly enjoys a new family arrangement made possible by the death of the wife/mother, anticipates many of Chabrol's later bourgeois fictions, from *La femme infidèle* (*The Unfaithful Wife*, 1969) to *La Cérémonie* (1995) and *La fleur du mal* (*Flower of Evil*, 2003), which present flawed but endearingly naive families who seem unable to conceive of any other way of behaving. Nonetheless, Varda's *Cleo from 5 to 7* and *Sans toit ni loi* (*Vagabond*, 1985) earn much more praise and attention from historians and cultural critics today than does *Le bonheur*, which also deserves continued consideration and analysis.

During a time when most European art films were still shot in less expensive black and white, the lush color in *Le bonheur*, with its obvious references to Jean Renoir as well as his father and French Impressionist paintings, seemed like a comment on the artifice of the characters to some critics, but also a suspicious attempt at entering the mainstream to others. However, *Le bonheur* also alternates the soft, sunny impressionist color with bright, bold, flat compositions that mimic modern poster art. Varda does not regress to classical realism. For instance, Varda cuts from François and Emilie's first embrace in her barren new apartment to an idyllic family picnic in a beautiful, sun-drenched shot, with sunflowers clustered in the background around the festive François as he opens the champagne. A few moments later François and the happy Thérèse, in her bright flowery dress, lie beneath a willow tree and discuss having more children. There is a natural, rich beauty that contrasts with the previous scene's limited palette of flesh and white as well as the next scene of François in bed with Thérèse. Occasionally Varda also works with bold, flat colors, as in the transition after François agrees to help Emilie move. Varda cuts from Emilie in blue to François sitting silhouetted against a blue wall featuring the word "azur," then cuts on a blue truck passing, which acts as a blue wipe to the next shot of a bright yellow truck and wall, then a jump cut on two red trucks passing, then back to the yellow truck as François pulls up in his little truck with the yellow sign. The next scene opens with him painting a blue square. Varda's set design alternates the nostalgic impressionist nature scenes with a flat poster style and primary colors that one might expect to find in a Godard film. Further, she also includes color fades between scenes, including fades to yellow, blue, and white that seem to mimic 1950s Hollywood romantic comedies such as *Will Success Spoil Rock Hunter?* Perhaps by this point her color style was being influenced by her relationship with the bold colorist Jacques Demy as much as her own love of visual arts.

Varda's staging in *Le bonheur* incorporates both flashy discontinuous montages and subtly elegant long takes. The most daring sequences show off her penchant for reflexive techniques in editing, shot scale, and even focus. The film opens with a haltingly edited montage of sunflowers framed in various positions of the frame, while François and his family slowly approach, out of focus, in the distance. In retrospect, it is unclear which blonde woman is with him. This sequence is jarring, with an average shot length of barely two seconds, while the film's overall ASL is over thirteen seconds. Twice Varda also offers montages of the woman's domestic work, including shots of the woman kneading dough, watering flowers, ironing, and putting the kids to bed. This montage, which is repeated near the end with Emilie having taken over Thérèse's routines, is often cited by critics as commentary on the value and place of women in the home, that pretty women, who can also clean, cook, and take care of the children, are exchangeable.

However, during its first appearance, this montage also provides an excellent glimpse into the subtleties of Varda's *cinécriture*. Immediately after the eleven-shot household montage, Varda continues with a twelve-shot montage of François driving to Vincennes. The gold sign "Porte Dorée" (Golden Gate) is followed by two gold statues, then the sign again and shots of François speeding along in his truck with the yellow sign, as if perhaps he is in some golden chariot. Next, several shots of lions are intercut with images of François driving past the zoo. A shot of a male and female lion snuggling is followed by some startled birds, and we hear "What a lovely

Figure 8.20. *Le bonheur* title sequence

bird," then cut to a bird stamp being handled by Emilie in the post office. The twelve shots move him from home to Emilie in twenty seconds. The domestic female-centered housework montage is thus followed with the male "on the hunt" montage, which acts as a clever transition between François' two worlds. That the scene continues with Emilie smiling at a postage stamp of a bride and groom also adds a bit of ironic foreshadowing.

With *Le bonheur*, Varda continues to explore a number of her earlier techniques and strategies. Beyond the long takes and montages, there are several subjective inserts. While François and Emilie sit at a café and discuss possibly visiting the nearby castle, there are inserts of them smiling at the camera, out of focus, as each seems to imagine their happy visit. During the scene when François discovers the drowned Thérèse, there are repeated shots of him lifting and hugging her limp body. The lack of any sound reinforces the nightmarish effect of her death. Brief inserts reveal her in the water, clinging to a branch, but it is unclear whether these are reliable flashbacks or François' imagination. Varda then eliminates any inquiry into the death by quickly cutting to a pile of dirt at the funeral. This shift from an intricately busy scene to a minimalist one-shot funeral is typical of the unusual pacing of *Le bonheur*. Even the August vacation that François takes is reduced to a single, still photograph of his smiling extended family. Varda claims this sort of image was at the root of her film project: Many family photos reveal happy faces, but she wonders whether happiness is merely a representation or something real.

One of the most functional methods of staging action in *Le bonheur*, however, involves carefully choreographed camera movements that arc and track, following characters from point to point. Varda frames an action in a medium-long shot, then as the characters move, the camera suddenly begins to track with them, then they stop at the other end of the track where the camera may tilt or zoom in on them. The scene where François and Thérèse wander off from the picnic to lie beneath the willow provides an excellent example, as does their final conversation, when the camera observes Thérèse arrange the mosquito netting over the children then follows her back to François, constantly reframing in their medium-close up on the blanket. During this shot Varda often shifts the actors' bodies so that they turn to and away from the camera, creating the equivalent of shot/reverse shots and isolated close-ups, all without editing, until the camera delicately pulls away as the couple undresses and begins making love. This technique allows Varda to begin casually, but by the end it becomes clear this was a carefully conceived set-up, with intricate pacing and blocking. Varda's productive camera movements and the long takes do not generate the same sort of deep space as in the staging of Jean Renoir or Louis Malle, but she guides our attention in creative ways while simultaneously reminding us there is a narrator organizing our view of this world, sometimes with long, subtle takes, and other times with jump cuts and jarring inserts. The result is a very personal and dramatic sort of narrative space.

Varda is adamant in maintaining personal control over the entire production process, and owning her own production company, Ciné-Tamaris, guarantees great independence while providing a small team of pleasant, devoted employees and colleagues who often function as her extended family. She engages actively in the management of every aspect of filmmaking, from finding funding to writing song lyrics and editing the final cut. Importantly, unlike other New Wave directors who gave up on documentaries after moving into fiction, she has continued to work in both fiction and documentary throughout her career. Two of her most successful films, the narrative *Vagabond* and personal documentary *Les Glaneurs et la glaneuse* (*The Gleaners and I*, 2000), have kept her at the top rung of French film directors. Varda has also fought to preserve high quality prints of her films, and those of Jacques Demy, and she personally prepares and distributes new DVD release versions and bonus materials. In 2005 she was accorded the honor of serving on the jury at Cannes. Thus, she has remained the most enduring and productive woman filmmaker in the world, fifty years after *La Pointe Courte*. Importantly, her fiction films refuse to simplify or explain psychologically "realistic" characters and her narrative strategies further complicate our identification with their decisions. The spectator's perception and recognition of character traits is thus impeded by the distancing narrative tactics that seem to come from contradictory cinematic traditions. The endings remain open, if not puzzling, in many regards. To conclude, we should return to the praise given *La Pointe Courte* by Bazin and recognize this unique experimental style for what it is able to accomplish: It is an evocative cinema that is realistic and dreamlike at the same time, obeying nothing but the desires of its auteur. Across her career, Varda's cinema is the freest sort because it recognizes no boundaries and bows to no producer's whims. Agnès Varda is unique, but she is also a product of that rich cultural moment that was New Wave–era France.

If Resnais and Varda remain less known than Truffaut, Godard, and Rohmer, it is due in part to the differences in their personalities. Since the *Cahiers* directors all began as critics, and brash critics at that, they were much more used to marketing themselves and their films. Resnais, Varda, and other directors associated with the Left Bank Group tended to be more contemplative, more akin to visual artists than high profile members of the culture industry. Additionally, the label "Left Bank" was used to distinguish certain aspects of this one trend among young French filmmakers from the New Wave at large. Jean-Michel Frodon points out that *rive gauche* really stands for the entire intellectual, philosophical environment centered around St. German des Près in Paris from 1945 up to May 1968. This milieu was very different from that of the *Cahiers* filmmakers who were an internal cinema group, unified around specifically cinematic concerns.[80] But as Sandy Flitterman-Lewis notes, "the preoccupation with modes of cinematic discourse" united the New Wave with the Left Bank Group.[81] Varda and Resnais, as well as their colleagues Chris Marker, Henri Colpi, and Jacques Demy, were products of, and key participants in, the new French cinema.

Already in 1960, *Cinéma* named as "beneficiaries" of the New Wave those directors, such as Resnais, Varda, and Demy, who had made successful short films during the 1950s but needed the excitement brought on by Truffaut, Chabrol, and Godard in order to find producers willing to give them a chance to continue with feature films.[82] Yet, as we have seen, the revitalization of French production depended as much on *La Pointe Courte*, *Night and Fog*, *Hiroshima, mon amour*, *Last Year at Marienbad*, and *Cleo from 5 to 7,* as *The Cousins, The 400 Blows,* and *Breathless.* Resnais and Varda rose to the top in part because they were able to capitalize on their own unique preparation for careers in filmmaking. They took advantage of opportunities of the moment. They also managed to establish consistent auteurist trajectories, directing a rich body of work over the next forty years, helping to shape French cinema through the latter half of the twentieth century. Certainly their most lasting effects have been on the blending of documentary and narrative strategies as they rethought and reworked representational modes in new, demanding, and ultimately incredibly rewarding ways.

CONCLUSION:
A NETWORK OF CARRIER WAVES

I think that fundamentally the New Wave was a cinema of amateurs. By becoming more professional it perhaps lost its force, which helps explain why French cinema has since returned to a situation similar to that of the 1950s.

—ERIC ROHMER, *La Nouvelle vague 25 ans après*

The Nouvelle Vague should have led us to anticipate films more like Jacques Demy's than the actual knottier works of Truffaut, Godard, or Chabrol. . . . His films are the work of a pure *metteur en scène*.

—GINETTE BILLARD, "Jacques Demy and His Other World"

W H E N I first began this project, my goal was to return in depth to the nouvelle vague, one of the eras in film history that had motivated me to study the cinema in the first place. Rather than rely upon the standard texts as a starting point, however, I took the detour of trying to rediscover how the New Wave presented itself initially to contemporary observers in the late 1950s. I knew the standard history, and had seen a good number of the less canonical films from that era, but I was suspicious about historical accounts claiming that the French had indeed "taken the world by surprise" with these groundbreaking films that were said to startle everyone as overnight a "wave had crashed on their shores." I was curious to see what contemporary accounts in film journals such as *Cinéma 59, Positif, Le Film français*, or even *Variety* thought of the on-going changes during this period. Initial tasks included finding out just when critics began making lists of who "was" nouvelle vague, whether those lists matched up, and whether there were competing conceptions of the New Wave even as it was still developing. I wanted to know just what the term nouvelle vague meant in film circles around 1960. In addition, I wanted to let those contemporary observers guide my inquiry as I searched for a purer understanding of the French New Wave. Certainly, an almost romantic quest was at work here. This book is the first summary of some of those findings. But it also sets the stage for future inquiry that will build upon this history of the New Wave's rise.

Overall, I was surprised to learn how fundamentally important the small core of *Cahiers du cinéma* directors, especially Claude Chabrol, François Truffaut, and Jean-Luc Godard, had been, right from the very beginning. My assumption was that *Cahiers du cinéma* had played such a strong public-relations role in championing the first films by its own members that it had permanently warped public perception of the New Wave. And to a certain degree that is true. As mentioned in the introduction to this study, that famous November 1962 issue devoted to the nouvelle vague already advanced "the big three" as the central players. Tests of popular and even competing journals reveal that Chabrol, Truffaut, and Godard were indeed the key figures, for better or worse, for most contemporary observers of the New Wave. Their critical audacity, avowed debt to great auteurs from both distant and recent film history, their marketing savvy, technical innovation, and narrative experimentation all seemed to set these three apart from their peers of 1960. Contemporary observers found these fellows to possess all the important youthful traits expected of New Wave filmmakers, while many other directors shared only several of those most pertinent qualities. Thus this book ended up concentrating on the initial development of the New Wave and its manifestation in the films produced by the filmmakers attached to *Cahiers du cinéma*. Those directors provided the most coherent body of decidedly nouvelle vague movies.

However, not all observers of world cinema were so welcoming to the innovations of the New Wave. Another interesting facet of the New Wave's definition involves evaluating its reception outside France. The American trade journal *Variety* provides a valuable chronicle of the developments by this new generation of directors and producers. *Variety*'s columnists report, often with a mixture of amusement and criticism, on the unusual tactics of what they call "the wave boys." *Variety* first uses the phrase "new wave" in June of 1959, but by January 1960 they already dismiss it in the past tense in an article entitled "Parisian Film Pros Ridicule New Wave": "During 1959 there was an effort here in Paris to recognize a so-called 'New Wave.' . . . This may be what [we know] as malarky, a calculated pose and pretense by young, or upstart directors to call attention to themselves."[1] By May, their Paris writer Gene Moskowitz wrote that the New Wave was "dead champagne" and had only managed to generate "a wave of mediocrity."[2] *Variety*'s accounts of the New Wave tend to concentrate on all the mischief caused by these youthful films, including censorship hurdles, technical shortcomings, and over production in the face of a dwindling French audience. Sources such as *Variety* help remind us why some established observers were so leery of these innovative films, which typically chose to shoot on location, compounding the crises in French commercial studio production. For industry insiders, the New Wave really did appear reckless and unwelcome.

Beyond my own personal fascination with this era and its filmmaking is the reality that the New Wave has earned an almost unique place among the great movements and schools of international cinema. Like Soviet montage, Italian neorealism, New German Cinema, and the Chinese Fifth Generation, the French New Wave has become more than a staple segment of film history classes. Each of these movements dramatically changed notions of just what the cinema could be and then pointed the way for others to experiment on their own, revising modes of production and narrative strategies. They also reinforced the cinema's cultural significance. Interestingly, the New Wave continues to be one of the most universally inspiring of these movements today, in part because many cinema students can more easily identify with an impassioned group of young film buffs, impatient to leap into the act of making movies, than they can with ideologically determined geniuses of the silent Soviet cinema or the impoverished desperation of the postwar Italians. Even the New Germans of the 1970s and Fifth Generation of the 1980s now look like brief though exciting moments in time rather than watershed periods rewarding anyone with a will to film new stories in new ways. That Claude Chabrol, Jean-Luc Godard, Agnès Varda, Jacques Rivette, and Eric Rohmer continue to make marvelous movies fifty years after their first short projects of the 1950s adds an impressive weight to their relevance as resilient exemplars of the modern cinema.

The critical context for the French New Wave was permeated with concern for individual cinematic stylists who developed distinct personal works. Auteurism was the battle cry for many of the *Cahiers* critics, and they certainly struggled to create their own thematic, mise-en-scène, editing, and sound strategies. Today, with the remnants of psychoanalytic film theory still affecting so many of the concerns of cultural studies, many express open hostility at the longevity of auteur criticism. It is quite true that any rigid belief in the ability of great geniuses to descend from the skies to remake the cinema is wrongheaded and naive. But that is not to say that the concept of auteurism, or the importance of the individual, should be minimized, or that the study of directors who prove to be consistently important should be seen as an embarrassment. Rather than offering a simplistic, auteurist cause-effect historical narrative here, I have labored to concentrate on all individuals, including cinematographers, actors, musicians, producers, writers, and editors as well as directors, for the complex ways their input shaped the New Wave and its concrete products, the movies themselves. I have also limited biographical accounts to information pertinent to the practical choices and decisions. For instance, I refer to where Agnès Varda spent her teenage years because it affected where she shot *La Pointe Courte,* or mention Louis Malle's wealthy family more than Jacques Doniol-Valcroze's because that background affected the former's conditions of production even more than the availability of a vast château and estate for the latter. Yet I would encourage anyone interested in the personal lives of all these amazing people to pursue that path. Their lives all provide fascinating material, partly because they lived in a very thrilling, transitional era, but mostly because they displayed the sort of creative problem solving that allowed them not only to succeed but to gain the attention of the world.

Auteur criticism does not have to slip into hero worship or get bogged down in detailed biographical reconstruction. But biography can provide unexpected insight into films such as those written and directed by these young critics-turned-directors, who already valorized the "personal" in films and were aware of just what sort of specific markers of story and style might cause others to celebrate *them* as auteurs. Thus, noting that Truffaut rarely enjoyed eating, while Chabrol feasted grandly, is hardly significant to film history until the historian uses those facts to help understand why Chabrol's characters so often reveal their true character at the dinner table, whereas Truffaut's characters prefer to explain themselves one-on-one in more intimate settings. It is helpful to expect that plot points such as these may depend as much upon the directors' lives as do the sorts of films and novels they had seen and read, suggestions by the crew or cowriters, or even the critical reactions to their earlier films. The point is simply that thinking in terms of authorship is appropriate and even essential in the historical evaluation of this era and its movies.

Thus, for this study I have tried to follow models that acknowledge the decisive role of the individual director as an essential component of the intricate process of filmmaking. One basic assumption has been that directors are not only shaped by their culture, but they actively and rationally participate in it. Social, technical, and aesthetic contexts help determine the material conditions for filmmaking at any given point, but the variety of responses to those set conditions are in part produced by active artists.

David Bordwell eloquently explains the concept of the filmmaker as rational agent in his study of Yasujiro Ozu, and that model has provided a solid foundation to the analyses of films and social settings in this book. According to Bordwell, rational agents make concrete decisions and choices within a complex set of social and industrial constraints.[3] New Wave directors are particularly appropriate for illustrating the power of individual actions since they defined themselves in opposition to many established industrial and narrative norms, as they struggled to establish themselves as unique auteurs. Yet each of these directors was also immersed in a historical situation that provided many determining factors over which they had no control, such as changes in the audience, the diffusion of new, inexpensive mobile cameras and sound equipment, and modifications in Film Aid rules. The resulting diversity of films, however, provides valid testimony to the variety of ways the same material conditions could be manipulated by various individuals. This history has thus tried to account for some of the reasons that the inexpensive films by these directors did not resemble "tradition of quality" films such as Claude Autant-Lara's *The Red and the Black*, while also clarifying some factors that help account for the decisive differences between Louis Malle's *The Lovers*, Godard's *Breathless*, and Pierre Kast's *Le Bel âge*.

As explained in the introduction, this book does not pretend to simplify and reduce the French New Wave to events leading up to and including the *Cahiers du cinéma* filmmakers. While the *Cahiers* critics-turned-directors proved to be some of the most popular and persistent directors to come out of the 1958–1964 era, they are just one subset among several that comprise the New Wave. This study readily acknowledges that the history of the New Wave must continue to explore fellow young French filmmakers of the New Wave. For instance, Jean-Pierre Mocky's playfully satiric *Les Dragueurs* (*The Chasers*, 1959), Jacques Rozier's meandering *Adieu Philippine* (1962), Michel Deville's *Une balle dans le canon* (*A Slug in the Heater*, 1958), *Ce soir ou jamais* (*Tonight or Never*, 1960), *Adorable menteuse* (*Adorable Liar*, 1962), Henri Colpi's striking *Une aussi longue absence* (*A Long Absence*, 1961), and Robbe-Grillet's challenging *l'Immortelle* (*The Immortal One*, 1963) were all part of this new French cinema. Their inexpensive films featured location shooting, innovative editing and camerawork, the reworking of genres, and New Wave actors such as Marina Vlady, Anna Karina, Charles Aznavour, and even Jacques Doniol-Valcroze. The next stage of the New Wave's history reevaluates their incredible contributions and narrative innovations.

One particularly important figure from the era who has never fit comfortably in everyone's definition of the New Wave is Jacques Demy. Demy (b. 1931), like Alain Resnais, began with several short documentaries in the 1950s, which served as training grounds for his leap into increasingly rigorous and fantastic narratives, culminating in some of French cinema's most visually spectacular films, including *Lola* (1961), *Les Parapluies de Cherbourg* (*The Umbrellas of Cherbourg*, 1964), *Les Demoiselles de Rochefort* (*The Young Girls of Rochefort*, 1967), and *Peau d'âne* (*Donkey Skin*, 1971). Demy's trajectory gradually led him further from the norms of his New Wave colleagues, but all his films involve stylish narrative experimentation. Demy worked repeatedly with the same creative team, including his good friends designer Bernard Evein and composer Michel Legrand, to fashion a distinct and modern sort of personal cinema. "From *Lola* on," Claire Clouzot explains, "Demy's Proustian universe, arranged around his themes of chance, absence, and waiting, is in place."[4] Demy referred to the fictional worlds created in his films as *en chanté*, a play on the words for sung and enchanted; music and fairy tale structures were fundamental to their plots.

Demy proves exemplary as a young French filmmaker who thrives in the same cultural and economic environment as the rest of the New Wave, forging his own distinct cinema. He was often considered a "fellow traveler" with the *Cahiers* directors, but also separate.[5] As Demy explains in Varda's *l'univers de Jacques Demy* (*The World of Jacques Demy*, 1995), "I made *Lola* thanks to Godard. Jean-Luc was the first to find a fellow named Beauregard." Demy pitched his idea for *Lola* but it would cost at least $400,000 with color, costumes, and musical numbers. "Beauregard told me, 'Look, it's a sweet project but *Breathless* cost $65,000. If you can do yours for $70,000 it's a deal.'" Demy shot silent, in five weeks, with mostly available light and a tiny crew. While *Lola* did not do well commercially, selling only 43,000 tickets in France, it nonetheless established Anouk Aimee as an iconic New Wave actress. For its international distribution package, the movie was bundled with *Adieu Philippine* and *A Woman Is a Woman*. Beauregard sold the British, American, and Canadian rights for $75,000. The deal also stipulated that if local censors demanded cuts in any or all the films, or even banned them, the full amount still had to be paid.[6] Thus, foreign audiences often saw these frank, sexy films one after the other, reinforcing the perception of a unified wave of striking French films. Moreover, *Lola* fit much of what one expected of New Wave films. It made reference to other movies and directors, from von Sternberg's *Blue*

Angel and Max Ophuls right up to *Breathless*. It also inserted references to Hollywood genre films, including dancing American sailors and an enormous white Cadillac. Gene Kelly appears in person in *The Girls of Rochefort*. Demy also worked closely with his small, devoted cast and crew, lending a sense of unity and coherence to his rapidly growing auteurist oeuvre.

According to Demy, "The New Wave blew the old system apart and brought in new blood. It was the evolution of technology that created the New Wave." Especially fast film stock and magnetic sound recording, which allowed them to leave the studios. "The only thing that united the New Wave was technique. They all filmed with the same methods but each made their own cinema. . . . But the two headlights, in my opinion, were *Hiroshima, mon amour* and *Breathless*."[7] Nonetheless, as Varda explains, Demy's first feature became a legendary film in its own right: "*Lola* was quickly recognized as an exceptional film, but it did not 'sell.' *Lola* is one of those films, like *Rules of the Game*, that had no commercial success, but gained a marvelous reputation." *La Baie des anges* (*Bay of Angels*, 1962) and *Umbrellas of Cherbourg* continued his shift toward increasingly artificial worlds in which strong young women, played by Jeanne Moreau and Catherine Deneuve, live, like Lola, at the center of a closed universe. Demy remains a perfect example of a director who shares in the stylistic and technical revival of the New Wave, yet whose films can benefit from study in their own right. Demy, along with Colpi, Rozier, Deville, and many others, is a central player in the *jeune cinéma français*. They all free up the language of modern cinema. Yet Demy also found a large audience. His immensely successful *Umbrellas of Cherbourg*, which sold 351,000 tickets in Paris during its opening four weeks alone, went on to become the number one hit in France for 1963–1964, selling 1.4 million tickets.

While the New Wave was an intricate collection of people, films, and cultural forces, its ultimate legacy is a vast network of effects upon international cinema and its history. One of the first concrete results was that it inspired other filmmakers in a wide variety of national cinemas, from Poland to the United States to Africa, to rethink how the dominant genres, techniques, and modes of production could be altered or circumvented in order to open up new options. Young men as diverse as Roman Polanski, John Cassavetes, and Ousmane Sembene saw parallels between their own situations and the French New Wave. If award winning films could be shot in Paris for sixty thousand dollars, think how cheaply an equivalent production could be made in Senegal or Warsaw, some pondered. In this way, the New Wave can be thought of as generating carrier waves; young people in France and internationally were motivated to participate in the fervor over a new generation coming to the foreground. The New Wave transmitted a new and vital excitement throughout the world's cinemas, motivating wildly diverse responses to their bold examples.

A second result was an increased attention to modern European cinema and authorship in the newly growing discipline of film studies within universities globally. Thousands of Japanese, British, and American French literature students who had just begun reading Alain Robbe-Grillet, the New Novel, and French theory, could now enroll in classes that granted Jean-Luc Godard equal status with Jean Renoir and Ingmar Bergman. The nouvelle vague, like the *nouveau roman*, helped lend a trendy urgency to teaching radical, contemporary texts. Film studies gained a bit of legitimacy, especially when one could include both the movies and the "theories" of mise-en-scène and auteur criticism alongside one another. As universities grew, cinema history classes grew, and the New Wave entered into a symbiotic relationship with the academic college curriculum of the 1960s. New aesthetic and cultural journals now regularly began to include articles on the semiotics of the cinematic image by Roland Barthes and Christian Metz, so the films coming from Paris at the same time as these essays seemed particularly appropriate for serious critical study. The nouvelle vague, like the *nouveau roman*, came along at an opportune moment in the development of higher education.

A third and more immediately visible legacy can be witnessed in the ongoing output of the surviving members of the *Cahiers* directors. In the final five years of the twentieth century, for instance, Godard shot thirteen different video and film projects, including the six-part *Histoires du cinéma* and a two-part study of the origins of the twenty-first century. During those same five years, Eric Rohmer and Claude Chabrol each shot four features, while Jacques Rivette, who had been incredibly prolific throughout the 1990s as a whole, made three features and one short, and Agnès Varda produced three features. This output is amazing, considering that Chabrol and Godard, the youngest of the five, turned seventy years old and Rohmer, the oldest, reached eighty in the year 2000. And they have all continued to produce important new features and documentaries since that date, including Rohmer's *l'anglaise et le duc* (*The Lady and the Duke*, 2001) and *Triple Agent* (2004), Rivette's *Va savoir* (2001), Chabrol's *La fleur du mal* (*The Flower of Evil*, 2003), Godard's *Eloge de l'amour* (*In Praise of Love*, 2001) and *Notre musique* (2004), Resnais' *Not on the Lips* (2003), and Varda's *The Gleaners and I* (2000). Their combined filmographies are staggering in terms of sheer numbers of productions and variety of length and format, with Chabrol alone having filmed more than fifty features, not including all his made-for-television feature-length productions. Most of these directors have now worked in new media, including digital video, and blurred the boundaries between documentary, television, and narrative cinema. Making, editing, and exhibiting sounds and images occupy nearly all their time. The Turks may not have been so young any more, but they are still among the most consistently interesting and challenging directors in the world at the beginning of this new century.

NOTES
BIBLIOGRAPHY
INDEX

NOTES

Introduction

1. Michel Marie, *La nouvelle vague;* Jean Douchet, *French New Wave;* Antoine de Baecque, *La nouvelle vague;* and de Baecque and Charles Tesson, eds., *Cahiers du cinema, nouvelle vague.*

2. James Monaco, *The New Wave;* Roy Armes, *French Cinema* and *French Cinema since 1946,* vol. 2; and Alan Williams, *Republic of Images.*

3. de Baecque, *La nouvelle vague,* 52.

4. Pierre Billard, "40 moins de 40," 5.

5. Françoise Audé, *Ciné-Modèles, cinéma d'elles,* 20.

6. Marie, *La nouvelle vague,* 19.

7. "New Directors," *Le film français* 765–66 (January 30, 1959): 70.

8. Richard Neupert, "Dead Champagne," 225.

Chapter 1. Cultural Contexts

1. Evelyn Ehrlich, *Cinema of Paradox,* 172–73.

2. For excellent summaries of the purification and revitalization of French postwar cinema, see Alan Williams, *Republic of Images,* and Ehrlich, *Cinema of Paradox,* 172–77.

3. Jill Forbes and Michael Kelly, eds., *French Cultural Studies,* 141.

4. Jacques Durand, *Le cinéma et son public,* v.

5. Maurice Larkin, *France since the Popular Front,* 179.

6. Ibid., 211.

7. Forbes and Kelly, *French Cultural Studies,* 143.

8. Jean-Claude Batz, *A propos de la crise de l'industrie de cinéma,* 63.

9. Ibid., 64.

10. Colin Crisp, *The Classic French Cinema,* 73.

11. "Box Office Foes: Cars, TV, Prosperity," *Variety,* November 27, 1963, 4.

12. Batz, *A propos de la crise,* 68.

13. Pierre Autré, "Autos et 'deux roues' concurrent no 1 de cinéma," 1.

14. Roland Barthes, "La voiture, projection de l'ego," 92. For more on cars, France, and the film industry, see Kristin Ross, *Fast Cars, Clean Bodies.*

15. Tino Balio, *The American Film Industry,* 401–2.

16. André Bazin, "Le Cinemascope," 672–83.

17. Forbes and Kelly, *French Cultural Studies,* 172.

18. "La recherche d'un public," *Le Film français* 828 (April 8, 1960): 1.

19. Batz, *A propos de la crise,* 64.

20. Ibid., 71.

21. René Bonnell, *Le cinéma exploité,* 46.

22. Ibid., 52.

23. Ibid., 55.

24. Batz, *A propos de la crise,* 69.

25. "La machine à laver tourne-t-elle dans le sens de l'histoire?" *L'Express,* March 1, 1957, 14.

26. Edgar Morin, *Stars* and *Le cinéma ou l'homme imaginaire.* Morin went on to work with Jean Rouch on the famous documentary, *Chronicle of a Summer,* in 1961 and became editor of *Communications,* the leading journal on sociology, anthropology, and semiology in France.

27. "La machine à laver tourne-t-elle dans le sens de l'histoire?" 14.

28. Françoise Giroud, "Une grande enquête nationale: Répondez!" 18.

29. Luisa Passerini, "Youth as Metaphor for Social Change," 319–20.

30. Coleman quoted in ibid., 319–20.

31. Françoise Giroud, *La nouvelle vague.*

32. "Rapport national sur la jeunesse," *L'Express,* December 5, 1957, 19.

33. Jacques Siclier, *Nouvelle vague?*

34. Maurice Bessy, "Nouvelle vague . . . de spectateurs," 1.

35. Forbes and Kelly, *French Cultural Studies,* 164.

36. Georges Duby, *Histoire de la France,* 3:432.

37. Germain Brée and Eric Schoenfeld, introduction to *La jalousie,* 5.

38. Alain Robbe-Grillet, personal interview, Athens, Georgia, May 1999.

39. Forbes and Kelly, *French Cultural Studies,* 164.

40. Alain Robbe-Grillet, *For a New Novel,* 8.

41. "En retard ou en avance?" *L'Express,* October 8, 1959, 31.

42. Robbe-Grillet, *For a New Novel,* 9.

43. Ibid.

44. Ibid., 26.

45. Forbes and Kelly, *French Cultural Studies,* 150.

46. Jonathan Culler, *Structuralist Poetics,* 4.

47. Rosalind Coward and John Ellis, *Language and Materialism,* 12.

48. Roland Barthes, *Mythologies,* 9.

49. Forbes and Kelly, *French Cultural Studies,* 168.

50. Duby, *Histoire de la France,* 3:409.

51. Wallace Fowlie, *Dionysus in Paris*, 16–17.

52. Jacques Guicharnaud, *Modern French Theatre from Giraudoux to Genet*, 216.

53. Forbes and Kelly, *French Cultural Studies*, 157.

54. Ibid., 160.

55. Colin Crisp, *Eric Rohmer*, 15–16.

56. Jean-Paul Sartre, "Quand Hollywood veut faire penser . . . *Citizen Kane,* Film d'Orson Wells," 3–5, 15. See also André Bazin, "The Technique of *Citizen Kane,*" 231–39.

57. Jacques Rivette, "*Under Capricorn.*"

58. Antoine de Baecque, *Les cahiers du cinéma*, 1:51–52.

59. Jean Douchet, *French New Wave*, 91.

60. Michel Dorsdale, "Le cinéma est mort."

61. Antoine de Baecque and Serge Toubiana, *Truffaut*, 74.

62. Jim Hillier, introduction to *Cahiers du Cinéma: The 1950s*, 12.

63. Pierre Billard, *L'age classique du cinéma français*, 565.

64. "Porquoi nous combattons," *Positif* 1 (1952): 1.

65. Ibid., 2.

66. Quoted in Antoine de Beacque and Charles Tesson, "Tout a changé en Bretaigne," 15.

67. Michèle Firk, "*Le beau Serge* et *Les cousins,*" 58–60.

68. Roger Tailleur, Paul-Louis Thiraud, et al. "Quoi de neuf?" 1.

69. "Dictionnaire partiel et partial d'un nouveau cinéma français," *Positif* 46 (June 1962): 27, 22.

70. Introduction, *Cinéma 55* 1 (November 1954): 1–2.

71. "Les Responsables, les voici!" *Cinéma 59* (March 1959): 6.

72. Interview in *Cinéma 55* 2 (December 1954): 26.

73. Pierre Billard, "40 moins de 40," 5.

74. Crisp, *The Classic French Cinema*, 418.

75. Introduction, *Cinéma 55* 1 (November 1955): 4.

76. Ibid., 6.

77. "French Aid Law Finally Signed," *Variety* (June 24, 1959): 65; and "Still Argue Over French Aid Law," *Variety* (July 22, 1959): 18.

78. "Quality Demand of Malraux Collides with French Export Needs," *Variety* (October 14, 1959): 7.

79. "Coin-With-Script Spells Dull," *Variety* (November 11, 1959): 15.

80. "French Finance Minister Replaced," *Variety* (January 27, 1960): 7.

81. Francis Courtade, *Les malédictions du cinéma français*, 273.

82. "In France Too, Bankers Like Stars," *Variety* (April 20, 1960): 28.

83. René Prédal, "De bonnes recettes pour faire des économies," 73.

84. "La nouvelle vague," *Le Film français* 785 (June 5, 1959): 7.

85. Douchet, *French New Wave*, 205.

86. Ibid., 6.

87. Jean-Pierre Biesse, "Qu'est-ce que l'Art et l'Essai?" 120–22.

88. Prédal, "De bonnes recettes pour faire des économies," 77.

89. Michel Marie, *La nouvelle vague*, 58.

90. Courtade, *Les malédictions du cinéma français*, 273.

91. Quoted in Jean-Michel Frodon, *L'age moderne du cinéma français*, 117.

92. "French Film-going Lags but Trade Sees a Rebound," *Variety* (September 16, 1959): 11.

Chapter 2. Testing the Water

1. Alexandre Astruc, "The Birth of a New Avant-Garde," 17.

2. Jean Douchet, *French New Wave*, 39.

3. Alan Williams, *Republic of Images*, 306.

4. Douchet, *French New Wave*, 39.

5. Astruc, "Birth of a New Avant-Garde,"17.

6. Ibid., 17–18.

7. Ibid., 20.

8. André Bazin, *What Is Cinema?* 1:40, 1:113.

9. Astruc, "Birth of a New Avant-Garde," 20–21.

10. René Prédal, *50 ans de cinéma français*, 133; and Kristin Thompson and David Bordwell, *Film History*, 507.

11. Williams, *Republic of Images*, 306.

12. Claire Clouzot, *Le cinéma français depuis la nouvelle vague*, 7.

13. Georges Sadoul, *Dictionary of Films*, 312.

14. Clouzot, *Le cinéma français depuis la nouvelle vague*, 7.

15. Jacques Rivette, "Beauty Lies in Accuracy," 29.

16. Quoted in Sadoul, *Dictionary of Films*, 394.

17. Jean-Luc Godard, *Godard on Godard*, 95–96.

18. Ibid., 96.

19. Ibid., 91.

20. Jean-Michel Frodon, *L'age moderne du cinéma français*, 82.

21. Williams, *Republic of Images*, 307.

22. Frodon, *L'age moderne du cinéma français*, 82.

23. Prédal, *50 ans de cinéma français*, 134.

24. Frodon, *L'age moderne du cinéma français*, 83.

25. Alison Smith, *Agnès Varda*, 3.

26. Ibid., 5.

27. Pierre Billard, *L'age classique du cinéma français*, 624.

28. Pierre Uytterhoeven, "Agnès Varda de 5 à 7," 1–2.

29. André Bazin, "*La Pointe Courte:* Un film libre et pur," in *Le cinéma français de la liberation à la nouvelle vague,* 194.

30. Billard, *L'age classique du cinéma français,* 624; Bazin, *Le cinéma français de la liberation,* 195.

31. Georges Sadoul, *Dictionary of Films,* 288.

32. Michel Marie, *La nouvelle vague,* 46.

33. Smith, *Agnès Varda,* 6–7.

34. Gerald Mast and Bruce F. Kawin, *A Short History of the Movies,* 372.

35. Colin Crisp, *The Classic French Cinema,* 281.

36. Susan Hayward, *French National Cinema,* 192.

37. Billard, *L'age classique du cinéma français,* 603.

38. Jacques Zimmer and Chantal de Béchade, *Jean-Pierre Melville,* 43.

39. David Bordwell, *On the History of Film Style,* 57–58.

40. Prédal, *50 ans de cinéma français,* 73.

41. Billard, *L'age classique du cinéma français,* 604.

42. Claude Chabrol, "Jean-Pierre Melville," 75.

43. Williams, *Republic of Images,* 334.

44. Peter Hogue, "Melville,"18.

45. Billard, *L'age classique du cinéma français,* 604.

46. Zimmer and de Béchade, *Jean-Pierre Melville,* 41.

47. Cited in Marie, *La nouvelle vague,* 45.

48. Crisp, *Classic French Cinema,* 82.

Chapter 3. New Stories, New Sex

1. Roger Vadim, *Memoirs of the Devil,* 66.

2. Ibid., 93.

3. Ibid.

4. Quoted in Françoise Audé, *Ciné-modèles, cinéma d'elles,* 25.

5. Michel Marie, *La nouvelle vague,* 94.

6. Audé, *Ciné-modèles, cinéma d'elles,* 25, 30.

7. Antoine de Baecque, *La nouvelle vague,* 19.

8. Ibid., 20.

9. Audé, *Ciné-modèles, cinéma d'elles,* 24.

10. Susan Hayward, *French National Cinema,* 178.

11. Audé, *Ciné-modèles, cinéma d'elles,* 25.

12. Jean-Luc Douin, "La république des gamins et des copains," in *La nouvelle vague 25 ans après,* 17.

13. Nick Roddick, "*And God Created Woman,*" 106.

14. Pierre Billard, " La jeune académie du cinéma français," 33.

15. Jean-Luc Godard, "Sufficient Evidence," 47.

16. Jean-Pierre Jeancolas, *Histoire du cinéma français*, 74.

17. "Interview with François Truffaut," in *The New Wave*, ed. Peter Graham, 92.

18. Jeancolas, *Histoire du cinéma français*, 74.

19. "Cent soixante-deux nouveaux cinéastes français," *Cahiers du cinéma* 138 (December 1962): 75.

20. Alan Williams, *Republic of Images*, 340.

21. Ginette Vincendeau, *The Companion to French Cinema*, 99.

22. Philip French, ed., *Malle on Malle*, 8.

23. Ibid., 10.

24. Williams, *Republic of Images*, 341.

25. Jacques Siclier, *Nouvelle vague?* 63.

26. French, introduction to *Malle on Malle*, xiii.

27. Quoted in *"Les Amants* et la presse," *Avant scène* 2 (March 15, 1961): 36.

28. French, *Malle on Malle*, 19.

29. The band that night included Kenny Clarke on drums, Barney Willen on tenor sax, René Urtreger on piano, and bassist Pierre Michelot.

30. Richard Williams, *Miles Davis*, 72–73.

31. Ibid., 73.

32. Georges Sadoul, *Le cinéma français*, 136.

33. French, *Malle on Malle*, 16.

34. Ibid., 11–12.

35. Noel Calef, *Ascenseur pour l'echafaud*, 61.

36. French, *Malle on Malle*, 22.

37. Pierre Billard, *L'age classique du cinéma français*, 107.

38. Jacques Doniol-Valcroze, "Le pouvoir de la nuit," 43.

39. André Bazin, *Avant scène* 2 (March 15, 1961): 36.

40. Eventually, the Ohio Supreme Court ruled in favor of Allen S. Warth of the Art Theatre and overturned the fine and correction farm sentence.

41. T. Jefferson Kline, *Screening the Text*, 28.

42. Ellen Fitzpatrick, review of *The Lovers*, 561–62.

43. See Michel Chion, *Audio-Vision*, 182–83.

44. Michel Flacon, review of *Les Amants*, 105.

45. From an interview on *Fresh Air*, National Public Radio, May 1994.

46. French, *Malle on Malle*, 22.

47. Eugen Weber, "An Escapist Realism," 11.

48. French, *Malle on Malle*, 21–24.

49. David Bordwell, *On the History of Film Style*, 65.

50. Review of *Les Amants*, *Le Film français* 755 (November 21, 1958): 17.

51. René Prédal, *50 ans de cinéma français*, 132.

52. Peter Graham, "New Directions in French Cinema," 578–80.

53. French, *Malle on Malle*, 30.

Chapter 4. Claude Chabrol

1. Claire Clouzot, *Le cinéma français depuis la nouvelle vague,* 29.

2. See, for instance, Roy Armes, *French Cinema since 1946,* 2:43; and Joel Magny *Claude Chabrol,* 9. Charles Ford even calls *The Cousins* "the most representative and masterful film of the New Wave" (Ford, *Histoire du cinéma français contemporain,* 159).

3. Claude Chabrol, *Et pourtant je tourne.* In the acronym AJYM, *A* is for his wife Agnès, *JY* for son Jean-Yves, and *M* for son Mathieu. The fact that Chabrol began his career thanks to Agnes's inheritance was responsible for his eventual loss of AJYM and most of his earned capital when he divorced her several years later.

4. René Prédal, "De bonnes recettes pour faire des économies," 76.

5. Note also the biographical aspects of *Le beau Serge:* the Chabrols lost a first child, and Claude had recently suffered from a lung disease; both events occur in *Le beau Serge.* Moreover, Chabrol, who liked *Bob le flambeur,* used its cinematographer, Henri Decae, and the actor Claude Cerval as the curate.

6. Claude Chabrol and Gilbert Salachas, "Claude Chabrol," 163.

7. Prédal, " De bonnes recettes pour faire des économies," 76.

8. Jean Curtelin, "Marée montante? En ligne droite de Melville à Chabrol," 6; and Prédal, "De bonnes recettes pour faire des économies," 76.

9. Chabrol, *Et pourtant je tourne,* 138–39.

10. Ford, *Histoire du cinéma français contemporain,* 158.

11. Jacques Siclier, *Nouvelle vague?* 67.

12. Roy Armes, *French Cinema,* 177; Ford, *Histoire du cinéma français contemporain,* 160.

13. Georges Sadoul, "Un film néo-romantique: *Les cousins,*" 7.

14. Robin Wood and Michael Walker, *Claude Chabrol,* 8.

15. Luc Moullet, "La balance et le lien," 31.

16. Magny, *Claude Chabrol,* 41.

17. Don Allen, "Claude Chabrol," 55.

18. Magny, *Claude Chabrol,* 83.

19. André S. Labarthe, cited in Guy Braucourt, *Claude Chabrol.*

20. Siclier, *Nouvelle Vague?* 67.

21. Rainer Werner Fassbinder, "Insects in a Glass Case," 205.

22. Charles Derry, "Claude Chabrol," 131.

23. An example of Chabrol's role in complicating his own political stance is evident in *Et pourtant je tourne* when he claims to have been a leftist Catholic in the middle 1950s; yet he occasionally frequented a right-wing hangout of Jean-Marie Le Pen, the notorious racist, fascist politician who later bragged of having tortured and killed Algerians during the war. See pages 81–83 and 144.

24. Braucourt, *Claude Chabrol.*

25. James Monaco, *The New Wave,* 257.

26. René Prédal, *50 ans de cinéma français*, 235.

27. Raymonde Borde, "Cinéma français d'aujourd'hui," 30.

28. Fassbinder, "Insects in a Glass Case," 252.

29. Braucourt, *Claude Chabrol*, 58.

30. Allen, "Claude Chabrol," 58.

31. David Overbey, "Chabrol: Game of Mirrors," 81.

32. R. P. Kolker, *The Altering Eye*, 184.

33. Claude Chabrol, "La peau, l'air et l'inconscient," 24.

34. Magny, *Claude Chabrol*, 40.

35. Derry, "Claude Chabrol," 132.

36. For more on point of view procedures and vocabulary, see Edward Branigan, *Point of View in the Cinema*, 103.

37. Chabrol, "La peau, l'air et l'inconscient," 24.

38. Alan Williams, *Republic of Images*, 345.

39. Paul Monaco, *Ribbons in Time*, 43–44.

40. Wood and Walker, *Claude Chabrol*, 13.

41. Chabrol, "La peau, l'air et l'inconscient," 24.

42. Marc Ruscart, "Des petits matins de la Cinémathèque au foyer des *Cahiers*," 33.

43. Antoine de Baecque, *La nouvelle vague*, 89.

44. Guy Austin, *Claude Chabrol*, 7.

45. See Michel Mardore, "Entretien," 8.

46. J. L. Cros, "*Les cousins*," 33.

47. Mardore, "Entretien," 9.

48. Ruscart, "Des petits matins," 33.

49. Cros, "*Les Cousins*," 33.

50. The ad campaign by North American distributor Joseph E. Levine featured the line "His women always meet their match" while a caricature of Landru, complete with a riding crop, stands under the portraits of eleven women.

51. Wood and Walker, *Claude Chabrol*, 81.

52. Magny, *Claude Chabrol*, 117.

53. Stanley Kauffman notes that the sets never look like places of murder or a murderer's home. Moreover, Fernande's apartment looks like something right out of a Colette novel (*A World on Film*, 256).

54. Austin, *Claude Chabrol*, 5.

55. Ibid., 34.

Chapter 5. François Truffaut

1. Kristin Thompson and David Bordwell, *Film History*, 525.

2. See, for instance, François Truffaut, *Correspondence;* Anne Gillain, *Le*

cinéma selon François Truffaut; Antoine de Baecque and Serge Toubiana, *Truffaut;* and Wheeler Winston Dixon, *The Early Film Criticism of François Truffaut.*

3. From an interview in *Arts* (March 20, 1968) reprinted in François Truffaut, *Truffaut by Truffaut,* 33.

4. Truffaut, *Truffaut by Truffaut,* 60.

5. Jean-Michel Frodon, *L'age moderne du cinéma français,* 47.

6. De Baecque and Toubiana, *Truffaut,* 89.

7. Gillain, *Le cinéma selon François Truffaut,* 83, 42.

8. See, for instance, Alan Williams, *Republic of Images,* 349; Williams argues that Madeleine's dowry helped make *Les mistons,* and then Morgenstern wanted to see Truffaut's "comeuppance" so lent him money for *The 400 Blows.*

9. Gillain, *Le cinéma selon François Truffaut,* 84.

10. Michel Marie, *La nouvelle vague,* 72.

11. Ibid., 101.

12. Truffaut, *Correspondence,* 111.

13. See, for instance, Annette Insdorf, *François Truffaut,* 106.

14. Ibid., 145.

15. Michèle Firk, "L'anachronique jeunesse du cinéma français," 67.

16. de Baecque and Serge Toubiana, *François Truffaut,* 124.

17. Ibid., 126.

18. Truffaut, *Truffaut by Truffaut,* 57.

19. de Baecque and Toubiana, *François Truffaut,* 128.

20. For a detailed study of *The 400 Blows* and its narrative strategies, see Richard Neupert, *The End,* 75–110.

21. Gillain, *Le cinéma selon François Truffaut,* 25.

22. For more on the fascinating details of Truffaut's childhood, see ibid., 15–25; de Baecque and Toubiana, *Truffaut,* 3–45; and Truffaut, *Truffaut by Truffaut,* 11–18.

23. Aline Desjardins, *Truffaut,* 40.

24. Murray Smith, "Altered States: Character and Emotional Response in the Cinema," 41.

25. Review of *The 400 Blows, Cinéma 60* 42 (January 1960): 14.

26. Franz Wegerganz, review of *The 400 Blows, Amis du film* 50 (October 1959): 2–3.

27. James Monaco, *The New Wave,* 21.

28. For more on the soundtrack, see Richard Neupert, "The Musical Score as Closure Device in *The 400 Blows.*"

29. Gillain, *Le cinéma selon François Truffaut,* 92.

30. Wegerganz, review of *The 400 Blows,* 2.

31. "Questions à l'auteur," *Cinéma 61* 52 (January 1961): 7–11.

32. Hélène Laroche Davis, "Interview with François Truffaut," 121.

33. Truffaut, *Truffaut by Truffaut,* 69.

34. Quoted in de Baecque and Toubiana, *Truffaut*, 157.

35. René Lefevre, *"Tirez sur le pianiste,"* 26.

36. Cited in de Baecque and Toubiana, *Truffaut*, 171.

37. Review of *Shoot the Piano Player, Cinéma 61* 53 (February 1961): 101.

38. Peter Brunette, *"Shoot the Piano Player* as Postmodern Text," 17.

39. Bosley Crowther, review of *Shoot the Piano Player*, 158–59.

40. Colin Crisp, *François Truffaut*, 65.

41. Truffaut, *Truffaut by Truffaut*, 75.

42. "Woman-on-Shuttle in *Jules and Jim* Amoral," *Variety* (May 2, 1962): 7.

43. "Janus Films Fights Legion Ratings of *Jules and Jim* by Plugging 'Condemned' Tag," *Variety* (October 29, 1962): 11.

44. René Prédal, *50 ans de cinéma français*, 233.

45. T. Jefferson Kline asserts that the beetle on the window is an accident of shooting but nonetheless offers different interpretations of its possible significance. See *Screening the Text*, 15–16.

46. Frodon, *L'age moderne du cinéma français*, 50.

47. David Nicholls, *François Truffaut*, 36.

Chapter 6. Jean-Luc Godard

1. Colin MacCabe, "A Life in Seven Episodes (to date)," 16.

2. Wheeler Winston Dixon, *The Films of Jean-Luc Godard*, 11–12.

3. Antoine de Baecque and Serge Toubiana, *Truffaut*, 151.

4. Michel Marie, "It Really Makes You Sick! Jean-Luc Godard's *A bout de souffle*," 201.

5. "Statements: François Truffaut," in *Breathless*, ed. Dudley Andrew, 177.

6. Antoine de Baecque, *La nouvelle vague*, 82.

7. "Statements: Raoul Coutard," in Andrew, *Breathless*, 176.

8. "*Cahiers* Interview with Godard," in Jean-Luc Godard, *Godard on Godard*, 173.

9. François Truffaut, "The Original Treatment," 160. For another early version of Truffaut's proposed ending see Michel Marie, *A bout de souffle*, 36.

10. James Monaco, *The New Wave*, 98.

11. David Bordwell and Kristin Thompson, *Film Art*, 399.

12. David Bordwell, "Jump Cuts and Blind Spots," 5–6.

13. For more on Godard and dysnarration, see Richard Neupert, *The End*, 137–38.

14. Marie, "It Really Makes You Sick!" 208–9.

15. Michèle Manceaux, "Learning Not to Be Bitter: Interview with Jean-Luc Godard," 26.

16. Frodon, *L'age moderne du cinéma français*, 54.

17. Godard, "Interview with Godard," *Godard on Godard*, 178–79.

18. Manceaux, "Learning Not to Be Bitter," 27.

19. See "Une femme est une femme," *Cahiers du cinéma* 98 (August 1959): 46–51. The names of the principal characters in that version are Josette, Emile, and Paul. The full script, though with some errors of translation and description, is reprinted in English; see Jean-Luc Godard, *A Woman Is a Woman, A Married Man, Two or Three Things I Know about Her: Three Films*.

20. Monaco, *The New Wave*, 116.

21. Manceaux, "Learning Not to Be Bitter," 30.

22. André S. Labarthe, quoted in Jean Douchet, *French New Wave*, 179.

23. Alain Bergala, "La couleur, la nouvelle vague et ses maitres des années cinquante," 128.

24. Noel Benoit, *L'histoire du cinéma couleur*, 210.

25. Ibid., 209.

26. Jacques Rivette, "The Age of Metteurs en scène," 275, 279.

27. Quoted in Bergala, " La couleur, la nouvelle vague et ses maitres des années cinquante," 130.

28. Godard, *"The Pajama Game," Godard on Godard*, 87.

29. Jacques Aumont, *L'oeil interminable*, 229.

30. Benoit, *L'histoire du cinéma couleur*, 213.

31. David Bordwell, *The Cinema of Eisenstein*, 189.

32. Aumont, *L'oeil interminable*, 247.

33. V. F. Perkins, *"Vivre sa vie,"* 33.

34. Godard, "Interview with Godard," *Godard on Godard*, 180.

35. Ibid., 185.

36. Perkins, *"Vivre sa vie,"* 32, 32–33.

37. Dixon, *Films of Jean-Luc Godard*, 32.

38. Perkins, *"Vivre sa vie,"* 33; see also David Bordwell, *Narration and the Fiction Film*, 281–82.

39. Bordwell, *Narration and the Fiction Film*, 281.

40. Godard, "Interview with Godard," *Godard on Godard*, 182.

41. Ibid., 188.

42. Douchet, *French New Wave*, 209.

43. Jacques Siclier, "Et la presse," 42.

44. Dixon, *Films of Jean-Luc Godard*, 39; note that Dixon bases his claim on the alternations of *Breathless*, followed by *Le petit soldat*, then *A Woman Is a Woman*, followed by *Les carabiniers*, but he leaves *Vivre sa vie* out of the sequence.

45. Bordwell, *Narration and the Fiction Film*, 321.

46. Anne Gillain, *François Truffaut*, 293.

47. Richard Roud, *Godard*, 99.

Chapter 7. The *Cahiers du cinéma* Cohort

1. Colin Crisp, *Eric Rohmer*, 19.
2. Joel Magny, *Eric Rohmer*, 7.
3. Antoine de Baecque, *Les cahiers du cinéma*, 1:221.
4. Crisp, *Eric Rohmer*, 3.
5. Ibid., 17.
6. Claude Chabrol, *Et pourtant je tourne*, 86–87.
7. Crisp, *Eric Rohmer*, 23.
8. François Truffaut, *Correspondence*, 131.
9. Magny, *Eric Rohmer*, 107.
10. Jean Collet, *Le cinéma en question*, 168.
11. Jean-Michel Frodon, *L'age moderne du cinéma français*, 61.
12. Crisp, *Eric Rohmer*, 28.
13. Ibid., 29.
14. Claude Beylie, "*Le signe du lion*," 111.
15. Jean Douchet, *French New Wave*, 172.
16. Crisp, *Eric Rohmer*, 34.
17. Frodon, *L'age moderne du cinéma français*, 62, 63.
18. Crisp, *Eric Rohmer*, 38.
19. Ginette Vincendeau, *The Companion to French Cinema*, 129.
20. Douchet, *French New Wave*, 173.
21. Quoted in Magny, *Eric Rohmer*, 120.
22. Michel Marie, *La nouvelle vague*, 64, 76.
23. Douchet, *French New Wave*, 173.
24. Magny, *Eric Rohmer*, 28.
25. Eric Rohmer, *The Taste of Beauty*, 39.
26. Ibid., 67.
27. Claudine Bouché, Denise de Casabianca, and Agnès Guillemot, "Montage, notre beau souci," 46.
28. Ibid.
29. Chabrol, *Et pourtant je tourne*, 109.
30. Jacques Rivette, "On Imagination," 104–5.
31. André Bazin, Jacques Doniol-Valcroze, Pierre Kast, Roger Leenhardt, Jacques Rivette, and Eric Rohmer, "Six Characters in Search of *Auteurs*," 31.
32. "Dictionnaire partiel et partial d'un nouveau cinéma français," *Positif* (June 1962): 35.
33. Jacques Rivette, "*Paris nous appartient*," 34–35.
34. James Monaco, *The New Wave*, 308.
35. Roy Armes, *French Cinema since 1946*, 2:94.
36. Frodon, *L'age moderne du cinéma français*, 59.
37. Marie, *La nouvelle vague*, 75.

38. " Dictionnaire partiel et partial d'un nouveau cinéma français," 35.

39. Claire Clouzot, *Le cinéma français depuis la nouvelle vague*, 142.

40. Bazin, et al., "Six Characters in Search of *Auteurs*," 43.

41. "Lexique de la nouvelle vague," *Cinéma 60* 45 (April 1960): 98.

42. Marie, *La nouvelle vague*, 89.

43. *"L'eau à la bouche," Le Film français* 819 (February 5, 1960): 24

44. Gérard Langlois, "Françoise Brion," 111.

45. Ibid.,109.

46. Louis Marcorelles, "Jacques, ou la soumission," 54, 56.

47. Freddy Buache, *Nouvelle vague*, 61.

48. Marcorelles, "Jacques, ou la soumission," 56.

49. de Baecque, *Les cahiers du cinéma*, 1:216.

50. Gérard Langlois, "Pierre Kast," 155.

51. Louis Séguin, "Questions à Pierre Kast," 29.

52. Marie, *La nouvelle vague*, 89.

53. Frodon, *L'age moderne du cinéma français*, 83.

54. Ibid.

55. Antoine de Baecque, *La nouvelle vague*, 100.

56. Frodon, *L'age moderne du cinéma français*, 83.

Chapter 8. On the New Wave's Left Bank

1. Raymond Lefevre, "Où va la nouvelle vague?" *Image et son* 130 (April 1960): 5.

2. *Variety* (31 October 1962): 24.

3. Robert Benayoun, *Alain Resnais*, 17–19; see also James Monaco, *Alain Resnais*, 15–17, in which he writes that Resnais was able to "reconcile the adventures of Albertine with the drastically contrasting exploits of Terry and the Pirates"; and John Ward, *Alain Resnais, or the Theme of Time*, 7, 14–15.

4. Alain Resnais, *Ciné-Club* 3 (December, 1948); cited in Alain Fleischer, *l'Art d'Alain Resnais*, 60.

5. Jean-Luc Godard, *Godard on Godard*, 115–16.

6. Roy Armes, *The Cinema of Alain Resnais*, 31.

7. Quoted in ibid.

8. Gaston Bounoure, *Alain Resnais*, 127.

9. François Chalais, "Television Interview," *Cinépanorama*, 1961 (available now on Criterion *Hiroshima, mon amour* DVD).

10. Frédérique Lebelley, *Duras ou le poids d'une plume*, 184.

11. Benayoun, *Alain Resnais*, 65.

12. Marguerite Duras, "Resnais Travaille comme un romancier," 8.

13. Bernard Pingaud, "A propos de *Hiroshima mon amour*," 2.

14. Roy Armes, *The Cinema of Alain Resnais*, 27.

15. Richard Neupert, "'Dead Champagne,'" 227.

16. Jean Domarchi, Jacques Doniol-Valcroze, Jean-Luc Godard, Pierre Kast, Jacques Rivette, and Eric Rohmer, *"Hiroshima, notre amour,"* in Hillier, *Cahiers du Cinéma: The 1950s*, 60–61, 69.

17. Jacques Chevalier, *"Hiroshima mon amour,"* *Image et son* 124 (October 1959): 24.

18. James M. Vest, *Hitchcock and France*, 190.

19. Christophe Carlier, *Marguerite Duras, Alain Resnais*, 6.

20. Max Egly, "Rencontre avec Alain Resnais," *Image et son* 128 (February 1960): 7.

21. Marguerite Duras, *Hiroshima mon amour*, 13.

22. Domarchi et. al., *"Hiroshima, notre amour,"* 69.

23. Pierre Marcabru, "A Film That Pierces the Darkness," *Combat* (13 June 1959), quoted in Douchet, *French New Wave*, 131.

24. Kristin Thompson and David Bordwell, *Film History*, 449.

25. Robert Sklar, *Film*, 336–37.

26. Susan Sontag, *"Muriel,"* 23.

27. André S. Labarthe and Jacques Rivette, "Entretien avec Resnais et Robbe-Grillet," 13.

28. Alain Robbe-Grillet, *Last Year at Marienbad*, 46.

29. Thompson and Bordwell, *Film History*, 450.

30. By contrast, John Ward argues that it is a straight forward tale, in which M kills A for her affair with X, and X is "left alone to mourn" at the end. See *Alain Resnais, or the Theme of Time*, 39.

31. Fernaldo di Giammetteo, "'Marienbadism' and the New Italian Directors," 20.

32. "French Producers: 'Watch our speed in American playoff during 1962,'" *Variety* (December 20, 1961): 3.

33. James Reid Paris, *The Great French Films*, 183.

34. Robert Benayoun, *"l'année dernière à Marienbad* ou les exorcismes du réel," 36–37.

35. T. Jefferson Kline, *Screening the Text*, 55–57.

36. Ado Kyrou, *"l'année dernière à Marienbad*, Les rencontres parallèles," 66–67.

37. "International Sound Track," *Variety* (September 5, 1962): 15.

38. André S. Labarthe, "Marienbad Year Zero," in Hillier, *Cahiers du Cinéma: The 1960s*, 54–55.

39. For examples of such devices in *l'Immortelle* see Richard Neupert, *The End*, 140–41.

40. Fleischer, *l'art d'Alain Resnais*, 32–33.

41. See Max Egly, "Varda, Resnais, Marker," 5.

42. André Gardies, *Le cinéma de Robbe-Grillet*, 14–15.

43. Rémi Fournier Lanzoni, *French Cinema from Its Beginnings to the Present*, 229.

44. Jean Douchet, *French New Wave*, 190–93.

45. James Monaco, *Alain Resnais*, 74.

46. Susan Sontag, "*Muriel*," 24.

47. Jean Cayrol, *Muriel*, 15.

48. Claude Bailblé, Michel Marie, and Marie-Claire Ropars, *Muriel: histoire d'un recherche*.

49. Michel Marie, *Muriel d'Alain Resnais*.

50. "Deux poles d'une modernité," *Cahiers du cinéma* 147 (September 1963): 42; "Petit journal du cinéma," *Cahiers du cinéma* 145 (August 1963): 36; and "Les malheurs de *Muriel*," *Cahiers du cinéma* 149 (November 1963): 20–34.

51. Jean-Luc Douin, *La nouvelle vague 25 ans après*, 17.

52. "Resnais' Own Credo 'Commonsensical'," *Variety* (December 13, 1961): 16.

53. David Bordwell, *Narration in the Fiction Film*, 213.

54. Agnès Varda, University of Wisconsin–Madison, October 3–5, 2002.

55. Agnès Varda, *Varda par Agnès*, 229.

56. Ibid., 230.

57. Paul Davay, cited in ibid., 231.

58. Sandy Flitterman-Lewis, *To Desire Differently*, 227.

59. Jean Douchet, *Arts* 726 (July 10, 1959).

60. François Truffaut, *Cahiers du cinéma* 84 (June 1958): 42; Jean-Luc Godard, *Cahiers du cinéma* 92 (February 1959): 36.

61. Agnès Varda, *Varda par Agnès*, 57.

62. Yvonne Baby, interview with Varda, *Le Monde* (April 12, 1962).

63. Agnès Varda, University of Wisconsin–Madison, October 3–5, 2002.

64. Sandy Flitterman-Lewis, *To Desire Differently*, 268.

65. Alison Smith, *Agnès Varda*, 101–2.

66. Janice Mouton, "From Feminine Masquerade to Flâneuse," 12.

67. Claudia Gorbman, "Cleo from Five to Seven," 46.

68. Claudine Delvaux, "Agnès Varda cinéphotographe,"25.

69. Roger Tailleur, "*Cléo, d'ici à l'éternité*."

70. Bosley Crowther, *New York Times* (September 5, 1962): 43, 4.

71. Agnès Varda, *Varda par Agnès*, 65.

72. Bosley Crowther, *New York Times* (May 24, 1966): 55, 2.

73. Alison Smith, *Agnès Varda*, 45.

74. Georges Sadoul, *Dictionary of Films*, 39.

75. Alan Williams, *Republic of Images*, 358–59.

76. Claire Johnston, "Women's Cinema as Counter-Cinema," 216.

77. Sandy Flitterman-Lewis, *To Desire Differently*, 232–33.

78. Pam Cook, *The Cinema Book*, 308.

79. *"Le bonheur," Le film français* 1083 (February 26, 1965): 13.

80. Jean-Michel Frodon, personal interview, June 24, 2005, Paris.

81. Sandy Flitterman-Lewis, *To Desire Differently*, 262.

82. *Cinéma 60* 44 (March, 1960): 6.

Conclusion

1. Gene Moskowitz, "Parisian Film Pros Ridicule New Wave," *Variety* (January 6, 1960): 43.

2. Gene Moskowitz, "'New Wave': Dead Champagne; but Gave France Passing Tonic." *Variety* (May 11, 1960): 5.

3. David Bordwell, *Ozu and the Poetics of Cinema*, 162–63.

4. Claire Clouzot, *Le Cinéma français depuis la nouvelle vague*, 150.

5. Jean-Pierre Berthomé, *Jacques Demy et les racines du rêve*, 109.

6. Jacques Demy files, Ciné-Tamaris.

7. Tassone, *Que reste-t-il de la nouvelle vague?*, 98.

BIBLIOGRAPHY

Allen, Don. "Claude Chabrol." *Screen* 11, no. 1 (January–February 1970).

Allombert, Guy. "*Le beau Serge.*" *Image et son* 115 (February 1959): 16.

Andrew, Dudley, ed. *Breathless.* New Brunswick, N.J.: Rutgers University Press, 1995.

Armes, Roy. *The Cinema of Alain Resnais.* New York: A. S. Barnes, 1968.

Armes, Roy. *French Cinema.* New York: Oxford University Press, 1985.

Armes, Roy. *French Cinema since 1946.* Vol. 2. London: A. Zwemmer, 1970.

Astruc, Alexandre. "The Birth of a New Avant-Garde: La Caméra-stylo." In *The New Wave,* edited by Peter Graham, 17–22. First published as "Naissance d'une nouvelle avant-garde: La caméra-stylo" in *L'Ecran français* 144 (March 30, 1948).

Audé, Françoise. *Ciné-modèles, cinéma d'elles: Situations de femmes dans le cinéma français, 1956–1979.* Paris: L'Age d'homme, 1981.

Aumont, Jacques. *L'oeil interminable: Cinéma et peinture.* Paris: Seguier, 1989.

Austin, Guy. *Claude Chabrol.* Manchester: Manchester University Press, 1999.

Autré, Pierre, "Autos et 'deux roues' concurrent no 1 de cinema." *Le Film français* 852 (September 30, 1960).

Bailblé, Claude, Michel Marie, and Marie-Claire Ropars. *Muriel: Histoire d'un recherche.* Paris: Editions Galilée, 1974.

Balio, Tino. *The American Film Industry.* Madison: University of Wisconsin Press, 1985.

Barthes, Roland. "Eléments de sémiologie." *Communications* 4 (1964): 91–135.

Barthes, Roland. *Image / Music / Text.* Translated by Stephen Heath. New York: Hill and Wang, 1977.

Barthes, Roland. *Mythologies.* Translated by Annette Lavers. New York: Vintage, 1993.

Barthes, Roland. "La voiture, projection de l'ego." *Realités* 213 (October 1963): 92–97.

Batz, Jean-Claude. *A propos de la crise de l'industrie de cinéma.* Brussels: Université Libre de Bruxelles, 1963.

Bazin, André. *Le cinéma français de la libération à la nouvelle vague (1945–1958).* Paris: Cahiers du cinéma, 1983.

Bazin, André. "Le Cinemascope." *Esprit* 21, nos. 207–8 (October–November

1953): 672–83. Reprinted as "Will Cinemascope Save the Cinema?" translated by Richard Neupert and Catherine M. Jones, *Velvet Light Trap* 21 (summer 1985): 9–14.

Bazin, André. *French Cinema of the Occupation and Resistance.* Translated by Stanley Hochman. New York: Frederick Ungar, 1981.

Bazin, André. "The Technique of *Citizen Kane.*" In *Bazin at Work,* edited by Bert Cardullo. New York: Routledge, 1997.

Bazin, André. *What Is Cinema?* Vol. 1 Translated by Hugh Gray. Berkeley: University of California Press, 1967.

Bazin, André, Jacques Doniol-Valcroze, Pierre Kast, Roger Leenhardt, Jacques Rivette, and Eric Rohmer. "Six Characters in Search of *Auteurs.*" In *Cahiers du Cinéma,* edited by Jim Hillier.

Beauchamp, Cari, and Henri Béhar. *Hollywood on the Riviera: The Inside Story of the Cannes Film Festival.* New York: William Morrow, 1992.

Benayoun, Robert. *Alain Resnais: Arpenteur de l'imaginaire.* Paris: Stock, 1980.

Benayoun, Robert. "The King Is Naked." In *The New Wave,* edited by Peter Graham, 157–80. New York: Doubleday, 1968.

Benayoun, Robert. "*L'année dernière à Marienbad* ou les exorcismes du réel." *Positif* 44 (March 1962).

Benoit, Noel. *L'histoire du cinéma couleur.* Croissy-sur-Seine: Press Communication, 1995.

Bergala, Alain. "La couleur, la nouvelle vague et ses maitres des années cinquante." In *La couleur en cinema,* edited by Jacques Aumont. Paris: Cinémathèque Française, 1995.

Berthomé, Jean-Pierre. *Jacques Demy et les racines du rêve.* Nantes: L'Atalante, 1996.

Bessy, Maurice. "Nouvelle vague . . . de spectateurs." *Le film français* 793–94 (August 21, 1959).

Beylie, Claude. "*Le signe du lion.*" In *La nouvelle vague,* edited by Antoine de Baecque and Charles Tesson, 105–20. Paris: Cahiers du cinéma, 1999.

Biesse, Jean-Pierre. "Qu'est-ce que l'Art et l'Essai?" *Cahiers du cinéma* 161–62 (January 1965): 120–23.

Biette, Jean-Claude, Jacques Bontemps and Jean-Louis Comolli. "Entretien avec Eric Rohmer." In *La nouvelle vague,* edited by Antoine de Baecque and Charles Tesson, 131–63. Paris: Cahiers du cinéma, 1999.

Billard, Ginette. "Jacques Demy and His Other World." *Film Quarterly* 18, no. 1 (fall 1964): 23–27.

Billard, Pierre, "40 moins de 40: La jeune academie du cinéma français," *Cinéma 58* 24 (February 1958).

Billard, Pierre. *L'age classique du cinéma français: Du cinéma parlant à la nouvelle vague.* Paris: Flammarion, 1995.

Billard, Pierre. "La jeune académie du cinéma français: Conclusions provisoires." *Cinéma 58* 24 (February 1958): 31–34.

Bonnell, René. *Le cinéma exploité.* Paris: Editions du Seuil, 1978.

Borde, Raymonde. "Cinéma français d'aujourd'hui." *Prémier Plan* 10 (June 1960).

Bordwell, David. *The Cinema of Eisenstein.* Cambridge, Mass.: Harvard University Press, 1993.

Bordwell, David. "Jump Cuts and Blind Spots." *Wide Angle* 6 (1984): 5–6. Reprinted as "La saute et l'ellipse," *Revue belge du cinéma* (summer 1986): 86–87.

Bordwell, David. *Narration and the Fiction Film.* Madison: University of Wisconsin Press, 1985.

Bordwell, David. *On the History of Film Style.* Cambridge, Mass.: Harvard University Press, 1998.

Bordwell, David. *Ozu and the Poetics of Cinema.* Princeton, N.J.: Princeton University Press, 1988.

Bordwell, David, and Kristin Thompson. *Film Art.* New York: McGraw-Hill, 2000.

Bost, Pierre. "Dialogue à une voix." *Cinéma 55* 2 (December 1954): 25–28.

Bost, Pierre. "Pourquoi nous combattons." *Positif* 1 (May 1952): 1–2.

Bouché, Claudine, Denise de Casabianca, and Agnès Guillemot. "Montage, notre beau souci." *Cahiers du cinema, nouvelle vague: Une légende en question* (special issue 1998): 46.

Bounoure, Gaston. *Alain Resnais.* Paris: Seghers, 1974.

Branigan, Edward. *Point of View in the Cinema.* New York: Mouton, 1984.

Braucourt, Guy. *Claude Chabrol.* Paris: Seghers, 1971.

Brée, Germain and Eric Schoenfeld. *La jalousie.* New York: Macmillan, 1963.

Brown, Royal S., ed. *Focus on Godard.* Englewood Cliffs, N.J.: Prentice-Hall, 1972.

Brunette, Peter, ed. *Shoot the Piano Player.* New Brunswick, N.J.: Rutgers University Press, 1993.

Brunette, Peter. "*Shoot the Piano Player* as Postmodern Text." In *Shoot the Piano Player*, edited by Brunette.

Buache, Freddy. *Le cinéma français des années 60s.* Lausanne: Five Continents/Hatier, 1987.

Buache, Freddy. *Nouvelle vague.* Paris: Serdoc, 1962.

Burch, Noel. "Qu'est-ce que la nouvelle vague?" *Film Quarterly* 13, no. 2 (winter 1959): 16–30.

Buss, Robin. *The French Through Their Films.* New York: Ungar, 1988.

Calef, Noel. *Ascenseur pour l'échafaud.* Paris: Arthème Fayard, 1956.

Cameron, Ian, ed. *The Films of Jean-Luc Godard.* New York: Praeger, 1970.

Carlier, Christophe. *Marguerite Duras, Alain Resnais: Hiroshima mon amour.* Paris: Presses Universitaires de France, 1994.

Cayrol, Jean. *Muriel.* Paris: Editions du Seuil, 1963.

Chabrol, Claude. *Et pourtant je tourne.* Paris: R. Laffont, 1976.

Chabrol, Claude. "Jean-Pierre Melville: L'homme au stetson." *Cahiers du cinéma* 507 (November 1996): 74–75.

Chabrol, Claude. "La peau, l'air et l'inconscient." *Cahiers du cinéma* 83 (May 1958).

Chabrol, Claude, and Gilbert Salachas. "Claude Chabrol." In *La nouvelle vague 25 ans après,* edited by Jean-Luc Douin.

Champagne, Roland. *Literary History in the Wake of Roland Barthes.* Birmingham, Ala.: Summa Publications, 1984.

Chevalier, J. "*Hiroshima mon amour* et *Les 400 coups.*" *Image et son* 124 (October 1959): 24–25.

Chion, Michel. *Audio-Vision.* Translated by Claudia Gorbman. New York: Columbia University Press, 1994.

Cléder, Jean, and Gilles Mouellic. *Nouvelle vague, nouveaux rivages.* Rennes: Presses Universitaires de Rennes, 2001.

Clouzot, Claire. *Le cinéma français depuis la nouvelle vague.* Paris: Nathan, 1972.

Collet, Jean. *Le cinéma en question.* Paris: Editions du CERF, 1972.

Cook, David A. *A History of Narrative Film.* New York: Norton, 1990.

Cook, Pam, and Micke Bernick, eds. *The Cinema Book.* London: British Film Institute, 1999.

Courtade, Francis. *Les malédictions du cinéma français.* Paris: Alain Moreau, 1978.

Coward, Rosalind, and John Ellis. *Language and Materialism: Developments in Semiology and the Theory of the Subject.* Boston: Routledge, Kegan, Paul, 1977.

Crisp, Colin. *The Classic French Cinema, 1930–1960.* Bloomington: Indiana University Press, 1993.

Crisp, Colin. *Eric Rohmer: Realist and Moralist.* Bloomington: Indiana University Press, 1988.

Crisp, Colin. *François Truffaut.* New York: Praeger, 1972.

Cros, J. L. "*Les cousins.*" *Image et son* 122–23 (May–June 1959): 33.

Crowther, Bosley. Review of *Shoot the Piano Player.* In *Shoot the Piano Player,* edited by Peter Brunette.

Culler, Jonathan. *Structuralist Poetics.* Ithaca, N.Y.: Cornell University Press, 1975.

Curtelin, Jean. "Marée montante? En ligne droite de Melville à Chabrol." *Prémier Plan* 9 (May 1960).

David, Michel. "25 ans de réflexion." In *La Nouvelle vague et après.* Paris: Cinémathèque Française, 1986.

Davis, Hélène Laroche. "Interview with François Truffaut." In *Shoot the Piano Player*, edited by Peter Brunette.

de Baecque, Antoine. *Les cahiers du cinéma: Histoire d'une revue.* Vol. 1, *A l'assaut du cinéma, 1951–1959.* Paris: Cahiers du cinéma. 1991.

de Baecque, Antoine. *La nouvelle vague: Portrait d'une jeunesse.* Paris: Flammarion, 1998.

de Beacque, Antoine and Charles Tesson. "Tout a changé en Bretaigne: Table ronde avec Jean Douchet, André S. Labarthe et Luc Moullet." *Cahiers du cinema, nouvelle vague: Une légende en question* (special issue 1998).

de Baecque, Antoine, and Serge Toubiana. *Truffaut.* Translated by Catherine Temerson. New York: Alfred A. Knopf, 1999. Originally published as *François Truffaut* (Paris: Gallimard, 1996).

Delvaux, Claudine. "Agnès Varda cinéphotographe." *La Revue Belge du cinéma* 20 (1987): 25.

Derry, Charles. "Claude Chabrol." In *International Directory of Films and Filmmakers.* Chicago: St. James Press, 1990.

Desjardins, Aline. *Truffaut.* Paris: Ramsay, 1987.

di Giammetteo, Fernaldo. "'Marienbadism' and the New Italian Directors." *Film Quarterly* 16, no. 2 (winter 1962–63): 20–24.

Dixon, Wheeler Winston. *The Early Film Criticism of François Truffaut.* Bloomington: Indiana University Press, 1993.

Dixon, Wheeler Winston. *The Films of Jean-Luc Godard.* Albany: State University of New York Press, 1997.

Doniol-Valcroze, Jacques. "Le pouvoir de la nuit: *Les amants.*" *Cahiers du cinéma* 89 (November 1958): 43–45.

Dorsdale, Michel. "Le cinéma est mort." *Cahiers du cinéma* 16 (October 1952): 55–58.

Douchet, Jean. *French New Wave.* Translated by Robert Bonnono. New York: Distributed Art Publishers, 1999.

Douin, Jean-Luc, ed. *La nouvelle vague 25 ans après.* Paris: Editions du CERF, 1983.

Duby, Georges. *Histoire de la France: Les temps nouveaux, de 1853 à nos jours.* Vol. 3. Paris: Librairie Larouse, 1972.

Durand, Jacques. *Le cinéma et son public.* Paris: Sirey, 1958.

Duras, Marguerite. *Hiroshima mon amour.* Translated by Richard Seaver. New York: Grove Press, 1961.

Duras, Marguerite. "Resnais travaille comme un romancier." *Avant-Scène Cinéma* 61–62 (July 1966).

Egly, Max. "Fascination de Marienbad." *Image et son* 142 (June 1961): 39–40.

Egly, Max. "Rencontre avec Alain Resnais." *Image et son* 128 (February 1960): 7–9.

Egly, Max. "Varda, Resnais, Marker." *Image et son* 128 (February 1960): 2–6.

Ehrlich, Evelyn. *Cinema of Paradox: French Filmmaking under the German Occupation.* New York: Columbia University Press, 1985.

Fassbinder, Rainer Werner. "Insects in a Glass Case." *Sight and Sound* 45, no. 4 (autumn 1976).

Firk, Michèle. "L'anachronique jeunesse du cinéma français." *Cinéma 59* 39 (May 1959).

Firk, Michèle. "*Le beau Serge* et *Les cousins.*" *Positif* 30 (July 1959): 58–60.

Fitzpatrick, Ellen. Review of *The Lovers. Films in Review* 10, no. 9 (November 1959): 561–62.

Flacon, Michel. Review of *Les amants. Cinéma 58* 32 (December 1958): 104–8.

Flaud, Jacques. Interview with André Bazin and Jacques Doniol-Valcroze. *Cahiers du cinéma* 71 (May 1957): 4–15.

Fleischer, Alain. *L'Art d'Alain Resnais.* Paris: Centre Georges Pompidou, 1998.

Flitterman-Lewis, Sandy. *To Desire Differently: Feminism and the French Cinema.* Urbana: University of Illinois Press, 1990.

Flot, Yonnick. *Les producteurs: Les risques d'un métier.* Paris: 5 Continents, 1986.

Forbes, Jill, and Michael Kelly, eds. *French Cultural Studies: An Introduction.* New York: Oxford University Press, 1995.

Ford, Charles. *Histoire du cinéma français contemporain (1945–1977).* Paris: Editions France-Empire, 1977.

Fowlie, Wallace. *Dionysus in Paris.* New York: Meridian, 1962.

French, Philip, ed. *Malle on Malle.* London: Faber and Faber, 1993.

Frodon, Jean-Michel. *L'age moderne du cinéma français: De la nouvelle vague à nos jours.* Paris: Flammarion, 1995.

Gardies, André. *Le cinéma de Robbe-Grillet: Essai sémiocritique.* Paris: Albatross, 1983.

Gillain, Anne. *Le cinéma selon François Truffaut.* Paris: Flammarion, 1988.

Gillain, Anne. *François Truffaut: Le secret perdu.* Paris: Hatier, 1991.

Giroud, Françoise. *La nouvelle vague: Portraits de la jeunesse.* Paris: Gallimard, 1958.

Giroud, Françoise. "Une grande enquête nationale: Répondez!" *L'Express,* October 3, 1957.

Godard, Jean-Luc. *Godard on Godard: Critical Writings.* Edited by Jean Narboni and Tom Milne. New York: Viking, 1972.

Godard, Jean-Luc. "Sufficient Evidence." In *Cahiers du Cinéma: The 1950s,* edited by Jim Hillier, 47–52.

Godard, Jean-Luc. *A Woman Is a Woman, A Married Man, Two or Three Things I Know about Her: Three Films.* London: Lorrimer, 1975.

Gorbman, Claudia. "Cleo from Five to Seven: Music as Mirror." *Wide Angle* 4, no. 4 (1981).

Graham, Peter. "New Directions in French Cinema." In *The Oxford History of*

World Cinema, edited by Geoffrey Nowell-Smith. New York: Oxford University Press, 1996.

Graham, Peter, ed. *The New Wave*. Garden City, N.Y.: Doubleday, 1968.

Grasset, Pierre. "Melville." *Cahiers du Cinéma* 507 (November 1996): 76–77.

Guicharnaud, Jacques. *Modern French Theatre from Giraudoux to Genet*. New Haven: Yale University Press, 1967.

Hardt, Hubert. "*Cléo de 5 à 7.*" *Amis du film et de la TV* 78 (July–August, 1962): 6–7, 22.

Hayward, Susan. *French National Cinema*. London: Routledge, 1993.

Higgins, Lynn A. *New Novel, New Wave, New Politics*. Lincoln: University of Nebraska Press, 1996.

Hillier, Jim, ed. *Cahiers du Cinéma: The 1950s*. Cambridge, Mass.: Harvard University Press, 1985.

Hillier, Jim, ed. *Cahiers du Cinéma: The 1960s*. Cambridge, Mass.: Harvard University Press, 1992.

Hogue, Peter. "Melville: The Elective Affinities." *Film Comment* (November–December 1996): 17–22.

Holmes, Diana, and Robert Ingram. *François Truffaut*. New York: Manchester University Press, 1998.

Insdorf, Annette. *François Truffaut*. New York: Cambridge University Press, 1994.

Jacobowitz, Florence, and Richard Lippe. "French New Wave: Fortieth Anniversary." *Cineaction* 48 (1999): 1–7.

Jeancolas, Jean-Pierre. "Années cinquante?" *Avant scène du cinéma* 370 (April 1988): 3–7.

Jeancolas, Jean-Pierre. *Le cinéma des français: La ve république (1958–1978)*. Paris: Editions Stock, 1979.

Jeancolas, Jean-Pierre. *Histoire du cinéma français*. Paris: Nathan, 1995.

Johnston, Claire. "Women's Cinema as Counter-Cinema." In *Movies and Methods*, vol. 1, edited by Bill Nichols, 208–17. Berkeley: University of California Press, 1976.

Kauffman, Stanley. *A World on Film*. New York: Harper and Row, 1966.

Kline, T. Jefferson. *Screening the Text: Intertextuality in New Wave French Cinema*. Baltimore: Johns Hopkins University Press, 1992.

Kolker, R. P. *The Altering Eye*. New York: Oxford University Press, 1983.

Kyrou, Ado. "*L'année dernière à Marienbad*, Les rencontres parallèles." *Positif* 40 (July 1961).

Labarthe, André S. *Essai sur le jeune cinéma français*. Paris: Le Terrain Vague, 1960.

Labarthe, André S., and Jacques Rivette. "Entretien avec Resnais et Robbe-Grillet." *Cahiers du cinéma* 123 (September 1961).

Langlois, Gérard. "Françoise Brion." In *La nouvelle vague 25 ans après*, edited by Jean-Luc Douin.

Langlois, Gérard. "Pierre Kast." In *La nouvelle vague 25 ans après*, edited by Jean-Luc Douin.

Lanzoni, Rémi Fournier. *French Cinema from Its Beginnings to the Present*. New York: Continuum, 2004.

Larkin, Maurice. *France since the Popular Front*. Oxford: Clarendon Press, 1988.

Leak, Andrew. *Barthes: Mythologies*. London: Grant and Cutler, 1994.

Lebelley, Frédérique. *Duras ou le poids d'une plume*. Paris: Grasset, 1994.

Lefevre, René. "*Tirez sur le pianiste*." *Image et son* 138 (February 1961): 26.

Levi, Giovanni, and Jean-Claude Schmitt, eds. *A History of Young People in the West*. Translated by Carol Volk. Cambridge, Mass.: Belknap Press of Harvard University Press, 1997.

L'Herbier, Marcel. "Vers les etats généraux du cinématographie." *Cinéma 55* 2 (December 1954): 2–6.

MacCabe, Colin. "A Life in Seven Episodes (to date)." In *Jean-Luc Godard: Son & Image*, edited by Raymond Bellour and Mary Lea Bandy. New York: Museum of Modern Art, 1992.

Magny, Joel. *Claude Chabrol*. Paris: Cahiers du cinéma, 1987.

Magny, Joel. *Eric Rohmer*. Paris: Rivages, 1986.

Maillot, Pierre. *Le cinéma français: De Renoir à Godard*. Paris: M. A. Editions, 1988.

Manceaux, Michèle. "Learning Not to Be Bitter: Interview with Jean-Luc Godard." In *Focus on Godard*, edited by Royal S. Brown.

Marcorelles, Louis. "Jacques, ou la soumission." *Cahiers du cinéma* 105 (March 1960).

Mardore, Michel. "Entretien." *Cinéma 62* 64 (March 1962).

Marie, Michel. *A bout de souffle*. Paris: Nathan, 1999.

Marie, Michel. "It Really Makes You Sick! Jean-Luc Godard's *A bout de souffle*." In *French Film: Texts and Contexts*, edited by Susan Hayward and Ginette Vincendeau. London: Routledge, 1990.

Marie, Michel. *Muriel d'Alain Resnais*. Neuilly: Editions Atlande, 2005.

Marie, Michel. *La nouvelle vague: Une école artistique*. Paris: Nathan, 1997. Reprinted as *The French New Wave: An Artistic School*, translated by Richard Neupert (Malden, Mass.: Blackwell, 2002).

Martin, Marcel. *Le cinéma français depuis la guerre*. Paris: Edilig, 1984.

Martin, Marcel. "France, jeune cinéma: La guerre est finie." *Cinéma 66* 108 (July–August 1966): 36–40.

Mast, Gerald, and Bruce F. Kawin. *A Short History of the Movies*. Boston: Allyn and Bacon, 1996.

Michalczyk, John J. *The French Literary Filmmakers*. Philadelphia: Art Alliance Press, 1980.

Monaco, James. *Alain Resnais*. New York: Oxford University Press, 1979.

Monaco, James. *The New Wave: Truffaut, Godard, Chabrol, Rohmer, Rivette*. New York: Oxford University Press, 1976.

Monaco, Paul. *Ribbons in Time*. Bloomington: Indiana University Press, 1988.

Morin, Edgar. *Le cinéma ou l'homme imaginaire*. Paris: Editions de Minuit, 1968.

Morin, Edgar. *Stars*. Paris: Editions du Seuil, 1957.

Morrissette, Bruce. *Novel and Film: Essays in Two Genres*. Chicago: University of Chicago Press, 1985.

Morrissette, Bruce. *The Novels of Robbe-Grillet*. Ithaca, N.Y.: Cornell University Press, 1975.

Moullet, Luc. "La balance et le lien." *Cahiers du cinéma* 410 (July–August 1988).

Mouton, Janice. "From Feminine Masquerade to Flâneuse: Agnès Varda's Cleo in the City." *Cinema Journal* 40, no. 2 (winter 2001): 3–16.

Neupert, Richard. "Dead Champagne: *Variety*'s New Wave." *Film History* 10, no. 2 (1998): 219–30.

Neupert, Richard. *The End: Narration and Closure in the Cinema*. Detroit: Wayne State University Press, 1995.

Neupert, Richard. "The Musical Score as Closure Device in *The 400 Blows*." *Film Criticism* 14, no. 1 (fall 1989): 26–32.

Nicholls, David. *François Truffaut*. London: B. T. Batsford, 1993.

Nogueira, Rui. *Le cinéma selon Melville*. Paris: Editions Seghers, 1963.

Overbey, David. "Chabrol: Game of Mirrors." *Sight and Sound* 46, 2 (spring 1977).

Paris, James Reid. *The Great French Films*. Secaucus, N.J.: Citadel Press, 1983.

Passerini, Luisa. "Youth as Metaphor for Social Change." In *A History of Young People in the West*, edited by Giovanni Levi and Jean-Claude Schmitt, 319–20.

Payne, Michael. *Reading Knowledge: An Introduction to Barthes, Foucault, and Althusser*. Oxford: Blackwell Publishers, 1997.

Perkins, V. F. "*Vivre sa vie*." In *The Films of Jean-Luc Godard*, edited by Ian Cameron.

Pingaud, Bernard. "A propos de *Hiroshima mon amour*." *Positif* 35 (July–August 1960). Reprinted in *Positif 50 Years: Selections from the French Film Journal*, edited by Michel Ciment and Laurence Kardish, 49–58. New York: Museum of Modern Art, 2002.

Pochna, Marie-France. *Christian Dior: The Man Who Made the World Look New*. Translated by Joanna Savill. New York: Arcade, 1996.

Porcile, François. "L'age du microsillon." In *La nouvelle vague 25 ans après*, edited by Jean-Luc Douin, 54–67.

Prédal, René. "De bonnes recettes pour faire des économies." In *La nouvelle vague 25 ans après*, edited by Jean-Luc Douin, 73–86.

Prédal, René. *50 ans de cinéma français (1945–1995)*. Paris: Nathan, 1996.

Rivette, Jacques. "The Age of Metteurs en scène." In *Cahiers du Cinéma*, edited by Jim Hillier.

Rivette, Jacques. "Beauty Lies in Accuracy." In *French New Wave*, edited by Jean Douchet.

Rivette, Jacques. "On Imagination." In *Cahiers du Cinéma*, edited by Jim Hillier.

Rivette, Jacques. "*Paris nous appartient.*" *Avant scène cinéma* 7 (September 15, 1961): 33–36.

Rivette, Jacques. "*Under Capricorn.*" *Gazette du cinéma* 4 (October 1950).

Robbe-Grillet, Alain. *For a New Novel: Essays on Fiction*. Translated by Richard Howard. Evanston, Ill.: Northwestern University Press, 1989. Originally published as *Pour un nouveau roman* (Paris: Les Editions de Minuit, 1963).

Robbe-Grillet, Alain. *Last Year at Marienbad.* Translated by Richard Howard. New York: Grove Press, 1962.

Roddick, Nick. "*And God Created Woman.*" In *Magill's Survey of Cinema*, edited by Frank N. Magill. Englewood Cliffs, N.J.: Salem Press, 1985.

Rohmer, Eric. "Premier accessit: *Ascenseur pour l'échafaud.*" *Cahiers du cinéma* 80 (February 1958): 59–60.

Rohmer, Eric. *The Taste of Beauty.* Translated by Carol Volk. Cambridge: Cambridge University Press, 1989.

Rosenbaum, Jonathan, ed. *Rivette: Texts and Interviews.* London: British Film Institute, 1977.

Ross, Kristin. *Fast Cars, Clean Bodies: Decolonization and the Reordering of French Culture.* Cambridge, Mass.: MIT University Press, 1995.

Roud, Richard. *Godard.* Bloomington: Indiana University Press, 1970.

Ruscart, Marc. "Des petits matins de la Cinémathèque au foyer des *Cahiers.*" In *La nouvelle vague et après*. Paris: Cinémathèque Française, 1986.

Sadoul, Georges. *Le cinéma français.* Paris: Flammarion, 1962.

Sadoul, Georges. *Dictionary of Films.* Translated by Peter Morris. Berkeley: University of California Press, 1972.

Sadoul, Georges. "Quelques sources du nouveau cinéma français." *Esprit* 285 (June 1960): 968–78.

Sadoul, Georges. "Un film néo-romantique: *Les cousins.*" *Lettres françaises* 765 (March 19, 1959).

Sartre, Jean-Paul. "Quand Hollywood veut faire penser . . . *Citizen Kane*, Film d'Orson Wells," *L'Ecran français* 5 (August 1, 1945).

Sauvy, Alfred. *L'Europe et sa population.* Paris: Les Editions Internationales, 1953.

Séguin, Louis. "Questions à Pierre Kast." *Positif* 34 (May 1960).

Siclier, Jacques. "Et la presse." *Avant scène* 171/172 (July–September 1976).

Siclier, Jacques. *Nouvelle vague?* Paris: Editions du CERF, 1961.

Sklar, Robert. *Film: An International History of the Medium.* Upper Saddle River, N.J.: Prentice-Hall, 2002.

Smith, Alison. *Agnès Varda.* Manchester: Manchester University Press, 1998.

Smith, Murray. "Altered States: Character and Emotional Response in the Cinema." Cinema Journal 33, no. 4 (1994).

Soila, Tytti, Astrid Soderbergh Widding, and Gunnar Iversen. *Nordic National Cinemas*. London: Routledge, 1998.

Sontag, Susan. *"Muriel." Film Quarterly* 17, no. 2 (winter 1963–64): 23–27.

Sterritt, David. *The Films of Jean-Luc Godard: Seeing the Invisible*. Cambridge: Cambridge University Press, 1999.

Tailleur, Roger. *"Cléo, d'ici à l'éternité." Positif* 44 (March 1962): 1–27.

Tailleur, Roger, Paul-Louis Thiraud, et al. "Quoi de neuf?" *Positif* 31 (November 1959).

Tassone, Aldo. *Que reste-t-il de la nouvelle vague?* Paris: Stock, 2003.

Thompson, Kristin, and David Bordwell. *Film History: An Introduction*. New York: McGraw-Hill, 1994.

Truffaut, François. "A Certain Tendency of the French Cinema." In *Movies and Methods*, edited by Bill Nichols, 224–37. Berkeley: University of California Press, 1976. Originally published as "Une certain tendance du cinéma français," *Cahiers du cinéma* 31 (January 1954): 15–29.

Truffaut, François. *Correspondence: 1945–1984*. Edited by Gilles Jacob and Claude de Givray. Translated by Gilbert Adair. New York: Farrar, Straus and Giroux.

Truffaut, François. *The Films of My Life*. New York: Simon and Schuster, 1975.

Truffaut, François. "The Original Treatment." In *Breathless*, edited by Dudley Andrew.

Truffaut, François. "Positif: Copie 0." *Cahiers du Cinéma* 79 (January 1958): 60–62.

Truffaut, François. *Truffaut by Truffaut*. Edited by Dominique Raboudin. Translated by Robert Erich Wolf. New York: Harry N. Abrams, 1987.

Uytterhoeven, Pierre. "Agnès Varda de 5 à 7," *Positif* 44 (March 1962): 1–2.

Vadim, Roger. *Memoirs of the Devil*. Translated by Peter Beglan. London: Hutchinson, 1976.

Varda, Agnès. *Varda par Agnès*. Paris: Editions Cahiers du Cinéma, 1994.

Vautier, René. "Et la guerre d'Algérie, Bordel!" In *La nouvelle vague 25 ans après*, edited by Jean-Luc Douin, 209–12.

Vest, James M. *Hitchcock and France*. Westport, Conn.: Praeger, 2003.

Vincendeau, Ginette. *The Companion to French Cinema*. London: Cassell and British Film Institute, 1996.

Vincendeau, Ginette. *Stars and Stardom in French Cinema*. New York: Continuum International Publishing, 2000.

Ward, John. *Alain Resnais, or the Theme of Time*. Garden City, N.Y.: Doubleday, 1968.

Weber, Eugen. "An Escapist Realism." *Film Quarterly* 13, no. 2 (winter 1959): 9–16.

Wegerganz, Franz. Review of *The 400 Blows*. *Amis du film* 50 (October 1959).

Williams, Alan. *Republic of Images: A History of French Filmmaking*. Cambridge, Mass.: Harvard University Press, 1992.

Williams, Richard. *Miles Davis*. New York: Henry Holt, 1993.

Woo, John. "Le Style Melville." *Cahiers du cinéma* 507 (November 1996): 80–81.

Wood, Robin, and Michael Walker. *Claude Chabrol*. New York: Praeger, 1970.

Zimmer, Jacques, and Chantal de Béchade. *Jean-Pierre Melville*. Paris: Edilig, 1983.

INDEX

WISCONSIN
studies in film

General Editors
David Bordwell, Vance Kepley, Jr.
Supervising Editor
Kristin Thompson

Film Essays and Criticism
Rudolf Arnheim

Post-Theory: Reconstructing Film Studies
Edited by David Bordwell and Noël Carroll

Reel Patriotism: The Movies and World War I
Leslie Midkiff DeBauche

Shared Pleasures: A History of Movie Presentation in the United States
Douglas Gomery

The Imperial Screen: Japanese Film Culture in the Fifteen Years' War, 1931–1945
Peter B. High

Lovers of Cinema: The First American Film Avant-Garde, 1919–1945
Edited by Jan-Christopher Horak

The Wages of Sin: Censorship and the Fallen Woman Film, 1928–1942
Lea Jacobs

Settling the Score: Music and the Classical Hollywood Film
Kathryn Kalinak

Early American Cinema in Transition: Story, Style, and Filmmaking, 1907–1913
Charlie Keil

Patterns of Time: Mizoguchi and the 1930s
Donald Kirihara

A History of the French New Wave Cinema
Richard Neupert

The World According to Hollywood, 1918–1939
Ruth Vasey

The Magic Mirror: Moviemaking in Russia, 1908–1918
Denise J. Youngblood